The Rebel

Leonor Villegas de Magnón

Edited and Introduced by
Clara Lomas

Arte Público Press
Houston, Texas
1994

This volume is made possible through grants from the National Endowment for the Arts (a federal agency), the Lila Wallace-Reader's Digest Fund, the Andrew W. Mellon Foundation, and the Rockefeller Foundation.

Recovering the past, creating the future

Arte Público Press
University of Houston
Houston, Texas 77204-2090

Cover design by Mark Piñón

Villegas de Magnón, Leonor.
The rebel / by Leonor Villegas de Magnón : edited by Clara Lomas.
p. cm.
ISBN 1-55885-056-2
1. Villegas de Magnón, Leonor. 2. Mexican Americans—Biography. 3. Feminists—United States—Biography. 4. Revolutionaries—Mexico—Biography. 5. Feminists—Mexico—Biography. I. Lomas, Clara. II. Title.
E184.M5V53 1993
973'.046872'0092—dc20
[B] 93-3607
CIP

The paper used in this publication meets the requirements of the American National Standard for Permanence of Paper for Printed Library Materials Z39.48-1984.⊗

This book is dedicated to those who have been my sources of inspiration:

María Luisa and Alberto Lomas, my parents, and Luis;

my children, Luis Alberto, Cecilia and Alma;

my mentors, Rosaura Sánchez, Carlos Blanco Aguinaga, Sylvia Lizárraga and Angie Chabram;

and 'las tres Leonores.'

C.L.

Contents

Preface

In Search of an Autobiography: On Mapping Women's Intellectual History of the Borderlands

The archaeological pursuit which led to the recent recovery of Leonor Villegas de Magnón's life stories—from an old family trunk nearly destroyed by burglars who broke into the Magnóns' vacant Laredo, Texas, house—is not unlike the many similar endeavors to retrieve, restore and preserve the historical, cultural legacy of the Latino communities in the United States. Withered by time, ignored and silenced by ethnocentrism, destroyed by the flames of arsonists, lost to unscrupulous publishers, among other reasons, myriad forms of historical/cultural documentation have been disintegrating, depriving us of answers to our personal, intellectual and academic queries about the past of our Latino communities.

In an attempt to fill in some of the numerous historical lacunae as well as to contribute to the massive 'archaeological' recovery project under way by several scholars,[1] I eagerly responded to several hints by historians of the existence of an intellectual community of women who were involved in the Mexican Revolution of 1910. Non-traditional literary sources such as Southwest Spanish-language newspapers and oral interviews of *fronterizos* (border area people) proved to be invaluable documentation of community activity.[2] Perseverance and patience paid off after three years of sifting through various archaeological layers. I conducted research at the Special Collections of the University of Texas Benson Latin American Collection and Barker Texas History Libraries, the Bancroft and Huntington Libraries in California, and the International Institute of Social History in Amsterdam. My correspondence with border-area librarians of public and private institutions revealed the whereabouts of many single issues of periodicals. Concurrent with this research, interviews with border-area residents uncovered data of inestimable worth. I was able to identify and retrieve from periodicals writings of several women who, at the turn of the century, exercised interpretative power by penning their views on their times and lives. The most extensive text I located was Villegas de Magnón's autobiographical narrative entitled "La Rebelde," published in serial form in the Spanish section of *The Laredo Times,* from March 19 through June 7, 1961.[3] As official history nearly erased the memory of the nurses' involvement in the Mexican Revolution, especially those from the Texas-Mexico border area who constituted La Cruz Blanca (The White Cross), Villegas de Magnón made it her duty to leave both written and pictorial documentation of that participation. Published posthumously at the request of her daughter, Leonor Grubbs, the daily literary installments, together with multiple visual images, pieced together, for the *fronterizos* of the early 1960s, the numerous fragmented memories of revolutionary times told orally by parents and grandparents.

Coincidentally, during the same days I located Villegas de Magnón's autobiographical narrative, I had finally secured a response from her granddaughter, Leonor Smith, who, for several months, had not responded to my letters and telephone calls regarding information leading to retrieval of her grandmother's narratives. Unhonored contractual negotiations with a publisher ten years earlier had scarred Leonor Grubbs so profoundly that she had given up in her efforts to carry out her mother's last wish: to have her story published in book form. Mrs. Grubbs' ill health had drawn her daughter's energies and attention away from all other matters.

Fortunately, I was able to interview Leonor Grubbs only a few months before she died; both her daughter and I promised to carry out her mother's final wish. Hoping to work on what read as a highly edited version of an autobiography, I began to study the serialized "La Rebelde." Soon thereafter, I received a telephone call from Leonor Smith. She wondered whether I would be interested in some recently salvaged materials she had in her possession. Nearly damaged and haphazardly returned to an old trunk, Mrs. Smith explained, the contents consisted of manuscripts, photographs, books, correspondence, telegrams and scrap books with old newspaper clippings. I traveled to Texas, surveyed the documentation, and made an inventory of all the materials. We soon realized that the contents of the trunk were what was left after Mrs. Grubbs' publisher took his first selection of the materials that Leonor Villegas de Magnón had willed to her children. The publisher never returned the originals. From that moment we began to piece together a legacy which to this date remains fragmented, marked by multiple ruptures.

Villegas de Magnón's autobiographical narratives allow us a glimpse, nonetheless, at women's historical struggles in appropriating a discursive voice to document their own social contributions. She left two versions of her life story. The first 300-page Spanish text, entitled "La Rebelde," probably written sometime in the late teens or early twenties, was directed to a post-revolutionary Mexican audience. After various unsuccessful attempts to have the Mexican government publish what they labeled "novelized memoirs," Villegas de Magnón wrote, during the late forties, a 483-page English version directed toward a United States audience.

The following English version of her work, entitled *The Rebel*, and the collection of photographs included here represent a selection from those fragile, crumbling materials from the old trunk. Taking into account the precarious history of Villegas de Magnón's compendium of self-representational documentation, we cannot ascertain whether this text is the final version she would have had published or whether it is one of several drafts. Thus the enigma remains unresolved, exemplifying those life stories that remain on the boundaries, peripheral to both countries, fragmented by a geopolitical border.

This retrieval enterprise required both human labor and financial support. I would like to thank the Ford Foundation, The Colorado College for its Benezet Award and Jackson Fellowships, and the University of California at Los Angeles Faculty Research Award, all of which supported various aspects of my research. I owe special gratitude to the Coordinators of the Recovering the US Hispanic Literary Heritage Project, Teresa Marrero and Elsie Herdman-Dodge, for their constant encouragement, and to the Project Director, Nicolás Kanellos, for his foresight. Research assistants Eleuteria Hernández and Xóchil from UCLA and Alma Lomas, Katherine Eastman and Kris McNeil from The Colorado College merit special recognition. I would also like to acknowledge the valuable comments and suggestions of María Daniels and Victor Nelson-Cisneros. For their persistence, we owe appreciation to the three generations of women of the Villegas de Magnón family, las tres Leonores (the three Leonors), who have striven to share with an audience beyond their immediate family the story of many other border women and men who temporarily left their families to carry out a humanitarian mission: assisting Mexico's revolutionaries in their struggle for justice, liberation, equality and a better future for the majority of its people.

Las tres Leonores. From left to right Leonor Grubbs (daughter), Leonor Villegas de Magnón and Leonor Smith (granddaughter), 1943.

Introduction

Revolutionary Women and the Alternative Press in the Borderlands

> [O]nly an imaginary line divides "México de Adentro" (Mexico as a territorial unit) from "México de Afuera" [Mexico abroad, specifically the United States]. This line is easy to cross, legally or illegally.
>
> —Américo Paredes[4]

> [A woman's] role in the alternative press movement is important because she belonged to that movement on both sides of the border, and in effect, through her life story, provides one more example of how the border often becomes erased when considering the experience of the Mexican people and their response to domination and oppression.
>
> —Inés Hernández[5]

Villegas de Magnón's *The Rebel* provides a stage on which the deeds of Mexican historical revolutionary figures such as Francisco I. Madero, Venustiano Carranza, and Francisco (Pancho) Villa are dramatized along with those of a cast of border area political activists. Villegas de Magnón protagonizes an "aristocratic" rebel whose task is to immortalize the border activism of *los fronterizos,* to move them from a marginal backstage to center stage. Her story provides yet another instance of the struggle for authority and interpretative power waged by the various revolutionary factions of the borderlands through one of the most powerful mediums of their oppositional discourse, the alternative press.

The United States-Mexico border area, especially the urban centers of Laredo, San Antonio, El Paso and Los Angeles, served as important centers for some of the precursory work for the first major revolution of the twentieth century, what has come to be known as the Mexican Revolution. Through various phases between 1900 and 1920, numerous political and military factions struggled first to oust Porfirio Díaz, Mexico's dictator for 34 years, and then to attain executive power. A significant part of this activity was documented by the many periodicals of the border region. According to José Valadez, there were over 170 Spanish-language newspapers published in the U.S. Southwest during this period.[6] Some of these newspapers had been established long before the revolutionary movement and the vast majority of these supported the Mexican dictatorship.[7] More than 30 newspapers, however, were founded by political exiles, such as Ricardo Flores Magón and members of the Partido Liberal Mexicano (PLM, Mexican Liberal Party) as well as by US citizen sympathizers to propagandize for an armed revolution.[8] During the second and more violent phase of the revolutionary movement, initiated in 1913, *juntas revolucionarias* (revolutionary groups) launched their own revolutionary periodicals while still other exiles established their newspapers in support of either "peace and harmony" or the counterrevolution, such as Ignacio Lozano's *La Prensa*, founded in San Antonio, Texas.[9]

Parallel to this explosive political journalism, the revolutionary sentiment recorded through letters, memoirs, autobiographies and through oral tradition preserved in songs and folklore attests to the erasure of the geopolitical border by the peoples of the border region, as noted above by both Paredes and Hernández. Despite the intersection of boundaries of two sovereign states, each with distinct national cultures, the social position of Mexican women in the borderlands was much dictated by traditional Mexican social mores. As the revolutionary movement developed, it provided a fertile arena for the resurgence of nationalist sentiment among the Mexican population, and created the space to recode the position of women in society. The liberalism of this movement reinforced the secular perspective, openly defying the master narrative of the Catholic church, which had long defined Mexican women's social role. The winds of war that swept Mexico had uprooted, snatched and carried hundreds of thousands of rural and urban lower-class women who accompanied their soldiers and were later known as "soldaderas." There were also a good number of women primarily, but not exclusively, of middle- and upper-class origins, however, who actively sought involvement in the struggle either against the anticlerical leadership of the revolution or in favor of the social struggle for revolutionary goals.[10] According to Anna Macías, as pointed out in her germinal study, *Against All Odds: The Feminist Movement in Mexico to 1940,* many of these women "were trained and educated in the vocational and normal schools and molded in the incipient feminist movement of the Porfirian era."[11]

Macías noted the following six fundamental reasons Mexican women faced overwhelming odds in their endeavors to assume agency, to act on their own: (1) the problem of machismo which compelled women to begin by educating "Mexican men to view women as persons and not as symbols or objects"; (2) the enormous influence of the church whose hierarchy "discouraged even the most moderate brand of feminism, refusing to countenance the establishment of any feminine organizations not controlled by the hierarchy"; (3) the disagreement among feminist factions on issues, tactics and programs as well as the high incidence of "burn out" among leaders; (4) "little support and encouragement from government leaders, especially between 1900–34," who were "suspicious of all women because of prevailing male attitudes" and who felt they were "politically unreliable due to their attachment to the church;" (5) "little support but much ridicule from the press"; and (6) most active politically Mexican women "came from the middle class and had to work for a living. Most of them were elementary schoolteachers."[12] Mexican women of the borderlands did not escape these moral, ethical and sociopolitical constraints.

Although few women in the borderlands had the cultural capital required to express themselves in writing, those who did were able to create an alternative means to do so, through the independent Spanish-language press. Villegas de Magnón was one of these well-educated schoolteachers of the border region whose activism not only effected the lives of many other women of various classes on both sides of the international border, but, through that activism, also contributed to the erasure of the imaginary border line and its intruding socially imposed boundaries. More importantly, her written stories afford us the narrative space and historical context for a journalistic activism which contributed to placing gender issues in the fore of the collective consciousness of that region. Along with Villegas de Magnón's indictments of the 34-year-old Porfirio Díaz dictatorship, the publishing efforts of Sara Estela Ramírez, Jovita Idar, Andrea and Teresa Villarreal, Isidra T. de Cárdenas and Blanca de Moncaleano projected new gender subject positions and identities.

Ramírez, the Villarreal sisters and Cárdenas were directly involved in the political activities of the Flores Magón brothers and other members of the PLM during their US exile and their many imprisonments. In 1901 teacher and poet Sara Estela Ramírez established the periodical *La Corregidora* (The Mayor's Wife) in Laredo, offered it as a tool for the PLM, and nine years later introduced the literary journal

La Voz De La Mujer

SEMANARIO LIBERAL DE COMBATE

Defensor de los Derechos del Pueblo y Enemigo de las Tiranías.

La mujer forma parte integrante de la gran familia humana; luego tiene el deber y el derecho de exigir y luchar por la Dignificación de su Patria

AÑO I. EL PASO, TEXAS, SEPTIEMBRE 6 DE 1907. NUM. 9

LABOR DE FIGAROS.

El flagelo de nuestra fusta ha sangrado los escamosos morrillos de la burguesía altanera. Nuestras rebeldías no han conocido valladar que contenga las justas iras emanadas contra el sistema atentatorio con que los impunes sueñan en reivindicar su historia de oprobio; por que, impotentes para combatir con razonamientos, son tenaces, tambión para reicidir, enfangados en el estercolero que les sirbe de lecho.

Á nuestra mesa de redacción nos llegan distintas quejas de los atentados que cometen en la ínsula de los contrabandos los bandidos caciques investidos de autoridad.

El primer fustazo que nuestro semanario asestó al contrabandista en funciones de Jefe Político, Silvano Montemayor, lo hizo convertirse en réptil, se enroscó, y dió un chillido, le robó a nuestro papelero unos ejemplares y lo amagó con hospedarlo en el *hotel de su propiedad*, si volvia a vender "La Voz de la Mujer." Nuestra protesta cargó sobre el cacique vulgar, castigando su insolencia como lo merecía.

Un Castrado ascendido y cornamentado ha tomado a su encargo molestar a los abonádos y repartidores de nuestro periódico, amagándolos con cárcel ¿Con qué derecho lo hace este Musa? ¡Tales son los méritos de los bandidos de uniforme!

Hoy nos visita una nueva querella: Un paquidermo que *ruge* de cobrador en el mercado de C. Juáres, y de eunuco de antesala, se opone a viva fuerza á que circule "La Voz de la Mujer," en la cafrería donde cree tener, en símil el derecho de usufructo.

Éste estulto cuadrúpedo no está conforme con andar en cuatro remos, sino que, persiste en escarbar con la trompa.

La impudicia de tales molúscos los congestiona, padecen sonambulismo y sueñan en el exterminio de la prensa independiente. ¡Falaz creencia! para que los ideales mueran, se necesita destrozarnos, ya que odiados somos; sólo que ese odio nos eleva por que prueba nuestra honradez, desde el momento en que los tiranos no nos estiman. Por esto los flagelamos para despertar su encono, seguras de que si socumbimos debe ser levantando ámpula; nuestra vacante será substituida con nuevas energías, con plumas viriles empapadas en luz fevas.

Nuestros carácteres están enteramente trocados: nosotras, rebeldes, ellos serviles; nosotras honradas, ellos bandidos; nuestro medio no es el de ellos; el espíritu de rebeldía tonifica nuestros cerebros y es el talismán que nos hace prepotentes en los azares políticos, en la cruenta lucha que sostenemos con los burgueses; somos pobres y la pobreza es maga cuando va emparejada con honradez y abnegación; porque en los mayores infortunios, el porvenir nos sonríe, nos da fuerza y nos acaricia. Esto no pasa con los tiranos criminales: su existencia es mezquina y ruin; sus espíritus siempre están emponsoñados por el crimen y la maldad; sus morbosos y enfermisos cerebros a diario se sienten atacados por la misma ruindad que los deprime; no tienen convicciones propias y viven en continuo asecho de victimas que aseguran sus canonjías; sus almas siempre sernosas sólo piensan en el mal; jamás se preocupan por nada loable.

¡Horrible torcedor para los tiranos, pensar en día de las represalías! ¡La hora suena, inecsorable y justiciera contra los autores de tanto crimen! ¡Oidlo, bien, tiranos y bandidos y si es que lo olvidáis, nosotras os lo recordaremos!

¡Vivid tranquilos!

DEFUNCION.

En San Antonio, Texas, rindió tributo á la Natraleza el rebelde liberal Aurelio N. Flores, dejando un vacío en las filas liberales.

¡La muerte se engalanó al apoderarse de alma tan noble! El Partido Liberal perdió un valiente luchador. ¡Paz á sus resto! ¡Consuelo á sus deudos!

Front page of *La voz de la mujer.*

Aurora (Dawn)[13]. According to the front page of *La Voz de la Mujer* (Women's Voice), Cárdenas established the bi-weekly in El Paso in 1907. *La Voz de la Mujer* included excerpts from the PLM's Los Angeles *Revolución* in order to communicate revolutionary ideas to the readership of El Paso and to send public messages to Roosevelt and other national leaders pleading for Flores Magón's freedom from prison[14]. Andrea and Teresa Villarreal, sisters of Antonio Villarreal, prominent member of the PLM, founded *La Mujer Moderna* (The Modern Woman) in San Antonio in 1910 and Teresa later established the short-lived periodical *El Obrero* (The Worker)[15]. In Laredo from 1898 through 1914 and under the pseudonym of "A. V. Negra" (which phonetically translates to "Black Bird"), Jovita Idar wrote about the discrimination which Mexicans suffered in the United States as well as about the revolutionary struggles for *La Crónica,* her father's newspaper.[16] After her father's death, Idar worked for several periodicals in southern Texas—*El Eco del Golfo* (The Gulf's Echo) in Corpus Christi; *La Luz* (The Light) in San Benito; *La Prensa* (The Press) in San Antonio—and in 1916, with the assistance of her brothers, Clemente and Federico Idar, founded the daily *Evolución.* In the 1940s she co-edited *El Heraldo Cristiano* (The Christian Herald) in San Antonio.[17] After Villegas de Magnón created the Cruz Blanca in 1913 to provide medical relief for the revolutionaries during the violent phase of the Revolution, her brother Leopoldo Villegas helped finance the daily *El Progreso* (Progress) to inform the border regions of the new developments. Blanca de Moncaleano published the anarchist-feminist *Pluma Roja* (Red Pen) in Los Angeles from 1913 through 1915.[18]

Through their publishing efforts, these women's involvement in the formation of women's socio-cultural organizations fomented intellectual growth. Sara Estela Ramírez was a prominent member of "Regeneración y Concordia" (Regeneration and Harmony) before the Revolution erupted in 1910; Jovita Idar created "La Liga Feminista" (The Feminist League) in 1911 as part of the "Primer Congreso Mexicanista" organized by her family; and in 1913 Villegas de Magnón formed "Unión, Progreso y Caridad" (Union, Progress and Charity). According to Gómez-Quiñones, "The feminist Club Liberal Leona Vicario, ostensibly an educational reform group, raised money for the PLM."[19]

At the turn of the century, Ramírez, the Villarreal sisters, Villegas de Magnón, Idar and the staff members of *La Voz de la Mujer* and *Pluma Roja* were organic intellectuals of their times who revealed different discursive positionings of women within their societies, posi-

INSTITUTO EVANGELICO

LA CRONICA

SEGUNDA EPOCA.

DISPONIBLE.

Tomo III. Laredo, Texas, Jueves Octubre 19 de 1911. Numero 41

Liga Femenil Mexicanista

Sentida Defunción

"El Estudiante."

Cambio de residencia

EL PRECIO FIJO

Esta recibiendo cada dia el surtido mas completo y variado en mercancias de invierno que su propietario compro personalmente.

Si usted nos hace una visita y examina lo elegante y barato de nuestras mercancias quedara convencido de que en el proximo invierno

· · EL PRECIO FIJO · ·

tendra el surtido mas completo para dar satisfaccion al gusto mas exquisito.

De Regreso.

AL PUBLICO.

S. S. S.
AUG. C. RICHTER.

Mercedes L. Peña

Personales.

Por el Electrico

LA PERLA

S. Guimberg & Co.

Strouse & Bros.

PESQUIZA.

Leonard Shaw and Bean.

La Mona Lisa.

DE UD. AFMO S. S.
M. VIZCAYA SIERRA.

Juan F. de la Garza

TOMEN NOTA.

ESCUELA "LA LUZ"

JULIAN M. TREVIÑO.

Abarrotes Nacionales y Extranjeros en General, por Mayor y Menor.

EL AMIGO DE LOS POBRES Y LOS RICOS Y EL MAS POPULAR. TANTO PORQUE VENDE A LOS PRECIOS MAS BAJOS, como por su trato fino y especial, pues su lema es: "VIVIR Y DEJAR VIVIR"

Se atienden con especialidad las ordenes a domicilio para familias.

J. MAXCY PACE.

CALLE ITURBIDE No.

AYUDA A LOS HUELGUISTAS.

INSTITUTO DOMINGUEZ
FUNDADO EN 1880.
S. G. DOMINGUEZ, Director y Propietario
TELEFONO 526
CALLE HOUSTON, NO. 806.

Front page of *La Crónica.*

tionings informed by the master narratives of nationalism, religion and anarchism. Until now these women's work as publishers and their written contributions have remained virtually unrecognized. Either because of political affiliations or gender discrimination, their work has not been recognized in Mexico. In the United States, these factors, as well as linguistic biases, have relegated their work to oblivion. These women's stories and their publishing efforts, nonetheless, capture the realities of a people, the significance of whose daily existence transcends the limitations imposed by political and national borders.

Nineteenth-Century Borderlands

While official history of the Mexican Revolution has focused on male political intellectuals and military leaders, *The Rebel* attempts to highlight the contributions of some of the aforementioned women as well as other borderlands heroines. Quick strokes attempt to capture brief moments of lives, deeds, social mores, customs, landscapes and historical events filtered through the memory of Villegas de Magnón. Ironically, her autobiographical text is written in the third person. She suppresses, silences at times, the "I" to tell the story of "The Rebel." In the style of revolutionary romanticism, at moments too high-flown and melodramatic for our taste, we learn of the Rebel's life, from her birth in 1876 to the death of one of the major figures of the Revolution, Venustiano Carranza, in 1920. The first quarter of her story narrates the transformations undergone by the protagonist from a highly sensitive child and lonely orphan into a brave woman with an altruistic sense of duty and loyalty.

Leonor Villegas was born on June 12, 1876, in Nuevo Laredo, Tamaulipas, only days from Porfirio Díaz's attempt to take Mexico City from Lerdo de Tejada. At her birthday, her father affectionately called her "La Rebelde" (The Rebel), because military men searching the area for insurgents suspected that the newborn child's cry was that of a hiding rebel. Later, she would grow into the name when she opposed the Díaz dictatorship, the conventions of her aristocratic class and the traditional role of women in her society.

Leonor's father, Joaquín Villegas, of Santander, Spain, had ventured to Cuba in the 1860s, then to Texas to seek his fortune in the ranching business. He married Valerianna Rubio, the daughter of one of the well-established families of Matamoros, who brought him a handsome dowry. Villegas' wealth later extended from ranching and mining to import and export marketing. Leonor, along with her brothers

EVOLUCION

DIARIO LIBRE

TOMO I | Laredo, Texas, Viernes 2 de Marzo de 1917 | NUM. 106

LA INTRIGA ALEMANA SOBRE MEXICO

LA HIPÓTESIS DEL DIA

EL SENADO AMERICANO SORPRENDIDO POR LA NOTICIA DE UNA INFLUENCIA ALEMANA ACERCA DEL GOBIERNO DE MEXICO Y EL JAPÓN, OLVIDA LAS ANTIGUAS DISENSIONES Y APOYA AL PRESIDENTE WILSON

EL PROBLEMA DEL DIA

Operaciones Militares en el Norte

CONFERENCIA ANGLO-FRANCESA

EL GOBIERNO MEXICANO NO ACEPTA LA SUGESTION ALEMANA

Movimiento Marítimo.

EL GOBIERNO Y PUEBLO AMERICANOS OTORGARAN GARANTIAS A LOS EXTRANJEROS

100 MILLONES PARA ARMAR LOS BUQUES AMERICANOS

LA DEFENSA CIVIL OBTIENE UN ESPLÉNDIDO TRIUNFO

NOTAS DIVERSAS

Front page of *Evolución*.

Leopoldo and Lorenzo and her sister Lina, were raised in the Mexico-Texas border area in the idyllic aristocratic world created by their parents. The narrator in *The Rebel* foregrounds Joaquín Villegas' ranching endeavors by describing the special *patrón-peón*/servant relationship documented by David Montejano in *Anglos and Mexicans in the Making of Texas, 1836–1986*:

> While Mexicans proved reluctant to perform farm labor, work on the ranches continued to be mediated by the old practice of debt peonage. Although peonage was formally illegal, most men and women on Texas ranches nonetheless looked to a *patrón* to provide them with the necessities of life, to give them work, to pay them wages, and, finally, there was a loyalty to the ranch and its owners that acknowledged and repaid a *patrón's* sense of noblesse oblige.[20]

The Rebel's childhood is deeply marked by what she recalls as her parents' noble relationship with their workers/servants. Several decades later, after reading a version of this story entitled "The Lady Was a Rebel," Seb S. Wilcox, Recorder and Official Historian of the counties of Dimmit, Jim Hogg, Webb and Zapata, would comment on her distinctive depiction of those times in his December 17, 1951, letter to Villegas de Magnón:

> [R]eading your work has given me an insight into the early home life of an aristocratic Spanish family along the Texas border that I have not heretofore had the pleasure to fully understand. And your early life and training fitted you for just such a venture as you so nobly carried out during the Carranza revolution.

Similarly significant in this section is the narrator's emphasis on spatial, national and genealogical links which suggest the obliteration of geopolitical borders. Leopoldo had been born in Corpus Christi, Lorenzo in Cuatro Ciénegas, Coahuila, and Lina in San Antonio—"two under the American flag, two under the Mexican, but their mother declared: 'I shall wrap the flags together and they will be like one.'"[21] Their unity, however, was unraveled when their mother died prematurely and their father remarried, a trauma Leonor Villegas would later explore in her autobiographical narrative. Their new "Americanized" stepmother, Eloise, sent them off to boarding schools, and thus began Leonor's unique educational path. From 1882 to 1885 she attended the Ursuline Convent in San Antonio. In 1885 she was

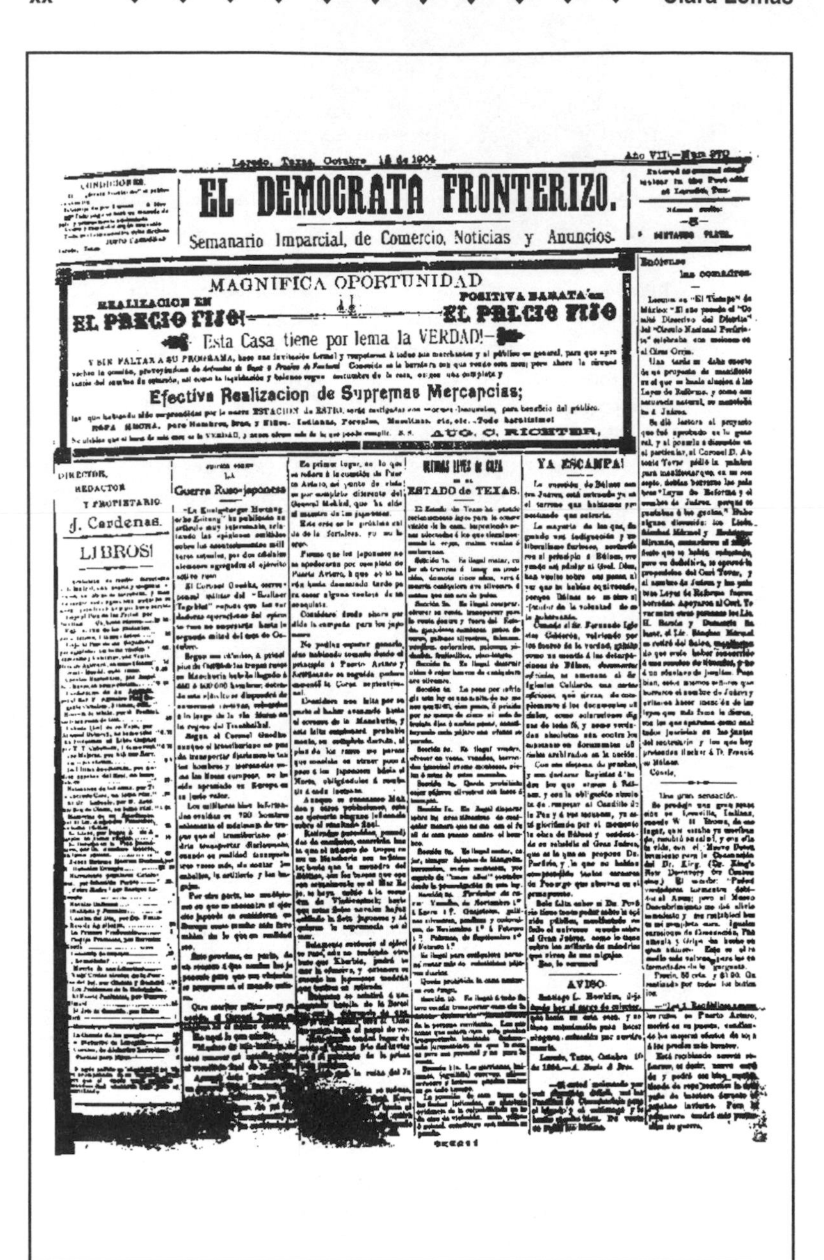

Laredo, Texas, Octubre 15 de 1904

EL DEMOCRATA FRONTERIZO.

Semanario Imparcial, de Comercio, Noticias y Anuncios.

MAGNIFICA OPORTUNIDAD

REALIZACION EN EL PRECIO FIJO!

POSITIVA BARATA en EL PRECIO FIJO

Esta Casa tiene por lema la VERDAD!

Efectiva Realizacion de Supremas Mercancias;

AUG. C. RICHTER,

DIRECTOR, REDACTOR Y PROPIETARIO.

J. Cardenas.

LIBROS!

La Guerra Ruso-japonesa

ULTIMAS LEYES de CAZA en el ESTADO de TEXAS.

YA ESCAMPA!

las comadres.

AVISO.

Front page of *El Democrata Fronterizo.*

transferred to the Academy of the Holy Cross in Austin, where she remained until 1889. Ostensibly to procure the finest education for her stepchildren and keep them as far away from home as possible, Eloise sent the children to New York. Leonor entered Mount St. Ursula's Convent to study education. Although she had contemplated the idea of becoming a nun, in 1895 she graduated with honors and teaching credentials and returned to Laredo with the intention of teaching. As Wilcox noted, she was very well trained—perhaps one of the best-educated women in Laredo—to carry out what her story suggests was her "destiny." The narrator of *The Rebel* claims:

> Pressing her hands together she looked at the burn scar on her hand. It was her destiny to be bound to the country across the river [Mexico] and its people.

Historical and personal events and incidents are intertwined to reflect a predestined life line: the date of her birth, her nickname, the burn on her right hand identical to Carranza's, her mother's foresight. Her life's deeds refused to take national boundaries into account.

The Anti-Porfirista Phase: The Precursory Movement and Maderismo

> [...] this is the collection of commercial interests which profits by the Díaz system of slavery and autocracy, and which puts no insignificant part of its tremendous powers to holding the central prop upright in exchange for the special privileges that it receives. Not the least among these commercial interests are American, which I blush to say, are quite as aggressive defenders of the Díaz citadel as any. Indeed, as I shall show in future chapters, these American interests undoubtedly form the determining force in the continuation of Mexican slavery. Thus does Mexican slavery come home to us in the full sense of the term. For the horrors of Acetin and Valle Nacional, Díaz is to blame, but so are we; we are to blame insofar as governmental powers over which we are conceded to have some control are employed under our very eyes for the perpetuation of a regime of which slavery and peonage are an integral part.
>
> —John Kenneth Turner, *Barbarous Mexico* (1910)

On January 10, 1901, Leonor Villegas married Adolfo Magnón and moved to Mexico City, where Magnón worked as an agent for several steamship companies. During the following nine years Villegas de Magnón lived in what she referred to as "the zenith of glory and wealth" of the *porfiriato,* the Díaz dictatorship. Her class origins, superior education and Franco-American husband afforded her the economic and cultural capital required to socialize comfortably with the capitol's bourgeoisie during the dictatorship. Her Ursuline upbringing, however, tinted her perception of the glorious Porfirista *orden, paz y progreso* (order, peace and progress). The autobiographer tells us that while the Rebel "was enchanted by the lives of the wealthy, she could never accept it completely, seeing the sorrows and oppression of the poor." Her US citizenship and the fortune amassed by her father during the *porfiriato* undoubtedly led her to critically evaluate her own moral sense of accountability in relation to Mexico's deplorable poverty. Morally, ethically and ideologically instilled with democratic ideals, like those of John Kenneth Turner—and surely other US citizen's in Mexico—she felt obliged to become part of a movement against the blatant injustices of the *porfiriato.*

While in Mexico City, Villegas de Magnón inevitably learned of the proletarian strikes and rural revolts and their ensuing brutal suppression by the *porfiriato*'s "peaceful Iron Hand." Stable "progress," evident through constant stimulation of industrial, commercial and banking growth with extensive foreign investment, somehow did not justify flagrant exploitation of the majority of the population. General discontent and profound and organic national discord gave way to a precursory movement characterized by many political factions: liberalism, anarchism, anarcho-syndicalism, a burgeoning agrarian movement and a democratic movement from the followers of Francisco I. Madero. The liberal and later anarchist and anarcho-syndicalist ideals of Ricardo Flores Magón and the PLM, ideals which constituted the intellectual ammunition aimed at the *porfiriato* and fired through the alternative press, resonated strongly throughout the entire country. From its US exile, the 1906 PLM Program manifested its very progressive liberal ideas which greatly influenced middle- and upper-class intellectuals. It is worth highlighting some of the program's proposed reforms, since they were the basis of the Constitution of 1917 and were ideas supported by Villegas de Magnón. Politically, the program called for a four-year presidential term, no reelection, free elections and elimination of forced military service. It also proposed secular public education, mandatory instruction until the age of 14, required manual training and increased instructors' salaries. It demanded new labor laws to guarantee eight-hour days, Sundays off, abolishment of the *tienda de raya* (company store), eradication of child labor, the establishment of retirement and workers' compensation plans and workers' rights, as well as special protection of the indigenous population. Regarding foreign policy, prohibited purchase of real estate by foreigners, it prohibited Chinese immigration, and proclaimed the importance of establishing links with other Latin American countries.

With the assistance of US officials and detectives, however, Díaz's repressive fist successfully crushed the PLM's opposition at home and abroad. In 1909 a book entitled *La sucesión presidencial en 1910: El Partido Nacional Democrático*, authored by a wealthy northerner, Francisco I. Madero, began to circulate in Mexico City. Soon the new party founded an anti-reelection periodical and launched its campaign against Díaz's impending reelection. After her three children, Leonor, Joaquín and Adolfo were born, Villegas de Magnón became involved with the sympathizers of Madero and the anti-reelection campaign. Without her husband's knowledge of her actions, she often visited the Café Colón, where Madero met with fellow liberals to plan the opposition campaign. Exposed to discussions of Madero's liberal democratic ideals and inspired by them, Villegas de Magnón began writing under her family name "fiery articles" against the dictatorship. Shortly before the revolutionary movement broke out in 1910, she left for the border with her children to see her gravely ill father. On his deathbed, he expressed admiration for her courage, but informed her that the majority of their Mexican properties had been confiscated because of her writings. These included their metallurgy, iron and steel mines in the states of Durango, Zacatecas and Saltillo, as well as their ranches around the Río Grande. Her previous political essays, however, were only the beginning of her collaboration with the revolutionary cause.

On June 5, Díaz had Madero imprisoned in San Luis Potosí and had himself "reelected." In October, Madero escaped from prison, fled to the United States, and announced his "Plan de San Luis Potosí," which declared the elections null and called for an armed uprising for November 20. Aquiles and Carmen Serdán were forced to begin the armed struggle a few days early in Puebla. The forces of Pancho Villa and Pascual Orozco captured Ciudad Juárez in 1911. A month later Díaz resigned and left Mexico for exile in Europe. Separated from her husband during the first year of the Revolution, Villegas de Magnón became actively involved in the political arena in the Laredo, Texas area, as a member of the Junta Revolucionaria. She housed political exiles and contributed articles reporting on the latest developments of the revolutionary movement to the Idar family's *La Crónica* as well as to *El Progreso* and *El Radical*.[22]

After Madero took power in 1911, Villegas de Magnón opened one of the first bilingual kindergartens in the area. She became active in local socio-cultural endeavors and founded the organization Unión, Progreso y Caridad (Union, Progress and Charity). Careful not to offend male egos and sensibilities nor to perturb the status quo too much, Villegas de Magnón would use her organization to call for the extension of women's domestic chores to the public sphere: education of children, city beautification, charity work, cultural and social events.

Across the international border, however, the Revolution continued brewing as rivalries between different factions provoked numerous revolts against Madero. Emiliano Zapata, from the state of Morelos, promulgated the "Plan de Ayala," recognizing Pascual Orozco as chief of the Revolution and calling for agrarian reforms and redistribution of lands to disenfranchised campesinos. A year later, Orozco revolted with his "Plan Orozquista" and also demanded labor reforms. In 1912, Madero sent in Victoriano Huerta to defeat Orozco. In 1913 Porfirio Díaz's nephew, Félix Díaz, together with Bernardo Reyes, escaped from prison and placed Mexico City under a state of siege. During the ten days known as "La decena trágica" (Tragic Ten Days), Huerta betrayed Madero by leading an uprising against the government. Conspiring with Henry Lane Wilson, the US ambassador to Mexico, and General Aureliano Blanquet, he arrested President Madero and Vice-President Pino Suárez and forced their resignations. Two days later, Madero and Pino Suárez were murdered. In the following months, Pancho Villa, Venustiano Carranza and Alvaro Obregón all rebelled against Huerta under the "Plan de Guadalupe," which initiated the second, violent phase of the Mexican Revolution. Carranza proclaimed himself First Chief of the Constitutional Forces and initiated an armed revolt against Huerta.

The Violent Phase: Constitutionalism and Dissension

Notwithstanding Villegas de Magnón's earlier revolutionary involvement, she did not deliberately set out to become an active participant in the violent phase of the Revolution. On the dawn of March 17, 1913, upon…

> Hearing the fire, the Rebel dressed quickly. She called her aunt's home in Nuevo Laredo. Getting no answer, she called several friends. There was no answer to any of her calls. Rushing out into the street, she stopped a big new car

> driven by a chauffeur. Directing him to drive to the offices of *El Progreso,* she told him to wait for her. She painted a red cross on a piece of paper and had it pasted on the windshield. Telephoning her friends, she told them her plans to go to Mexico and help take care of the wounded; she needed volunteers. With her faithful friend, Jovita Idar, a writer for *El Progreso,* the Rebel encouraged four other young women to join them in offering immediate help.

Thus began the work of the group that was to become La Cruz Blanca. Their participation in the revolutionary effort nonetheless would become the most significant part of Villegas de Magnón's own life story. In effect, the last three quarters of her autobiographical narrative read as a compilation of her memoirs from 1913 to 1920, focusing extensively on the work of La Cruz Blanca from March 17, 1913 in Laredo through September 14, 1914, when, as part of the Constitutionalist forces, La Cruz Blanca triumphantly entered Mexico City.

The narrator of *The Rebel* often reminds the reader that she is not by any means attempting to write official history, but merely her own version of what she saw. It is worthwhile to quote at length the only "official account" that I have been able to locate thus far which includes Villegas de Magnón as one of the protagonists of the revolutionary struggle. In *Laredo and the Rio Grande Frontier,* historian J. B. Wilkinson offers us a parallel account of the events of early 1914. The Constitutionalist revolutionary forces attacked federally fortified Nuevo Laredo on January 1, as an assault on the counterrevolutionary Huerta regime. Villegas de Magnón thus began to use all her resources—her inheritance, her social and family contacts and any other means at her disposal to create a medical relief group of women and men that was soon to become known as La Cruz Blanca. Wilkinson writes:

> The colonel closed the bridge to Nuevo Laredo during and immediately after the battle. He did this to prevent the passage of spies, smuggled ammunition, and sight-seers. The US consul at Nuevo Laredo protested, and General Bliss urged the colonel to rescind his order. The bridge was reopened on January 5. By that time the defeated Constitutionalists had by-passed Nuevo Laredo, as Gonzales [*sic*] probably reported it, or had been driven off, a more accurate statement, to a position opposite San Ygnacio.
>
> Over a hundred wounded Carranzistas [*sic*] escaped to the left bank of the river, where they were first cared for

by the Red Cross. They were later quartered in the rented home and garage of Mrs. Magnón, whose husband has been identified with the Reyes revolution, and in a school she conducted. By the end of the month, the number of refugee soldiers had been reduced to no more than 50; the rest had recovered enough to leave Mrs. Magnón's "hospital" and lose themselves in the Laredo population, presumably to find a way back to General Gonzales' small army.

On January 26 Lieutenant A. H. Jones was, rather belatedly, to intern the wounded men still in Mrs. Magnón's care. Dr. Lowry was the attending physician. The lieutenant found the doctor cooperative and quite willing to turn the men over to the army. Mrs. Magnón, a redoubtable lady, opposed the move. All Jones could do was to post sentries. But the wounded men had many visitors, and these milled about so much and became so mingled with the convalescents that the sentries were unable to tell one from the other. Jones reported that Mrs. Magnón added to the confusion by having the visitors exchange clothing with the prisoners, by having prisoners pose as attendants, and so on. Ten of fifteen men escaped internment by walking away. The more seriously wounded, however, were not able to take advantage of Mrs. Magnón's hullabaloo, and Jones finally was able to move 37 men into custody at Fort McIntosh.

Mrs. Magnón did not let it rest at that. She hired a lawyer. He pleaded that the men were not belligerents who fled the battle to surrender to a third party, but wounded brought across the river to safety by friends, a distinction without much difference. He threatened to have a writ of habeas corpus served on President Wilson. Mrs. Magnón made a personal effort to interest Governor Colquitt of Texas, who couldn't have helped much if he had wanted to, but Mrs. Magnón said with feminine vehemence that the governor refused to help because he did not favor the Constitutionalist cause. Senator Morris Shepart of Texas was persuaded to write to the war department, which insisted that the internment was a matter for the state department. William Jennings Bryan was still secretary of state, and when the argument reached his attention, Mrs. Magnón had won her case. Bryan didn't bother to investigate; he hastened to oblige the lady and ordered the release of the interned Carranzistas. Apparently no one bothered to ask them whether they wanted to return to Gonzales' army, and the US army doubtless was happy to have its war with Mrs. Magnón settled on any terms.[23]

Wilkinson's interpretation of these events is telling of his cavalier attitude toward *The Rebel*'s protagonist. Moreover, it provides a unique point of comparison to Villegas de Magnón's own narrative.

After these two events, the work of La Cruz Blanca reached the ears of one of Carranza's generals, Pablo González, who would soon ask her to officially head the medical relief group which would travel with the Constitutionalist forces. Through a letter dated February 25, 1914, included in the old trunk, Villegas de Magnón reveals much of the gender and factional politics which she judiciously "silenced," that is either not included or subdued in her narrative. She claims to be working for the newspaper *El Radical* and discloses the names of so-called "revolutionaries" who in fact are profiting from the arms sales. The letter further uncovers the reason she and her husband were separated:

> [T]rabajo con dificultades pues mi marido es de distinta opinión, por eso vivo separada y estoy resuelta de no ir a México hasta que triunfe la revolución, ni aceptar ni un centavo de él hasta que cambie él de opinión.
>
> (I work with difficulties because my husband is of contrary opinion, that is why we are separated and I am resolved not to return to Mexico City until the Revolution truimphs and not to accept a penny from him until he changes his opinion.)

The narrator of *The Rebel* mildly explains her relationship to her husband as the Rebel and the first Cruz Blanca brigade leave their homes and families in Laredo and head toward El Paso to cross the border to Ciudad Juárez:

> With no opportunity but to go forward, the Rebel had left her three children with her brother and his wife, and with an indefinite idea of her husband's attitude towards the Revolution, she had set out on an unknown expedition. Before the small band of volunteers stood the available future to which every human being is entitled; that future was their own. Behind them would soon be an abyss which would separate them from the past, from those they loved, their inheritance. They did not speak of home, nor the ones left behind, but kept their eyes on time. The time piece on their wrists regulated their lives; every minute was counted, every minute belonged to duty at a bedside, at an operating table, at a disinfecting process, or writing letters to someone dear to a dead soldier.

Through her account of La Cruz Blanca's performance in the revolutionary stage, the narrator discloses the medical corp's numerous ventures to unify, harmonize and pacify the otherwise massive, chaotic, destructive revolutionary hurricane. Featuring a romanticized Venustiano Carranza as "Mexico personified," the narration focuses on the Constitutionalist faction of the revolutionary struggle. Subsequently, dissension by other revolutionary leaders such as Villa, Zapata, Orozco and Felipe González is viewed unfavorably through the eyes of a fervent, loyal Constitutional. *The Rebel* gives a detailed account of the historical events surrounding the violent phase of the Revolution, and the "Chronology of Events Surrounding the Mexican Revolution" (Appendix I) and the "Bio-Bibliography of Historical Characters" (Appendix II) should facilitate reading of Villegas de Magnón's own narrative.

The Rebel ends rather abruptly, with a eulogy to Carranza and with the following lines:

> Too many memories were gathered in the recesses of her mind to allow her to be content with the peace of forgetfulness.
>
> Commanded by the dead, and wishing to do justice to the worthy nurses and brave women who so patriotically defended their country, the Rebel watches the outcome of the years that flamed a white heat in the fiery crucible of the Mexican Revolution.

Thus concluded the work of La Cruz Blanca and that chapter of Villegas de Magnón's life. Her activism, however, was far from concluding with that episode.

The Post-Revolution: Silencing The Self

> En las chozas, en los templos, en los palacios, en los campos de batalla, pides esa limosna [de amistad sincera] y nada encuentras, ¿y por qué? ¿Tan sólo por el delito de ser mujer?
>
> —Leonor Villegas de Magnón, from her poem entitled "Soy una triste peregrina"
>
> (In huts, in temples, in palaces, and in battlefields, you beg for that charity [of sincere friendship] and you get nothing. And, why not? Is it only for the crime of being a woman?)
>
> —from her poem entitled "I Am a Lonely Pilgrim"

During the second half of her life, Villegas de Magnón carried out several significant projects unnoted, silenced in her autobiographical narrative, but revealed through correspondence and newspaper clippings recovered from the old trunk in the vacant Magnón house. She spent her post-revolutionary years producing various versions of her story, marketing them, securing means to financially support herself and her family, and participating in governmental activities both in the USA and Mexico. Five medals acknowledging her own participation in the Revolution, along with numerous periodical clippings, attest not only to her activism through the 1950s, but also to ample public recognition for her own individual accomplishments.

With her abundant inheritance exhausted in the revolutionary effort, Villegas de Magnón was briefly supported by her brother Leopoldo in the early 1920s while she set up her kindergarten again. During the 1930s, she also worked for the Women's Division of the Texas Democratic Executive Committee. In 1940, in dire economic need, she returned to Mexico City to solicit employment with the Bloque de Veteranos Revolucionarios de Sindicato Unico de Trabajadores de la Secretaría de la Economía Nacional (a division of the Veteran's Administration). She soon became a member of the Club Internacional de Mujeres (Women's International Club). Together with other women who had taken part in the revolutionary struggle, she lobbied for decades to receive official recognition as veterans of the Revolution. Leaving a comfortable position at the National Department of Statistics in Mexico City, in 1946 she volunteered to work her own "parcela" (agricultural plot) in Rancherías Camargo, Tamaulipas. After two unsuccessful years, her credit and family's financial gifts expended, and disillusioned with the failure of agrarian programs, she returned to Laredo. Her last duty, she notes in her story, was to attempt "to do justice to those worthy nurses and brave women who so patriotically defended their country" by narrating their heroic deeds, lest they be relegated to oblivion. She died before she received her veteran's pension and three days after she had made her last attempt to have her story published.

Other correspondence tells of the tremendous difficulties of that endeavor. More than 26 letters of rejection from numerous U.S. and Mexican publishing houses suggest that attempting to have *The Rebel* published became a major enterprise between 1920 and 1955. Her daughter, Leonor Grubbs, would continue her efforts through the 1980s. Two letters from Mexican officials chronologically frame this collection of correspondence from 1919 to 1959. Dated February 9, 1919, a letter from Carranza hints at the possibility that she could have written the Spanish language version of the narrative even before 1920:

> No puede el gobierno facilitar a Ud. la cantidad que me dice para la edición del libro que desea Ud. publicar. Pero puede editarlo aquí en los talleres del gobierno que hacen trabajos tan buenos como los que se hacen en ese país. Si regresa Ud. a éste hablará Ud. sobre el asunto conmigo.
>
> (The government cannot help you with the amount that you have asked for to edit the book you wish to publish. But we can edit it here in our government offices which produce works just as good as those from that country. You will have to speak to me about this issue if you return to our country.)

A letter from Antonio Díaz Soto y Gama, prominent member of the Instituto de Estudios Históricos de la Revolución (Institute of Historical Studies of the Revolution), to Mrs. Grubbs, dated July 9, 1959, attempts to justify the Institute's rejection of "La Rebelde":

> Ya di cuenta al Patronato de Estudios sobre la Revolución con las memorias de la señora madre de usted y excelente amiga mía.
>
> Las encontró el Patronato muy interesantes, pero a la vez estimó que la forma novelada que esas memorias revisten, no da lugar a su publicación por el Patronato, que sólo pública historias o crónicas sobre la Revolución.
>
> Pedí yo, en tal virtud, que la copia de esas memorias pasase a manos del Sr. Gral. Urquizo, a fin de que éste hiciese lo posible por que aquéllas sean publicadas por la agrupación oficial de veteranos de la Revolución, a quienes seguramente inspirarán interés por la justicia que se hace a las esforzadas integrantes de la Cruz Blanca Constitucionalista.
>
> El Gral. Urquizo aceptó la comisión y de su resultado daré cuenta a usted oportunamente.
>
> (I presented to the Board of Historical Studies of the Revolution the accounted memoirs of your mother, my excellent friend.
>
> The Board found them very interesting but at the same time expressed that the novel format of her memoirs does not meet the Board's requirements. The Board only publishes histories or chronicles on the Revolution.

> I requested instead that this copy of her memoirs be passed to Gen. Urquizo, with the hope that he will make it possible for them to be published by an official group of Revolutionary veterans, whose interest I'm sure will be inspired by the justice of the courageous members of the Cruz Blanca Constitucionalista.
>
> Gen. Urquizo accepted the commission and I will inform you on its result soon.)

Even though these two letters seem promising, neither yielded concrete results. The other letters of rejection are from such publishers as Simon and Schuster, McMillan, Harper and Brothers, P. J. Kennedy and Sons—all of New York—and The Bruce Publishing Company from Milwaukee, Wisconsin.

Why did Villegas de Magnón not succeed in communicating her story to her intended audiences in Mexico and the US between 1920 and 1955? Surely a woman of her class, education and undeniable resourcefulness should have met with success. Why did her various privileges not afford her the satisfaction of seeing her manuscripts in book form? The Villegas de Magnón papers located thus far give a clue to one answer: the mixed response of those who read the work in manuscript form. More specifically, I would like to suggest that the many readings—from those of friends and fellow revolutionaries, to scrutinizing professional writers and editors, to her own readings of her texts, her life and times—generated critical valuation which significantly sealed the fate of her story. The following subsections contextualize these readings within two distinct national "literary" traditions: the Mexican post-revolutionary memoirs and the tradition of autobiographical writing in the English-speaking world. I submit that various marginalizations situated her story within precarious borders, in particular the marginal status of women's autobiographies. The autobiographical/memoir genre imprisoned her story within a narrative form which has historically privileged male authority, authorship and discourse, and ignored or devalued those same female qualities.

Reconstructed Memories/(Re)Constructed Selves

> Hers [the woman autobiographer's] is always a complex, ultimately precarious capitulation, open to subversive elements both without and within the text. Although her "life" reenacts the figures and supports the hierarchy of values that constitute patriarchal culture, it remains nonetheless the story of a woman. No matter how conscientiously it

> pays tribute to the life of man, no matter how fiercely it affirms its narrative paternity, the testimony of life and text is vulnerable to erasure from history because it is, on the one hand an "unfeminine" story and, on the other, merely the "inferior" word of woman.
>
> —Sidonie Smith, *A Poetics of Women's Autobiography*

In this passage, Sidonie Smith's remarks capture the complexity, precariousness and erasure of women's life testimonies, of their historical struggle to grapple with the ambivalences, contradictions, subversiveness and betrayals inherent in making those testimonies public within a patriarchal culture. Villegas de Magnón confronted these perils. Numerous ruptures in her narratives subtly suggest, or overtly disclose, ruptures in her life, subject positionings (with regard to class, nationality, gender, religious beliefs) and ideological postures (concerning political alliances). By aspiring to make public the story of a woman who rebelled, however tenuously or ardently, against her class origins, religious upbringing, family expectations, political affiliations and patriarchal social mores, she reveals the multiplicity of selves linked to her socio-historical context. She depicts a rebel who subsequently escapes the normal destiny of a bourgeois woman of the borderlands through her own agency. Ironically, as a means to find a public for her autobiographical narrative after she feels betrayed by the Revolution, she returns to that lady that she had cast off. Doubly ironic is the fact that she did not succeed in reaching that public during her lifetime.

In order to give written form to her anecdotes, remembrances, historical and heroic deeds, ventures, treasure stories and love tales, she inevitably entered into a communicative process which demanded awareness, conscious or intuitive, of her self as a writer, of her narrative text as a medium of unique communication and of her potential readers as receptors of an ignored part of history.

Life Writing in Mexico: Revolution, Catalyst for Memoirs

> "Go straight to General Herrera," [Federico] Idar said rapidly. He had the fire and fearlessness of a Comanche. To him a patriotic duty was a moral command. "Tell the General that he is being betrayed."
>
> "But will he believe me?" she insisted. "I am only a woman in the hospital service."

As Villegas de Magnón experienced La Cruz Blanca's erasure, and sensed its dilution into folklore—following the fate of the revolutionary female image into the mythified "soldadera," "Adelita," "Marieta"—she unrelentingly sought to reinscribe a 'real' image into historical memory through the first, Spanish version of her story, "La Rebelde."[24] Her portrayal of "rebel women" derived from different social classes—from rural, destitute soldiers' companions to middle-class teachers, journalists, propagandists, printers, telegraph operators, nurses and to bourgeois socialites—subverts the Mexican social text. Just as subversive is her own self-portrayal as an independent, intelligent, and extremely outspoken woman. By doing so, as Claudia Schaefer explains, she was a threat to the status quo:

> Even the women who had taken part in the Revolution itself became mythified [sic] by society. The *soldaderas,* for example, became the image of women who take orders faithfully, conceive and give birth to children on the battlefield, and follow their men unhesitatingly and supportingly wherever they go. [...] If a woman spoke up, she was no longer dependent on others, nor on their interpretation and control of social reality, and consequently she was a threat to the status quo. This was particularly true in the halcyon days after the 1910 Revolution when men (politicians, philosophers, military leaders) were forging mechanisms of power and held a monopoly on all varieties of social discourse.[25]

In asking from the 1920s to the 1950s the Mexican government and publishing industry to provide book form for the performances and experiences of "real" women in the revolutionary theater, Villegas de Magnón seems to have been alone. By assuming authorship and authority to shift women's image from object to subject, she openly defied Mexican social gender codes. She ripped through the "double corset" of which Mexican historian Carmen Ramos speaks in her study of the "señoritas porfirianas" of 1880–1910:

> La mujer porfiriana, sobre todo la burguesa, estaba presionada por un doble corsé, el físico, que afinaba su talle hasta hacerle perder la espontaneidad y la libertad de movimiento, y el más opresivo corsé de una moralidad rígida [...][26]
>
> (The Porfirian woman, especially the bourgeois woman, was pressured by a double corset. The physical corset refined her waist until she lost her spontaneity and freedom

> of movement, but the more oppressive corset was that of a rigid morality[...])

Furthermore, she claims, the parameters of feminine morality and immorality were established by masculine judgment:

> A la mujer burguesa se le predica y exige sumisión, abnegación, desinterés por el mundo de la política, de las cuestiones sociales, aislamiento absoluto de todo lo que vaya más allá del ámbito doméstico, reducto desde donde dirige a un ejército de sirvientas que mantienen inmaculado el sagrado recinto del hogar. Ese hogar se entiende como un ámbito especial, intocable, a donde no llegan las tensiones, un espacio reservado exclusivamente para la vida familiar, totalmente desligada del mundo social. Más allá del hogar, fuera de éste y desconectado de él, está el ámbito de la vida pública, del mundo de los negocios y las grandes decisiones, el mundo de los varones. Los ámbitos público y privado quedan así claramente divididos para cada sexo.[27]
>
> (Submission, self-denial and disinterest in the world of politics and social concerns are preached and insisted upon for the bourgeois woman. In absolute isolation from everything that extends beyond the domestic environment, she directs an army of servants who keep the sacred area of the home immaculate. This home is understood to be a special, untouchable environment reserved exclusively for family life, free from tensions and totally free from the social world. Beyond the home, outside of it and disconnected from it, is the sphere of public life, the world of business and big decisions, the man's world. The public and private environments thus remain clearly divided for each sex.)

Villegas de Magnón's story depicted quite a different image. A schoolteacher from Monterrey, María de Jesús González, becomes a revolutionary spy, then requests that the First Chief Carranza give her a post within the ranks of his army. María de Jesús relates her own story:

> [...] in hopes of an audience with the First Chief [...] I prepared myself carefully. [...] I started with a flood of information about the battle of Matamoros, Nuevo Laredo, and the White Cross. [...] "I want a commission in the army," I told him. "I want to be in the calvary." [...] Slowly he said, "We will think over how best you can serve. Call again." Then I thought that I could easily pass for my brother,

> dressed in soldier's clothes. [...I] went to a barber shop. "Give me a man's haircut." The shocked barber went about his business. It was a perfect hair cut. I gave him a big tip.

The narration depicts an articulate, strong-willed protagonist who defies men who attempt to give her orders to follow.

> Señor Múzquiz told the Rebel that the next day she must send one of the corps with a card to the First Chief saying the Constitutional White Cross was at his orders.
>
> "Señor Múzquiz," she said patting his right hand that was holding his fork. "You don't know me. I am a sensible rebel. No one, as yet, has ordered me to do anything. My father, my husband, and my brother always let me do anything."

She also advises, almost scolds, revolutionary leaders. When the Rebel notices that Carranza mistreats one of his officers, the Rebel attempts to apologize for him. He disapproves of her interference and she responds:

> "You can argue, but you cannot fill my mind with doubt. You need many friends. The army without you can accomplish nothing. You are their standard of hope. But you can do nothing without your followers. There can be no retracing of steps now until you bring peace, and so justice to the oppressed millions."

Villegas de Magnón's subversion of both narrative and social texts undoubtedly alarmed her potential Mexican publishers.

Generic boundaries further aggravated gender constraints. The three predominant narrative forms utilized in publishing the historic significance and essence of the Mexican Revolution—the historical narrative, the novel and personal memoirs—have invariably privileged male protagonists. Scholars of Mexican life writing note that only four women have received recognition for autobiographical narratives focused on the Revolution.[28] Well-known Nellie Campobello has received critical attention for her lyrical memoirs of the cruelty and violence of the Revolution from the naive perspective of a child witness in her *Cartucho: Relatos de la lucha en el norte de México* (1960) and *Las manos de mamá* (1960).[29] Less well known are the memoirs of Consuelo Peña de Villarreal, *La Revolución en el Norte* (1968), whose hybrid text assumes more the voice of a historian than a memoirist;

Sara Aguilar Belden de Garza, *Una ciudad y dos familias* (1970), renders a *costumbrista* portrayal by a Monterrey aristocrat who recalls her family's role in the Revolution; and the oral autobiography of Luz Jiménez, *De Porfirio Díaz a Zapata: Memoria nahuatl de Milpa Alta* (as compiled by Fernando Horcasitas from the Nahualtl Recollections of Luz Jiménez and published in 1974), whose story focuses more on her village than on her self-image.[30] It is important to note that these four memoirs were published after Villegas de Magnón's death.

Critic and bibliographer Richard Woods claims that although self-referential writing is almost an anomaly in the Spanish-speaking world, the Mexican Revolution served as the catalyst for its production in Mexico. Encompassing a 450-year period, Woods identified more than 325 published life writings, from *crónicas* of Conquest to recent *testimonios*. More than 20 percent of these dramatized the tumultuous events surrounding the Revolution and its impact on the lives of the authors. Appendix III lists the 30 autobiographical texts which, according to Woods' extensive study, were published in Mexico during the decades Villegas de Magnón sought publication of her Spanish-language version, "La Rebelde." Evidently no women succeeded in the enterprise.

The Villegas de Magnón papers reveal her sustained contact with numerous authors included in Appendix III, some of whom were readers of her Spanish-language version. An overview of these narratives further suggests that, in molding her story faithfully, Villegas de Magnón adhered to conventions of what was emerging as the canon of Mexican memoirs. Defining Mexican autobiographical writing as memoir, Woods' bibliographical study describes this genre's salient characteristics in the Mexican context:

> When speaking of Mexican autobiography, one is automatically referring to memoir, easily the favored form of life writing. [...] Memoirs simply are the recording of a fragment of years from a life. Usually they will be what the author perceives to be his significant years as a participant in an historical event or his nearness to celebrity or frequently, as in the case of Mexico, a justification for one's actions and a refutation of one's enemies. They lack both the formality and completeness of autobiography proper. To illustrate, the Mexican Revolution has been the greatest catalyst for memoirs. Furthermore, the memoir, rather than an intense self examination, is usually a refraction of events external to one's life. The author, recalling action in which he was a participant, may so distance himself from

> this that at times he assumes more the role of historian than autobiographer.[31]
>
> Since being in the world rather than becoming in the world characterizes the memoir, the self as an evolving personality, more the object of autobiography proper, rarely is portrayed in memoir. The creator, perhaps egotistically concerned that his role in an historical event be recorded, finds the memoir with its limited self-portrayal as a natural vehicle.[32]

Both the English and Spanish versions of Villegas de Magnón's autobiography, *The Rebel* and "La Rebelde," fit well all these generic descriptors. An examination of some of Villegas de Magnón's particular narrative strategies in light of those memoirs that were actually published between 1920 and 1955 reveals that in form and content her text conforms to, rather than challenges, their autobiographical conventions.

Written mostly by professionals, such as journalists, lawyers, diplomats, politicians and doctors, many of the narratives are written in a distanced, highly impersonal, documentary style similar to that conveyed by the third-person narrator in *The Rebel*. From the outset, the narrative voice establishes an internal distancing, an "articulated connection, a tension, between identity and difference" through the use of the third person.[33] Philippe Lejeune points out that, with this transposition from one code to another, the third-person

> autobiographer is authenticating his [her] own discourse instead of assuming it directly; he [she] takes a step down and, in fact, divides himself [herself] into a double narrator. One has the feeling he [she] is talking to us in a simultaneous translation.[34]

With the construction of the "fictive witness," Villegas de Magnón creates an internal distancing which also expresses personal confrontation. Throughout the entire Spanish manuscript, the subject is referred to as the child, the young lady, or the Rebel. Her proper name is never used. It is this "other" who rebels against the ideology of her aristocratic class, against the boundaries set by society with regard to women's role.

Similar to the memoirs published by Ediciones Botas, Toribio Esquivel Obregón's *Mi labor en servicio de México* (1934), Francisco L. Urquizo's *Recuerdo que...": Visiones de la Revolución* (1934), Manuel González's *Contra Villa: Relatos de la campaña, 1914–1915* (1935), Felix Fulgencio Palavincini's *Mi vida revolucionaria* (1937), and

Querido Moheno's *Mi actuación política después de la decena trágica* (1939), *The Rebel* interpolates an impressive compilation of documents: official military correspondence and telegrams, transcribed speeches and a massive collection of photographs. La Cruz Blanca had an official photographer, Eusebio Montoya, who visually documented all their work. Evidently the Rebel was well aware of the value of photographs as history and, as a shrewd capitalist, of the value of making them her private property: "'Montoya,' the Rebel said repeatedly to him, 'photographs are history, and you must not let anyone have a negative or sell the pictures. They are my personal property. I pay for the supplies.'"

As Francisco Vázquez Gómez's *Memorias políticas* (1909–1913) (1933) and Manuel González's *Con Carranza: Episodios de la revolución constitucionalist*, 1913–1914 (1933), *The Rebel* included long lists of names and tributes to political luminaries who surrounded La Cruz Blanca staff. Unlike these other memoirs, however, its focus was names of the women of the various Cruz Blanca brigades as well as vignettes of women turned spies, female military officers dressed as men and valiant heroines. Although the temporal structure is that of traditional chronological discourse, Villegas de Magnón interrupts the chronological narration to remind the reader of her objective in writing her story. After a detailed account of the journey of the revolutionary forces and the Cruz Blanca battling the federal troops from the border area down to Mexico, she disrupts the third-person narration, inserts herself in first person with an outcry against what official history is negating. As the narration describes the events of La Rebelde's 38th birthday, June 12, 1914, when La Rebelde finds herself absorbed in "vague melancholic thoughts," offended at the ingratitude shown toward the Cruz Blanca's work, the disruption discloses the following:

> ¿Qué acaso ha habido al pie de la tumba del Mártir Madero o del Mártir Carranza, cuando los grandes oradores recuerdan los actos de los héroes y sus hazañas, quién se acuerde de mencionar la valiosa colaboración de la Cruz Blanca?
>
> Aquellas mujeres abnegadas jamás encontraron en los hospitales de sangre a las esposas de los generales. ¿Dónde estaban? En el extranjero esperando el toque del clarín para recibir, por lo menos una palabra de reconcimiento.
>
> Por eso precisamente escribo esto, para glorificar a las enfermeras patriotas y desinteresadas de entonces. [...]
>
> Todas ellas habían probado ya su lealtad y su eficacia; no dudaba la Rebelde que en su corazón jamás habría

> traición; por eso cada una se convertía en cabeza ya probada y aprobada.
>
> (When great orators remember the deeds and feats of heroes, has there been someone who has remembered to even mention the collaboration of the Cruz Blanca?
>
> Those unselfish women never saw the Generals' wives in the hospitals. Where are [those selfless women]? They are abroad awaiting the bugle call to at least receive a word of acknowledgement.
>
> This is precisely why I am writing this, to glorify those patriotic and selfless nurses. [...]
>
> All of them had already proven their loyalty and efficiency. La Rebelde had no doubt that in their hearts there would never be any trace of treason. Every one of them therefore [had become] a proven and approved entity.)

The Rebel understood that as US citizens their national alliance was continually being questioned. Her narrative was to point to their deeds as acts of an international social justice which knew no national boundaries. For her all border area participants, regardless of gender, were just as important as anyone else. Continued narrator interruptions in the story line boldly protest calculated omissions by official history:

> [...] la historia se ha encargado de relatar los hechos, pero se ha olvidado del importante papel de los pueblos de Laredo, Texas, Nuevo Laredo, Tamaulipas y otros fronterizos que en esos momentos se unieron en un fraternal acuerdo.
>
> ([...] history has assumed responsibility for documenting the facts, but it has forgotten the important role played by the communities of Laredo, Texas, and Nuevo Laredo, Tamaulipas and other border cities which united themselves in a fraternal agreement.)

The narration includes long lists of the *fronterizos'* names and their accomplishments such as the those of Clemente and Federico Idar, Jovita Idar's brothers, focusing on their labor and political activism.

> Clemente M. Idar, viril periodista y orador de gran fuerza moral, llegó a adquirir fama internacional en sus esfuerzos en pro del trabajador mexicano establecido en Estados Unidos, y en aquel tiempo era un infatigable propagandista del "Maderismo," y luego del "Constitucionalismo," a cuya obra redentora dio las primicias y el

fuego de su juventud. Más tarde, es el único líder obrerista que logra distinguirse en tierra extraña. Organizador general del trabajo en aquella región, levanta el obrerismo latino como ningún otro campeón. Su magnífica oratoria y sus notables esfuerzos le valieron la estimación de Samuel Gompers, Presidente de la Federación del Trabajo Americano, y de William Green, líder del Trabajo de los Estados Unidos, a quienes a veces representó en importantes comisiones.

Su fervor fue tan extremado, que en sus últimas palabras, en el lecho del dolor, hizo reiteración de sus doctrinas de civismo, unión y progreso. En su cámara mortuoria, recibió el tributo de miles de obreros, que desfilaron ante su féretro con la cabeza inclinada. Derramando lágrimas, se despidieron de su campeón fraternal.

Más tarde, su hermano, Federico, que había recorrido los países de la América Latina sembrando las mismas ideas, sacrificó la vida defendiendo los intereses superiores de los ferrocarrileros, pues a causa de esa actitud fue asesinado en la capital, siendo Senador de la República.

(Clemente M. Idar, a forceful journalist and a public speaker of great moral strength, gained international fame for his efforts in support of Mexican workers established in the United States. At that time he was a tireless propagandist for Maderism and later for Constitutionalism, a redeeming work to which he gave the fire and first fruits of his youth. Later, he was the only labor leader who was able to distinguish himself in a foreign country. As general organizer of laborers in the region, he raised Latino workers to a level previously unreached. His magnificent public speaking and his notable efforts earned him the esteem of Samuel Gompers, President of the American Federation of Labor, and of William Green, leader of the United States Labor Union, both of whom Idar represented in important commissions.

His enthusiasm was so extreme that his last words—while he was suffering great pain—reiterated his doctrine of citizenship, union and progress. Thousands of laborers saluted him upon his death, passing his coffin with their heads bowed. With tears overflowing, they said goodbye to their leader and champion.

Following his death, Idar's brother Federico travelled through Latin America spreading the same doctrine. He dedicated his life to defending the interests of railroad

> laborers, an act for which he was assassinated in the capital as Senator of the Republic.

The narration then continues with the following denunciation against Mexico's contempt for US citizens of Mexican descent,

> Estos son ejemplos de los llamados "Pochos" que tanto desprecian en la capital y que guardan en ambos puños fuertemente apretados el honor y el decoro internacional de una psicología incomprensible y grandiosa. De ellos se servía la Rebelde y ellos fueron su inspiración.
>
> (These are examples of the so-called "Pochos" who are so despised in the capital [Mexico City] and who hold in their clenched fists the international honor and decorum of an incomprehensible and magnificent psychology. La Rebelde received assistance and inspiration from them.)

Through the discursive mode of memoirs, then, the narrator lists paragraphs of names of those whose lives as labor, political and revolutionary leaders were dedicated to social change. As such, "La Rebelde" stands as one of the few documents produced between 1910 and 1920 which challenges the stereotypes of Texas Mexicans held by both Mexican and US dominant societies.

The memoirs which most parallel Villegas de Magnón's narratives are those written by Urquizo, one of "La Rebelde's" readers. "Recuerdo que..." is highly impersonal, gives priority to detail and anecdote, and basically personalizes the memoirs by the narrator's presence. Whereas both Urquizo's and Villegas de Magnón's explicit admiration of Carranza serves as one of the primary impetuses for their memoirs, their intent is not to provide an organized history of events nor to offer partisan views or ideological approaches to the Revolution. The narrator of "La Rebelde" seems to be suggesting that as an "ambassador of good will," La Cruz Blanca carried out a magnanimous mission beyond mundane political disputes, divisive personality conflicts and fratricidal turmoil, a claim which could have been read as naive.

Like the vast majority of Mexican memoirists, Villegas de Magnón consciously does not exploit the memoir for its aesthetic possibilities. Notable exceptions to this practice by Mexican memoirists are Martín Luis Guzmán's *El águila y la serpiente* (1929), which is considered one of Mexico's finest autobiographical novels, and José Rubén Romero's *Apuntes de un lugareño,* valued for its humorous, picaresque style. Unlike most memoirs, these two autobiographical pieces are recognized for their formal unity, sense of completeness and introspective, explorative nature as well. Interestingly, the narrative strategies employed by Villegas de Magnón in the first quarter of her story interpolate the intimate processes of self-formation utilized by these writers.

Villegas de Magnón seems to explore the Rebel's childhood episodes in order to examine whether the religious background forged at the Catholic boarding schools in San Antonio and New York to which her stepmother had sent her off, or her loneliness, or perhaps her stepmother's materialism were the motivating forces which lead her to rebel against her aristocratic social class. Directly and indirectly exposed to the ideals of the revolutionary leaders in Mexico City and the border region, the narration seems to be asking whether it was a sense of altruistic justice which guided the Rebel to recognize the plight of the exploited. Her own life, the Rebel reasoned, had supplied her with several significant motives. Her mother had intuitively known the Rebel's vocation early on ("Here, Leonor, you carry this [a white towel], and march between your brothers. Women also go to war. They carry a white flag and take care of the soldiers."). Carranza's pronouncement had further determined her fate ("In your capacity of President of the White Cross I will allow you to observe the silent passages of my life. It will be your privilege later on to report facts about me and my revolt that will be unknown to others"). Villegas de Magnón gave closure to *The Rebel* by expressing yet another motive: her desire to give homage to her nurses. These enquiries and motives however are not posed directly through a revelation of the Rebel's thoughts. Rather, they are "articulated" through the description of her acts.

Instead of revealing an introspective self who reflects, contemplates and arrives at self-knowledge, the narrator creates a persona who acts. The focus of the narration is on the events, incidents and experiences themselves. Her conception of the "word" seems to follow the Hebraic biblical concept of "davhar," which means not only "word" but also "deed." As Harold Bloom explains:

> *Davhar* is at once "word," "thing" and "act," and its root meaning involves the notion of driving forward something that initially is held-back. This is the word as a moral act, a true word that is at once an object or thing and a deed or act. A word not an act or thing is thus a lie, something that was behind and was not driven forward. In contrast to this dynamic word, the *logos* is an intellectual concept, going back to a root meaning that involves gathering, arranging, putting-into-order. The concept of *davhar* is: speak, act, be. The concept of *logos* is: speak, reckon, think. *Logos* orders

> and makes reasonable the context of speech, yet in its deepest meaning does not deal with the function of speaking. *Davhar,* in thrusting forward what is concealed in the self, is concerned with...getting a word, a thing, a deed out into the light."[35]

What is concealed in the self, from the perspective of the narrator of "*La Rebelde,*" is the sense of moral mission, duty, responsibility to drive forward the deeds of the women and men of the border which were being held back by official historians. Her word, however, is not meant to merely gather, arrange and render an intellectual account of their actions. Rather, her narration focuses on the acts and events which she attempts to have speak for themselves. At times, however, especially when alluding to "bandits," "Indians" and "servants," that omniscient narration cannot suppress the author's class biases.

As compared to the Mexican memoirs which did appear in published form, Villegas de Magnón evidently accommodated her text to suit the protocol demanded of it. With its subversion of assumptions about gender and nationality contrary to dominant discourse, however ambivalent and ambiguous, it could have been dismissed as a suspect feminine text. Besides questioning, it challenged the common female archetypes depicted in the narrative forms of the Mexican Revolution: the doll-like beauty, the subjugated wife and mother, and the prostitute, as well as Mexico's condescension toward the *fronterizos*.[36]

Acts of Translation: Marketing Autobiographical Writing in the USA

Although the Spanish and English versions of her work render the same story, comparison of the two reveals insights into the implied readers whom Villegas de Magnón thought she was addressing. In the Spanish version, relating events and mentioning names was most important. The implied reader would be familiar with the historical drama. In contrast, detail becomes important in the expanded English version; the "foreign" reader requires explanatory remarks. The first quarter of the narrative elaborates on Mexican borderlands' traditional customs, mores, culinary habits and historical background.

Conscious of her "historical task," she appropriates the dominant discourse and "markets" her commodity. Her September 26, 1953, form letter to US publishers reads:

Dear Sir:

Would you be interested in a M.S.S. [manuscript] concerning life in a changing Mexico, from Díaz's 1876–1920, when a new Mexico was emerging? [It contains] approximately 100,000 words. The authentic story, ["The Rebel was a Lady"], follows the life of a wealthy Spanish merchant's daughter.

The first seven or eight chapters describe life on both sides of the Río Grande, where the "good neighbor policy" was practiced in a crude way and has existed for over a century.

"Land of Mañana" is a thing of the past, it is now the land of the future. As years roll on the Rebel becomes part of the rumbling against aging dictator Díaz and finally establishes the National White Cross, the nursing organization of the Carrancistas. The Rebel and her brigade accompany Venustiano Carranza's forces through the revolution until triumph in 1916. Then she watches helplessly the disintegration of Carranza's power and his downfall.

One of her nurses [was] "Adelita," who was to become the inspiration for the song by that name, [t]he famous marching and fighting song of the revolution. From the same source of inspiration, The White Cross, came successively "La Marrietta" [*sic*] and "La Valentina," equally popular and provocative to deeds of valor.

The unpredictable Villa passes through the Rebel's swift moving drama, as does General Felipe Ángeles, General Pablo González, ex-President Abelardo Rodríguez and many other high veterans.

She presents new and intimate pictures of President Carranza during the civil strife in Mexico.

If desired there are telegrams, letters to accompany the text.

Yours very truly,
Leonor Villegas Magnón

Lv/iba

Ironically, within the US context, Villegas de Magnón attempts to market her story by capitalizing on popular, uncritical notions of female images of the Mexican Revolution. Was this a desperate maneuver on her part to "sell" her story? Was it shrewd manipulation of gender discourse?

The following letter is indicative of the type of responses of rejection Villegas de Magnón received. On October 29, 1951, Orrin Keepnews, Associate Editor for Simon and Schuster, answered Villegas de Magnón's publication inquiry, noting:

> I'm sorry to report that we don't feel sufficient enthusiasm for the material to warrant our taking it on for publication.
>
> There is undeniably a great deal of colorful and important material here. But your story is basically a detailed description of a historical situation in which the general book-buying audience in this country actually has no deep and immediate interest, and we doubt that it would have a very wide appeal.
>
> This does not mean that we feel the manuscript is not worthy of publication, but simply that we believe that it is comparatively too limited in its potential market to make it particularly well suited for our list. We are primarily concerned with, and best equipped to handle, books that we believe to have a very wide, general potential audience, and our editors don't seem to regard your story as fitting that description.

Villegas de Magnón was not, however, to remain silent to such reading of and rejection to her story. On November 25, 1951, she retorts:

> Your answer of Oct 09, 1951 has become a fathomless script of knowledge. I love the way you raise my hopes then, suddenly dash me against a pitiless world of chaos and tumbled ideas.
>
> I will keep up my good work in the Río Grande as a union rather than a division.
>
> We need each other. This hemisphere must be united morally and spiritually. Whenever and however we can add even a tiny link to that chain of thought we should do it. I wish we had more such valiant souls like those who co-operated with me during the days of tragic civil strife in México.
>
> Since there is no law that prohibits pleasure in the accomplishment of one's duty, I shall hold a very special place in my life for you. Thanks for the mss that was returned in perfect shape.

Her rejoiner to Miss Jean Holloway, editor for the University of Texas Press, the following year (January 26, 1952) also exemplifies her continual defense of her work:

> No, my story is not a literary gem, it has been written in a hurry, but I intend to keep it just the way it is as I want it to reach a certain class of eager readers of the present day.
>
> I did not dwell on disagreeable things such as the 22 of Feb 39 years ago when at the American embassy Mr. Wilson and Huerta offered toasts to the Genesis of the Mexican Revolution exactly at the time Madero was being assassinated. With a smothered sob the Latin Americans today celebrate Washington's birthday when it could have been a precious memory for us all. My mss is only a synopsis of what I experienced [...].
>
> The sequel of the story should be The Martyr of the Apocalypse or Rebirth of the Mexico Nation. [...]
>
> I am anxiously awaiting the appearance of "Genesis under Madero" by Dr. Charles C. Cumberland so that I will have the pleasure of presenting it to next president, Adolfo Cortines who is my friend as was Pres. F. I. Madero. [...]
>
> I shall keep up my work of establishing the Río Grande as a union rather than a dividing line. [...][37]

This letter suggests Villegas de Magnón's desire to reach a broad audience, perhaps the new generation of middle-class readers who would not necessarily have interest in reading a literary gem but would read a personalized version of history, much in the Mexican tradition. Apparently, she was quite aware of the severity and significance of avoiding any critical remarks or analysis of US-Mexico relations.

Yet another letter from another editor gives evidence of the fact that Villegas de Magnón did substantial rewriting, both expanding and, more importantly, deleting at the recommendations of her readers:

> Our Mss would need going over, and elimination of a good many purely local matters, particularly names and characters that would have no special force in the story telling, for a nationwide audience. Streamline, cut down, I think it would have more force.

Evidently because of advice such as this, Villegas de Magnón deleted many sections on the *fronterizos,* including those quoted above on the Idar brothers and the "pochos." These responses and suggestions, indeed demands, from her readers were informed by a US cultural context. Valuative criteria for autobiographical writing have changed dramatically in the past four decades allowing for new readings not available to Villegas de Magnón's manuscripts during her lifetime.

"Critical Fictions" of Autobiographical Writing: the US Cultural Context

Since Villegas de Magnón's writing of the English version of her work during the 1940s through 1950s, critical studies of autobiographical writing have developed their generic definitions based on theories of selfhood. At different historical moments, distinct readings of autobiographies have given rise to distinct definitions and criteria to evaluate the success of any particular autobiographical narrative. The various philosophical theories of selfhood since the 1940s have centered their analysis anywhere from "facticity [the search for 'truth'] to psychology [the search for a 'true self'] to textuality [the search for the many significations of a text]."[38] An outline of several generations of autobiographical critical practices reveals critical traditions which have highlighted either the *autos* (self), the *bios* (life) or the *graphia* (writing) of the autobiographer.[39] Inevitably, the critical practices of any generation will be highly influenced by the philosophical assumptions of their times. The brief discussion of these critical approaches that follows will attempt to note, in very broad terms, the appropriation of historically-determined philosophical assumptions adopted by the readers/evaluators of autobiographical writings, an appropriation which has implications for both the writing and reading of women's self-representational projects. I contend that the readings by US editors were affected to various degrees by the philosophical and theoretical assumptions of two generations of critics who searched for "truth" and a "true self" in Villegas de Magnón's autobiography and evidently were unsatisfied with their findings. Moreover, I suggest that a new third generation of readers/critics now has at its disposal other assumptions which will allow us to approach the reading of *The Rebel* differently, asking new questions of it, searching for new answers.

Critical social theorists have used historical periodization terms such as the "modern" and the "postmodern" epochs to refer, in broad terms, to the periods approximately between 1475 and 1875 as the "Modern" age and since 1875 as the "post-Modern" age of Western history. Modernism has been characterized by traditional values of Protestantism, Victorianism, Enlightenment, rationalism and humanism. Depicted as "ranging from the philosophical project of Descartes, through the Enlightenment, to the social theory of Comte, Marx, Weber and others,"[40] much modern theory has been characterized by its focus on individuality, the notion of an unchanging human nature, purity, unity, as well as unproblematical trust in science, art, reason, ethical absolutes and certainties. Advocating a rational and unified subject, modern philosophy claimed access to absolute truth and objectivity. Ideologically, its foundation for knowledge was based on a "binary metaphysics"—subject/object, reality/appearance, speech/writing, voice/silence, man/woman, reason/nature, rational/instinctive, public/private, fact/fiction, etc.—which constructed a hierarchy of values, upholding in each case the "superiority" of the first term over the second.

Both the first and second generations of literary critics valorizing writings of self-representation during the 1940s and 1960s appropriated many of these modern values to give validity to the autobiographical genre within the sanctioned literary canon. Through the process of genre legitimacy, which privileged a rational and unified subject with a truthful, factual, eminent, public voice, it became evident that "universal" selfhood as defined by the economic, sociopolitical and cultural formations of the modern epoch was indeed masculine selfhood. I suggest that some of the following critical assumptions of the first and second generations of critics informed the editors/readers of *The Rebel* during the 1940s and 1950s.

A first generation of critics placed the most value on the moral implications of the *bios,* the quality of the lived experiences of the author, and the "truthfulness," the biographical veracity, of the narrative. The emphasis was on the cultural significance of the "individual personalities," the "self-assertion of the political will" and the "intellectual outlook revealed in the style of an eminent person," as well as "the relation of the author to his work and to the public" which was "bound always to be representative of [his] period," to capture "the spirit of his time."[41] Consequently, historical valorization of individuality, the ideal model, self-formation, independence, distinctiveness, public life, public voice and public self-disclosure in the autobiographical project inescapably privileged male discourse and virtually negated or ignored women autobiographers.

The concern with the *autos,* self-representation, of the following generation of critics led them to stigmatize the psychological significance of questions of identity, selfhood, self-definition, self-creation and authenticity of the self. By submitting the "autobiographical act" to methodical literary analysis, they disclosed a subject capable of being "made and remade according to such criteria as naturalness, originality, essentiality, continuousness, integrity and significance."[42] Grounded in "universal" ideologies of selfhood and metaphysical, essentialist notions of self and individuality, these studies continued to privilege male authority.

In view of the plurality, often conflicting, of postmodern positions, we cannot talk of a unified postmodern theory. I will select, however, some key concepts adopted by critics which should give a glimpse of the theoretical positionings of the following generation of autobiographical readers and which may be useful in our contemporary reading of *The Rebel*. According to some social theorists, postmodernism opposes some of the oppressive aspects of modernism and modernity and "calls for new categories, modes of thought and writing, and values and politics to overcome the deficiencies of modern discourses and practices."[43] Many postmodern literary theorists celebrate the breakdown of literary and cultural tradition and the subsequent high-low art distinction; critics call for a new postmodern criticism that "abandons formalism, realism, and highbrow pretentiousness, in favor of analysis of the subjective response of the reader within a psychological, social and historical context." Postmodern critics valorize eclecticism, pastiche, discontinuity, fragmentation, difference, decentered subject and multiplicity of selves, otherness, pleasure, insouciance, playfulness and novelty. These critics also place stress on the "arbitrary and conventional nature of everything social—language, culture, practice, subjectivity, and society itself."[45] They give primacy to "discourse theory" which claims that "meaning is not simply given, but is socially constructed across a number of institutional sites and practices."[46] The postmodern theorization of the intimate connection between knowledge, multiple forms of power and domination has opened useful analytical possibilities for the study of women, in general, and female subjectivity, in particular.

This third, and more recent, generation of critics of self-representational writings, then, utilizes some theoretical assumptions of postmodernism to move beyond generic valorization of self-representation. No longer are rigid, "universal" genre classifications "imposed" on the readings of autobiographical writings. Moreover, the autobiographical text can be approached as a narrative artifice. The development of new theoretical paradigms in the fields of psychoanalysis and linguistics during the past two decades have posed challenges "both to the concept of a speaking subject and to the belief in language's transparency."[47]

> [These] have shattered the epistemological certainties and ontological legitimacy of what French theorists call the "master narratives" of the West, autobiography among them. As notions of an authoritative speaker, intentionality, truth, meaning, and generic integrity are rejected, the former preoccupations of autobiography critics—the nature of its truth, the emergence of its formal structure, the struggle with identity, even the assumption of a motivating self—are displaced by a new concern for the *graphia,* "the careful teasing out of warring forces of significations within the text itself."[48]

The expansion of women's studies during the past few decades has not only tremendously influenced, but stigmatized as well, the theoretical debates on the status of self and the nature of language and of self-representation. Shifting cultural configurations have led critics interested in the feminine subject to both clarify and question extant systems of valuation of self-writing. They "explore the many 'lines' women have devised to speak of themselves for themselves and for their readers, going beyond the constraints of traditional boundaries."[49] Highly critical of exclusionary practices, feminist scholars promote the inclusion of previously "illegitimate," "marginal," "feminine" writings such as diaries, letters, memoirs, etc. Textual critics, interested in the writing, the text, shift their focus to the "reader" of the autobiography to examine both the "fictive" implied reader of the autobiographical writing as well as the author who "rereads literary and cultural conventions" of his or her times.[50] The "self" created by the author of a life story becomes a rhetorical construct. Those critics influenced by psychoanalytic assumptions scrutinize the "subjects in process"—both author and reader—and examine the multiplicity and instability of "selves." The autobiographical narrative is seen as both "a mode of reading" and "a mode of writing."[52]

It is precisely this new moment of critical discourse, of new approaches to evaluate the autobiographical writings, that creates the space from which new readings of *The Rebel* may take us beyond commentary illustrative of literary and cultural conventions, beyond the "critical fictions" of *The Rebel*'s 1940s–50s readings which rendered the testimony of Villegas de Magnón's life "unmarketable" both in Mexico and in the USA. Among the multiple new possibilities, we can now pose questions such as the following to evaluate the significance of this text. How do we now valorize the self-representational project of a bourgeois Mexican woman raised in US Ursuline convents who donated her entire inheritance to humanitarian, altruistic causes on both sides of the Mexico–US border? Why are her fragmented, contradictory autobiographical narratives, of both or either languages, relevant to our understanding of gendered voices which attempt to transcend national, class and religious boundaries? Why is Villegas de Magnón's use of language to capture a moment of social and political crisis as she "unconsciously" reveals a struggle to define her subjectivity a significant contribution to our comprehension of a historical/fictional narrative? Given our historical, social and psychological context, how do we respond to an "informal," "novelized," gendered account of the first revolution of this century? How is Villegas de Magnón attempting to construct new meaning with regard to the Mexican Revolution? How is she illuminating the connection between knowledge, power and domination? In light of the multiple forms of self-representational documentation (multiple versions of autobiographies in two languages, visual images of her self and her life, correspondence, telegrams, etc.) Villegas de Magnón consciously left to posterity, how can the reader (re)construct her "reading" of her social context?

Within this new space, we can tease out "warring forces of significations within the text itself," as critic Barbara Johnson has suggested, to explore not only the text's integrity and unity but its ruptures, fragmentations, silences, contradictions, ambivalences and ambiguities. These distinct readings delineate new insights into the multiplicity of boundaries—historical, linguistic, geographic, cultural, political, as well as those of class, nationality and gender—crossed by those peoples of the borderlands. Unearthing, recovering and preserving stories such as *The Rebel,* along with other narratives in their multiple oral and written forms, will further allow us the historical reconstruction of our Latino communities and critical evaluation of our cultural heritage.

Notes

[1]Scholarship on literary historiography has been conducted for the past three decades by literary critics, historians and librarians, most of whom form part of the Advisory Board of the Recovering the US Hispanic Literary Heritage Project: Edna Acosta-Belén, Antonia Castañeda, Rafael Chabrán, Richard Chabrán, Rodolfo Cortina, Onofre DiStefano, José Fernández, Juan Flores, Erlinda González-Berry, Ramón Gutiérrez, Inés Hernández, María Herrera-Sobek, Nicolás Kanellos, Luis Leal, Francisco Lomelí, Alejando Morales, Felipe Ortego, Genaro Padilla, Raymund Paredes, Tey Diana Rebolledo, Juan Rodríguez, Rosaura Sánchez and Charles Tatum.

[2]Herminio Ríos and Lupe Castillo, "Toward a True Chicano Bibliography: Mexican-American Newspapers: 1848–1942." *El Grito* 3 (Summer 1970): 17–24.

[3]I am grateful to Texas historian Ruthe Winegarten who first introduced me to the work of Leonor Villegas de Magnón.

[4]Américo Paredes, "El folklore de los grupos de origen mexicano en Estados Unidos," in *Folklore Americano* (Lima, Peru), 14 (1964): 146–63; translated by Kathleen Lamb and reprinted as "The Folk Base of Chicano Literature." I have quoted from the translation, page 7.

[5]Inés Hernández, "Sara Estela Ramírez: The Early Twentieth Century Texas Mexican Poet" (Diss., University of Houston, 1984): 112.

[6]"Más de cuatrocientos periódicos en español se han editado en Estados Unidos," *La Prensa,* San Antonio, Texas, domingo 13 de febrero de 1934: 9–11.

[7]Richard Griswold del Castillo, "The Mexican Revolution and the Spanish-Language Press in the Borderlands," *Journalism History* 4, issue 2 (Summer 1977): 42–47.

[8]Dirk Raat, Revoltosos: *Mexico's Rebels in the United States, 1903–1923,* College Station: Texas A&M University Press, 1981: 38.

[9]Luis Leal, "The Spanish Language Press: Function and Use," *The Americas Review* 17, issues 3–4 (Winter 1989): 157–162; Dennis J. Parle, "The Novels of the Mexican Revolution Published by the Casa Editorial Lozano," *The Americas Review* 17, issues 3–4 (Winter 1989): 163–168.

[10]See Anna Macías, *Against All Odds: The Feminist Movement in Mexico to 1940* (Westport, Connecticut: Greenwood Press, 1982): 26–57.

[11]Macías 25.

[12]Macías xiii–xv.

[13]See Inés Hernández's excellent study of one of these prominent figures, "Sara Estela Ramírez: The Early Twentieth Century Texas Mexican Poet" (Diss., University of Houston, 1984). This dissertation stands as one of the first extensive studies on a single Mexican American writer from the turn of the century.

[14]*In Revoltosos: Mexico's Rebels in the United State*s, 1903–1923 (College Station: Texas A&M University Press, 1981): 33, Dirk Raat cites the existence of this periodical. I have located a few issues at the International

Institute for Social History in Amsterdam and at the Bancroft Library at the University of California, Berkeley—number 5 (July 28, 1907), number 7 (August 11, 1907), number 9 (September 6, 1907) and number 13 (October 27, 1907)—and have briefly examined them in "Mexican Precursors of Chicana Feminist Writing," in *Multi-Ethnic Literature in the United States.* Cordelia Candelaria, ed. Boulder: University of Colorado, 1989: 21–34.

[15]Both Juan Gómez-Quiñones, in *Sembradores: Ricardo Flores Magón y el Partido Liberal Mexicano; A Eulogy and Critique* (Los Angeles: Chicano Studies Center Publications, University of California, 1973), and Dirk Raat, in *Revoltosos: Mexico's Rebels in the United States, 1903–1923* cite the work of these women. In "The Articulation of Gender in the Mexican Borderlands," published in Recovering the *U. S. Hispanic Literary Heritage* (Houston, TX: Arte Público Press, 1993): 293–308, I study an issue of *El Obrero.* Very little has been written on Andrea Villarreal except for references to her as one of PLM member Antonio I. Villarreal's sisters. Together with her sister Teresa, Andrea worked to free the PLM Junta members when imprisoned during their exile in the USA. Due to her oratory skills the *San Antonio Light and Gazette* refers to her as the "Mexican 'Joan of Arc'" in the article "Women Will Plead Cause of Refugees" (August 18, 1909: 1). The article is an announcement of a meeting in which Andrea and Mother Jones were to speak on behalf of imprisoned PLM members. The column begins:

> The power of woman's oratory will be used in the effort to win freedom for Tomás Sarabia and José Rangel, alleged Mexican revolutionists, now in jail here. Andrea Villarreal, the Mexican "Joan or Arc" will be a speaker with Mother Jones of national fame at the "freedom" meetings to be held at the old tent theater on East Houston Street, commencing Saturday evening.

In *Antonio I. Villarreal: Vida de un gran mexicano* (Monterrey, Nuevo León: Impresora Monterrey, 1959): 17–18, Fortunato Lozano, Antonio Villarreal's biographer, wrote the following of the importance of Andrea's involvement in the revolutionary effort.

> En esos días [en los del frustrado levantamiento de "Las Vacas", hoy Villa Acuña, Coahuila, el año de 1908] y no obstante la férrea preponderancia del gobierno porfiriano aun en el territorio estadounidense, la intrépida hermana de Villarreal, la entonces Srita. Andrea de propio apellido (hoy Vda. de Heredia), había llegado desde San Antonio, Texas, al pueblo ribereño de "Del Río" con un buen bagaje de armas y parque; y mientras tanto, animaba a los hombres del lugar con fogosos discursos, preparándolos para la acción.

[16]See José Limón's excellent analysis of the Idar family's political activism in "El Primer Congreso Mexicanista de 1911: Precursor to Contemporary Chicanismo," *Aztlán* 5 (1974): 85–117.

[17]Letter from Jovita López (Jovita Idar's niece) to Clara Lomas dated April 4, 1989.

[18]A note of appreciation to Rafael Chabrán who called to my attention the existence of *Pluma Roja*. In "The Articulation of Gender in the Mexican Borderlands" published in *Recovering the U. S. Hispanic Literary Heritage,* I offer a brief study of several issues of *Pluma Roja*.

[19]Juan Gómez-Quiñones, *Sembradores*: 40.

[20]David Montejano, *Anglos and Mexicans in the Making of Texas, 1836–1986* (Austin: University of Texas Press, 1987): 78–79.

[21]This is also noted by Ms. Bessie Lindheim in her "Comments on 'The Lady Was a Rebel,'" presented at the Laredo Historical Society Meeting (Laredo, Texas), May 8, 1970; I quote from her comments.

[22]Some of her articles include: "Evolución mexicana," *La Crónica* 7 September 1911: 1; "Adelanto de los mexicanos de Texas," *La Crónica* 19 September 1911: 4; "Cuentas de la Cruz Blanca Local," *El Radical* 5 March 1914, np.; "Justas aclaraciones," *El Progreso* 11 June 1915, n. pag.

[23]J.B. Wilkinson, *Laredo and the Río Grande Frontier* (Austin: Jenkins Publishing Co., 1975): 387–389.

[24]See María Herrera-Sobek, *The Mexican Corrido: A Feminist Analysis* (Bloomington and Indianapolis: Indiana University Press, 1990).

[25]Claudia Schaefer, *Textured Lives: Women, Art, and Representation in Modern Mexico* (Tucson: The University of Arizona Press, 1992): 6–7.

[26]Carmen Ramos, "Señoritas porfirianas: Mujer e ideología en el México progresista, 1880–1910," in *Presencia y transparencia: La mujer en la historia de México,* México DF: El Colegio de México, 1987: 150–151.

[27] Carmen Ramos 150–151.

[28]Richard Donovon Woods, compiler, *Mexican Autobiography/La Autobiografía mexicana: An Annotated Bibliography/ Una bibliografía razonada,* trans. Josefina Cruz-Meléndez (New York: Greenwood Press, 1988); Raymundo Ramos, *Memorias y autobiografías de escritores mexicanos* (Mexico: Universidad Nacional, 1967). Woods' book was an invaluable guide to Mexican life writings.

[29]Both books were published in México by Compañía General de Ediciones in 1960.

[30]Consuelo Peña de Villarreal, *La Revolución en el Norte* (Puebla, Mexico: Editorial Periodística e Impresora de Puebla, 1968); Sara Aguilar Belden de Garza, *Una ciudad y dos familias* (Mexico: Editorial Jus, 1970); and Luz Jiménez, *De Porfirio Díaz a Zapata: Memoria nahuatl de Milpa Alta,* comp. and trans. Fernando Horcasitas (Mexico: UNAM, Instituto de Investigaciones Históricas, 1974).

[31]Woods xiii.

[32]Richard Woods, "An Overview of Mexican Autobiography," *Auto/Biography Studies* 3 (Summer 1988): 13–14.

[33]Philippe Lejeune, "Autobiography in the Third Person," *New Literary History* 9, issue 1 (Autumn 1977): 32–35.

[34]Lejeune 35.

[35]Harold Bloom, *A Map of Misreading* (New York: Oxford Univ. Press, 1975): 42–43. Quoted from Douglas Atkins, *Reading Deconstruction, Deconstructive Reading* (Lexington, Kentucky: The University Press of Kentucky, 1983): 43–44.

[36]Margarita Peña, "Santa: Un arquetipo de prostituta," in *Entrelíneas, Textos de Humanidades*, 34 (México: UNAM, 1983): 98–100.

[37]The University of Texas Press published Cumberland's *Mexican Revolution: Genesis under Madero* in 1952.

[38]William C. Spengemann, *The Forms of Autobiography: Episodes in the History of a Literary Genre* (New Haven and London: Yale University Press, 1980): 189.

[39]See Sidonie Smith, *A Poetics of Women's Autobiography*, Chapter 1. The sketch which follows is derived from Smith's succinct revision of this autobiographical critical tradition.

[40]Steven Best and Douglas Kellner, *Postmodern Theory: Critical Interrogations* (New York: The Guilford Press, 1991): 4.

[41]See Georg Misch, *A History of Autobiography in Antiquity*, trans. E. W. Dickes (Cambridge: Harvard University Press, 1951): 12–14, and Karl Joachim Weintraub, *The Value of the Individual: Self and Circumstance in Autobiography* (Chicago: University of Chicago Press, 1978).

[42]Francis R. Hart, "Notes for an Anatomy of Modern Autobiography," *New Literary History* 1 (1970): 492. Also see: Margaret Bottrall, *Every Man a Phoenix: Studies in Seventeenth-Century Autobiography* (Chester Springs, PA: Dufour, 1958; Paul Delany, *British Autobiography in the Seventeenth Century* (London: Routledge & Kegan Paul, 1969); William L. Howarth, "Some Principles of Autobiography," *New Literary History* 5 (1974): 363–81; Roy Pascal, *Design and Truth in Autobiography* (Cambridge: Harvard University Press, 1960); and William C. Spengemann, *The Forms of Autobiography: Episodes in the History of a Literary Genre* (New Haven and London: Yale University Press, 1980).

[45]Best and Kellner 30.

[46]Best and Kellner 11; also see Leslie Fiedler, *The Collected Essays of Leslie Fiedler,* vol. II (New York: Stein and Day, 1971): 379–400; and Ihab Hassan, *The Postmodern Turn: Essays in Postmodern Theory and Culture* (Columbus, 1987).

[45]Best and Kellner 20.

[46]Best and Kellner 26.

[47]Smith 6.

[48]See Smith 6. Within the quote Smith cites Barbara Johnson, *The Critical Difference: Essays in the Contemporary Rhetoric of Reading* (Baltimore: Johns Hopkins University Press, 1980): 5.

[49]See Germaine Brée's foreword to *Life/Lines: Theorizing Women's Autobiography,* eds. Bella Brodzki and Celeste Schenck (Ithaca and London: Cornell University Press, 1988): ix–xii.

[50]See Nelly Furman, "Textual Feminism," in *Women and Language in Literature and Society,* eds. Sally McConnell-Ginet, Ruth Borker and Nelly Furman (New York: Praeger, 1980): 49–50.

[51]See Nancy K. Miller, "Women's Autobiography in France: For a Dialectics of Identification," in *Women and Language,* 271.

The Rebel

Leonor Villegas de Magnón

Map of the railway system in Mexico during the Revolution.

CHAPTER I
The Rebel Is a Girl

The Río Bravo or Río Grande defines the dividing line between the two nations, Mexico and the United States. As the years pass the river appears to be in a state of inactivity. Its waters seek a lower level, until it eventually leaves its banks exposed. In some places it becomes a thin stream that can be easily crossed on foot. The least cautious, or perhaps the most daring and hard-pressed people, take advantage of the fertile soil and, at their own risk, build huts, plant vegetables, raise chickens, cows, and a pig or two. The river maintains this happy mood for years, and the poor are hopeful that it will thus continue.

By some whim of nature, or it may be that Neptune, God of the Seas, wishes to amuse himself, the water awakens from its tranquil slumber and transforms itself into a gigantic serpent that crawls slowly, but gains a momentum of such menacing form that carries with it everything that it contacts. Soon on its surface floating with the torrent cows, sheep, chickens, snakes, and huts struggle to keep above the waters until they are finally engulfed by the churning undercurrent. Nothing escapes the furious waters that rush on as if in answer to a challenge presenting a grotesque contrast to the many years of defiant lethargy.

On a night like this, the twelfth of June, 1876, the shrill whistle of the night guards gave the alarm. Civil guards on horses rode from town to town along the river, warning the inhabitants of the approaching peril. Shrill cries and terrifying screams filled the air and the Laredos, two border towns across the river from each other, rose to the emergency. The darkness of the night became more terrifying as thunderclap after thunderclap intermingled with the cries of those in danger. The lightning illuminated their path momentarily only to leave it again and again in intense darkness.

The trees whipped by a gale of wind blew back and forth, beating against the walls of the big homes, while rampant waters gaining ground curled around the foundations, menacing homes and huts till they yielded to the mighty pressure of the water and fell like sugar toys.

The poor who lived on the edge of the river were making powerful efforts to save the little they possessed. They moved forward like beasts of burden, carrying as much as their strength allowed them. Women with children tied to their back in *rebozos* had their hands free to drag their animals. Men burdened with chattel also dragged their beasts, going ahead to find a safe foot path to scale the river banks. If they dared to halt, those behind gave a cry of warning.

"Go up higher! Higher! Higher!"

Again they redoubled their steps in an effort to gain safe ground; the waters were already flooding Nuevo Laredo on the Mexican side. The town was in darkness; only the lanterns carried by helpers provided the means to light the way of the refugees. The *mozos,* caretakers of the rich ones, were kept busy guarding the homes, and running back and forth with news of the rising water, its level, its perils, providing an excuse for wild excitement.

Emperor Maximilian had been dethroned, tried, and executed. Benito Juárez and Porfirio Díaz had dickered for power between themselves. After overthrowing the government of Lerdo de Tejada, General Profirio Díaz had taken the Capital of Mexico proclaiming his *Plan de Tuxtepec.* Slow means of communication and the rapid changes in governments left many guerrilla bands of either side scattered over the country. These groups, unaware of peace, continued to roam about attacking towns.

A band of these scattered rebels, taking advantage of the storm-frightened people of the little town of Nuevo Laredo, found it opportune to attack and loot the homes which had been temporarily abandoned or neglected either from fear of the rising river or out of curiosity to view the damage. The terror of the night meant nothing to the rebel looters. They rode unchallenged to the heart of town, determined to break down the gates of a rich Spanish merchant to whom it was rumored a large consignment of fine wines had recently arrived by barge from the Gulf of Mexico.

Quickly they made their way through the darkness to the front of a strong gate, or *portón,* with the master's name, Don Joaquín, on the stone arch overhead.

"This is the place," they yelled, banging on the gate with the butts of their guns. "Open the gate! Open!"

Don Joaquín, a prudent man, ordered the gate opened. Pancho, the *mozo,* was accustomed to obeying orders, but he hesitated.

"Go, Pancho. Open the gate."

Slowly Pancho proceeded to accomplish the task which was always so easy, but tonight his trembling fingers refused to pull the heavy lock that held the door tight.

"Señor," he said "they are bandits."

"You cannot do it, Pancho? I will do it myself." Don Joaquín, carrying a lantern in one hand, approached and opened the door that yielded softly.

Pancho hid behind the door. The Indian guessed the reason for this visit. Holding his lantern high, Don Joaquín got a quick view of the intruders. He saw the group of armed bandits and at once guessed their motive.

"Follow me," he said in a low voice, escorting them down the tile-paved courtyard.

Don Joaquín's establishment covered a long city block on the main plaza, a quarter of a mile from the river. Surrounded by a thick wall well over a man's height were the house, the *bodega* (warehouse), and the store. In the house lived the young master and his family. In rooms built along the side of the warehouse lived the young boys who had come from Spain to learn the merchandising business. Along the back wall was an open space behind the house and the *bodega,* where garlic was stored.

Entering the warehouse, Don Joaquín led the way down into the cellar where the big assortment of Spanish wines has been stowed away. The intruders at once became his guests, sitting around on the benches, but still holding their guns in a prominent position. Wine casks stacked on top of each other lined the sides of the room. The light from Don Joaquín's lantern on the rough wooden table was reflected in the tin wine cups. Where the wine had dripped from the spigots there were stains on the stone floor. The sweet smell of wine was heavy in the air.

Serving the wine Don Joaquín drew, Pancho faltered among the rough men. Grabbing a cup from Pancho, the leader held it up close to his eyes to see if it was full. Then flinging back his head he poured it down his throat. Putting his cup back on the table with a heavy thump he looked meaningly at Pancho.

"His cup, Pancho. We do not want our friends to leave thirsty." Don Joaquín held out his hand for the empty cup.

"Ah, we are not leaving yet, Señor. Not until we have searched the house." The leader nodded to his men who forgot their wine and jumped up.

Don Joaquín pushed through the men and started toward the door near the gate, but the men were already attracted by a closed door across the patio, where voices were heard coming from within.

"Open this door, Señor," commanded the boldest one making a sign to his companions to present arms. "Open this door."

Without hesitating, the master raised his lantern to throw a better light in the dimly lit room. At that moment cries of a newborn baby broke the silence.

Outside, the increasing fury of the stormy night threatened at any moment to demolish the house. The waters were slapping against the walls, slipping in through the low windows. Inside the bandit-held mansion, beaten by the wind, threatened by the water, a woman in majestic dignity had given birth to a child.

The rebels were touched by the familiar sacredness of the scene. Putting away their guns, some among them made the sign of the cross on their foreheads and on their hearts. They returned to the patio to resume their drinking.

"Pardon, señor," the leader murmured.

But before the band could descend to the wine cellar, loud knocks and threats of breaking in the gate were heard. A Federal commander in command of his own troops demanded entrance to search for bandits. Frightened by the Federals, the rebels scattered wildly over the courtyard, climbing the wall in back of the warehouse and escaping in the opposite direction.

Gripping his lantern, the master walked to the gate. He again held his light high. Opening the door, he signaled to the Federals to walk in and be quiet.

"Follow me," said Don Joaquín, starting toward the wine cellar.

The Federals in their anxiety to find some victim on whom to discharge their fury, pushed one another into the hall, some bouncing clear across the patio.

"The rebels are here," the commander said, seeing that Don Joaquín was leading them away from the direction of the house.

"Sí, señor," answered Don Joaquín quickly. "I am hiding one rebel." He walked toward the door, hesitated, then flung it open. The crying of the baby silenced the men.

"A man child, señor?" asked the commander.

Pancho shook his head at Don Joaquín.

"No, señor," the master answered. He drew himself up in pride. "My rebel is a girl."

"A girl!" one of the men said, and making excuses for their intrusion, turned away from the door.

"Pardon us, señor. We already knew that you were an honest man. But in these awful times, what about it? Anything may happen. All the people are alarmed with so many rumors of bandits."

Don Joaquín ushered the Federals to the same cellar where the bandits had just been. With their cups filled, the men held them high and offered a toast of welcome to the new arrival, the Rebel. They drank a second toast to the mother of the baby.

"This toast we offer," the commander said, "to the mother of this border town on the banks of the Río Bravo." He wished to appear in a good light before the eyes of the owner of such good wines.

"¡Viva! ¡Viva!" the men called out in high spirits because their bandit hunt had turned into a party.

Finally, Don Joaquín, who was impatiently awaiting their departure, began to show signs of restlessness. Pancho appeared with his lantern to lead the way out. As the Federals filed out of the gate, passersby reported that the river was now at a standstill and the storm had abated.

Pancho, lantern in hand, did not think it time to go to bed, but preferred walking the streets, telling the double good news of the baby and the dying storm. As he started out the gate, Don Joaquín called, "Pancho, go put on dry clothes while Julia makes coffee for us all."

Julia was considered part of the family. She was a young Indian girl whom Doña Valerianna, Don Joaquín's wife, had taken as a child and raised.

Meanwhile, Don Joaquín personally examined all the doors and windows; though the storm had ceased, the strong wind might blow them open. While he was walking about the place, his thoughts were filled with scenes from the year. He remembered that just one year before, his first son had been born in Corpus Christi.

"Strange coincidence," he recalled. On the night Leopoldo was born there had been a tempest and the waves had lashed his home on the bay.

"My son born on American soil. My daughter in Mexican territory, and I, a Spanish subject. Who will be more powerful, he or she?"

In bed, Doña Valerianna held her child in a warm embrace, whispering a benediction.

"A Mexican flag shall be yours. I will wrap it together with your brother's. His shall be an American flag, but they shall be like one to me."

Her eyes searched into the darkness for her husband's flag, murmuring in her semiconsciousness, "His country I shall never see; it is beyond the great ocean."

CHAPTER II
Life at Rancho San Francisco

Two years passed. Days went by with happiness and tender solicitude for the young parents, Don Joaquín Villegas and his beautiful wife Doña Valerianna, had but one ambition in life, to amass a fortune for their children's education and inheritance. Don Joaquín's business prospered. His large warehouses were full of rich imported goods; his storehouses filled with harvests of corn, beans, chili, garlic and onions, all raised on his own farm.

Doña Valerianna and the two children spent the winter in town and the summer months at the hacienda. That season of the year provided interesting pastime for the children and their mother, who enjoyed the country life with them.

There were hundreds of hands employed on the hacienda. They also served as protection in case of an attack by Indians, who maintained a war-like attitude toward the *hacendados*. The Comanches had been driven from their lands during the late civil war and they were seeking to regain their old hunting grounds along the border.

The courtyard of the *patrón*'s house was surrounded by high walls; only one gate permitted entrance. Pancho was the custodian of this entry, which was closed at night and opened at an early hour in the morning. The house was a two-story building of massive rock. The family occupied the upper story, sitting room and two bedrooms. A porch surrounded by a two foot brick curb was the children's playground during the day and a place to sleep at night. Cement arches and columns supported the tile roof over the porch. From here there was an unobstructed view of miles of brush country. Anyone approaching the ranch could be seen from a great distance. The lower part of the house had a large hall that served as a dining room and a sitting room. During the winter months, its huge fireplace gave warmth and comfort to the visiting family of Don Joaquín and to many wayfarers. The kitchen was next to this room. It was equipped as only the Mexican aristocratic families of that time could afford.

In the center of the kitchen was a semi-circular brick stove, a *bracero,* about two-feet wide, eight-feet long, and three-feet high. On the top were hollow squares covered by iron grills. Underneath each top opening was a space for charcoal; the ashes fell freely into a container bellow. Big *cazuelos,* pots, rested on cement borders just above the iron grills. The large coffee pots had their special place on the round openings at one end of the stove. A *bracero* was easy to keep clean. Ashes from the fire were mixed with water and scrubbed on with a stiff brush after each meal. The ashes took the place of modern disinfectant.

Ash water, too, was used to wash clothes. Two barrels were put one on the other, the clothes in the top. Then ash water was poured on them, dripping into the bottom barrel. When the water that dripped through was clean, the clothes were ready to hang out.

On the wall behind the stove was a tall, open wooden safe. Here were hung all the cooking utensils. There were *cazuelos* of all sizes with looped handles on each side, and hand-hammered copper pots, their red copper color long lost beneath a coating of green patina and charcoal smoke.

Early in the morning the children were alert watching for Pancho to take them to help milk the cows and feed the animals. As soon as Julia had fed them, Leopoldo and Leonor took their tiny pails, which Pancho had filled earlier with foamy milk for them to drink. Swinging the empty pails, they began the daily routine of feeding the chickens. All morning they searched the chicken coops, filling their pails with eggs. When their mother paid them for the day's work, they put their money in clay piggy banks.

The children went with Julia as she carried the daily washing for the family. Through the lanes between the adobe houses of the peons they passed. Straight haired, smiling children peeked at them from holes in the walls that were windows. Away from the great house and the peons, Julia washed clothes in the creek, beating them clean on a rock that lay like an island in the water. When she had hung the clothes to dry on mesquite trees, she undressed the children and herself and led them out in the clear, tepid water to bathe.

At noon, Pancho put on his white apron and, with a clean, white towel over his left arm, proceeded to set the table. Dinner was always the ceremonious affair at the ranch that it was in town.

After resting in the afternoon, Doña Valerianna went with her children for long walks in the country. They gathered wild cactus fruits, tunas from the prickly pear, tiny strawberry-tasting fruit from the *pitahaya.*

One afternoon, the children impatiently awaited their mother. It had rained and the frogs and the butterflies, excited by the cool dampness, filled the courtyard with their activity. Doña Valerianna was late in joining her children. The Little Rebel ran to her mother's room to see what had delayed her.

Doña Valerianna had been slow in finishing her flowers for the church. They were tall, stiff floral designs. Each flower on the spray proclaimed its own individuality. In a large barrel on the porch there was a rose bush covered with roses. One of these Doña Valerianna had picked to use as a model for the color and form of the petals of her cloth flowers.

As she got up to meet Leonor, the rose fell from her lap. Quickly the child picked it up.

"Oh, it has pricked my finger," she cried. "Oh, Mamá, why has this beautiful rose hurt me? The ones you make do not have thorns."

Laying the rose gently on the dresser, Doña Valerianna reached for the alcohol and bandages, explaining while she dressed the tiny finger, "My little child, even if they are beautiful, real roses have thorns to protect themselves. In our lives, when things are beautiful and good we are happy, then things change and we are sad. The roses I make to offer on the altar to God have no thorns, because we offer only what is good to Him." Wrapping the little finger, the mother visualized her daughter in the future in a far away land, her heart pierced with thorns of ingratitude.

At sunset, everyone came home from the day's work in the fields and pastures. Supper was served in the hall while the cowhands and shepherds gathered in the courtyard to render account of the day to the *patrón*. Don Joaquín had been riding among the cattle and the sheep. As he rode up to the house, the children clapped their hands. Doña Valerianna looked at him with pride. She adored her husband and lived only to please and serve him.

The usual supper was barbecue beef, red beans, tortillas, cream cheese, and plenty of milk for the children. The adults drank fine claret.

After supper, Don Joaquín in his *charro* suit would greet his men. "Well, Amigo, what good news do you bring? Have you increased your wealth?"

A certain percent of the calf and lamb crop went to the men who took care of them. Beside their salary, each one became a part owner. In the course of time, they had land and cattle of their own. Don Joaquín carried on his business in town in the same way. His clerks, salesmen, and manager all had an interest in the business. They looked forward to the inventory and balancing of accounts which took place twice a year. As time passed, they, too, became part owners, shareholders, as they decided. Don Joaquín saw to it that if good employees left him, they could start a business of their own.

Although Doña Valerianna was not strong, she took an active part in her husband's business affairs. When Valerianna Rubio had married at fourteen, her mother had given Don Joaquín a bag of forty thousand Mexican gold pesos as dowry. She had brought her husband a small fortune.

The moment Valerianna felt her husband stir in the morning, she arose. Smoothing her long hair away from her face, she stood for a moment looking at the dull lights in the adobe huts of the peons. Taking her rosary, she knelt down. With the first light of day Don Joaquín and his wife were in the courtyard waiting for their horses. Riding together, they went to the corrals where the cattle and sheep were held. When the animals were turned out, Don Joaquín and Valerianna followed the cattle for a little way.

Coming home one morning, they saw a bull that should have been with the herd. Startled by the sound of Don Joaquín's galloping horse, the bull swung around and charged. The horse, rearing in fright, plunged wildly out of control. Spurring her mare, Valerianna rode up beside her husband and grabbed his horse by the reins. Both horses ran along together for awhile, Don Joaquín's horse jerking against his twice held bridle. With a final lunge, he pulled Valerianna from her horse. Hanging for a moment by the great horn of the sidesaddle, her skirt covering the horse, she slid softly to the ground. Pulling his horse with all his strength, Don Joaquín jumped off and ran back to where his wife was sitting, dazed.

"Here, my wife, let me help you." Don Joaquín slid the gun she carried from her shoulder.

"Can you stand?" he asked, holding out his hands and pulling her up.

She swayed against him and he felt the pounding of her heart.

"No, my husband, I am not injured," she whispered.

Walking over to an old mesquite, Valerianna fell on her knees in prayer. Don Joaquín stood for a moment waiting. Then putting his arms about her, kissed her warmly, holding her close.

"You saved my life, Valerita. Yet I think it is not just today, but everyday, you are my star of good fortune."

She closed her eyes resting in his arms. I must remember this moment, she thought, for they come so seldom. I desire this always.

The smile on her face dimmed when she thought of her mother standing in the stuffy parlor before her on her wedding day. In her tight fitting black dress it was Mamá who had laid the first weight on her heart.

"My daughter, it is a wife's duty to serve her husband in every way. Whatever he wishes you must not question."

"Of course, Mamá," she answered smiling. "I love him. I will do anything."

"Love has nothing to do with it. Forget that, it will be easier." Mamá's mouth drew into a tight line. "Neither laugh too loud nor shed too many tears. Love would make you do that."

Valerianna had laughed and cried only for a little while for her husband did not approve.

Valerianna opened her eyes as she felt Joaquín's body stiffen. She knew he was again the man whose sense of responsibility to his family had made him austere and cold at twenty-four. They began walking toward the *hacienda*. Someone would find their runaway horses and soon be after them.

As the routine of ranch life went on, things became more interesting for the children. During the hot months the cattle were branded, the sheep sheared. Shepherds began a month before shearing time to bring in big ox-drawn carts filled with fodder. They covered the tops of the long sheds, which were divided and sub-divided for the shepherds who sheared their own flock. Each shepherd had a leather apron with many pockets for scissors, a can of ointment, a soft mop, and all the necessities for shearing.

Pancho, Julia and the children would climb up on the big log fence and sit watching how the shepherds tied the sheep's legs in preparation for the "undress," as the children would say. Jumping down to go to help the shepherd, they scampered back to the fence when they saw the overseer approaching.

Pancho held up his hands in alarm. "What awful children! You must not interfere. This work has to be done quickly. The wool must get to the factory in time to make our blankets and winter clothes."

"And the fine dresses for your mother," added Julia.

This work finished, the impatient overseers rendered their accounts. Then the cowhands began corralling cattle for branding. Mules, donkeys, oxen and cows, new calves and lambs, all had to pass inspection for a brand. The children insisted on watching the branding operations.

Covering her face, Leonor would shudder and wail, "Those awful hot irons. It will burn them badly."

At night when the children were in bed, they talked in the darkness. Leonor called to her brother.

"Why do they burn the animals with that horrible iron?"

"I don't like it either," answered the little boy. "But our dear Papá will lose his animals if they are not branded with a V on the right side."

"I don't like it, not at all," said the little girl. "It is cruel." She would cry until she fell asleep.

Besides her mare, Doña Valerianna loved her guitar. In the days of her courtship, she had won her husband with the strains of her love songs as she sat in the iron-barred window of her home in Brownsville, waiting for her lover. Now it was a means of entertaining everyone on the Hacienda de San Francisco.

At night on hearing the first strains of music, the men, women, and children on the place would gather in the courtyard for an evening of pleasure. Doña Valerianna learned the shepherds' songs, the songs of the cow hands, and their dance music. Some of the men had harmonicas, drums, and fiddles. Soon she was directing her little band. It made her husband happy to see the harmony and union that existed. It was a rest for him from his busy town work and his hard days on the ranch.

Before the gathering broke up, Julia approached her mistress and kissed her hand. Taking the guitar, she gave Doña Valerianna her silver-flecked, ruby rosary. The women knelt down, bowing their heads. The men took off their hats and held them over their hearts. Prayers over, the peons lined up to pay their respects to the *patrón* and his wife, kissed Doña Valerianna's hand and shook Don Joaquín's hand in the limp Spanish fashion. When the last peon was gone, Pancho rang the great copper bell and bolted the heavy gate.

As time drew closer for the family's leaving, Doña Valerianna, the children, and the peons close to the family became melancholy. The children savored each day's adventure, knowing the days left were few. They had learned the vastness of the sky and the earth, the bleating of sheep, and the mad rush of cattle. They felt God in his infinite greatness.

Pancho was a hero of great knowledge. Often on his walks with the children he would kneel down and put his ear to the ground. When he listened for too long a time, the children became impatient.

"Pancho, what do you hear?"

Holding up his hand he would point one, two, or more fingers. "Someone is riding this way. It is a man on horseback," he would say clarifying his signs.

He knew the sound of mules, oxen, carts, carriages, and wagons. Taking the children, Pancho would rush up the stairs behind the great chimney of the house. There in a tower used for the night watch, they scanned the countryside for dust rising, showing that someone was approaching the hacienda.

From the shepherds the children had learned the ways of nature. The sheep would warn the shepherds of an approaching storm by huddling together. Rams encircled the ewes, and the lambs packed together into the center of the milling circle. On dark nights when even the sound of snapping twigs was frightening, the shepherds' hearts were light and fearless. They sang in happy, carefree strains. As the night grew into daylight, the rhythm had been caught by all the shepherds and became a song to God in thanksgiving for the new dawn.

The lonely shepherds were fascinating to the children. Julia explained their strange costume. The sheep fleece fastened about their necks by tiny hoofs were the shepherds' pallet at night. The colored sash wrapped about them in many folds was used for carrying their sling, and their small flute, or harmonica. Their *huaraches* tied with colored strings scared away the rattlesnakes; the rabbits' feet dangling from the sash brought good luck. But Julia's lips were closed regarding the many shepherd suitors who had strings tied to her fickle heart.

The shepherds in their attire were outshone by the gallant, swashbuckling vaqueros. The vaqueros had saddles glittering with silver, sombreros trimmed with bright braid and tight rolled serapes strapped to the back of their heavy Mexican saddles. Jugs of wine and water were tied in front.

The children knew the signs that guided the vaqueros, too. On nights of storm, burros whirled about chasing their tails, warning the cattle. Insects crawled to newly burrowed holes. The vaqueros calmed their nervous cattle by singing soothing whooping songs to them.

An insensitive fate was arranging events so that the family of Don Joaquín would never again return to the Hacienda de San Francisco. This would be Doña Valerianna's last visit to her beloved ranch where she felt close to her husband and children. Often during the last days there she had felt a sharp pain tugging at her heart. She prayed incessantly, kneeling before the painting of the Blessed Trinity in her room, repeating prayers in her mind as she sat making flowers.

"Dear Lord, if you must call one of us, let it be me. My heart is full of fears for the future of my little children. I could not bear the burden alone.

CHAPTER III
"V" Is for Villegas

Doña Valerianna returned to town with her family in the winter with gay expectancy. Church work occupied much of her time: making flowers for the altar, embroidering vestments and fine linens, and sewing altar cloths. Young matrons vied with each other in supplying the costly gifts of perfumes and incense for the church. Social gatherings were intimate and exclusive; celebrations, such as balls, teas, dinners, and religious feasts, were held in the spacious private homes.

Familiar envelopes brought by messengers filled Doña Valerianna with excitement. Clasping an unopened invitation, she fluttered about the sitting room, placing it first against a vase, then on the mantel, finally, by the lamp near Don Joaquín's favorite chair. Running through her mind were ideas for her party gown. Her thoughts were of sleeves and tight waists, white damask, red velvet, black taffeta, curled hair falling in ringlets glittering with jewels, fans, long white gloves, and satin slippers. By nightfall she was all plans and hopes.

Sitting embroidering, Valerianna watched her husband first notice the envelope. Then casually picking it up, he fingered it thoughtfully before opening it. If it were of no consequence, he would put it aside, saying nothing. She knew if it were rejected, she would bend her head over her work to hide quick tears. Since it was to his liking, he ceremoniously announced, "We will accept this cordial invitation."

All the random ideas immediately took shape in her mind. For the dress she would go to the fine stores that sold Parisian goods and foreign laces and materials. Even people from San Antonio made the month's trip to shop in the elegant border stores of Spanish merchants. Consultations with Mamá and the seamstress, hurried exchanges of notes and fashion plates kept a messenger running all day between friends' houses.

On the wonderful night, Don Joaquín escorted his wife to the ballroom, finding his own entertainment in chess and dominoes. As the hour grew late, Valerianna sought out her husband to remind him of the time.

"Yes, yes. It is time we thought of our children," he answered.

Taking his wife by the arm, they walked into the ballroom to make the rounds, saying good night. Don Joaquín kissed the ladies' hands; Valerianna made a deep bow, her dress rippling about her on the floor. Her tall Spanish comb held the lace mantilla that fell about her bare shoulders. Driving away in their carriage, Valerianna was pleased with the lackey and the driver in their smart blue dress uniforms, the crest on the horses' blankets, and of her husband who provided her with such beautiful luxury. Going immediately to the children's room, she startled the sleepy-eyed Julia who sat on a little chair between the beds. After kissing the half-awake children, she stood before the Guadalupe for a moment's prayer. The flickering light of the candle in its red glass cast only a dim glow in the room so that to the children their mother seemed to float in a cloud of soft lace, smelling of sweet cologne.

"Mamá, did the carriage have the coat of arms?" Leopold asked.

"Yes, my son."

"And the driver, and the horses' blankets, and the lackey, all of them?"

"Yes, everything has a great gold V for your Papá's house."

"A V on everything, Mamá? Oh, no!" Leonor cried out. Why must you always brand everything that is ours?"

Julia comforted the sobbing child as the mother turned again to the Virgin's picture.

After pacing the great patio several times, Don Joaquín appeared in the door. "My dear, first you dance, then you pray."

Looking at her husband, she heard again the last strains of the waltz, felt the quick step of the polka. There were new tunes tonight, tomorrow she would try them on her guitar.

"Pardon, your *copita*. Yours, too, my lady." Pancho stood waiting for them, holding a tray with two glasses of wine.

She was coquettish now, the *copita* stirred her blood, and she was defiant of their strict conventional way. Don Joaquín buried himself in the soft wool mattress. Removing her comb and mantilla, Valerianna knelt by his bed, giving him a lingering kiss that brought a smile to his lips and a dreamy look to his eyes.

"Pardon me," she whispered, rushing into his arms. Gathered in his warm embrace, she expressed her love for him.

When Don Joaquín began planning his long business trip through northern Mexico, Doña Valerianna made preparations to accompany him with the two children. Although the distance was not far, the journey would take months. Roads were little more than deep ruts, and the way beset with suspected dangers. When Valerianna's mother, Doña

Damianita, found out about his wife's condition it was already too late to change plans. Valerianna needed him. She would go on the trip as they had at first decided.

Before daybreak on the day of departure, Doña Valerianna, in her starched ruffled dress with great balloon sleeves and lace collar held with a diamond pin, briskly directed last minute packing. Seeking peace, she went to her room and knelt in prayer.

When the door opened behind her, she turned to see Pancho standing inside, unannounced. His close-knit figure filled a handsome charro suit Don Joaquín had given him. There were silver buttons on the jacket, silver bars on the shoulders, and silver stripes down the sides of the trousers. Pancho held his heavy sombrero nervously in his stubby hands.

Doña Valerianna sat down in wonder, looking at the transformed Pancho. Just then, Julia's black head peeped over his shoulder.

"Say it, Pancho. Say it." She pushed the reluctant Pancho toward their mistress.

Falling on his knees before her, Pancho placed his hat carefully beside him. Closing his eyes as if in prayer, he hesitated.

"Say it, Pancho," Julia roused him.

"My dear mistress, it is but natural that I beg your permission. Julia and I want to be married before we leave on the trip."

Kneeling confidently beside Pancho, Julia looked Doña Valerianna in the eye, speaking rapidly lest her mistress stop her. "Please, dear Señora, give us your blessing. Let us be married. This trip will be a dangerous one. I will need someone to defend me if we are attacked by Indians. Please, dear mistress."

Looking at the clock, Doña Valerianna smiled at them. "Pancho, mass is at six. Go tell the padre I want the church adorned with flowers; to be ready to marry you immediately. Tell the father it is urgent. Don Joaquín and his wife will be there."

Everything had been packed and put away in lavender branches and cinnamon sticks, but in her valise Doña Valerianna had a fine white muslin gown. Julia slipped out of her skirt and blouse. The softly draped gown fitted her well. Pulling down a lace curtain from the parlor window, her mistress made Julia a train. She pinned the veil from her traveling hat about Julia's shiny black hair. A little powder, a rosary, and the bride was ready.

Pancho returned perspiring. He stared at the bedecked Julia, then turning to his mistress he spoke breathlessly. "Señora, the padre says come at once. It is time to ring the bell for mass."

As Valerianna got them in the carriage, Don Joaquín watched the whole proceedings with amusement. Then the master and mistress walked across the plaza to the church, Valerianna carrying her triangular white lace mantilla and her rosary.

Kneeling at the altar rail waiting for the priest, Pancho leaned over to Julia, who knelt with downcast eyes, her lips moving. "Julia," he whispered, "do you see how bright the silver buttons shine on my suit. Look at the V."

"Pancho, how can you be thinking of how fine you look?" Julia whispered back loudly. "Smell the perfume Doña Valerianna sent to be sprinkled on the carpet. There on the altar are the flowers she herself makes. All this for us."

"My, how vain you have become with all your finery," was Pancho's amused answer.

Just then the priest entered. Doña Valerianna, from her place near the front of the church, recalled her own sumptuous wedding, thinking how nice was this simple ceremony. She had ordered a wedding breakfast for them of coffee and sweet breads laid in the patio.

Giving the bride and groom each a bag of gold coins, Don Joaquín advised Pancho to take care of his bride, but hurry up with the preparations for the trip.

During the excitement of the wedding, the Little Rebel had slipped into the parlor and stood beneath the portrait of Pope Leo XIII. She had great fear of this picture. It was unjust. When Leonor was troublesome, she was turned over to the housekeeper. The old woman would lead the child into the dark parlor, forcing her to accuse herself. Drawing a small table under the picture, Doña Damianita would heave herself up with great effort. Invoking powers from the unknown, she mounted the table with a show of ruffles and laces of her undergarments that always delighted the child. Questioning the great man regarding Leonor's guilt, she slyly put her hand behind the loosely hung picture. The pope would agree shakily with the housekeeper that Leonor must be punished.

Looking longingly at the picture, Leonor wished for some message. She did not want her family to go on the long trip that made her grandmother cry so often.

"Come, child, you will be left behind." Julia found her and carried the little girl out to the carriage.

The caravan of Don Joaquín Villegas, Spanish merchant and importer, was a long and impressive one. Leading the procession were four mounted guards, who served at times as scouts. Next came the two coaches with four guards on each side carrying rifles and jars of water. These guards were the messengers for the travelers in the coaches. Dressed in grey traveling uniforms, they had command of the lesser guards, who were the servants.

Don Joaquín drove the first coach. Doña Valerianna sat beside him with the eager Leonor between them. In the back sat Doña Damianita with Leopold, who held his sling ready to shoot attacking Comanches. In the second coach was the family doctor, his wife Doña Isabelita, and their three-year-old son.

This child, Pepito, kept the caravan in an uproar with his bad behavior until he was sent back to Julia and Pancho with Leopold as company. Third in the procession was the big spring wagon driven by Pancho. Covered by an awning, this wagon carried the camping equipment for the two families along with the cook, his wife, and two maids. Next followed the ten wagons filled with barrels of water, provisions, feed for the animals, and camping equipment for the servants and guards.

Across the vast, arid state of Tamaulipas they traveled, taking winding unused roads to avoid attacks of bandits and Indians. At night the caravan stopped near water to camp. The peons built a big fire and rolled logs to camp to be used as benches. Wagons and carriages were driven into a circle about the fire. The cook prepared beef on a spit, hung the coffee pot on a tripod over the coals. Unpacking the *metate,* the maids ground corn for the tortillas they would cook on an iron skillet. Doña Valerianna played her guitar, and the whole camp sang. Lastly, she recited the rosary to calm the fears of the wild place and the darkness.

The *patrones* slept in their carriages, the peons on pallets spread around the fire. All night the men worked in shifts, tending to the animals, giving water and feed, making ready for an early start. In the dim light of dawn, coffee and bread and eggs were served to the family. Soon the camp was behind them as they traveled in the cool morning.

As they left the barren country of Tamaulipas and entered Nuevo León, the scenery changed completely. Surrounded by great mountains, chill winds blew about them. They crossed more creeks and rivers. Hurrying west, they wanted the caravan to reach Coahuila before the cold of autumn overtook them.

One afternoon soon after entering Coahuila, they drove confidently toward a town, hoping to reach it before nightfall. Suddenly one of the scouts who had gone on ahead returned in a gallop, making signs for the procession to stop.

"Be careful, *Patrón,* the Indians are coming this way. They are behind that hill," he said, pointing west.

The sun was setting and scarcely had the man finished speaking when the Indians, riding their horses in a cloud of dust, came over the hill towards them. Don Joaquín sent word immediately along the line.

"Do not draw arms unless I give the order," he commanded.

He threw the reins of his horses on his wife's lap. "Hold them steady," he told her.

In her efforts to catch them, she dropped her rosary on the floor of the coach. The Little Rebel slid off the seat, picked up the rosary and held it concealed in her fist. She scrambled off the coach to stand beside her father. Doña Valerianna had not taken her eyes from the approaching cloud of horsemen, who came shouting warlike cries, waving their bows, and preparing their arrows. No one noticed the child.

Don Joaquín stood with open arms, facing the Indians. The silver buttons on his dusty, tan charro suit shone brightly in the rays of the setting sun. His richly trimmed sombrero, ablaze with the beautiful twilight, had the desired effect on the Indians. There was no sign of hostility as the Indian tribe came nearer to the still caravan. Suddenly, the Comanche chief made a sign to his men to stop.

"I will advance alone."

Don Joaquín serenely awaited the approaching Indian. The moral courage of both men drew them to one another.

"Only God can save us," the grandmother mourned. When the prancing horse of the Indian was almost to him, Don Joaquín took off his sombrero and flung it to the chief. He caught it. Well pleased, he examined the silver string around it and the ornaments, turning it slowly in his hard hands. No one noticed the Little Rebel as she drew close to the chief's horse. The Comanche's moccasins were studded with bright beads. Reaching out, the child ran her fingers over the soft leather, caressing the Indian's foot. He looked down at her with wonder. It pleased him to be well treated. Doña Valerianna was faint with fear, but she kept her lips tightly closed.

Placing the sombrero on the horn of the saddle, he dismounted and took the little girl in his arms. "Brave little one, open your hand and pull a feather from my headdress. They are fine, too."

He caught her tightly closed fist and forced it open. As he did the rosary fell across his brown arm like so many drops of blood. Noticing Doña Valerianna's pale face, he walked over to her with the child.

"Take her, we would not harm any of you," he said kissing the chubby hand with the rosary.

Don Joaquín ordered jugs of wine, blankets, food, and boxes of fine things to be unloaded. The Comanche chief made a sign to his men to draw nearer. The Indian, seeing Julia, pulled off his feathered headgear and placed it on her head. Pancho was proud. She was his queen.

Only the chief could speak the Spanish language; the others made signs to the servants in the caravan. They exchanged their hides for blankets, moccasins for *huaraches*. Don Joaquín gave them bags of coins. Doña Valerianna gave the Indian women, who had followed the men, sacks of coffee, sugar, and flour. Leopold gave his father's tobacco; Pancho showed them how to make corn cob pipes.

It grew dark. The chief ordered his people to go back a little way and to keep guard for the generous *patrón*. In view of the caravan, the Indians pitched their tents, began their fires, and started beating their drums that sounded softly, rhythmically all night.

Don Joaquín ordered a halt, and camp was set up as a marked sign of trust to the Indians. Two scouts, however, rode on to find out the distance to the town. It was urgent to get there soon. The shock had been too great for the young *patrona*. The trip was already three months spent, and her time was near.

CHAPTER IV
Two Hands Are Burned

The encounter with the strange Indians gave the whole camp a topic for conversation and made the travel light. Leopold thought the Indians brave and wild as the horses they road. Julia provokingly tossed her head to show off her feathered crown. When they stopped by a creek to eat, the party gathered around the *patrona,* solicitous of her health.

"Oh, I will be all right," she told them. "I will sing tonight."

"What a narrow escape, how fortunate we were," the grandmother recalled, which was enough to start them all chattering again about the Indians.

Doña Valerianna remembered the band of outlaws that had raided their home in the city the night her girl was born, and she marveled at her husband's adroit way of handling serious situations.

Once more on their way, Doña Valerianna took her sleepy little girl on her lap. She sat close to her husband and caressed his hand.

"Dear one, how good God has been to us."

Seeking to comfort her, Don Joaquín said quietly, "Please do not worry, my darling, just remember the Indians of fine physique riding on their alert horses, their feathers moving in the air, and their loyalty to their chief."

"They had bows and arrows, knives, and *rachetes,*" she added grimly.

"Yes, I admit, they appeared fierce, yet they gave us many beautiful things, fine furs, beads, and moccasins, They are the last of a noble race that once owned Mexico. Now they are wanderers in their own land. These men are good at heart, just like all of us. If they are approached in a friendly manner, they quickly respond. The world is not actually against anyone. It is fear and misunderstanding that make people fight." He stopped talking and gave his wife's hand an impatient pat for her fears.

They rode on without losing time, but showing the usual reaction to a long trip. They were tired. How they looked forward to a rest from traveling. The first days of December found this caravan passing through the fertile lands of Coahuila. Here among well-bred and prosperous people who retained the unassuming character of those who live from the land, Doña Valerianna could relax and rest before proceeding to larger cities in the same state. This was a state full of historic memories of days of past glories.

Two of the advanced guard sent the previous night to explore had returned by daylight. The other two had stayed behind to prepare quarters for the travelers.

In the town of Cuatro Ciénegas a fashionable wedding had just taken place, the festivities lasting several days. At high noon, the bridal couple had left on a long honeymoon to New York. On their return they would live in the new home the bride's parents had given them.

When Señor Hernández, a rich merchant and father of the bride heard of the approaching convoy, he called his *encargado* and gave him orders.

"*Vete pronto,* go quickly. Meet these travelers and greet them in my name. Take a message of welcome. They must be our guests."

It was late afternoon before Don Joaquín's party reached town. Their advance guard met them at the outskirts of the city with broad smiles on their dust covered faces. They signaled the caravan to follow, leading them through town to the imposing home of Señor Hernández's daughter.

At the wide open portals, the *encargado* was standing and bowing in greeting and holding in his hand a ring of large keys.

"*Pase Ud.*, Señor Villegas," he kept repeating.

The court yard was a cool green garden. There was a wide-mouthed well covered by an arbor of vines and flowers. A bucket hanging from the frame dripped water slowly back into the well. A giant pecan tree shaded the center of the yard.

"How very inviting, this dreamy place," Don Joaquín remarked. Turning around to the rest, he said, "Wait, do not dismount."

"What is this?" he inquired of the genial caretaker who walked along beside him. The man was dressed in a dark blue charro suit with silver trimming like those used by Don Joaquín's men on state occasions.

"Here, Señor," the caretaker said, handing him the keys. "My *patrón* sends greetings and says you are to take possession of this humble house while you are here."

"But, my good *amigo,* are there no inns, no *posadas* in this town?"

"Yes, Señor, but my *patrón* and his wife have been informed by your men that your wife is ill, so he wants you to occupy his daughter's bridal home. She will be away some time. My *patrón* will call on you as soon as you are settled."

"And your *patrón*'s name? Don Joaquín inquired.

"He is Señor Hernández," replied the man driving himself proudly.

Doña Valerianna, anxiously awaiting her husband, grew restless. She decided to join in the conversation and know the reason for the delay. On seeing her alight, her husband graciously thanked the caretaker. He introduced his wife, his mother-in-law, and the doctor's family.

Meanwhile, Pancho had taken possession of the keys and Julia proceeded to open the door.

"How beautiful," she exclaimed, throwing up her hands. *"Dios mío, qué bonito."*

Don Joaquín gave her a stern look that quieted her. Then taking his wife's arm, he stepped across the threshold into the reception hall. They stood there waiting for Doña Damianita, the children, and the doctor and his wife. Leaning on her husband's arm, Doña Valerianna asked her people to wait until she and Don Joaquín looked over the house. She would then assign them their quarters.

The bridal suite overlooking the blooming garden growing with fragrant flowers would be theirs. Next to this bedroom she would have her mother and the children. There was a side door opening on a tile-paved veranda, which made an ideal place for the grandmother to pray and Julia to tell the children stories at night. Another bedroom was further on down the corridor. It overlooked a patio with potted plants and many bird cages. Overhead a pagola, covered with grape vines from which hung ripe white and dark red grapes, lent its shade to complete the artistic harmony of the whole place. Here the doctor and his family would stay. Pepito would run out whenever he pleased to play with the dog and kittens. The noise would not disturb anyone.

After admiring the beautiful place with its exquisite furniture, marble topped tables, its tall mirrors with gilt frames and the great oil paintings on the walls, they were grateful for the elegant house. They returned to those waiting to tell them of their good fortune.

"Please go to the quarters that I have assigned you and rest. You will be called in time for supper." Doña Valerianna spoke now as hostess and mistress of the place.

Don Joaquín knew that Pancho, his *mayordomo,* would find the stables, the coach house, and servants' quarters. They would not unload until early morning. The traveling utensils and other unnecessary equipment were to be left packed.

Smoking quietly, Don Joaquín was sitting by a window overlooking the front gate. He was overcome by the spontaneous demonstration of hospitality. He thought to himself, "It is just what I would do if others were placed in the same position."

Slowly, the big gate opened. He half arose in surprise. "It must be someone who has a key and a right to open the doors," he thought to himself.

In came the caretaker in Don Hernández's livery, followed by four *mozos* walking noisily in *huaraches* and dressed in white coats and pants. They moved quickly towards the side of the house, bearing great silver platters, big pots, and a big can of milk, which they carried by means of a stick placed through the handle on top. They did not speak to anyone.

In a few minutes Pancho came to notify Don Joaquín, "Señor, they have sent you a banquet! The *mozos* have laid out a table in the dining room. Plenty of milk, coffee, a roast *cabrito, aguacates,* lettuce, tomatoes, bread, and a big cake. Shall I ring the bell hanging over the dining table and call the family?"

Don Joaquín nodded as Pancho continued.

"For us there is a big pot of beans, chili sauce, and many tortillas. I shall tell Julia to get things ready in the kitchen for the servants."

Don Joaquín sat at the head of the table, Doña Valerianna and their children at his right, on his left Doña Damianita. The doctor and his wife Doña Isabelita were on the right and Pepito was at the other end of the table. These were to be their places all during their stay. Pancho would see that Julia and Rosita would properly wait on the table. Rosita was the maid that Doña Valerianna had assigned to the doctor's family.

By this arrangement at the table, Pepito was opposite the Little Rebel who received her ample share of kicks under the table. He snatched her food when he could, though he was afraid of the *patrón*.

Doña Valerianna, being very tired, sat in a Chippendale arm chair, her feet on a fancy four-leafed-clover-shaped stool. Julia had removed her mistress's shoes and put on her soft slippers. Petting her little feet Julia said, "Now, *mi ama* will be rested."

After supper, Valerianna begged Doña Isabelita to pray the rosary. They would retire soon afterward. Doña Isabelita was young, very fair, and inclined to be frivolous. She combed her hair like Doña Valerianna, in two braids crossed at the back and wound around her head, a big comb holding the braids in place. She wore long earrings with sparkling stones, and the traditional gold brooch to hold the lace around her shoulders. She had a mellow, sweet voice, which meant nothing, but covered a multitude of sins.

Doña Valerianna tolerated her, but was not close to her; neither did she like the doctor. But her husband had engaged them, so she accepted them graciously for his sake.

Doña Isabelita rushed through the prayers, hoping to sit around and talk, but Julia took care of that.

"My mistress is tired so I will put out the lights."

Standing on tiptoe in her soft shoes, Julia began blowing out the candles one by one. The silver candelabras reflected the twinkling orange lights until the last candle was extinguished. To the children standing below them, the tall candleholders looked like gleaming lyres on tall pedestals.

"Julia, take my mother and the children to their room; we will follow." Her mistress rose and prepared to go.

The next morning, the servants who had gone to mass and others to market came back with news of great activity in town. It lacked but a few days before the feast of the Virgin of Guadalupe on the twelfth of December. They had left Nuevo Laredo on the same date in September.

Julia was ordering the maids to help with the unpacking of the *patrona*'s personal effects. Rosa was talking incessantly, heedless of the frowning Julia and the restlessness of Doña Valerianna.

"Rosa," Valerianna spoke to the maid, "please ask my mother to come here."

Doña Damianita was found picking figs.

"Here she is, Señora," the pretty Rosa said. "We cannot keep her away from the fruit, and the flowers, and the birds."

"Daughter, there are about forty cages hanging in the back portal, birds of every kind."

"These people are of good taste. They must be very fine," Doña Valerianna remarked. "They will probably visit us after the fiestas. Señor Hernández's wife must be very busy."

"Yes, indeed," the maid spoke up quickly. "Her daughter, the one just married, is very beautiful."

"Well, Rosa, run along. You can tell me later on. I must not keep my mother waiting."

Doña Damianita took a traveling bag from Rosa's hand.

"I suppose it is this you want. You asked me to take care of it."

"Yes, yes, mother, open it quickly. I am very tired and feel a bit faint."

Doña Damianita, who was a personified example of decorum, carefully closed the door. Then she spread the contents of the bag on a table.

"Daughter, here it is, mostly baby clothes. And something in this white paper."

"That is what I want, mother. Please place the baby clothes in the drawer of that chest while I attend to this."

She carefully unwrapped the roll and kissed it reverently. It was a fine oil painting of the Virgin of Guadalupe which she had carefully taken from its heavy Italian frame and rolled up in fine linen. In her home it occupied the place of honor in her room. She kissed it several times while looking for a fitting place where she could see it from her bed.

"There, that is fine. I shall pin it lightly, so that it will not mar this perfect tapestry." She said as she fastened it to the wall covered with pale blue brocade decorated with tiny rosebuds.

The painting had been given to her by Doctor Plutarco Ornelas, Mexican consul in San Antonio, Texas, on the Little Rebel's first birthday in 1877. Under the title of Virgin of Guadalupe, the mother of Jesus is greatly honored in Mexico. It was her image that the liberator Padre Miguel Hidalgo had placed on the flag when he started the revolution that overthrew an empire. It is the greatest feast day of the year that commemorates the appearance of the Dark Virgin of Guadalupe to an Indian shepherd on the cold mountain of Tepeyac.

It was on this great and memorable day that Doña Valerianna gave birth to a third child, a boy whom she named Lorenzo. Amid the joys that always accompany birth, the household had gathered around the fireplace to hear the happy news. Everyone was excited. The servants rushed about aimlessly chattering about the new baby. The first cold norther had blown in, and the great fireplace was filled with sweet smelling logs of pine and fir trees. The *mozos* wore their colored woolen ponchos over their shoulders, and the women wrapped long, somber *rebozos* about their bodies.

Doña Isabelita sat near the fire and watched the children roast chestnuts over the hot coals. Leonorcita, tired of playing, crawled up on Doña Isabelita's lap, leaving the boys. When the doctor came into the room with good news of Doña Valerianna's progress, Pepito rushed up to him.

"Papá, please lend me your knife."

The doctor, who was greatly agitated from his long hours with the mother and baby, handed the boy his knife. It was a large pearl-handled one and so clumsy and hard to open that Pancho had to open it for Pepito.

The Rebel, from Isabelita's lap, watched Pepito go to the fire. He held the knife over the bright coals, taking it out to look at it several times. She noticed sleepily that it was almost transparent with heat. How pretty and bright it was.

On close examination it seemed to satisfy Pepito, who stood up. Coming quickly to the Little Rebel, he pushed the blade roughly against her left hand, which rested on his mother's breast. The blow was so hard that the hot knife buried itself in the chubby hand. The child shook it off with a scream of pain. As much as it hurt, she remembered her mother and began to cry softly.

Pepito triumphantly jumped about taunting her saying, "Now you will not sit on my mother's lap."

The doctor rushed over from his chair to see what had happened. Pepito kicked over a small center table on which was a lighted lamp. It started a blaze on the floor as he ran away to his room. The servants rushed to put out the flames.

Doña Damianita was indignant and told the doctor not to bother. She would take charge of the child and cure her. The doctor, seeing the awful burn, began curing and bandaging it. A knock at the door distracted the disturbed group at the fireplace.

Pancho opened the door. It was a *mozo* from a neighboring home.

"Please hurry, doctor. You are needed at the house of Colonel Jesús Carranza," said a breathless *mozo.*

"I will go immediately. Wait." The doctor finished wrapping the little hand, promising to return and chastise the boy.

On arriving at the home where he had been called, the doctor was received by the family. A young man about seventeen or eighteen held out his left hand to the doctor.

"I have been burned, and am afraid of an infection," he said.

"I have just doctored a child's burn. She was burned on the left hand, too."

"What a coincidence," the young Venustiano Carranza said softly.

His family listened silently in awe. It was not the first time he had spoken in this strange manner, half to himself, half audible, as if he were listening to someone else's voice.

"We will be in the same movement. I see many people around us. All of us in red flames."

"Who is this child?" someone asked.

"She is the daughter of Don Joaquín Villegas. We are staying at the house of Señor Hernández's daughter.

"Yes," young Venustiano spoke dreamily. "I have heard about them. My father and that *señor* were talking business some days ago."

On returning to the house, the doctor told the family about the incident and what the young man had said, adding that he seemed to have been far away, seeing things that were yet to happen. No one gave it any importance. They were all interested in events at the house.

When the Little Rebel went to her mother's bed, she found Doña Valerianna crying because she had heard of her child being burned.

"My poor little one. It must hurt you very much."

"Yes," she answered kissing her mother. "But Grandmother will cure me. And now, Mamá, I will never get lost. I will always be yours. I have been branded with a red hot iron like the little sheep on the ranch."

Under the watchful care of Doña Damianita, the burn soon began to heal. As the part of the hand burned by the end of the knife widened, it left a scar in the shape of a V.

The months of December and January were spent in the beautiful, peaceful city of Cuatro Ciénegas, owing to the delicate state of health of Doña Valerianna. She was surrounded by loving care and affection.

Time went by happily for the little mother, content to be surrounded by her family. Soon, she took up her guitar and always sang her baby to sleep. The townspeople were kind to her. They knew she could not make calls, but Doña Damianita received callers, and many loving messages were exchanged. The grandmother supervised the running of the house. Doña Isabelita's apartment was carefully done over so that no trace of Pepito's mischief remained. The doors and windows were closed, everything put in perfect order for the bride and groom on their return home. Don Joaquín made courtesy calls on the prominent families, offering them his home in Nuevo Laredo at any time it was convenient for them.

Don Joaquín's friends were notified that he was in the vicinity on a buying trip. He made short trips to nearby cities, taking some of his men and wagons on each trip, as they were to return to Nuevo Laredo in different wagon trains loaded with purchases. Led by one of Don Joaquín's wagons, merchants sent in their own wagons large shipments of corn, beans, chili, garbanzos (chick peas), spices, and piloncillos (raw sugar cones). The surrounding country near the cities of Nadares, Abasolo, Puerto del Carmen, Buena Vista, and Monclova were combed in search of merchandise. The towns of Saltillo and Monterrey were left until last.

One convoy was sent to San Luis Potosí to buy nonperishable goods, *rebozos,* gunny sacks, crude manta (unbleached domestic), and *huaraches*. The convoys had orders to travel as near the cities as possible; the open country was more dangerous for laden caravans. During the holiday season from the twelfth day of December until well past New Year, merchants brought their goods to sell at market. Burros loaded with fragile earthen wares, *cazuelas* and jugs, men and women loaded with toys and bird cages for the holiday market trotted along the roads.

Don Joaquín decided that the doctor's family should leave first, going directly to Saltillo to visit Doña Isabelita's people. It would be more pleasant for Doña Valerianna to be left quietly with her mother. Don Joaquín planned on leaving in February, returning slowly, taking a direct road that would bring them to Saltillo by March. He reserved for himself the stagecoach in which they had come. Only he and his wife would ride, taking the front seat for themselves; Rosita, the nurse, would ride with the baby on the back seat. In the second coach, Grandmother Damianita and the children would be taken care of by Pancho and Julia. There would be peons on horseback and two guards in livery. The *mozos* would attend to the camping outfit which was to be loaded in two wagons.

Once the necessary but disturbing doctor's family had left, Doña Valerianna made arrangements with a fine old lady to come in the afternoons and teach Julia to sew. She brought her guitar and would sing and play. She amused the children with her songs while Doña Valerianna embroidered baby clothes, often joining in the singing.

Don Joaquín and Pancho had stripped the coach that the doctor took. The money concealed in the lining, the pockets and the seats was transferred in bags and hidden in Pancho's wagon. The doctor's family took along two guards, two wagons with their personal property and necessary funds. All this relieved the *patrón* of a feeling of responsibility for them.

When things became somewhat quiet, the *patrón* took Pancho with him to the wagon that Pancho and Julia had traveled in.

"Remove the seat and take it to the dining room," Don Joaquín ordered.

It was so heavy for Pancho that the *patrón* had to help him. They returned for the other box that served as a foot rest. Pancho knew better than to ask questions. He judged that the contents were similar to those in the bags he had taken out of the doctor's coach.

"Look, Julia," he whispered. "so much money. The Indians would have killed us."

"Foolish one, the Indians are our people. Don't be too proud, Pancho," Julia chided him gaily.

They were glad to know that the money was now in the house and no longer in their unknowing care.

As time passed, Doña Valerianna's health did not improve. She waited only for her husband to finish his buying expedition, then begged him to hurry home. As they were nearing Nuevo Laredo, they decided that the family would cross by ferry to Laredo where they could take the train to San Antonio. Doña Valerianna could stay there until she regained her health.

On arriving at home, Don Joaquín was informed that, a few months after he had left on his trip, a band of horse thieves had attacked his Hacienda de San Francisco. Another change of government had provoked dissatisfaction in the country. The famous outlaw Don Catarino Garza took advantage of the unrest that had made all the ranches along the border almost untenable outposts. He had surprised Don Sereno Pérez, the *encargado,* or manager, and, under one pretext or another, had forced him to sign papers by which the ranch passed into the bandit's hands. Pérez had sent his best foreman, Sóstenes, on horseback, to notify the *patrón,* but the messenger never reached Nuevo Laredo. While crossing a swollen river, he and his horse had been drowned. The peon with him had returned to the ranch alone.

His wife ill, his business taking another trend and prospering, Don Joaquín thought it better to let go of the ranch that held so many memories of happier days. He, therefore, sent a trustworthy employee to San Antonio to look for a home for his family. On arriving, the employee contacted a friend of Don Joaquín's who found them a new cottage near the Sunset depot. It had a garden and shade trees. The family was pleased when they saw the "chalet," as the houses were called, and they soon settled in.

Under the care of their friends, Dr. Ornelas and Dr. Adolfo Herf, Doña Valerianna was kept in bed. Don Joaquín was told that his wife was expecting another child. Doña Damianita was ever vigilant for her daughter's comfort. She placed her daughter's bed near a big window overlooking the garden. From this place Doña Valerianna could see her children romping on the lawn under the watchful care of Pancho and Julia.

During their trip in Mexico, the children had learned many stories and tales about the Emperor Maximilian and Benito Juárez. The little boys wanted to play soldiers. Pancho pulled out flags. He gave the American flag to Leopold, and Julia gave the Mexican flag to Lorenzo.

"This is yours. You were born in Cuatro Ciénegas," she said.

Although Lorenzo could walk, Julia dragged him by the hand, marching proudly with him. The Rebel, who thought she had a prior right to that flag, argued and fought to get it. Doña Valerianna, hearing so much discussion and noise, finally leaned out of the window and called their attention by waving a white towel.

"Here, Leonor, you carry this, and march between your two brothers. Women also go to war. They carry a white flag and take care of the soldiers."

They were all happy then. Each had a flag to fight for. Reclining again on her pillow, Doña Valerianna fingered her rosary nervously.

"Dear God," she prayed, "may they always be united."

She watched the passing of travelers to and from the station along the shady street. Don Joaquín made frequent trips not only to Nuevo Laredo to receive stocks for his store, but to neighboring towns to make new acquaintances. After making new friends in San Antonio, he began to widen his scope of business, but he stayed close to his wife. This pleased Doña Valerianna.

One day she asked her husband to sit near her. She had something to ask of him.

"Do you see that long, dreary house across the street?"

Her husband nodded.

"Well, ever since we arrived, it has been my constant nightmare. I have prayed fervently and asked God to please send someone to live there. It is so dismal, like a haunted house."

"But, darling, what do you want me to do about it?" He smoothed back her hair.

She lovingly kissed his hand. "Precious one, I am going to give you some news. Last night, I was watching the arrival of the train. Some passengers carrying boxes and cases came to that lonely house and went in. Today, I saw a lady and gentleman, quite elderly, with many young people."

Don Joaquín sat listening, not wanting to stem her enthusiasm by talking.

"Please, dear one, tonight will you go to call on them? Tell them I am ill and cannot make a call, but I want them to know we will be at their service."

"We do not even know who they are, dear," her husband suggested.

"No matter, let us remember the kindness we received in our travels, especially in Cuatro Ciénegas," she insisted.

"My, you are a romantic. But I am going to please you. We shall have an early supper." He would have kissed her good night, but she held him off.

"Not good night, my darling. I shall be waiting for you. I want to hear about your visit."

Later she saw her husband walk across the lawn, cross the street, and knock at the door of the house. Did his wife realize that she was sending him to greet his future, or was it an inevitable call of fate? She saw the door open. It had been her wish. All the lights inside the house shone brightly for a moment, then the door shut and there was only darkness.

She dozed off. Hearing her husband's footsteps approaching her bed, she opened her eyes and dreamily inquired, "How about it? Was it an interesting adventure?"

"Yes, very," he said. "Are you sleepy? Do you want to hear about it?"

Eagerly she sat up and he put a pillow behind her shoulders.

"The old man is a Spaniard from Barcelona, a Presbyterian missionary. His wife is Swiss. They have eleven sons and daughters. All their children were born in different countries, as they have traveled much. Now they want to settle here in this city. They are looking for work. It seems urgent, as the older ones support their parents and the younger children."

"Dear one, you must help them to find work. You have so many friends." She lovingly begged her husband, who was already impressed by their struggle.

He promised to help them. After contacting his good friends, Don Joaquín soon had the family across the street in a flourishing condition. They were all as highly educated as the father, the Reverend Ramón Monsalvatge, who had taught them three languages. The oldest, Adele, became a professional translator. Her work soon piled up: almanacs for drug stores, catalogues for out-of-town mail orders, and correspondence. Eloise taught mathematics in high school, while two other sisters opened a private school in their home. Two brothers, Ullyses and Washington, were given credit by Don Joaquín to open a grocery business. Reverend Monsalvatge tended to the Presbyterian church and became known for his humanitarian work in the fever plague on the border. He wrote many books, mostly against the Catholic church. He had once been a Catholic monk. Doña Valerianna, a great admirer of education, saw only the good in the young members of the family, who were so dominated by their parents.

Every afternoon, Leopold and Leonor were bathed, carefully dressed, and brought to their mother's bedside for inspection. She would look them over and repeat to them the same instructions.

"Leopold, take your sister by the hand. I shall be watching you. Cross the street carefully and knock at the teachers' door. When someone answers, you say, "Good afternoon, my mother sends love, and wishes to know how you are all getting on. We are well, thank you, in case they ask about us. Then you say goodbye and come straight home. It will be time for your supper. I will give you your reward."

This was a task the Little Rebel did not like. She tugged at Leopold's pants for fear he might be tempted to accept an invitation to go in. Leopold did not like it either, but since it pleased his sick mother, he obeyed.

One morning the children awoke to the sound of great commotion in the house. The Little Rebel, tired of the neighborly visits, suspected something, so she went to her mother's room and crawled under her bed. Presently, Doña Valerianna moaned. Though Leonor would have rushed out to console her, it was impossible, as the bed was soon surrounded by people talking excitedly and moving quickly about. She could not understand why her mother sobbed, but she supposed those around her were the cause of her suffering. Leonor tried to attack them. Sticking her little hands out from under the bed, she pinched their legs. Her tiny fingers must have been as flea bites, because the people shook their feet and moved on. The sickness was so serious, they did not have time to give the matter any importance.

Presently, Leonor heard a baby cry and heard the doctor say it was a baby girl.

"A girl, indeed not. I am the only girl. I won't like her. She had made my mother suffer. I shall tell Leopold. He won't like her either," the little girl whispered to herself.

She waited until everyone left the room. Sticking her head out from under the bed to make sure there was no one around, she crawled out and went to the head of the bed. Her mother lay with closed eyes, praying very low. Leonor stood on tiptoe until she reached her mother. Kissing her and taking a nickel out of her apron pocket, she said consolingly, "Mamá, don't cry. I am leaving this nickel under your pillow for you."

Hardly had she finished speaking when Grandmother Damianita rushed into the room, grabbed her by the arm, almost dragging her out.

"Where have you been? We have all been looking for you." Shaking her for an answer, she repeated, "Where were you, Little Rebel?"

"Right here," said the child, pointing under the bed.

"Listen, my daughter, to what this child says."

"Well, mother dear, forgive her. Come here, mother. Look, now I shall have two daughters, one Mexican and one American. And two sons, one Mexican and one American. The Virgin of Guadalupe, my flag, shall keep them unified." She close her eyes and slept, exhausted by her effort to speak. When she awoke, she called for her husband.

"Well, dear, are you pleased?" she asked smiling up at him.

"Yes, indeed. Let us called her Lina. Dr. Ornelas and your sister, Adelita, will be her *padrinos*. We shall baptize her right away."

Seeing the happiness in his eyes, she was encouraged to speak.

"My dear husband. I have been a fortunate wife. I want to ask a great favor of you. Please take me back to my home. I am not too strong, but I will get well quickly there."

"Are you really in earnest?" he asked seriously. "We can leave in several days. The train will take us to Laredo and you can cross the river in an ambulance."

"But that is not all, dear one. I want the two children, Leopold and Leonor, to stay here. You can make arrangements with the teachers across the street to board and keep them, to teach them many things. You say they are smart, and I know how much the Little Rebel means to you."

"If that is what you wish, I shall talk to Don Ramón." Don Joaquín desired only to please her now, even if he was not in agreement with her plans.

"And the other two children, my dear. They are too small. Mother and Sister can take care of them at home."

So it was arranged. Doña Valerianna and her mother cried constantly. It was Adelita who was the bravest. Dr. Ramón and his family would profit by the two extra students, who would be well paid for. Don Joaquín completed plans to leave. Goodbyes were said to the children with promises to come for them very soon. All the toys and clothes piled about the little forlorn ones did not ease the feeling of foreboding they had. Sadness filled their hearts, making indelible marks for the rest of their lives. They drew close to one another, seeking comfort in the last semblance of their family, each other. Different flags, different countries, a muddy river separating them, it all meant nothing now or ever after.

The trip home for the sick mother was hard and, being without her children, increased her restlessness. There had been a heavy rainfall on the border. They rushed to place the ambulance on the barge and cross the river before the waters became too swollen. As they were crossing, Don Joaquín was close beside his wife.

"Dear," she said almost in a whisper. "Do you remember the night our Little Rebel was born. It was on a night like this." She smiled. "You knew what to do, you always do."

Her mind wandering, she spoke softly as if to herself. "I will see my little children very soon."

He, the strong man, the stern husband, became a little child. Impatiently brushing away his tears, he tenderly promised to bring them home very soon, as soon as she got well enough.

Everything was ready when Doña Valerianna arrived at home, but it seemed empty without her older children. Her rosary was her only consolation. She prayed, looking at the painting of the Guadalupe that had been hastily unpacked and put on the wall at the foot of her bed. Pancho and Julia went about sniffling, hiding their sobs. They went to the padre and asked him to pray for their mistress.

One evening, a few days after the family's arrival, the attending doctor shook his head. Taking Don Joaquín aside, he said, "She is very sick. She will not be here long. Go talk to her. It will relieve her mind. She may have many things to tell you."

Don Joaquín took his wife's hand, bending over her to hear her voice. He could not speak. She was the braver.

"Promise me, Joaquín, my husband, you will be a loving father. You will always take care of my little children."

Weeping over the hand he clasped, he repeated over and over again his promise, kissing her many times. Then he closed her eyes and she slept in her eternal sleep with her rosary in her hand, her mother and sister crying by her bedside.

Pancho and Julia covered the grave with fragrant, hard-blossomed flowers of cape jasmine and delicate blue plumbago sprays. They swore to be faithful to Doña Damianita, who would have charge of the two children at home, and not lose their vigilance over the two in San Antonio.

CHAPTER V
Second Marriage for Don Joaquín

The pent up love Doña Damianita felt for her lost daughter poured out in incessant attention and care for the two little ones left in her care. Their presence was a balm to sooth her aching heart against the longing to see the absent ones in San Antonio. She dared not speak of them to Adele, lest they both become a fountain of tears. Adele, too, burned the vigil lamp of love that kept her sister's presence alive. The little ones were not aware of their mother's death.

Don Joaquín gave the grandmother a block of land on the outskirts of town, yet within walking distance of the main plaza. Fenced in, shaded by pecan trees, it was converted into a playground where Doña Damianita spent most of the day. The children, hanging to her skirts, trotted along until they were quite exhausted. It did not take long to make a little farm. The block was divided in half by a wire fence. Under two big, shady mesquite trees, Pancho built a barn for two cows, two goats and a burro. There was a pig pen and chicken coops.

On one corner of the block there was a house big enough for the grandmother, Adele, and the two children. Near the house, Pancho built cages for the rabbits and a dove cote. There was a dog and a cat for the children. On the opposite corner there was a small house that gave Adele the idea of opening a grocery store. She fought for her independence, wanting to earn her own living and that of her mother.

Don Joaquín protested as he amply supplied the needs of his children and gave Doña Damianita an allowance, signing a legal document whereby he would take care of her the rest of her life. To please his sister-in-law, he nevertheless bought the store, stocked it with groceries and opened a credit account for her. Pancho took charge of selling, while Adele had charge of the cash. The burro was hitched to the wagon and, with a large barrel, Pancho hauled water from the river and delivered articles bought at the store by the neighbors.

On moonlit nights, Pancho filled the wagon with straw. Julia and the children, and sometimes Doña Damianita, went for rides out into the country along the river. All this was pleasing to Pancho, who enjoyed exchanging the stiff charro suit for the loose white jacket and wide white pants of unbleached muslin. He wore a red belt and a big sombrero like a peon. Julia seemed beautiful. She was now a mature little wife. She wore wide skirts of bright colors and flowered blouses, which were low-necked and provokingly coquettish. Her long braids were tied with colored ribbons. There was no other man about the place, so she lavished her smiles and songs to quicken the heart of her Pancho.

Julia was a consolation to the family. She was gay about the place, and sometimes she was moody. She kept the house spotlessly clean, pots boiling on the *bracero*. After the noon meal, she took the children with their serapes out under the trees. Spreading the blankets on the ground, she told them stories about two children who lived in San Antonio, and all they had once done on a big ranch, Hacienda de San Francisco.

A large comfortable apartment was fitted up for Don Joaquín at one end of the store, where he received his friends every night. The home remained locked. The huge bunch of black crepe hanging for weeks on the door, until it fell off, was a constant reminder of his tragedy.

He made secret visits to the house, but they were fruitless efforts to regain the peace he sought. Opening the door and going to his wife's room, the first thing that caught his eye was the guitar. Drawn to it by an irresistible impulse, he held it in his hands. Every string seemed to vibrate. It made him quiver. He heard the melodious voice drift from one song to another until the instrument dropped out of his shaking hands with an awakening thud. Only then did he realize that it had been stilled forever.

Catching his breath, the desperate husband wandered about the house torturing himself, looking at his wife's sidesaddle and riding habit.

"Merciful God! I hear her voice warning me. 'Joaquín, be careful, there is danger ahead. Dear,' her soft voice continued, 'we had better return. The children are waiting for us!'"

His wild eyes seemed to follow her as she jumped from her mare and ran to embrace her little ones. Holding his head between his hands, he rushed out of the house.

"I shall go mad." Bathed in cold perspiration, he thought he could never live again.

As this went on time and again, his friends began noticing a great change in him and became alarmed. They talked it over.

"Time passes and our good friend Joaquín cannot be consoled. He is young yet. Let one of us talk to him and give him advice," Señor Adolfo Larralde said.

"You, Pedro Regal, who are more closely connected with the family, you do the talking," spoke Medirichaga thoughtfully.

When Don Pedro went earlier than usual for his evening call on Don Joaquín, he found the disconsolate husband sitting alone, smoking. A bottle of wine was on a small table near him with glasses ready for the night's game of chess.

Speaking quickly, Don Pedro wasted no time in working up to his subject. "*Compañero,* I want to talk freely with you. May I be allowed to do so?"

"Mi amigo," Joaquín answered inquiringly, "anything gone wrong? Any trouble with your business? Your family?"

To all the questions Don Pedro shook his head. "No, *compañero,* it is you and you alone. Time goes by, you don't seem to be aware of it. Your children, in San Antonio, you have not seen for more than a year. You did not go at Christmas; it was too near your wife's death. It will soon be Christmas again. You should go to see your little ones."

"Yes," Joaquín answered sadly. "They do not know that their mother died. That is the reason I have not gone. I have not forgotten them. They are well supplied with clothes and money."

His friend continued. "My good friend, have you never thought of marrying again, getting your little ones all under one roof?"

Don Joaquín shook his head.

"Do you not think it is an injustice to your children? You nurse your grief, forgetting about them."

"No, I do not forget them," Joaquín insisted. "I have proposed to my sister-in-law, Adele. She will not consider it. She says that I have been like a father to her. She should not betray her beloved sister."

"Foolishness. But if that is the case, perhaps there are others." Don Pedro did not give up. Don Joaquín had to be brought to his senses.

"You are right." Joaquín looked his friend in the eye. He took out his watch, thoughtfully.

Was he again hearing his wife's voice? She seemed to be guiding him, urging him. "Go, Joaquín, dear one. Go and be nice to those people across the street."

Snapping the cover of his watch shut, Don Joaquín stood up. "It is six o'clock. At eight a train leaves for San Antonio. I shall go to see my children."

Don Pedro helped him pack and they both went to the station.

On saying goodbye, Don Joaquín promised to return soon. "Wait, Pedro, one more favor. Tell the *encargado* to take plenty of candy, toys, and money to my mother-in-law's house for the children. Will you tell her what I have done?"

In Mexico, at Christmas, there were no Christmas trees as a centralized idea of yuletide. A *nacimiento* was the typical way of celebrating the nativity. In the house, a manger was arranged in which the child Jesus was tenderly laid in straw. Nearby were the figures of Mary and Joseph. Angels floated above the manger, and a star was hung. Near the crib were the donkey and oxen, and scattered around the place in hay were the shepherds and their sheep.

Not so in San Antonio. Leonor and Leopold were sitting in front of a chimney, roasting chestnuts and remembering that their little brother had been born on such a night. The also thought of Pancho and Julia. It had been so long since they had seen their mother. A large Christmas tree near the fireplace was gaily decorated with cotton, icicles, candles of all colors, toys and cookies hung from branches tied with red ribbons. Candied apples and oranges were strung on silver cord.

The children were not happy. Don Ramón sat in an armchair, his feet curled under him, telling them Christmas stories. Finally, he said, "When you go to bed, ask God to give you anything you wish. Tonight is the birthday of his son."

"Anything?" the Little Rebel asked. "I wonder if he will really give us anything."

"I want, most of all, to see my mother," Leopold whispered.

"I do, too," Leonor answered. "And our brother and sister, and Pancho and Julia."

After a little while as they prepared to go to bed, a knock at the front door detained them.

"It may be Santa Claus," Don Ramón said to them.

The children could see through the door. The person who was outside waiting had many bundles. Hopping up from his chair, Don Ramón opened the door. It was no stranger. The children flew to their father's arms. He dropped his parcels to the floor. Leonor began hugging her father, her arms about his neck, as he picked her up. Leopold climbed up on a chair, so he too could reach his father's face.

"Where is mother? Is she coming, too? Are we going away with you?" Leopold asked. The children had not been happy with the two old people and the stiff, puritanical old maids.

Don Joaquín saw an opportunity while they were so happy. They might not feel the pain so much. He told them his news. "No, darlings. You cannot see your mother. She has gone away."

"We shall never see her again?" Leopold asked.

"Now, darlings, I shall tell you tomorrow. Take these toys. They are for you both. Take them to your room and go to sleep. I will see you tomorrow. Tonight I have business with Don Ramón."

Taking each other by the hand, the two children walked out. They knelt numbly by their beds. They did not pray for anything. They did not look at the toys. They had sobbed all the time they were getting ready for bed. Their beds were far apart, divided by the high, wide bed that belonged to Grandmother Rosalie, as they called Don Ramón's wife.

Lying in their beds, Leonor said to her brother, "I don't want any toys. I don't want to look at them. I will not go to sleep. I will just cry all night."

But she didn't cry. Instead, leaving her bed, she opened the drawer of Grandmother Rosalie's massive, marble-top dresser. Feeling about, she found what she was looking for. Then going to the foot of her brother's bed, she picked up his little shirt made of star-decorated material. How he hated to wear that shirt to church on Sundays. The boys always said he had a girl's waist.

Sitting down cross-legged near the door where the light came in from the hall, she pulled her long gown over her feet. Then carefully and completely, she began cutting out the white stars. When she finished, she got up, brushing off the stars that clung to her gown. Holding the riddled shirt up over her head, she smiled at all the empty spaces. No stars were left. Now her darling Leopold could never, never wear that shirt again. And she wouldn't be punished for cutting up the shirt because her father had come to take them away. She dropped the shirt back on the pile of clothes and went to bed and to sleep.

On arriving in San Antonio, Don Joaquín had gone to the elegant Menger Hotel. Many stores along the plaza were still open for late Christmas shoppers. He had bought the gifts for his children. It was going to be hard for him to see them, but he had made up his mind to live a new life. He was going to have his children at home again.

After the children had left the room, he spoke abruptly to Don Ramón. "Sir," he said, "you are a fine gentleman. You have a nice family. I am still young and have a good future. I have thought seriously of marrying again. I would like one of your daughters for a wife."

Don Ramón sat silently a few moments, then he asked, "Which one do you like?"

"The one you wish. You know me, and know which of your daughters would be most suitable."

Again Don Ramón sat silent, thinking. "I think Eloise will be best suited for you and your children. She is the one I love best."

"Very well," Don Joaquín said quietly.

Don Ramón arose and went into the next room where his wife sat crocheting and waiting. She had heard every word. So had her daughters. They were breathlessly awaiting Don Ramón's decision. Looking at Eloise, he made a sign, nodding his head toward the parlor. His wife Rosalie was grimly silent. In the same emotionless way, Don Ramón had proposed to her. She had known no love affair. Her marriage had been a matter of the expediency of business.

As Eloise entered, Don Joaquín rose, speaking as if he were opening a business transaction. "I need a mother for my children. I need a home for them. I am quite able to take care of you. Your parents will not lose your support. I shall give them an ample allowance as long as they live." Looking calmly into Eloise's startled blue eyes, he continued, "Will you be my wife?"

"If you have my father's consent, I will say yes," she answered, looking at him inquiringly. Then she left the room, as Don Joaquín said nothing more.

When Don Ramón returned, Don Joaquín took up the subject again. "I wish to marry very soon. It is now Christmas. I will stay here three weeks attending to business. I shall want to marry on the tenth of January."

He placed a bag of money on the table. He had dropped it on the floor when he had greeted his children. "Give this to your daughter so that she can buy herself a trousseau. I will be here in the morning for the children."

Instead of going to church with Grandmother Rosalie, Leopold and Leonor were standing side by side looking through a window pane, waiting for the arrival of their dear Papá. Sunday after Sunday they had stood in the same spot, sulkily looking out into the joyless world. Church was an ordeal, where they were frowned at and pinched by Doña Rosalie if they moved or talked. With their mother, they had prayed in Spanish. They had been coaxed to sleep with Mexican lullabies. They were sure that God did not understand them when they prayed in English, because He had not answered their prayers. He had not remedied their situation and taken them home to their mother. Waiting, they argued, and finally agreed that God must have heard their prayers at last.

Leopold, putting his hands in his pockets, found them empty. There was only the nickel that was to go in the collection basket. Smiling, he said to Leonor, "I'll have plenty of money and marbles in a little while."

Leonor, looking at her hand that was holding back the lace curtain, replied, "I'll have a gold ring like Lily's." Lily was the little Negro girl to whom Leonor gave most of her belongings.

Papá arrived in a coach and they drove off spellbound. It was the same princely Papá, but where was Mamá? They enjoyed the hobby horses and the pink lemonade at the park. Leonor, in pink satin slippers, jumped back and forth across the little San Pedro Creek.

As the bells rang for eleven o'clock mass, their father took a coach, and they were driven to the cathedral. Their eyes wide, holding hands, they reverently followed their father up, up to the front pew. Perhaps he was fascinated by the flowers on the altar, like the flowers he had seen his wife making so often. As they bowed their heads in silent prayer, the past rushed over them. Now more than ever they remembered Doña Valerianna. Each one filled with different emotions, swept by the memory of a past that had left an indelible imprint on their souls. The father, once, twice, passed his fine linen handkerchief across his face. It was Christmas Day. His tears were a wreath of pearls, a tribute of love he placed at Valerianna's shrine. After mass, the children walked to the crib where the Infant Jesus lay.

"Just like Julia used to tell us," Leonor whispered, "see the shepherds with their little sheep."

Leopold, looking up at the star above the crib, whispered to his sister, "Leonor, Mother told us about the Star of Bethlehem, the guiding star. Maybe it will guide us home."

Their hearts were full of joy as they proudly walked beside their father, who took them by the hand. Soon they arrived at the hotel. They ran up the carpeted stairs and into the beautiful rooms. Boxes of toys and candy were scattered everywhere.

"Wash your hands, my children, before we go down to dinner. You can enjoy your toys later. This afternoon we will go for a drive." Don Joaquín, looking at his children thoughtfully, took off his gloves.

Now they were really happy. Leonorcita had her ring. Leopold had one too and his pockets were full of pennies. They were so sure of going home that they did not ask any questions. They ate, listening to the orchestra playing, half-hidden in palms and artificial foliage.

All rested after dinner. Even Papá had a *siesta*. Perhaps he dreamed of Valerianna, of how pleased she would be now that her children were to be again under one roof. The porter knocked. "Your coach is waiting."

Sitting between the two little ones, Don Joaquín began to break the news. "I am going to be married very soon to Eloise. You like her, do you not? She is going to be your new mother."

They did not answer their father. They were bewildered by the idea of having another mother.

"I want you to have a home again. Your little brother and sister will be waiting for you." Don Joaquín tried again.

They seemed like bright flowers suddenly blasted by a hard, cold wind. Bent over and drooping, they stared ahead of them, not speaking. They were too far apart to whisper consolations to each other. They had learned from him that Eloise would share their father's love with them. They would never see their real mother again. Finally the fatal drive ended.

The activity around the house, the jokes among the sisters who were really jealous of Eloise, confused the children. They waited the outcome, because they were going to go home to their loved ones.

Eloise was duty-conscious regarding the children. She had dreams of love, but at the same time accepted the whole affair in a religious sense. The arrangement had pleased her father. She loved the children. She was in her late twenties, perhaps would not have children of her own, so she was determined to be a perfect mother.

In the early days of the new year, Eloise encountered a puzzling attitude among her family and friends. Little unkind remarks were made, showing how much they envied her chance to become the wife of a very wealthy and important man. Again and again she was asked, "Eloise, how can you marry a man with four children?

She smiled coyly, "Oh, I shall love them easily enough."

Her dressmaker, while trying on the wedding gown and mouthing pins, spoke with downcast eyes, averting Eloise's open gaze. "Why, Miss Eloise, you are so young, such a fine young lady. How can you marry a man with four children, who is taking you away to a foreign country?"

Each one had something to say, until the loving heart of Eloise began to be troubled, and she wondered if she could really love all four of the children. She had not seen the others, who were two and four years old. The children in San Antonio were six and seven. She resolved to handle her husband and his children.

The wedding took place in her home. The Presbyterian minister performed the ceremony. It was a sumptuous affair witnessed by Leonor and Leopold peeping through the half-opened dining room door. They had refused to officially attend. They were undermining the bride's sense of competence, very much to the displeasure of their father, who had exhausted his persuasive powers. Nothing consoled them. They were put to bed after kissing their Papá and their new Mamá good-night.

The bride and groom rode off to the hotel, where Don Joaquín had engaged the bridal suite. The next day the children were at bay. They did not dare return to their happy plans of Christmas. They loved their father. They would never lose faith in him. The atmosphere at Don Ramón's home changed. The children were being royally treated, although they heard many discussions about their future.

After a short honeymoon, Don Joaquín broached the subject of their departure for Mexico. He had closed his business deals and was ready to return. He was enchanted with Eloise, who entered charmingly into his business plans, quickly understanding his financial problems. While she was well educated, fluent in three tongues, Don Joaquín had still to fall in love with his bride.

Coaxingly, she suggested that it would be fine to spend a day visiting schools to be able to select two good ones where Leonor and Leopold could be properly taken care of and well educated. Their future depended so much on it. The two little children in Mexico would have a chance to get better acquainted with her, and learn to love her. So wise and practical was her idea that her husband was immediately in accord. She had his children in mind; their future was important. Leopold was to go to St. Mary's on the very outskirts of San Antonio, and Leonor, to the Ursuline Convent in town.

Early the next morning, Señor and Señora Joaquín Villegas drove up to her parent's home. The children were ready, and soon they were boarders each in his respective school. The Reverend Ramón was surprised to see the adroitness of Eloise's scheme. He said nothing, but he saw that many changes would take place in the Villegas family.

Leopold and Leonor, with a brief hand clasp and in mute appeal to each other, said goodbye. They were allowed to see each other seldom during the next three years. They accepted their school as a home. They were lavishly attended to by Don Joaquín in a businesslike way, by sending barrels of apples and baskets of oranges, enough to feed the whole school for days. The same day the children were put in school, Don Joaquín and Eloise returned to Nuevo Laredo.

It seemed quite natural to Don Joaquín to take his bride to his home. As the smiling *mozo* opened the door, Don Joaquín took his wife by the arm and escorted her to the parlor.

Eloise stood for a moment, surveying the whole room, suddenly turning only her head. Then she shook off her husband's arm. Her skirts swirling about her, she swung herself around so that she faced him, her face distorted with rage, fine beads of perspiration gleaming coldly on her upper lip. "What do you mean bringing me here where everything speaks of your dead wife?"

Eloise took Doña Valerianna's guitar and threw it. As it hit the tile floor small, white pieces of the onyx inlay bounced in little tapping sounds. For a second the sound fell on Don Joaquín's mind. It was like hearing again the light quick step of the dead Valerianna. Tearing a portrait of Doña Damianita from the wall, Eloise threw it down, the glass flying in a thousand shining pieces. Moving about the room, she quickly pounced on the riding habit that lay over a low chair. She jerked down the sidesaddle, as it was hidden by the voluminous skirt.

It was too much for Don Joaquín, who considered it a sacrilege. "Stop! Stop, I say!" Raising his voice for the first and only time. He was too much of a gentleman. Understanding her feelings, he looked quietly and sternly at her, saying in a commanding voice, "Eloise!" Then softly, "Marriage had never entered my mind until a few days ago. I was not quite prepared."

They were facing each other. He, the future provider of her numerous family. She, the woman yearning to kindle his love. As he was speaking, Eloise pulled her laced handkerchief from her sleeve. She crushed it into a moist ball in her hands. Realizing how she had shocked him, she looked at him imploringly. "Joaquín, please forgive me."

Seeing her momentary humility, he rushed to remind her of her other duties. Gently he said, "Eloise, the two little ones will be coming soon. Their grandmother, Damianita, has been advised of our marriage, of my wishes to have the children here. I do not want them to be frightened by this disorder. I will immediately send servants to take your orders. Transform the house as you wish."

At the door he hesitated. She ran to him, embracing him, whispering again and again, "Forgive me, please forgive me."

He looked tenderly at her, pity filling his soul. He remembered the gay young señorita whom he had wooed long ago. She, singing to him from her barred window; he, in his troubadour suit, throwing flowers to her. What a different courtship. It was the sacred recollection of those days that softened his heart. This one would be good to his motherless children and he would make it up to her. Valerianna's tenderness had unconsciously prepared the way.

In a short time, Eloise had the house running smoothly. In an empty room in back of the store she put away everything that belonged to Valerianna. They were piled up indiscriminately: guitar, riding boots, trunks full of beautiful gowns, fans, oil paintings, photographs, everything that might remind her husband of his first wife. The marble mantle piece had been scrubbed and new bric-a-brac replaced the old. All the wedding presents on display were in grand and good taste.

The children were delayed in coming. To them it was a surprise. Their dear grandmother was not going with them. Julia and Pancho already hated the stepmother. "Why should Don Joaquín take the children away?" Julia sighed passionately. "Will we never see them again?"

When Don Joaquín finally had to go for the two younger children, he found them tearfully clinging to their grandmother. Respectfully, he explained his plans regarding the other two children to Doña Damianita and his sister-in-law, Adele. "I shall never forget you. The children will come often to see you." On leaving, he added, "Tell Pancho and Julia I want to speak to them, to come tomorrow morning to the store."

Eloise embraced the little ones. They were too small to remember their mother, so they easily accepted her. She played up to the situation and firmly proposed to be a real mother to them.

Late the next morning, Pancho and Julia were in a rebellious mood. They walked into the store well clad in starched clothes, and into Don Joaquín's presence. He told them first about Leopold and Leonor. Not needing them anymore, he wanted them to be independent now. He would give them money and credit for whatever they wanted to do.

Julia spoke up, quickly sensing the situation at Don Joaquín's. She had promised Doña Valerianna always to take care of the little ones. She thought up a scheme to fulfill her vow. "*Mi amo,* we can sell candy on the streets. Each of us can have a little candy box trimmed with gay tissue paper, the box covered with a screen. We can stand on the corners of the busy streets selling our candy." Julia could make good pecan candy, the kind children liked and strangers always buy.

Don Joaquín was not in the humour to use his imagination. He simply nodded agreement. One of his clerks received the order for a sack of sugar, cinnamon, and pecans to be sent to them, also enough cash to buy their boxes and paper trimming.

"Now, Pancho, I have had a large wagon loaded with Doña Valerianna's belongings. You must go with the driver and deliver these things to Doña Damianita. Be very careful. She will keep some things for my children." He walked away from them to stand at the door to watch the two mules being hitched to the wagon. He was trying to adjust his thoughts to the new domestic arrangement.

Pancho and Julia, gaily clad, took up their position daily, waving little sticks topped with colored tissue paper streamers to attract attention. Standing across the street from Don Joaquín's house, on opposite corners, they could command a view of all the windows. The children were forbidden to talk to Pancho and Julia because they were inclined to share their candies with the children. The vigil kept on day after day, much to the chagrin of Eloise, who stood on guard knowing them to be faithful servants of the family. Wishing to obliterate every trace of the past, she began planning how best to set about doing so.

Eloise, who had been born in New Orleans, was an American citizen. She had imbibed American ways, yet retained the charm of her parent's foreign background. Her husband had ordered her a piano, a Kanabe, best suited to the warm climate. She had a beautiful soprano voice and played her own accompaniment. In the evenings, she sang for her husband, who now began inviting his friends to join them.

Feeling more secure in her husband's embrace, Eloise began, with great diplomacy, to coax him to transfer his business to the American side. She emphasized the growth and expansion of his business affairs. He did not have to leave his Mexican connections. He must continue his export business, exchanging products from one country to another. One morning, he sent cards to all his clients and friends, advising them that the firm of J. Villegas was moving to the American side, leaving in Nuevo Laredo a representative to handle his interests in Mexico.

Julia and Pancho, observing certain activities around Don Joaquín's house, ran back and forth to Doña Damianita's home, carrying what news they could gather from the household servants. Late one evening, they crouched in the shadows beside the house. Watching for them, Lorenzo and Lina crept out on the balcony, closing the tall double doors after them. Pressing their little faces against the wrought iron grating, they began talking to their dear friends.

"Pancho," Lorenzo said, "we are going away. We will never see you again."

"Don't say that. We will always follow you," Julia responded immediately.

"Mamá says she will make Americans of us. What is that, Julia?" Lorenzo felt important, impressed by Pancho and Julia's reaction to his news.

"It must be something good or the *amo* would not allow it," Julia consoled Pancho and the children.

They both kissed the little ones' hands repeatedly, promising not to abandon them. Pancho made a sign toward a shadow nearby. It was Grandmother Damianita. She could not speak, just stood weeping. She, too, began kissing them, until Lina began to cry out loud. Immediately the door flew open behind the children and Eloise dragged in the culprits, sticky with salty tears and brown sugar candy. Wrestling the bags of candy from them, she sent them off to bed.

As they turned the corner to leave, Pancho and Julia met Don Joaquín. "*Mi amo,*" Pancho said, "you are going to take the children away? They will be Americans?"

"Well, what of it? It is not bad." He laughed trying to dismiss their fears.

"But, señor," Julia began to cry, burying her face in her trembling hands, "they say your wife is not a Catholic. How can they ever see their mother when they die?"

"Now, now, you two go home and be good to Doña Damianita. I will take the children to church. I am a Catholic." Don Joaquín dismissed them smiling.

They went off sobbing. Suddenly Julia stopped. Wiping her face on her sleeve, she sniffed loudly. She pushed Pancho roughly. "Let us go across the river. I have a friend there whom we can trust."

Shaking his head, Pancho looked half pleased. "We may not find a boat to row us across. It is too late."

"Ah, Pancho, don't be afraid. You see I am not. I have the money the *amo* gave me. Let us go." Julia pulled Pancho by the arm. There was a skiff tied at the river bank. After a few minutes of bickering about the price, they stepped in and sat down on the damp board seat. The boatman pulled the little boat slowly across the dark river. When Pancho and Julia arrived in Laredo, they went to the friend's house nearby. They rented a little hut close to the landing. Here, spreading a *sarape* on the hard clay floor, they were soon asleep in each other's arms.

They waited the next day, sitting at the edge of the river. Don Joaquín and his family were rowed across on a big barge. It was late afternoon when they crossed, but Pancho and Julia, hidden in the tall river cane, were satisfied when the family had landed safely. After awhile, they decided they would sell their candy on the streets and keep watch over Doña Valerianna's children. Days passed and Julia and Pancho, night after night, sat at the edge of the river, looking across to their beloved Mexico, sighing for Doña Damianita and Adele. They saw the lights of the town go out one by one, then they turned to their humble hut. It was a long time before they dared walk the streets of the American city of Laredo.

Mr. Daniel Milmo, a rich Irishman, offered Don Joaquín the use of the building he was leaving. Don Joaquín accepted it while he built his own quarters. Once his business was established, he ordered an architect to make plans for his new home and place of business. Eloise was soon handling the building project. It would be a large building. The street floor was for the wholesale and export business. The second floor would be used for a home.

Eloise had traveled and knew much about city comforts. She ordered catalogues of home furnishings. She sent to New York for her furniture. Plumbers, electricians, and paper hangers were brought from San Antonio. Everything was thought of. She had time only for planning her home. Joaquín's children would have a beautiful home to grow up in. It took time to build a fine home. None of the modern comforts had reached the frontier. While there were beautiful riverfront Spanish homes, they were not equipped with conveniences later indulged in. Eloise insisted on luxuries, arguing that Don Joaquín's children should have the best. Thus, she kept before her husband his parental duty, kindling love for herself through the children.

Time passes quickly. The little ones accepted Eloise as their mother. She began to love them jealously. Lest the older children remind them otherwise, she quickly planned that Leopold and Leonor would be privileged to know and meet many friends. They were placed in other schools. Leopold in St. Edwards and Leonor in the Academy of the Holy Cross in Austin, Texas. There, brother and sister saw each other frequently and visited schoolmates' homes on holidays.

Leonor, with her rebellious streak, was often threatened by expulsion for her pranks. Life in a convent was too monotonous. She had to give vent to pent-up emotions. She gave no thought to punishment. "Her life is paved with good intentions," muttered the distracted nuns.

"You must be like your mamá," the Reverend Mother told the girl repeatedly.

Shaking her naughty head, Leonor remonstrated, "I want to be like my papá."

At home, Eloise reigned unchallenged. Young Lina sometimes went to church with her. Standing on tiptoe, she would peep into her hymn book, then, looking up into her stepmother's face, wondered how she could sing so beautifully. Pancho and Julia capitulated at their post. Waving their tissue paper switches, they won warm smiles from Mamá Eloise. She gave the children money to buy candy, watching them from the window as they crossed the street. Then the faithful pair would eagerly cross the river to tell the old grandmother how things were going at the house of Don Joaquín.

Fearing this overflow of outside affection, Eloise began finding fault with her house furnishings. She must choose new things to replace the fading old ones. "Joaquín, we must be planning for the future of our little ones. They must have the same advantages as the older two. They must go to school up north. Let us make a trip to New York. On our way we can take Leopold and Leonor with us. We will all be united."

Don Joaquín was overjoyed at the prospect of seeing his older children. Proud of their reports from school, he wrote them of the trip which would be their reward. Leopold and Leonor, now fourteen and thirteen, were serious-minded and well behaved. They wrote back quickly that they were overjoyed with the idea of traveling with their family.

Julia and Pancho were mystified at the family's absence. "Where can they be?" They asked the clerks at Don Joaquín's business house. "They are not ill?"

"Gone to travel," was the only answer. "They will be home soon."

Their charges gone, Julia coaxed Pancho to leave the candy business. "Let us stay at home and get acquainted with the people around us."

"What are you thinking about Julia? We have to earn our living." Pancho slapped his knees with his broad hands in astonishment.

"Yes, my Pancho. We will feed the men who work near our little hut and the people who cross the river. I will make the tortillas and coffee, and you can sell them."

Pancho made a little shed around the house, walling it in with branches and vines. Big earthen jars of water on the crude table and benches in the shade soon attracted weary travelers.

Don Joaquín's entire family traveled to New York City. They went sightseeing, and visited the popular watering places, Asbury Park, Ocean Grove, and Bay Ridge. Finally in September when school opened, Leopold and Lorenzo, now called Lawrence, entered Fordham College, Leonor and Lina, Mount St. Ursula Academy in Bedford Park. Leopold was to study law; Lawrence took commercial courses. Leonor chose to be a teacher, and Lina took elocution and drama. No one was to return home without a diploma.

Through the years, Eloise had in innumerable ways made herself indispensable to Don Joaquín. Her studied considerations for the children were always to work out so that she, too, would benefit. Don Joaquín loved her. She became absolutely necessary in his life. She wisely advised the children, writing them about their studies and their conduct toward their father. She emphasized the sacrifices he made for their welfare. He did not deny them anything. They had music, painting, all the fine arts. She never complained about expenditure at their costly colleges. Anything was worth the privilege of being with her wonderful husband. She lived those six years in a happy dream.

Then, the graduating year sped quickly upon her unruffled domestic felicity. Leonor graduated in 1895 with honors. Archbishop Corrigan of New York placed the laurel wreath on her forehead, a diploma in her hand. "You will have many roses, my dear," the bishop said. "But remember every rose has its thorns."

The young girl recalled the dim memory of her mother and her beautiful Mexican roses, the thorn that had pricked her finger. She looked at the Archbishop thoughtfully. "How calm he is." She actually forgave that forbidding Pope who shook his head accusingly at her so long ago in her mother's parlor.

Having fallen under the influence of religious training and the regularity of convent life, Leonor was half-inclined to become a nun. The sisters gently hinted it would be a fitting thing for her to do. At mass she would be transported to the filmy, feathery, heavenly regions, promising the dear Lord to be at his service forever. On leaving school, she said goodbye to the Reverend Mother in a warm embrace, tearfully promising to return and enter the convent. She had written her father that she wished to become a nun. He had written back tersely, asking her to come home first and think it over.

Don Joaquín knew his willful daughter. Under the rigid discipline of a nunnery, she would thresh herself with piety one day, and beat her hands in hatred against its confining walls the next. He smiled thinking of how many noble vows she had made only to do the opposite when the heat of her decision had cooled.

He met his returning children at the station. Leonor looked for him from the trim window and saw the almost blinding whiteness of his finely tucked shirt front, pierced by the hard, black brilliance of his black pearl studs. Rushing to him, she rubbed her cheek against his arm, laughing and holding his hand. She had been a long, long time coming home. Following Leopold to the baggage window, she saw a young man, and suddenly she was alone. There was no father, brother, or sister, just Leonor and the young man.

"How handsome he is. How princely. I shall marry that young man. He will be just like Papá." Her mind, in the breathless fashion of her heart, was making little clipped sentences. The dreamy-eyed young man looked her way indifferently. She forgot her vow to become a nun.

Leopold, after leaving Fordham, graduated from the New York Law School. Lawrence was delicate in health, having grown so rapidly. He was very much like his father. Ever watchful and solicitous, Mamá Eloise suggested he be sent to Switzerland to a good school in Zurich, where he could grow strong. Lina returned for two more years in New York

The two younger children gone, Eloise was reoccupied with Leopold and Leonor. The house had been completely renovated. Joaquín's children were welcomed in a fitting manner. A billiard room was made for Leopold, a darkroom for his photographic hobby, and another room for his hunting and fishing equipment. Leonor would continue her music.

Mamá Eloise watched with her large fathomless eyes the close companionship between Joaquín and his children. The three spent hours at the billiard table. There were early bicycle rides that Leonor and her father took to inspect the tannery on the heights near town. Leonor would translate orders to the manager, a husky German. She often softened her father's demands as she translated for him, fearing that the towering red-faced tanner might attack her slender father in rage. Riding home, Don Joaquín teased his daughter about her veracity as his intermediary.

In the evening after singing and entertaining her husband, Mamá Eloise would call Leonor, who had been sitting gloomily wondering what her brother was doing out in town. So charming was the request that the girl rose eagerly to sit by her majestic stepmother at the piano. Playing duets with the girl, Eloise felt that, at least, Joaquín's attention would not be divided between the girl and the woman.

The Spanish American War of 1898 that lasted two years was over. Many of the Laredo boys, who had gone off to fight with the Texas Rough Riders, had returned victorious. Laredo, dressed in holiday attire, was out to welcome them home. Leonor, standing at her bunting-draped balcony, sought eagerly among the crowd for the young man. She picked out a seemingly familiar head, her eyes discarding it quickly when the face became visible. Her sparkling diamond earrings trembled impatiently with each turn of her head. Her hands left wet marks of perspiration on the iron rail of the balcony. Almost beneath her stood her elusive quarry. Smiling slightly, his eyes shaded by his hat brim, he glanced indifferently up toward her now and then. That Villegas girl had fire, he thought, like the bright, clear stones of her earrings.

Just around the time for Lina to come home from school, Mamá Eloise suggested a trip to Europe. Her husband should go to visit his family in Spain. Furthermore, the girls' education was not complete without a European tour.

Lawrence was handsome. His slimness was graceful, and his manner gentle and charming. From his European school, he had returned polished and accomplished. He hunted and fished. In hunting season, he kept the household supplied with venison and quail. He and a group of young men about town became amateur bullfighters. Lawrence was the constant delight of Leonor, who would have loved some of his wonderful freedom for herself.

Lawrence soon found out about his sister's infatuation. He also found out that the young man had a beautiful sister. Letters began to pour in for Leonor. Serenades rose to her window on the still night air. At length, the conversations began. Pieces of sentences, words half lost by the distance, were exchanged by the slim girl on her balcony and the young man beneath it. Finally, the words, the letters, the tender serenades were not enough. The young man decided to write Don Joaquín. It was that fatal letter that set the family plans in rapid motion.

Don Joaquín, letter in hand, serious-eyed, knocked at his daughter's door. Carefully closing the tall double doors to gain time, he turned to face his daughter. "Leonor, you said you were going to be a nun. What is this letter? How can you love this young man when you don't know him?"

"But, Papá, I know him through his letters, our talks from my balcony." Leonor did not dare approach the window, lest her troubadour be standing across the street, waving his handkerchief to her after kissing it.

Surely the thoughts of his affectionate Valerianna and their courtship must have rushed to her father's mind, for he answered slowly. "I will tell him that you are going on a very long trip. Two years, or more. You will have time to make up your mind, meanwhile."

"I shall never be a nun. I will always love him. No one else matters," she began sobbing as her last defense.

"We shall see," Don Joaquín answered softly, knowing the answer even as he played for time. "You are to return his letters. You must not speak to him again."

Don Joaquín was please with the prospect of his trip. He had not seen his family for many years. He would make contracts for Spanish wool and garbanzos to exchange for chili and beans. That would more than cover the expenses of the lengthy trip. Passage was taken on the French steamer *L'Aquitain,* which sailed from New York to Le Havre, France. A party of twenty composed of families from Mexico met in

New York. They were all going to the Paris Exposition for six months. Then they were to separate, each going to their old homes in Spain. Later, there would be a trip to Rome before starting back to America.

Booked on the same steamer were members of the Metropolitan Opera Company: Emma Calvé, famous soprano, Emma Eames, coloratura, Paul Plançon, renowned baritone, the de Reszlse Brothers, tenors, all engaged to sing in Paris. There were others, the famous prestidigitator, Fre'goli, Count Lebonjeff, pianist, and José Guadalupe Aguilera, noted geologist from Mexico. The artists entertained the guests at the ship's concert in a never-to-be-forgotten show.

In Paris, the amused tourists hid behind screens to see the ladies dance at the Moulin Rouge. At the Louvre, Leonor was fascinated by the portrait of the Mona Lisa. Don Joaquín's family visited in the elaborate home of a French doctor who had relatives in America. One evening after supper, Leonor stood with her sister before a huge realistic painting of the doctor clutching the reins of two runaway horses that threatened the life of a beautiful woman. Leonor admired the fiery courage of the man and the wild strength of the horses. The painting and a medal for courage had been given to the doctor in commemoration of his bravery. Watching the doctor talking to her father, she recalled a daily scene on the banks of the Río Grande in America. Now she understood the character and background of the old man in his jet black wig, who day after day sat in state on his balcony, overlooking the plaza that bore his name, looking down on the people whom he governed as leader of a strong political faction.

CHAPTER VI
Adolpho Comes into the Rebel's Life

Fourteen years had passed since Doña Valerianna's death. Her four children living in the United States were completely obedient to the zealous authority of Mamá Eloise and her American culture. Don Joaquín, under pressure of his ever-watchful wife, was persuaded to become an American citizen. It meant much to his social standing in a community where he was loved, honored, and had prospered. The children were not consulted; they were minors and automatically became Americans. Now Joaquín Villegas, American, crossed the mountains from France to Spain. The Rebel, filled with romantic ardor for her father's country and his people, thought of him as a Spaniard. Eloise was not entirely at ease, regardless of Spain's being her father's country. She was already jealous of her husband's people, who might influence him to transfer some of his affections to those in Spain. She began planning against that possibility without realizing that Spain might get into her blood through her own family roots.

Don Joaquín deposited his letter of credit in the Banco de Madrid and called on his friend, the president of the bank. Leonor visited a schoolmate who had married Carlos Pereda, poet laureate of Spain. Don Joaquín's mother and his two sisters awaited the arrivals from America at their summer villa in Carandia. The famous bathing resort, "El Sardinero," was crowded with Spanish nobility. Don Joaquín's family had a chalet near the ocean. It was a gathering place for the family members to bathe during the days of summer.

Later, the Villegases proceeded to their villa and ancestral estates that had been in their family for three hundred years. The coat of arms carved in stone high on the bell tower had defied time and tempests. Once in a momentary act of rebellion during the Spanish-American war, Lawrence had climbed to the top of the tower of Don Joaquín's mother's estate, paint and brush in hand. "I shall paint it away," he said defiantly. "I will cover it. We are Americans now." Some unknown power held his hand. He stood transfixed as if he had seen a ghost. "No, I cannot do it. It means tradition. It means the honor of my forefathers, of my father whose name I bear." A light shone from his eyes. He realized a desire to do something for his father's people. The next day, Lawrence, the dreamer, the lover of art, cabled his father to obtain permission to establish a school in the village. It would be supported by his father, just as the village church had been cared for by his grandmother, the Countess Vicenta Pacheco.

Late one afternoon, Eloise stood on the terrace of the villa, overlooking the village of her husband's boyhood. Holding her wide brimmed hat, she looked down one of the narrow cobbled streets, picking out a small black figure coming toward the villa, skirts flapping. It was the priest. Approaching Don Joaquín's Protestant wife, Padre Alejo bowed slightly. He licked his lips. The climb up the hill had left him tired, his mouth dry. He hadn't expected to meet the American so abruptly. "Good evening, Señora Villegas. You are viewing our little town approvingly, I hope," he ventured a courtesy of speech.

"Yes, Father. I was thinking about the little Joaquín who once ran about these same streets." Eloise clung to her reverie despite the padre's presence.

"Señora, please sit down. Look out over the town. I will tell you about that strong-willed boy who defied an ageless tradition when he was but sixteen." Having told the story many times, he savored each retelling. Wrapping his cossack about his thin legs and sitting down on the terrace curb, not too close to Eloise, he closed his eyes and began talking.

"One spring vacation when he was home from school, young Joaquín sought out his father and told him of his desire to take a small part of his inheritance in gold and leave for the Americas. 'It is unfair to my brother and our two sisters for me to have everything because I happened to be the first born,' said the boy.

"'But, my son, it is the *mayorazgo*. The oldest son receives everything. You must take care of your mother when I am gone,' Don Lorenzo replied incredulously.

"Let me go, father. I will come back for you both as soon as I am established,' the boy spoke confidently. He had rehearsed the speech many times.

"Don Lorenzo gave in to his son's demands. He stood by the window, his head bowed. Then glancing outside, his eyes glowed. 'Joaquín, come with me!'

"The sun was setting and the grey olive trees were gold dipped in the warm light. Joaquín followed his father across the brick-paved courtyard until they came to the foot of a hill in back of the villa. Kneeling by a great round rock, Don Lorenzo rubbed its smoothness thoughtfully. 'Every evening at sunset I shall be here, facing the west, the country of your choice. I will remain in prayer until the sun has dropped from sight. Then I shall know that this sun here has reached you.'

"Year after year Don Lorenzo kept his prayerful vigil. As he grew older, he withered quickly. He was forced to stay in bed. One bright evening, the memory of his son was especially clear and he called his wife. 'Take me to the rock, Vicenta. I shall never see my son again. I must send him a last blessing.'

"At the foot of the hill, Doña Vicenta supported her husband as he knelt, whispering his old prayer to himself. 'He will come again to us,' his wife spoke bravely. The heavy limpness of his body told her it was finished. Her son had not returned in time. With a rush of tears long held back, she laid his head on the rock and ran to the house for the servants."

While Padre Alejo was talking, the Rebel had been sitting unnoticed in a low chair silently looking at the hill. Rising quickly, lest the padre stop what interested her so vitally, she knelt beside him saying, "Where did my father go when he left Spain?"

Laying his hand on her head, the old man continued. "Joaquín went to Cuba to an uncle in Havana, who was president of a bank. With him he deposited all his earnings. The boy had a home there."

"Did he stay long?" She begged him to continue.

"Until he was twenty-one. Then he heard of great sums of money to be made on the Texas ranches. He took a boat to Texas. Some time later, he met your sainted mother." He had more yet to tell. The old priest shifted his weight. Mamá Eloise now thought it time to stop the story. She saw tears in the Rebel's eyes. Her heart softened momentarily. They both felt a mutual love for Don Joaquín that bound them in spite of other things.

It was on the eve of one of their trips from the villa that Padre Alejo talked to Doña Eloise. His heart was heavy and troubled. What would the villagers think of her, the new wife of Don Joaquín, a Protestant and an American. They had known of Valerianna and loved her for her piety and her generosity to them.

"Señora Villegas, you are now the wife of our dear benefactor. Try to win the love of his people."

Eloise smiled graciously, nodding her head. "Yes, indeed, I want to continue the tradition." Being a patroness wasn't exactly an unenviable station. She liked the idea.

"Señora, it will be difficult for you." The priest hesitated before he finished.

It was in that moment that he unconsciously won his case. With the word difficult, Eloise had bridled. Nothing was too difficult where she was concerned with the pleasure of Don Joaquín. She was determined to succeed in whatever situation the little priest presented to her.

"Go to mass," he said. "At our little church we always offer up special prayers for Don Joaquín and his deceased wife. Let the people see you bow your head as they do. Stand beside your husband, greet them after mass." He finished hastily, fearing that he might have outraged the woman from America.

Eloise murmured assent. Words were unimportant. She had made up her mind. She would appear with Don Joaquín before the populace. It was through Valerianna that she had attained so much happiness. Why not show her gratitude? Besides, it would please her husband.

In the quaint village with its hanging bridge, its waterfalls, the old mill, and the well near the house shaded by persimmon trees, Eloise began to fall under the sway of Spanish romance, its aristocracy, its traditions, and its history. She willingly yielded to her husband's wishes to spend some time at the villa. From there they made trips to other places in Santander.

The family attended the coronation of Alphonso XIII, standing close by on a balcony where they could view the brilliant ceremony. The young king was sixteen. He was attended by his female family, his beautiful mother, María Cristina, and his two haughty sisters. Sightseeing, they were fascinated by the fish market noted for its beautiful country women. The women were combed as any court lady, beautiful as any dame with flashing eyes, rounded arms and busts. Jeweled hands skillfully showed the slimy, slick, wiggling fish they held up to buyers who could not resist their call. The family heard the fishermen's songs, and saw their graceful butterfly nets. At the summer villa at Carandia, they admired the walls of the great halls, hung with huge paintings of bulls wearing big rosettes of bright colors. The best bulls at the fair in Torre la Vega belonged to Lorenzo Villegas, the *alcalde,* or mayor, who always won the highest honors.

They attended the bullfights where Mazantini was the court favorite. King Alfonso and his mother sat in colorful glory with jeweled field glasses, watching the bulls that were offered them before the killing. Beautiful señoritas with naughty dresses, flowers at their bosoms, and combs in their shining black hair, gnashed their teeth if the *torero* missed his mark on the fierce bull's flank, or the matador made a slip with his sword.

The girls liked the "Romerías" that lasted all day and into the night. Everybody danced the *jota,* rhythmically clapping their castanets. This was life in Spain! Their Spanish kinsmen were not a sickly, anemic race who hugged their sorrows. No, they wisely said, "Let the wind blow away our grey hairs." How the Rebel loved it when she saw her dignified father, stirred by the throbbing gypsy music, clasp a partner and dance into the merry crowd. How many were the love letters, the flowers, the song birds at the balcony for the two girls from America. The Rebel hid her love, keeping the promise she had made her father.

Visiting many large cities, Don Joaquín searched for wool and export products to ship to Mexico. Eloise accompanied him in hopes of finding proper suitors for the Rebel and Lina. The girls were amiable and always ready to accept invitations. They visited the university. It was thrilling to see the young students in their black cloaks draped carelessly over their left shoulder, wearing student's caps called *boinas*. They were round woolen flat caps worn in Navarre and Biscay, but adopted by the students for their own wear. They trod noiselessly through the Royal Academy where the wise men of Spain met to deliberate on educational matters.

After two years in Spain, Don Joaquín approached Eloise and told her that he wished to take his mother, Doña Vicenta, with them to America. Although it meant an added burden, it alleviated the fear in her heart that her husband might be tempted to remain in Spain. Don Joaquín explained to her that his mother was very orthodox in her way of thinking. She had expressed the wish to live with his brother Quintín and his wife, Amelia.

Quintín had followed his elder brother's pattern of life. He had left Spain and gone to Cuba. There he married the only daughter of a wealthy doctor. Quintín had been twenty-two, his wife ten years older. Besides having plenty of money, she also had three maiden aunts. He brought them all to Texas and cared little for the laughter it caused about town. The aunts wore outdated hoop skirts with long pantalets decorated with many little starched ruffles, pretty soft slippers, and lace draped over their shoulders. Devout Catholics, they were constantly pattering up the aisles of the church, attending all the religious services.

In Texas, Doña Vicenta became a member of Don Quintín's household, where the old ladies, each in their peculiar way, spoiled Don Quintín's and Doña Amelia's only child, paving the way for her tragic ending.

Don Joaquín's life was full with his business and his family. Now that his mother had come to America, he felt the fulfillment of his old promise to support her. He visited her every morning, and on Sundays he came to see her after mass. Between the two brothers, Doña Vicenta was made independent of small worries. They each agreed to give her a twenty-dollar gold piece every Sunday and ten dollars in silver and small coins so that she could tip the *mozos* for errands and maids for extra attentions. This money was also for the collection at church.

Don Quintín's home was sumptuous with many servants. Doña Vicenta was considered the most important member of the family. The Latins have high respect for the older members of their family. When visitors called, she would be notified first. However, her radical ways were the cause of many wagging heads by friends and blushes by the family. As an introduction to the guests, she would invariably ask, "Do you speak Spanish?" If the answer was negative, she would show her surprise. Shaking her head dolefully, her white curls hanging from under a newly starched cap bobbed heavily. Studiedly smoothing the skirt of her neat dress, she commented softly, "Too bad. What have you done all your life?"

Her next question was equally as important. "Are you a Catholic?" She asked it easily with the assurance of a correct answer. If the answer was negative, we would wait a few moments while she excused herself by saying she would call Amelia, her daughter-in-law. She would not return to the drawing room. Instead, she hurried upstairs to her room. Lying flat on her back on her high bed, her face covered with a large white handkerchief, hands clasped over her breast, she prayed in a semi-audible whisper. "Dear Lord, I pray for the conversion of this person, whoever she happens to be."

Amelia had a hard case on her hands, but she never complained. She had brought three maiden aunts to her marriage. "After all," the Rebel often remarked, "Uncle Quintín has the hardest part of the job." Amelia and her spinster aunts kept a hawk's eye on Quintín, whose youth they couldn't forget. He was still a young man.

Scarcely two days had passed since the family's return, when Pancho came to welcome his master, hat in hand, tears in his eyes. "My *patrón,* this is not a joyful welcome." Stifling his tears, he continued. "Our beloved Doña Damianita is very ill. She wants to see Leonor. It has been many years since the girl was there. Please take her tomorrow."

"We will be there, Pancho." Don Joaquín was agitated by the bad news. Reaching in his pocket, he handed Pancho some gold pieces. "Tell Adele to get a good doctor."

"*Mi amo,* she has already seen one. She has been operated on her right side. She knows she will die soon." Jingling the money absently in his hand, he started off for Nuevo Laredo, Mexico.

Don Joaquín remained seated at his desk a long time, looking over his books, his accounts, and checking expenses. Then, fighting his emotion no longer, he buried his face in his hands, leaning heavily on his desk. He remembered how Doña Damianita had solemnly handed him her daughter's dowry, asking no recompense, no receipt. "It is true I have done for her all her life. I have never abandoned her nor Adele. Poor Adele, what will she do?" He called his secretary, dictated a letter and drew up a bill of sale, mentioning no value. He signed it and placed it in his vest pocket.

Next morning, he called Leopold to take Doña Vicenta his regrets for missing his planned call. "I am taking Leonor across the river to visit her grandmother Damianita. She is very ill."

This was Leonor's introduction to sorrow and illness. Solicitously, she sat at the foot of her grandmother's bed. Seeing her, the old woman began talking as if she had been waiting a long time for the girl to come. "Child," she began in a clear voice, looking straight at Leonor, "do your duty, leave to God the rest." Then her eyes wandered indifferently about the fading, familiar room. Seeing her granddaughter, she began speaking again.

"You are a young lady, more like me. Your sister is like your mother." Lowering her eyes, she said, "Perhaps you will be married soon. Always," she looked up, "you will find your answer in the sky. All these years," she began to cry. "All these years I have seen your mother in a cloud, shining light about her. Have faith. Pray as I have prayed."

Little by little, Leonor had moved nearer to her until she grasped a little wrinkled hand in her small, firm one. Now Doña Damianita was whispering. "Be good to your Aunt Adelita. She is your mother's sister."

Adele tiptoed into the room and knelt on the other side of the bed. In the dimness of the room, Leonor noticed a blond, blue-eyed, middle-aged man standing by her aunt's side. He bent over her grandmother so that she might see him well before he began speaking.

"Dear lady, I have come for your blessing." His voice quivered. "Adele and I wish to be married." He stopped, but with a look of encouragement from Adele, he cleared his throat and went on.

"I have known her only a short time, but I have been watching her many days. She is a pearl in a haystack. I could never find a more perfect wife."

The Rebel tightened her grip on her grandmother's hand, drawing closer to hear what she would say. "What would she say?" thought the girl impressed by the romance and the grief that filled the room at the same time. A brief light shone in Doña Damianita's eyes, a smile flickered on her lips. Her trembling hand sought out her daughter's. She held up her other hand for the suitor Ignacio's. Then she clasped them together.

Turning her head toward the wide-eyed Leonor, whose tears were falling on her grandmother's bed, she whispered, "You, too, shall be happy. You shall have the one you love."

Adele placed her head on Ignacio's shoulder, weeping, and was comforted. Leonor smoothed her grandmother's pillow, looked into her hazel eyes and received her last sign. "What is life, after all, but the accomplishment of God's will." The words flowed into Leonor's startled mind before she had time to think.

Pancho and Julia, kneeling at the foot of the bed, quietly arose and led Leonor away, though not too far. She wanted to see everything in this new drama. Her Grandmother's body was not rushed off to an undertaking parlor. She was anointed with balm and sweet smelling herbs. Her beautiful hair was brushed into soft ringlets, her face bathed with attar of roses. Finally, she was shrouded in a fine linen sheet. The little household went about quietly getting ready, laying the body on a narrow bed covered with white embroidered sheets, removing all the furniture from the room. Late in the afternoon, Leonor, Adele, and Ignacio sat in the little parlor. Julia brought in black coffee on a tray with a large pitcher of hot milk. A rumbling sound of wheels on the hard dirt road was heard. Pancho alighted from the funeral coach.

"Leonorcita," he called softly. "Your father is here. I slipped away and told him the news." Behind him was her father, scrupulously dressed with a white, black-bordered handkerchief in his coat pocket.

Men were bringing in a shining casket lined in silvery, white satin. Lovingly, Pancho and Julia lifted the body. There was an unclouded peace about the half smile on Doña Damianita's dead lips. The satin cast a soft light about her face, like the halo one sees about the saints. All night, the family kept vigil around the bier. The flickering candles and repeated sighs of the mourners mattered not to the Rebel, who held communion with her own insatiable soul.

"She will surely see our mother and tell her of our love." She leaned toward her father and whispered this with such surety and piety that he felt his grief lighten for the moment.

The next morning Doña Damianita was laid in the powdery bottom land next to her beloved daughter, Valerianna. Don Joaquín and his children with Adele returned to the house. It was Lawrence who approached his father.

"My father, it was Grandmother's wish that Aunt Adelita marry Ignacio Beléndez."

Joaquín eyed Adele thoughtfully. She was no longer young. Her years of young womanhood had been spent freely in attentions to her mother. "Is this true, Adelita?" he asked kindly.

She nodded several times, not trusting herself to speak. She looked at Lawrence imploringly.

"Father," the boy began earnestly. "He is a customs cashier, well thought of by his fellow workers and the officials."

"When do you wish to be married, my sister?" Don Joaquín wanted to hear Adele express her wishes.

"Now," she whispered, wiping her nose, avoiding her brother-in-law's eyes.

"Very well. Lawrence, fetch the judge and the priest. Notify Señor Beléndez that his bride is awaiting him," Don Joaquín directed.

Pancho was given the keys to Don Joaquín's old home. It was to be opened and cleaned quickly for the bridal party. Receiving the keys from Don Joaquín, Pancho felt their warmth. "A part of himself still, that old house," he thought to himself.

"Now Adele," Don Joaquín spoke so jovially that she looked up startled. He felt young again, with wedding plans to arrange. I have the deed to the house. It was Valerianna's. Now it will be yours. It is the birthplace of our Little Rebel. Sell this other property. It has sad memories."

Adele opened her mouth to reply, but a sob came out instead. Don Joaquín patted her shoulder awkwardly. He had resolved to be gay for the bride's sake. "But," he sighed a little, "women have a way of mixing tears with joy until a man doesn't dare express his own feelings."

Mail had been piling up on Don Joaquín's desk. He was in no hurry to read it. As he leafed through his correspondence, a telegram from Mexico caught his eye. It was addressed to Leonor in care of her father. He did not open it, putting it in his pocket instead. He heard the *mozos* banging the doors, evidently trying to attract his attention. It was closing time. Taking his gold watch from his pocket, he snapped the lid open to make sure of the time. He smiled when he closed the lid. Lawrence had brought him the watch from Switzerland. He had hardly gotten off the train when he had shown his father how the opening and shutting of the lid would wind the watch. During the two hours of closing time at noon, Don Joaquín's family met for the noon meal, exchanging news about town and their friends. It was the first year that the family had all been united. Don Joaquín, in fine style, offered each one a cocktail. At the meal, they drank claret. Mamá Eloise served a bountiful table.

After dinner as they walked to their rooms, Don Joaquín, contrary to his usual habit of walking with his wife, caught up with Leonor. Handing her the telegram, he said simply, "No secrets, I hope?"

It was from Adolpho, Leonor's young man. "Have learned of your return. May I again approach your father?"

She looked into her father's face. Impulsively she kissed his hand. They had both witnessed so much deep emotion in the past few days, the death of Doña Damianita, the wedding of Adele. The Grandmother's prophesy was to be fulfilled in this ripe time.

"Father, I shall say yes. I will wire him to come."

Don Joaquín pressed her hand, kissed her forehead. It was settled for them both. He walked back down the hall toward Eloise, who was waiting for him at the door of their bedroom.

It was December. Many employees had short vacations. It was possible that Adolpho would arrive during the Christmas holidays. When the family had left for Europe, Adolpho had decided to go to Mexico City to find himself a lucrative position in hopes of being able to save some money. He had many friends and was soon the city ticket agent for the railroad lines operating in the United States. He was also agent for several steamship companies sailing to European ports. He made good connections and met influential people. In answer to Leonor's telegram, he boarded a train for Laredo, telegraphing on the road that he would be there for Christmas.

No one knew the plans but Leonor and her father. Mamá Eloise had a suspicion that something was going on. She approached her husband regarding Christmas festivities for the family, but he made no mention of anything extra to be planned for. Big stacks of mesquite wood were placed in each room, where fires burned gaily. Leonor helped decorate. The oak paneled fireplace in the dining room, the tiled ones in the parlor and living room were all trimmed with moss and holly. Lawrence added white cotton to remind him of Switzerland. One quiet evening when all the children were out visiting, Eloise walked down the long hall that divided the sleeping rooms from the living rooms. Entering the parlor she opened the folding doors into the living room, then those leading into the dining room. Strolling down the entire length of the three large rooms, her skirts rustling, her soft shoes sinking into the carpets, she saw a promising future: the happy years to come when the girls married and the boys chose wives. Again she alone would reign over the domain of her husband's undistracted attentions.

Leopold decorated the billiard and the music rooms, throwing wild animal skins from his hunting trips onto the polished parquet floors. He hung deer horns on the walls. But no one spoke of guests. There was a mutual understanding that this, being their first Christmas together, would be a family affair. Mamá Eloise had the *mozos* put up a great Christmas tree in the living room. She busied herself in making long lists of foods. Don Joaquín would see about the supply of fine wines.

Adolpho arrived on the twentieth of December and went to his sister's house. That same afternoon, he presented himself at the store, asking for Don Joaquín. Locked in the office together, Don Joaquín talked with Adolpho for the first time. Leopold and Lawrence, suspicious, notified Leonor of the happenings downstairs. Pacing up and down across her long room, she was oblivious to Mamá Eloise's repeated calls for advice about decorations.

Finally, rapping at the girl's room, she begged insistently.

"Leonor, what is the matter with you?" she asked. "You have worked so hard, now you stop. Your father has a distaste for disorder in the house. We must hurry and finish."

"Get Lina, Mamá Eloise," Leonor replied in a faraway voice.

"Lina's making decorations for the tree," she pleaded. "Wreaths for the windows still must be made. Please come out and help us, Leonor."

Leonor came out, but her help was so distracted that Mamá Eloise admitted failure and let her go back to her room.

That night when supper was over, Don Joaquín looked at his family thoughtfully before he spoke quietly. "You will please stay at home tonight. We are to have company, not a long visit, but you must be present."

Turning to his wife, he said, "Eloise, I wish to speak to you. Shall we go to your sitting room?"

He told her that Leonor would be married soon. He had had a long talk with the young suitor who had brought with him fine recommendations from his employers and two letters from Spanish merchants Don Joaquín knew. Adolpho made a good salary at a responsible position. While the young man had only come to ask permission to marry, Don Joaquín himself had fixed the date. Being very strict about his own employees' absences, he doubted if Adolpho would get another vacation soon. It might jeopardize his job.

"So, the sooner, the better," Don Joaquín finished his long speech jauntily. Then suddenly he threw his handkerchief over his face with a sob.

Eloise was touched. She stepped swiftly into her role of mother and dutiful wife. "Your plans are right, my dear. But you are not losing your daughter. She will always love you. Tonight, I shall have everything ready to receive our new son-in-law." She stroked the soft black hair of his bent head thoughtfully.

He went to his daughter's room. She was sitting by the window, watching for the shadow of the man who was to share her life.

Drawing a chair near her, Don Joaquín began speaking. "Daughter, can you prepare for your wedding soon? I do not like long engagements. Can you be ready by the tenth of January?" As he spoke he hesitated. It was the same date on which he had married Eloise.

"Yes, father, I will be ready by that time. I have lovely clothes from our European trip. I need only my wedding gown, and that, I beg you, let me have my matron of honor order for me."

"So you have already talked it over with her?" he asked. "Why not your mother?"

"It is customary for the matron of honor to do this. Besides we are both Catholics. The matron of honor attends to the church decoration, the wedding rehearsal, and the bridesmaid's dresses." Leonor spoke assuredly.

"Who are they?" her father asked. He was to do the only thing left for him. "I must send them a blank, signed check to cover the expenses."

"Mayor Vidaurri and his wife will be our sponsors. The two bridesmaids will be Lina and our cousin Herminia. I shall not give my wedding another thought," she concluded simply.

"So young, so sure." Don Joaquín smiled at her as he rose to go.

A discreet cough and a shadow passing across the street reminded them of their visitor.

Leonor was bewildered. She had never been close enough to Adolpho to clasp his hand. During the family gathering, between intervals of conversation, they exchanged glances and smiles, drinking their cocktails slowly and deliberately.

Don Joaquín broached the subject of the visit as soon as the pleasantries were over. "Daughter, in my talk to your fiancé I asked him to leave town until the eve of your wedding. He has relations in San Antonio. You may write to each other. Please me in this respect. I do not like publicity."

With bowed heads, they agreed silently.

"The wedding will be at my expense, and I shall give my daughter a generous dowry. The same that I will give to Lina when she marries." Don Joaquín rose, closing the interview for the family.

The days passed quickly. After Christmas Mamá Eloise ordered new china, cut glass, silver, embroidered tablecloths and napkins. She refused to borrow even a punch cup. Everything was to be perfect for the bride. Of course, it was understood without saying that everything would remain in the house as the personal property of Mamá Eloise. The wedding plans were completed without the Rebel's help, except for brief consultations. She was in love, and no one in love was expected to do much. All she ever remembered about the wedding was that it was a sumptuous, smoothly run success.

Because the mayor of the city was the best man, the wedding immediately became semi-official. The police force in white spats and white gloves directed the carriages at the church and at the reception afterwards. As a friendly act of courtesy to Don Joaquín, the merchants in town closed their stores during the morning so that everyone could attend the important affair.

Leaning on her father's arm as she stepped in the threshold of the church, the bride saw only her Adonis and his best man. "Were there ever more handsome men than those two? Only my father could be a rival," she thought with gay pride.

From the church loft, music of the stringed orchestra filled the church with delicate, soft strains. Down the aisle toward the warm light of dozens of burning candles, her long court train of satin trailing regally behind her, Leonor walked slowly in time to the music. Past the row of ushers, she glanced up at the handsome face of Lawrence. The lavender shepherdess' hats of her bridesmaids loomed like great screens between her and her beloved. In the family pew in the front part of the church sat Mamá Eloise in gleaming black satin, the plumes of her velvet hat hiding her face, diamonds sparkling on her hands and at her throat. On they walked, Don Joaquín straight yet at tremendous ease. The high-necked yolk of Leonor's dress pinched just a little. The diamond brooch pinned in her high combed coiffure holding her veil felt heavy.

They reached the altar, her father stepping back as Adolpho came to her side. It was only after the marriage vows were pronounced and the wedding ring had been slipped on her finger that she became aware of the solemnity of the act. Snuggling her knees on a soft, white satin cushion, she looked down. It was one she had embroidered for the bishop. She had made it at the convent in Austin and had her grandmother present it to Bishop Pedro Verdaguer. She recognized the familiar passionflower and the thorns she had carefully stitched on the pillow years earlier.

Looking up at the altar, she fixed her eyes on the figure of Christ, who stood with open arms, holding out his hands. She trembled when she remembered how many times in the little convent chapel she had promised to be a nun, to serve only the Lord. Now, here she was kneeling beside a handsome man, vowing to love him, honor him, and obey him. The sacrifice of the mass brought her to the stern realization that she must be destined to otherwise serve humanity. A deliciously sweet scent disturbed her reverie. Glancing toward her husband, she noticed for the first time his boutonniere of purple and white hyacinths. How like him, she smiled, to disturb my unworldly thoughts with the sweets of the earth. As if sensing her thoughts, he looked toward her and at her until she dropped her eyes.

Then it was over. The priest had given them his blessing and the orchestra had struck up the gay, light wedding march. Adolpho helped her to her feet, holding her arm tightly. They turned to face the crowded church brimming with crying, smiling faces. Outside the chimes pealed as wildly as young love.

On reaching the door, Leonor saw her two oldest and dearest friends, Pancho and Julia, holding each other's hands as if to stay one another in a determined effort to keep from breaking loose and embracing her. She rushed over and hugged them, her billowing veil enveloping all three of them. Recovering from his astonishment, Adolpho led the tearful Rebel away and into the waiting carriage. After the wedding banquet, Leonor left her father's house and boarded the train to Mexico with her husband.

CHAPTER VII
A Blessing for the Rebel

Mexico, that beautiful, paradoxical country, was to be the Rebel's home. Her husband's offices were in the Hotel Coliso in the center of Mexico City. They made plans to stay a few months in the suite of rooms above the office where Leonor would not be lonesome. The city of the well-to-do was a gay place and sometimes called "La cuidad de los palacios" (the city of palaces) and "La cuidad de los pecados" (the city of sins).

President Porfirio Díaz reigned supreme as he had done for almost fifty years. His wife, Doña Carmen Romero Rubio, daughter of a sagacious lawyer, had been instructed well regarding her power, both political and social. As an aristocrat at the side of her commoner, aging husband, she was conservative, religious, dignified, and cautious. From 1901 to 1910, Mexico was at the zenith of glory and wealth. The drawing rooms at Chapultepec Palace were unsurpassed in the beauty and elegance of the chosen people who gathered there. Men from all parts of the world came to render homage to the wife of the Mexican president and to seek her favor. Díaz ruled Mexico with an undisputed iron hand, surrounding himself with men of high culture and refinement, in strange contrast to his own rude background. The Rebel imbibed Mexican life. She was enchanted by the lives of the wealthy, yet she could never accept it completely, seeing the sorrows and oppression of the poor.

At their leisure, the young couple rode about town looking for a convenient place to live. It had to be modern and within walking distance of Adolpho's office, so that Leonor could accompany him every morning. On Juárez Avenue was the great iron figure of Charles V on horseback. The horse faced Bucareli Avenue. It was here, in the first block on Bucareli, that they found a newly furnished building with four apartments. Three were occupied by American families: a major from the American Embassy; Mr. and Mrs. Edward Butler, who established the Christian Science Church in Mexico; and a business man, Hoffman Pinther.

Her father's friends, having been notified of the marriage, began to call. She admired them because they were Don Joaquín's friends, but Adolpho thought their traditional society dull. Callers came at high noon. Men in immaculate morning clothes with high silk hats, their wives in feather boas and big hats, their diamonds sparkling in the cool brilliant sun. After their noon social visits, the wealthy families rode in their elegant carriages in the long circuit from the crowded Zócalo in the center of town up the leafy drive to Chapultepec hill. At two, the carriages disappeared from the proper streets for dinner and siesta. Again at six o'clock, the well-groomed horses pulled the carriages slowly along the same route. At times as many as eight carriages rode abreast, four going one way and four the other with their occupants visiting as the coachmen held the horses to a dignified walk. At eight o'clock, they went home to dress for supper.

Through others, Leonor met many Americans. But it was among the grandees that she met her best friend, a daughter of Benito Juárez, Soledad Juárez de Luchichi, whose husband was the official historian of Mexico. Leonor was impressed by their high spiritual and moral view of life. In their home was a life-size portrait of President Benito Juárez. Every time she visited them, she went reverently to the drawing room to see the masterpiece while Doña Soledad told her some new episode of the great man's life.

Adolpho's father had been a colonel during Juárez's time. An American of French descent living in New Orleans, he had equipped his own men to fight on Mexico's side during the French invasion in the 1860s. He had been wounded in the battle of Santa Isabel near Puebla.

During the five years that the Rebel and her husband lived on Bucareli they had three children, two boys and a girl. Adolpho had, during this time, organized three pilgrimages to Rome and the Holy Land, groups composed of five hundred or more wealthy families under the sponsorship of a high prelate from San Luis Potosí. They took with them jewels and gifts of such exquisite native workmanship that even in Italy they were unsurpassed.

On his last pilgrimage to Europe, Adolpho visited Spain. There he met Lawrence, who had returned on a pleasure trip to his old haunts in Spain and Switzerland. On a walking tour across the Alps, Lawrence had covered more ground than he was physically able, contracting a fever that was persistent and weakening. He was staying at a health resort in Avila, Spain. Adolpho cabled Don Joaquín to come immediately, as it would be a long time before Lawrence would be able to travel again. Don Joaquín and Eloise rushed to his bedside, arriving only a few days before his death. They buried him in Spain, the country of his ancestors.

Spain became a shrine to them. It was as if his ancestors had called Lawrence back to Spain to lie with them. The Rebel remembered the exquisite delicacy of perception and appreciation of his short, brilliant life. Don Joaquín and Mamá Eloise returned from Spain in 1906 changed persons. The son had been like the father, and Mamá Eloise loved his memory. The tragic loss of his young son enfeebled Don Joaquín.

Each year Leonor's parents visited her in Mexico City on their way to the famous health resort of mineral springs in Tehuacán, frequented by families of means. Originally a monastery with long wide corridors and stone archways, the rooms had large bay windows closed in with iron grills overlooking a silent, shady, square park. The bath houses had tile baths built in the ground with three tile steps leading down into the clear, health-giving waters. Two doctors were in constant attendance. In the evenings, the guests met in a large reception room to visit and discuss their ailments.

The Rebel was always invited to spend the months of April, May, and part of June with her parents there. She took two maids to take care of the children. Don Joaquín saw that they all had the best attention. Leonor's suite was adjoining that of her father and Mamá Eloise, who insisted on supervising the care of the children.

The last trip to Tehuacán was made in 1907. Among the guests there was General Bernardo Reyes and his family, who had the apartment adjoining the Rebel's. Leonor soon became the General's most ardent admirer, learning much from him about the army and politics. General Reyes, President Díaz's Minister of War, spent his time at the resort writing a book about his constant interest, the bettering of the soldiers' way of life. He sought to provide homes for their families, with schools and modern barracks for them.

The Rebel spent hours in the park listening to him read parts from his book. Beside the Rebel, there was a wealthy merchant and his wife, Señor and Señora Everardo Arenas, who were the General's companions. All of them sympathized with Reyes' cause and began to see in him a future opponent to President Díaz.

While reading parts from his book, the General would often stop to discuss certain problems that faced the government. It was during one of those times that Leonor interrupted him.

"General," she said almost gaily, "when you became president, will you let me visit those model soldiers' barracks?"

Looking over her head, the General met the stoic gaze of Señor Arenas. She saw the seriousness that lay in their eyes. Becoming president of Mexico would be a deadly, heartbreaking process.

As time went on, Porfirio Díaz began to catch rumors of his Minister of War's popularity and of his plans. Hurriedly, Reyes was sent off on a mission to Europe. This kindled the popular sentiment into a warm flame, and Mexico was soon ablaze, burning with red carnations on the lapels of military jackets and civilian coats. Women and children were daring in declaring their opposition in the coming elections. However, the shrewd Díaz and his partisans struck a *coup d'etat*. General Reyes was called home and imprisoned. When Francisco I. Madero rose up in opposition, all the Reyes sympathizers turned to him for leadership. Madero was destined to rule and become the idol of the people.

When the Rebel returned to her home in Mexico City, she and her husband agreed to move, because Bucareli Avenue was occupied by publishing houses where the great daily newspapers of the city were printed. Frequent riots occurred there among the vendors, opposing political factions, and laborers attacking the press. They found a beautiful apartment just two blocks from the Iron Horse on the Paseo towards Chapultepec, on Glorietta Colón. Nearby was a statue of Guatemozin, an Indian chief. Around him occasional demonstrations by students and aboriginal groups were held with patriotic fervor. Opposite the apartment was the popular Café Colón. Adolpho passed many hours there playing billiards, and he and Leonor had their noon meal often at the café.

The children went to kindergarten, always accompanied by their nurses. The spacious mansion where they lived was lonely with only one other tenant, Señora Sánchez Azcona and family. They too were Madero sympathizers. They had belonged to the radical party called Precursors, or forerunners, of the Mexican Revolutionary group. In 1907 one of the party leaders, Enrique Flores Magón had been imprisoned in California for political reasons, while others of the party had suffered alike in St. Louis, Missouri. The long arm of Porfirio Díaz reached his political enemies anywhere. The Azconas became friends of the Rebel's. Leonor was soon indoctrinated in the intricacies of opposition and rebellion.

From her windows the Rebel could look across the street into the Café Colón where a large glass-framed porch on the Paseo served as a dining room. She could hear the music from the orchestra as it played at night. There "Panchito" I. Madero, as he was popularly called, dined and met many of his followers. The Rebel made frequent visits to the Café, as the owner was a Spaniard, a friend of Don Joaquín's.

When Mexico wrested its independence from Spain in the early nineteenth century, the country was immediately plunged into a civil war which continued until the time of Díaz in 1876. President Díaz and his supporters boasted of a long peaceful reign, of economic stability such as the country had never seen. But for the enormous Indian population, the old Spanish system of peonage continued. The Indians in Mexico were never given the chance to taste European culture. The rich were privileged aristocrats; the poor, oppressed slaves.

By 1910 there was a noticeable undercurrent of dissatisfaction and unrest among all classes of the Mexican population. The middle class could find no openings for their skills. The agrarian question arose again, principally in Chihuahua, where enormous estates held the land inaccessible to new ownership and to complete production. The socialist idea had found ardent sympathizers all over Mexico. The wage problem developed in the northern states, whose proximity to the United States made workers conscious of their unfair treatment. Foreign-controlled capital was exploiting the oil richness of Tampico, and an interlude of religious character kept the inhabitants agitated.

All of these sore spots, Francisco I. Madero, who was an inspired idealist, had grasped and considered in his plan to modernize Mexico. Had he had the required time to organize his government, Mexico's history would have been vastly different. His plans were of great magnitude, requiring the uprooting of three centuries of Spanish rule that had left an indelible stamp on a virgin country owned by Indians. Madero became their savior, a divine missionary who would end their age-old wrongs. Probably no man could have served as ably or more fearlessly. Unfortunately, the hatred of the reactionaries was centered on his government. The Madero outbursts occurred sooner than planned. People followed him everywhere, anxious to see him and hear him speak.

One Sunday morning as the Rebel was on her way to church, she saw a multitude of people headed by Madero coming down the wide Paseo de la Reforma. Flags and banners bearing inscriptions of "Sufragio libre, no re-elección" (Free Elections, Not Re-Election) fluttered above the crowd. Telling the driver to turn back and follow the crowd, Leonor's carriage was soon full of eager boys, girls, and men who wanted to get ahead of those walking. The driver made a short cut toward Madero's residence, for it seemed the crowd was headed that way. They gained ground on the throng. Reaching Madero's front gate, they saw his devoted wife and two sisters hastily draping a balcony with tricolor bunting: red, white, and green. Scarcely had they finished, when Madero's diminutive figure appeared on the balcony.

A cry arose. "Viva Madero!" Again and again they hailed their leader. The Rebel's coach rocked to and fro like a boat on a choppy sea. The genial, smiling face of Madero was outlined against a background of Mexican flags. His mouth soon formed words, but no sound was heard. He raised his hand. The din was hushed. He spoke to his people in simple phrases.

"We have been slaves for forty-three years, but now I come before you like Moses to lead you across the red sea of passions into a promised land."

"Viva! Viva! Madero!" The crowd roared in rhythmical repetition.

Leonor's heart was in her throat. How superb he was, this small man who stood powerfully great. Glancing around, she saw that the walls of tall buildings, the electric light posts, the trees, all the high places were no longer there. Instead there was a moving sea of humanity. Her own coach would not be able to move an inch. She memorized everything he said, marveling at his bravery.

"I shall write fifty articles. I'll send them to the border to my friend, Idar. We will ignite the flame of love and friendship for Madero."

Nicasio Idar, a Liberal editor, was the owner of the only Spanish newspaper on the frontier, a weekly, *La Crónica.* They were to become staunch propagandists, she signing her full name to her incendiary outbursts of patriotism.

Adolpho did not return home until late evening. The Rebel was determined to conceal from her husband her part in the Madero demonstration. Adolpho, unable to keep his news, told her almost immediately that he too had followed eagerly the cheering crowd that had swarmed down the Paseo after Madero.

The Rebel and her husband had a long talk with their friend Juan Sánchez Azcona. He was leaving that night, but he did not tell them his plans. The Rebel, with a woman's instinct, felt the need for secrecy. Taking her husband's hand, she turned to their friend.

"You need not tell us your plans. You may be sure that we understand. We will be loyal to the common cause."

Hastily they parted. In the morning he was gone.

With the Madero Revolution gaining momentum, on August 10, 1910, the Rebel received a telegram from Laredo to come quickly to her father's bedside. He was not expected to live long.

Her first thought was to rush home. She boarded a train for the border. On leaving, she tucked away all her correspondence, putting it in her bag to read on reaching home. So many things took place on her arrival that the letters remained unopened for several weeks.

Upon arrival in Laredo, Leonor went immediately to her father's house. Unpinning her hat and veil, she stopped for a moment before going into her father's room. She smoothed her travel-wrinkled dress. Don Joaquín had heard the family's whispered greetings outside the bedroom door.

"Has my little brave one come?" He said raising his head expectantly.

Seeing him so ill, she felt a deep hurt. She knew her father had read her articles against the old system and that he had suffered losses because of them.

"You are not angry with me, my father, for the trouble I have caused you?" She buried her face, crying, at the side of his bed.

"No, daughter," he said feebly. "You know they will confiscate our properties in Mexico. We will have nothing there. But," he put his finger under her chin, lifting her face, "I forgive you. Remember, Leonorcita, I forgive you."

Mamá Eloise, kneeling on the other side of the bed, hastened to smooth his hair, her gold bracelets making a light, gay sound. The little jingling bells recalled the past to Don Joaquín.

Taking her arm gently, he said in a whisper as if speaking to a ghost, "Valerianna, the tinkling of your bracelet is like the notes of your soft guitar." Caressing her hand he pleaded, "Take them off, Valerianna."

Mamá Eloise slipped the bracelets over her trembling hand, letting them drop with a last bright sound onto the carpet.

His eyes closed, Don Joaquín weakly fumbled for something under his pillow. Sliding her hand beneath the pillow, Mamá Eloise drew out his gold watch. Placing it in his hand, she took Leonor's and put it over her father's.

"He wants you to have it. He has said so many times," she whispered, looking at her husband as she spoke.

Reaching under his pillow again, she found her husband's keys. Don Joaquín looked toward Leopold, who was standing close to the bed. He handed his only son the keys to his safe, his store, and his house. Over Leopold's shoulder Don Joaquín glanced at his beautiful young daughter-in-law, Inez. It was through them that he hoped that the family name would live. Resting his head on Eloise's arm, he closed his eyes. It was hard to drag her away. She clasped his lifeless hands, crying, covering them with kisses. She had been a loving and dutiful wife. Now she was surrendering his soul to Valerianna.

A few moments after Don Joaquín's death, Leonor was taken from his room unconscious. When she was revived, she begged to be taken across the river where Doña Valerianna had slept her last sleep. Her Aunt Adele was living there with her family. There, for three days the Rebel lay in a darkened room, fighting reality, talking to her father as if he were still alive. On the fourth day she had a strong reaction. She remembered her days of work for her country, her mother's country. She must resume her fight for Mexico. It was there in that same house where her father, opening the door of the room where she had been born, had said, "This is the only rebel in the house."

She dressed quickly and put a veil over her face. She left, crossed the bridge, the first bridge between the two border towns. She had not been in Laredo when it had been opened, but her brother, Leopold, had made a speech at its dedication. She had read and re-read it, finding an agreement in her heart. She knew the last paragraph by memory.

"As I close my eyes tonight, when the two cities are wrapped in slumber, two familiar forms appear at this bridge, and at this monument unite their hands. The tall form with the white wig, on the American side, will be George Washington. The other from the Mexican side is the monumental Hidalgo." Feeling as he did, she thought, her brother would help her and befriend her people of Mexico. She would gladly fight for and defend his country if need be.

As she reached the end of the bridge, her eyes sought the mighty Río Grande. The river was in a tranquil mood. A bright sun shone on it fondly, caressing its gently rippling waters. She stopped, leaning over the railing, eagerly looking along the river bank. It had been a long time since she had seen Pancho and Julia. She ran down the rocky street to the place where she remembered their hut to be. Pancho was sitting at the edge of the river near a little skiff.

"Pancho, guess who I am." She put her hands over his eyes.

The old man turned quickly, smiling. He was glad to see the Rebel again.

"Let us go to the house to see Julia," she said.

"My Julia is no more," he said, taking hold of her arm, shaking his head. "She died before your father. He came to see her and paid the doctor bills and funeral expenses for me." Turning stiffly, he faced the river.

"There is the boat he bought me. Now I fish and take passengers up and down the river to the little towns along the border." Pancho began to cry in his loneliness, and Leonor left quietly.

Faithful to Don Joaquín's wishes, ten days after the funeral the family gathered in the great reception room of Mamá Eloise's house for the reading of the will. Each member of the family had his own attorney. They all sat listening as the trustee solemnly read word by word the legal document. He was a family friend, and it must have been painful for him to execute it.

The children had an option of either giving their stepmother one half of all their father possessed or of contesting the will. They could claim their mother Valerianna's share with compound interest for twenty-eight years. The last choice would have meant less for Mamá Eloise. "He who nourishes and cherishes is by right the owner" goes a Hindu saying. The children gave Mamá Eloise her share, one half, in cash. She left the border, and lived for the next twenty years in a sumptuous suite in a New York hotel with two of her sisters who had also made wealthy marriages. At her death she had enough to will equal shares to her stepchildren and grandchildren, having spent only the interest from her money.

Leopold assumed the trusteeship for his sisters, supplying them with ready funds. Don Joaquín's estate would take years to settle. Lina went to Spain. Leonor's husband, having become involved in the Revolution, could not leave Mexico. Leonor decided to remain on the border where she would continue to aid the cause of Madero.

The Rebel took a small house in town, despite its reputation for being haunted. Across the back of the house was a long, cool porch. The park-like grounds were shaded by huge pecan trees. Her home soon became a popular meeting place for exiles coming from Mexico. Leonor always made them welcome. There was a steady exodus of wealthy *ciéntificos,* of Reyistas. Laredo was actually the hotbed of the Revolution.

The Madero Revolution, though not a bloody one, spread like wildfire. President Díaz was advised by his chief of police that the Maderistas were provoking riots. Madero had left Mexico City and was campaigning in the large cities in the northern states, where the Madero family was powerful and well-known. In San Luis Potosí, he was seized and put in prison. He did not remain there long. After October elections, in which Díaz again was elected president, he signed Madero's release. But Madero had already escaped. His followers advised him to take refuge in the United States and prepare himself for any emergency. They would carry on the campaign at home.

Madero's followers became more open in their campaigning, especially in the state of Puebla. The outbreak was more sudden than originally planned. Puebla, where Madero was much loved, was the state most feared. The political conflagration started here. The home of Aquiles Serdán was under suspicion. Arms and ammunition to supply

Madero partisans had been reported stored there. A party of sympathizers were in the house at the time it was raided by the Federales. Aquiles Serdán and his two sisters together with eight others were fired on. Finally, Serdán was killed with the others, and his sisters arrested. The resistance and brave stand at the Serdán house was like an electric charge. The revolution broke out openly three days prior to the date planned on, which was to be November 20, 1910. Carmen Serdán became the heroine of the Madero Revolution. She ignited the flaming torch that illuminated the path for democracy and hastened the overthrow of President Porfirio Díaz. Men say much about themselves. Do they not remember the brave women? Another woman who came to the aid of her struggling countrymen was Elena Arizmendi, who quickly organized the Neutral White Cross that served during the short-lived Madero Revolution.

On May 10, 1911, Madero with twenty-five men entered Mexican territory for the third time; this time he was victorious at Ciudad Juárez. The Federales capitulated to Pancho Villa. Against pleadings of Doña Carmencita and his political advisors, Díaz held on to the office he had filled for a quarter of a century. He finally resigned in the early morning of May 26, 1911. The document he signed admitted to no moral wrong during the years of his iron-handed peace in Mexico. His letter of resignation as President of Mexico to the President of the Chamber of Deputies has the characteristic Díaz blandness.

> I come before the supreme representatives of the nation in order to resign unreservedly the office of constitutional president of the Republic with which the national vote honored me. I do this with all the more reason since, in order to continue the office it would be necessary to continue shedding Mexican blood, endangering the credit of the country, dissipating its wealth, exhausting its resources, and exposing its policy to international complications.
>
> I hope, gentlemen, that when the passions have calmed down a more conscientious and just study will bring out in the national mind a correct judgment which when I die I may carry graven on my soul as a just estimate of the life which I have devoted and will devote to my countryman.

Díaz and Doña Carmelita sailed the last day of May 1911 for France on the German boat *Ypiranga*. Díaz lived there for the last years of his life and is buried in France.

CHAPTER VIII
Revolution across the River

One day a man called on the Rebel to bring her proofs of some articles he was going to publish. They decided that, since there was no Spanish daily newspaper on the border, it was absolutely necessary to have one now. In 1912, *El Progreso* was founded in Laredo, Texas. It was edited by two of the Rebel's friends, Santiago Paz, and Oswaldo Sánchez, and financed by Leopold and several other wealthy men, all Madero partisans. From the first edition, the popularity of the new paper was evident. It soon grew into a powerful tool, handling all the news from Mexico's fighting zones. Many prominent Mexican writers were pouring their souls into its columns. It had a tremendous circulation in South Texas along the border.

The first issue made a stir in the community for it was dedicated to helping the sufferers of a flood in León, Guanajuato. The Rebel invited the members of the Club BRDA, (Club Benéfico, Recreativo, de Amigas, or Beneficent, Recreative Friends' Club), and a select group of girls, to sponsor a drive to gather food, clothing, and money for the flood victims in Mexico. As the influx of Latin exiles continued to increase, the Rebel saw the advisability of forming a civic organization. It was called the UPC (Union, Progress, and Charity), and soon it numbered over a hundred members. The club had a wide scope for action. Madero had many relatives in Laredo: the Faries, the Vidarri, the Ortiz, and the De la Garza families. And since they consisted of large families of ten or twelve, the organization had a big drawing pool. A clean-up drive was sponsored by the club, and blessed by the mayor and sheriff, who ordered all available carts to join the drive. For money, the grandees of the town took part in amateur contests, vying with each other in the arts of a singing and dancing. Funds were used to supply some of the basic necessities for the local needy.

In Laredo at this time, opinion was divided concerning rival political factions in Mexico. Among the strong adherents and friends of General Reyes was Amador Sánchez, the sheriff. Across the street from the Rebel's house the jail waxed hot with intrigue and injustice.

The Rebel heard many of the heated arguments and plans of the Reyes group.

As long as she could remember, she had heard of Mexican revolutions, of the times when Laredo had been attacked by guerrillas and bandits. During a more recent incident General Quiroz, fleeing from Díaz, had taken refuge on this side of the Río Grande. He had built and lived in the small adobe house which the Rebel was now occupying. There were stories that he had buried his treasures there. The house seemed destined to be connected with activities of civil strife.

By strange coincidence, within a stone's throw of the fated house where General Quiroz had hoped for the downfall of Díaz, Reyistas such as Rodolfo Reyes, a prominent lawyer and son of the General; Antonio Magnón, his confidential friend; Marshall Hicks, his legal advisor, Sandoval, Figueroa, Reyes Retana, all lawyers; and General Jerónimo Treviño gathered for secret political meetings.

Two months after President Porfirio Díaz had resigned and left Francisco de la Barra as interim president, Francisco I. Madero and a handful of followers arrived at Mexico City and were at its portals. Entering Juárez Avenue, he made a rapid march up Plateros Avenue (now Francisco I. Madero Avenue), mounted on a superb white horse. He waved his *sombrero tejano* to the hurriedly assembled throng. On his march, he passed by his completely demolished home that had been burned shortly after his speech in 1910.

He was followed by thousands of citizens, making a compact formation that moved as a single body. He had no bodyguards, no military escort, just the good will of the people. They escorted him to the palace and from the balcony he made a speech to greet the people of a free, peaceful republic. He was soon joined by his vice-president, Pino Suárez; Ernesto Madero, his brother and Secretary of the Treasury; Secretary of the Interior Rafael Hernández; Antonio I. Villarreal, Secretary of Agriculture; and De la Huerta, Secretary of War.

A few days after that triumphant entry, such as no man in Mexican history has ever enjoyed, Madero was unanimously elected president. His term was of short duration; two years later, in 1913, he was assassinated. His partisans were always loyal, no one asking for favors; all were satisfied with the president of their choice. With the country still in arms, the first duty had been to disband the many armed groups and install faithful followers. De la Huerta, Minister of War, failed to do this. He let the reactionaries still hope they would get back in power. General Felipe Ángeles was sent off to quell the Indians, so General Victoriano Huerta had little opposition in plotting against the innocent and well-meaning Madero.

On February 12, 1913, a tragic national upheaval began. For ten days, the battle that cut short Madero's life and his plans raged throughout the city of Mexico. After seeking refuge in the American club, the Rebel's husband could not leave the place in safety. General Victoriano Huerta ordered federal troops under his command to surround the city. Before it could be brought under martial law, the followers of Reyes attacked the penitentiary where Reyes, who had been imprisoned by Díaz, was being held. Mexico was filled with the hopeful followers of Díaz and Reyes factions. General Felipe Ángeles, who had become military commander, turned all his guns against the fortified Huerta and began to demolish the stronghold. Along with Reyes, many Madero followers escaped to flee northward to join Villa's army.

General Bernardo Reyes, freed, riding a spirited horse, approached the National Palace. At the gates of the Palace he was shot and instantly killed. He died at the very portals where he had once ridden through daily, triumphant as the proud reformer of the Mexican Army, as the invincible war chief of the Díaz army. Those were days when even to think was treason.

When General Reyes was Minister of War in President Díaz's cabinet, he overstepped his signal post in life. He was a failure in his repeated plans to overthrow Díaz. General Reyes, as Minister of War, was quite in his place and reached the zenith of his abilities. He was, after all, only to be remembered as a military man, not as president, as his ambitious followers had schemed. The meter of President Díaz's waning popularity had become more evident. No one wanted Díaz's choice, Corral, the hated, heartless "bourgeois," for vice president. He was obnoxious to the Mexican people. Although tired of the same regime and tyranny of thirty years, no one dared openly oppose Díaz's wishes. Out of the bubbling caldron of hopes, the name that came to many minds was that of Bernardo Reyes. He commanded the whole army and was beloved by it. Perhaps he could have overthrown Díaz. But he remained an ill-starred candidate.

As her brother-in-law, Antonio Magnón, was closely connected to the Reyes faction, Leonor's house became temporary headquarters of the Reyistas in Laredo, much to her chagrin, for she lacked sympathy with the cause.

News of the overthrow of the constitutional government spread like wildfire over the republic. Consternation and chaos reigned in the convalescent nation. Just one year before, Díaz had been overthrown. The fires of patriotism were again fanned to wild flames by the dastardly deeds of Huerta. The news came to an astonished people in

Mexico. Already infuriated by Huerta's imprisonment of Madero, they learned that their beloved leader had become a martyr president.

The *coup d'etat* that overthrew Madero in early 1913 was in no way a popular revolution. It was a barracks plot, a conspiracy of a few army officers financed by *ciéntificos* living in exile and a few Spanish reactionaries. It was attended by circumstances of treachery so depraved, of villainy so fantastic, of cruelty so barbaric that the story is one which the mind has difficulty in accepting as credible.

After having amiably breakfasted with Raúl Madero, the president's brother, Huerta, the Minister of War, secured Madero's gun and ordered his arrest. He was then taken out and murdered. Huerta then proceeded with his staff to the National Palace, where he had President Madero and Vice President Pino Suárez arrested. They remained in custody for some days; General Felipe Ángeles, his devoted friend, remained with Madero. After signing deeds of resignation, Madero and Suárez were spirited away on the evening of February 22 and taken to the state penitentiary. Circling around to the back of the building, the two men were told to get out of the carriage. As they did they were shot in the back.

It was a day of deep mourning and shock for the nation. Huerta drank triumphantly to the restoration of peace at the American Embassy with ambassador Wilson. When news of Madero's death and the overthrow of his government became known in Laredo, an immediate meeting of protest was held. Thousands gathered in the plaza to show their indignation at the terrible crime. Laredo was already inundated by a flood of ex-Porfiristas. Ex-Maderistas, now exiled, came to swell the ranks. During this time the Rebel remained at her post in Laredo.

Through the instigation of *El Progreso,* Laredo became a propaganda center and aid base for the anti-Huerta forces. The columns of the paper fought all the Maderista battles, at first the imaginary ones. Later on, it was only through its pages that true information could be obtained. Three of the most powerful minds in Mexico were writing for the border paper. These writers were: García Virgil, who afterwards became governor of his native state of Oaxaca; José Ugarte, later Mexico's Minister to South America; and Carlos Samper, who controlled the Mexican associated press. The Rebel was proud of her three friends who advocated that government founded upon anything but liberty, justice, and equality could not and ought not stand.

Ugarte, whose nom de plume is Jorge Useta, wrote fifteen pamphlets appealing for a sane and honest return to national life. Thoroughly conversant with conditions in Mexico, Useta declined to count on Huerta, a military usurper who did not represent the people of Mexico. He insisted that the people fight for their rights and select a man of their own choosing.

Venustiano Carranzo protested against the crime and policies of Huerta. As governor of the state of Coahuila, he had a legal right to revolt. Saltillo, the capital of Coahuila, became the cradle of the Carranza revolution. With a handful of men, General Carranza immediately called on all patriotic Mexicans to rally to his standards in support of constitutional authority. He issued his famous Plan de Guadalupe, signed by over 150 anti-federalists at his Hacienda de Guadalupe near Saltillo. While this was taking place, loyalists in Laredo banded against Huerta, rallying around the prominent figure of Melquíades García, a lifelong friend of the Rebel.

In Mexico City, General Felipe Ángeles' forces were fighting while retreating, allowing Carranza's men to reach Sonora. Under censorship, horrors were enacted in the Mexican capital while the masses gathered silently. As Carranza and his men passed through revolt-inspired towns and villages, they were joined by inhabitants who left their towns, following the Chief until he reached Sonora.

When Carranza abandoned Saltillo on his famous march west, he left his brother, Jesús Carranza, in charge. Pablo González and Luis Caballero were to conquer the state of Tamaulipas and take possession of parts of Matamoros, Nuevo León, and Tampico. This move would cut off communications and prevent bringing in arms and ammunitions to the Federals. They made hurried marches. But once in power, having control of the railroads, Huerta commanded the immediate reinforcement of all border towns. Federal troops were rushed to state capitals. The Constitutionalists were limited to skirmishes and destruction of railroad communications and telegraph lines.

Generals Antonio I. Villarreal, Cesáreo Castro, and Pablo de la Garza operated in the state of Nuevo León, while General Jesús Carranza was to attack Nuevo Laredo. General Villarreal and his men were to cut off federal troops being rushed north. Pablo González, with the bulk of his army, was to simultaneously attack Matamoros. Villa was to attack Ciudad Juárez in the north; Obregón, Calles, and Maytorena had no trouble in taking possession of all territory and surrounding country of Sonora and Sinaloa. General Felipe Ángeles joined Villa's troops and, after conferring with him, went to Sonora to receive further instructions from the white-bearded chief, Carranza.

General Felipe Ángeles, who pointed his guns towards the Huerta forces, was a patriotic and loyal Mexican. He was convinced that the only right way was to uproot the evil from the heart of his country.

Placing himself subordinate to Carranza, he later rallied a powerful army in northern Mexico.

The Rebel had known General Ángeles when he was the director of the Military College in Chapultepec. She had learned much of Mexican history during her short visits to the college, where she had a cousin studying military tactics and engineering. At that time, Federico Cervantes, Jacinto B. Treviño, and Federico Montes were training for military careers. Later, the Rebel was to meet many of these young boys as generals on the battle fields of Mexico, leading their men to battle.

When they had walked on the beautiful terrace of the Military College, General Ángeles had pointed out to the Rebel the place where the brave young cadets, wrapped in a Mexican flag, had thrown themselves headlong over the rocky precipice to resist being captured by the enemy. There, too, when the General was in a sentimental mood he told her about Carlota and Maximilian, showing her the balcony where the tragic empress was frequently serenaded. Again in other moods, he sighed for the vast country where the Indians suffered continual persecution. The Rebel remembered his hands, firm but small, the hands of a writer. His quick mind sought liberty by action. To the Rebel, he was Mexico awakening.

General Aureliano Blanquet had become Minister of War and all the army was being mobilized under his command. He was sending his best generals to the frontier. On March 17, 1913, in the early dawn the small garrison of Nuevo Laredo was attacked by General Jesús Carranza. Unexpectedly, a group of civilians took up arms and aided the unprepared Federals. The Carrancistas advanced to the city limits. After a brisk encounter during which the outskirts of Nuevo Laredo was strewn with wounded, Jesús Carranza ordered his men to retreat. The Constitutionalists could have taken the town before the military train arrived bringing Federal reinforcements, but false news reached them that new aid was already arriving for the enemy.

Hearing the firing, the Rebel dressed quickly. She called her aunt's home in Nuevo Laredo. Getting no answer, she called several friends. There was no answer to any of her calls. Rushing out into the street, she stopped a big new car driven by a chauffeur. Directing him to drive to the offices of *El Progreso,* she told him to wait for her. She painted a red cross on a piece of paper and had it pasted on the windshield. Telephoning her friends, she told them her plans to go to Mexico and help take care of the wounded; she needed volunteers. With her faithful friend Jovita Idar, a writer for *El Progreso,* the Rebel encouraged four other young women to join them to offer immediate help.

Opening his pharmacy, Don Flavio Vargas gave her a basket of first-aid supplies. As she got in the car, he placed a towel-wrapped bundle behind her on the seat.

"You may need this," he said, patting her arm.

Told to drive to the international bridge, the chauffeur balked. He dared not take the car across the river into the battle-stricken town. Reaching behind her, the Rebel got the bundle. She felt the hard round object. Inside the towel was a long-necked bottle of whiskey. Unwrapping it, she pushed the hard bottle neck against the driver's back.

"Drive on," she ordered tersely.

As they neared the bridge in high speed, the Rebel leaned out of the car waving the white towel. The car was allowed to cross to the other side unhindered.

Leaving most of her girls at the hospital, the Rebel could be seen in the distance going south. The Rebel glanced towards a soldier. How she longed to run after him and give him the message to attack again quickly before Federal aid could arrive for the small garrison. She heard the captain's voice.

"So you are not one of us?" he said holding towards her the flag staff they had both advanced to get. "You may have this. It is yours to put your white flag on. Keep it." He handed it to her, gazing at the bronze eagle on the tip. It was not long afterwards that the Rebel heard that the captain had joined the forces of Carranza.

The hospitalized Carrancistas were held prisoners in the hospital. The problem after a few days was to get them to their post at Matamoros. All the men were in good shape to join the Constitutionalists that would soon attack the town of Matamoros. Aracelito, the Rebel's young secretary, seldom left her. She was well informed of all activities concerning the White Cross. The Rebel unfolded her plan for the prisoners' escape.

"As soon as we get news of the arrival of Federal reinforcements, we will take advantage of the excitement among the people," she said.

One morning soon afterward, Aracelito rushed to the Rebel.

"The troops arrive today. There will be a huge parade. Tonight there will be a big banquet and dance on the Main Plaza." The girl's eyes danced as she told the Rebel the news. The Rebel went about her duties and daily routine. Aracelito relayed the orders to the hospital corps to clean, disinfect, and prepare the hospital for inspection. Every bed was aired and clean linens put on. Only the Rebel and Aracelito changed the beds. As they did, they placed the prisoners' clothes beneath the mattresses. Each man was told to carefully dress himself at ten minutes before midnight. There was a big clock in the ward, and the men would be told when to start. Each bed had to be camouflaged after the soldiers fled. The nurses were told to entertain the guards at the right time. Jugs of pulque and tequila with tacos would be a banquet to the men while their *jefes* were gaily celebrating in the plaza.

The Rebel left the hospital to buy provisions, but instead crossed hurriedly to Laredo. She found Pancho eating. Together they shared the simple dinner. Their talk was full of reminiscing of the dead and absent ones.

"*Mi ama,*" Pancho said sadly, "it is only you and your brother Leopold now. Do as your mother always prayed: be united."

"There is no fear about that, Pancho," she replied. "He and Inés, his wife, are my guardian angels, always taking care of my children and loving them as their own."

"I am old and useless," he sobbed. "I want to go back to Mexico when this war is over."

"You shall, Pancho," she comforted him. "I will take you with me. My husband is kind. You shall live with us. Now," she said lowering her voice, "I am going to entrust a very important mission to you."

Pancho straightened up, his eyes shone. He was ready to serve his country. He looked young again.

"Please tell me what you want me to do, Little Rebel," he said smiling fondly at her.

"First of all, you must sleep this afternoon and be rested. At twelve tonight you will hear the church bells and see the fireworks in Nuevo Laredo. The people will be celebrating. Take your skiff and row toward the cave that is at the foot of the road leading to the hospital. Soldiers will be there, hidden. Ask them if the Rebel sent them. Then row them quietly down the river on the Mexican side. As soon as you pass the last post of the Federals, land them near a *jacal*. Call the sentinel; he belongs to General Pablo González's people. Return quickly before morning, as you must not be seen." She spoke slowly so that Pancho would remember it all.

"My Julia will help me. Her spirit will protect me." Looking out over the waters of the river, he made the sign of the cross. The Rebel embraced him with the firm faith in him that he had always inspired in her in her childhood.

Buying a few things, she returned to the hospital. There was a strong smell of disinfectant; all quarters were clean, and nurses were rushing about ready for the federal inspection.

It was a little before midnight. The prisoners had dressed and were gone. Sleepy, well fed guards looked over the wards, the dim lights helping to conceal the secret of the vacant beds. Laughingly, they returned to their posts. In a few minutes, there would be a changing of the guard. Hurriedly, the Rebel and Aracelito went past the great hospital portals and asked permission to go to the plaza for a little while. Most of the nurses had already left. The loyal nurses had taken a carriage to their homes across the river.

Aracelito and the Rebel walked to the bridge only two blocks from the plaza, which was ablaze with lights and crowded with newly arrived Federal troops celebrating with the townspeople. The hospital, eight blocks away, was in darkness and stillness. There were few people on the bridge. As the two women passed the monument in the middle of the bridge, the Rebel noticed that Aracelito was nervous and kept looking back. Someone was following them. The Rebel stopped as she heard the clock strike twelve. Anxiously looking towards the river bank, she thought she heard the rippling of water and the soft paddling of oars. She stood still and prayed. A young man had approached Aracelito and was speaking to her.

"Please believe me," he said earnestly, "ever since I first saw you, I have loved you. I am not a Federal. I am dressed as one, but I shall escape and go over to our people. Perhaps, tonight." He looked appealingly at the girl.

"I shall wait," she answered simply, unsmiling.

The young man disappeared in the darkness toward Mexico. The Rebel, anxious to be safely at Pancho's cabin, took Aracelito's trembling hand and pulled her toward the end of the bridge. Pushing open the door of Pancho's hut, they found a heavy dark blanket on the cot and on the dying coals a pot of coffee. They poured themselves coffee, then wrapping the blanket about them, walked to the edge of the river bank. They waited for Pancho's return.

"The young man who followed us," Aracelito began in a tremulous voice, "says he loves me, but I have not encouraged him. I thought he was a Federal. But he has told me that he will cross over to our people. I have promised to wait for him," she whispered, sobbing.

"Darling," the Rebel said, hugging her. "some night we will come here and Pancho will take a message for you to him."

They sat silently watching the lights across on the Mexican side go out, one by one. The hours of the clear moonlit night passed. Sometimes dozing, sometimes making plans, they kept vigil. Finally, they heard the soft ripple of water and drip of oars. They crouched down in the river weeds. The Rebel saw Pancho swiftly plying his oars. Behind him crumpled on the floor of the boat, her head on the seat, was a girl.

Lifting her gently in his arms, Pancho ran with his precious burden. The Rebel and Aracelito followed him to the cabin. Pancho placed her on his clean bed that Julia had always taken care of. Smoothing the pillow, he went for alcohol. The Rebel stood looking amazed at the beautiful girl, one hand hanging limp off the side of the bed, the other on her breast clutching something that was hidden under her blouse. There were blood stains on the other arm. They bandaged her arm, but did not try to move her hand. Whatever was there was sacred to her. She slept, exhausted. It was daylight when Pancho finished telling his part in the daring plot.

"I left here, *mi amita,*" he began as they sat drinking coffee, "just as you told me. Crossing the river, I rowed over towards the cave. I know it well; often Julia and I sat there after your mother died. I had only my skiff. I wondered what I would do if there were too many. Perhaps, I would have to make several trips. But as I was nearing the place, I noticed my *compadre*'s boat tied among the bushes at the river's edge. I tied it to my boat, saying all the time, '*Compadre,* I shall return it, God willing.'

"When I approached the cave, I was glad that I had taken the other boat. They all got in and helped me row. It was downstream; that made it easier. When we arrived at the hut past the last post, they left me. I rowed fast. Suddenly I heard a rustle of leaves in the shadows along the bank."

"Pancho, you are sure you took no enemy?" the Rebel asked clutching his hand.

"No, *mi amita,*" he said smiling at her fear. "I got the password from every one of them. They were quiet and kind."

"Well, go on," the Rebel insisted. "What was at the water's edge?"

"I heard a woman's voice, and out of the bushes a girl rushed to the water's edge toward me. '*¡Qué bonita!* Could it be the Virgin of Guadalupe herself coming to save me?' I thought to myself.

"Begging me to take her across the river she jumped into my *compadre*'s boat and helped me row. We rowed a little farther and then we heard a noise. It was Federals. They cried halt and fired a shot at us.

"'It is Pancho, the *esquifero*. I am going home.' I called to them and they let us pass. We were nearing my *compadre*'s place. The girl had jumped into my boat as the shot had made its mark in the skiff she was in and was filling with water. We cut off the boat and I hid it where I had found it. After that, she must have fainted, as she did not speak again." Pancho finished his story and got up to put some mesquite on the low burning fire.

"Let her sleep," said the Rebel, also rising. "Do not disturb her. If she awakens and wants nourishment, prepare nice food like Julia made.

I will come back as early as possible and bring you food and clothes. Tell no one of this; and let no one see her."

Making their way up the embankment silently, the two women parted, promising to meet again at mid-morning. People were beginning their usual daily routine, but there was excitement caused by the little newspaper vendors calling the news of the arrival of Federal reinforcements in Nuevo Laredo, and the daring escape of forty prisoners from the hospital.

Immediately, a meeting was called of all loyal nurses that had taken part in caring for the soldiers during the days after the combat. They sent a message to General Blanquet stating their displeasure regarding the Federal treatment of prisoners. While promising to care impartially for all wounded on the battlefield, they declared themselves strictly Constitutionalist sympathizers. Accordingly, the White Cross was no longer allowed to cross the frontier, and if so under penalty of death.

It was at the time of the Huerta outbreak that the Mexican National Red Cross, organized during the last years of the Díaz regime, failed in its principles of non-partiality and nonpartisanship. In its cause destined to aid the wounded were spies and ammunition for the Federals. It was in protest and to counteract it that the Constitutionalist White Cross was established in Laredo, Texas, serving throughout the Carranza Revolution. The Red Cross served the Federals. It was pledged that the White Cross would go with the Carranza army, organizing hospitals and replacing Federal personnel with loyal doctors and nurses. The White Cross had stayed in the hospital until every wounded Constitutionalist had escaped.

The Constitutionalists repulsed, Federal reinforcements had arrived under the command of General Quintana. Nuevo Laredo bustled with preparations against attack. Trenches were built; search towers were erected with powerful searchlights; cannons were mounted on hill tops; brush and trees were cut down to clear the horizon for miles around the surrounding country.

At the time agreed, the Rebel went to Pancho's hut. A noise among the bushes and a rapid opening and closing of the door told of Aracelito's earlier arrival. Everything within Pancho's house was still. The visitor must have been asleep.

Aracelito came to the door to greet her silently. She dare not waken the sleeping girl. Pancho came in and started the fire. The girl awoke. Slowly getting herself together, she sat up on the side of the bed, stretching both her legs as if to assure herself of her identity. Then she stretched her arms. Suddenly becoming conscious of her mission, she searched in her blouse pocket.

"How well I feel," she said in a sweet voice. "I have had a perfect rest. I know that I am among friends who fight for the same cause." Looking at each of them, she spoke confidently. "Tell me please," the girl said, looking at Pancho, "who is the Rebel? It is urgent that I get in touch with her."

The Rebel grew pale, a strange thing for her, who knew not fear. Could it be a message from her husband? She had not heard from him since the tragic death of the President. Who was this violet-eyed girl?

"I am the Rebel," Leonor answered in a quiet voice.

"Yes," said Pancho, nodding emphatically. "She is our *jefe*."

"Who are you and where do you come from?" The Rebel spoke hoarsely, sitting on the bed beside her.

Aracelito pulled up a bench and looked earnestly at the newcomer.

"I am María de Jesús González, a teacher from Monterrey. I have a friend in the telegraph office; we are both telegraph operators and Constitutionalists. Here are telegrams that we held back. They will prove our loyalty. We heard of you and your brave companions and resolved to become allied with your work. One of these messages is from General Jerónimo Villarreal in Nuevo Laredo for Secretary Blanquet, asking for reinforcements; they were expecting the second attack by General Jesús Carranza. We also heard of the Constitutionalist retreat. Two days later we had another telegram that reinforcements would arrive in Matamoros at any moment. I traveled on horseback night and day until I found this good man at the river's edge." The girl spoke rapidly as if she feared something might happen to keep her from delivering her news.

"There are messages for you from Sonora," she continued. "A companion, Marie Bringas de Carturegli; the telegraph operator, Trinidad Blanco; and her sister will be here as soon as they can travel in Coahuila. Also, a teacher from there will join you, and in Tampico, Juanita Mancha, a brave girl. There are two more in Monterrey, the Blackaller sisters, teachers." She concluded her long recital of names with relief.

María de Jesús was having a cool bath. Pancho had stretched a sheet across the back of his hut for privacy. Standing in a big wash tub, the girl poured cool water over herself from a Mexican dried-gourd dipper that had been Julia's. Her long red hair hanging down, dressed in a cool summer kimono, she sat down to a humble repast that Pancho had prepared for her.

"María de Jesús," the Rebel said, "you are fully aware of the dangers we will encounter. Will you obey orders?"

"Yes, I am ready," she replied firmly.

"Then you must leave tonight," said the Rebel, "for the nearest Constitutionalist camp. Pancho will row you there. Rest now, and we will return tonight."

That night, Aracelito and the Rebel were stealing down the hill again with more clothes and food and a little money. María de Jesús was listening. She and Pancho had their supper while they were awaiting orders.

María put on her boots. She tucked a dagger that Pancho gave her in her blouse. She wore trousers that the Rebel had brought. Her hair was neatly braided and wound around her head.

"María," the Rebel said tensely, "you will take these telegrams to General Lucio Blanco, or any of his staff. They will probably attack Matamoros before reinforcements arrive. Come back quickly. This letter is for General Pablo González. Listen for any news."

The girl jumped in the skiff with Pancho. Soon they were lost in the shadows of the mesquites along the river banks. Aracelito and the Rebel sat again by the river, alone. Pancho was not to return until the next day. They did not know whether María would return or not.

"I wish," Aracelito sighed, "I wish I was as brave as our brave companion. I would go and look for Guillermo. Perhaps he is already with General Lucio Blanco's forces."

CHAPTER IX
Laredo and the Constitutionalistas

On hearing the news of Matamoros' capture, the Rebel knew at once that María de Jesús had fulfilled her mission. She would, probably, return on the American side. Hurriedly she sought Pancho's hut. Telling him to be on the lookout, she promised to call frequently. Meanwhile she was expecting the Flores Blanco sisters from Monclova, where Trini was chief telegraph operator.

Beside the daily *El Progreso* newspaper that the Rebel loved, another equally interesting group was the newsboys who worked incessantly voicing extras at intervals during the day and night. It was the thrill of their lives when the Rebel photographed them, telling them that the First Chief Carranza would see their picture. They vehemently voiced the triumphs of the Constitutionalist activities in Cuidad Victoria, Matamoros, and the surrounding territory. As their bundles of papers were handed them, they were eager to learn where each general had opened his new campaign. Sitting on a corner or gathered in a group in a doorway, they discussed the fighting. Each one became a fighting unit for the Carranza commander. Sometimes, a little urchin from across the river would come and give them new information concerning the war.

The Rebel was now in communication with Marie Bringas de Carturegli, the beautiful wife of a prominent doctor. Señora de Carturegli had sent a message with María de Jesús offering her assistance. Seeing the possibility of her work, the Rebel thought it time to begin organizing over the expanding Republic.

Accordingly, without interfering with local affairs, she wrote Señora de Carturegli, asking her to be President of the Constitutional White Cross in Sonora. Accepting with profuse thanks, she and her husband equipped a Pullman car, turning it into an operating room with beds for the wounded. Her work in Sonora was effective and continuous. The Rebel was to meet her later in New York City, when the doctor was confidential financial agent for the still-fighting Carrancistas. Shaking her head sadly, Marie de Carturegli uttered the prophetic, fateful words that bespoke the years of dissention yet to come in Mexico: "We have apparently triumphed, but I cannot see the end."

While the organization of forces was going on in the Northern Zone, in Laredo the population was in a white heat. Every hour, every day, General Pablo González's army was expected to attack Nuevo Laredo. Finding a counterattack on Nuevo Laredo useless, as the town was strongly fortified, the Carrancistas joined forces and made a combined attack on Matamoros.

Early, at dawn, the firing started and the border town fell into the hands of the forces of Generals Pablo González and Jesús Carranza. The fleeing Federals joined the garrison at Nuevo Laredo. News of Matamoros' capture was a great incentive to the Carrancistas. The post was one of the principal ports through which arms, ammunition, and provisions were passed.

María Villarreal, who was now rested after working in the Nuevo Laredo hospital as a nurse, phoned the Rebel. "Hello, Mrs. Magnón," she said. "I have just learned that my namesake is back from the Matamoros fireworks. An officer told me."

"Come over and we'll take a walk," suggested the Rebel.

María de Jesús was sitting at the door of Pancho's hut, humming a tune softly when the Rebel and María Villarreal arrived. María de Jesús was happy to be back again. The clatter of dishes came from inside the hut, where Pancho was preparing a *merienda* of coffee and pan dulce.

"It seems that we are always ready to eat, no matter what our troubles are," said the girl joyfully as the four of them sat down.

The Rebel had been making plans. Suddenly she turned to the fair-haired María de Jesús and said, "Is it asking too much for you to leave right away?" Looking admiringly at the girl, she said, "You seem to fit into this scheme like a beautiful picture in the right place."

"Yes, I am ready to go at any time" was the girl's firm answer.

"María, you live close to the depot," the Rebel said to the other girl. "What time does the train leave for San Antonio?"

Hesitating a moment, María Villarreal replied, "I am sure it is at eight forty-five."

"Then please meet us at the station tonight. Buy one ticket to El Paso. Get a dress and a few things for María de Jesús to take with her," the Rebel directed.

"So easy as all that?" asked María de Jesús, raising her blond eyebrows and shrugging her shoulders.

"Oh," the Rebel replied, laughing, "nothing is impossible for María. She could be hospital supervisor over the whole republic. She is very resourceful, and like a good teacher, she bosses me. She has taught many boys in Laredo, and her word is their command. I think she would make a good general."

María went off, laughing heartily as she went along.

"Only an hour more to rest, María de Jesús," said the Rebel, looking fondly at this child scarcely eighteen.

"María de Jesús," the Rebel said when they were alone, "our first Chief is in Cuidad Juárez. Make every effort to see him. Tell him of the work of the White Cross. You need not mention names." The Rebel looked seriously at the girl. "You are so brave, you are better fit for the army. Beg Carranza to make you a cavalry lieutenant. You ride well and hard. I hate to lose you, but you would be better there."

"Señora, you make much of me," María de Jesús said clasping the Rebel's hand. "I shall go and do as you say. When and if we meet again, you shall know of my success or failure."

The girl arose. Looking in Pancho's little mirror, she pushed her bright hair under her cap. "Time to be off," she said jauntily. "Pancho, I'll see you soon." She shook the old man's hand warmly.

At the depot, María greeted them, bundle in hand. "You can dress here or on the train. I have spoken to one of my pupils; he will take care of you. They are all my friends, these railroad people." She handed María de Jesús an envelope with her ticket and some money.

"It will soon be Christmas time; perhaps, we will have Nuevo Laredo as a gift for our First Chief Carranza," María said thoughtfully.

They said good night. María sniffed several times.

"God bless you, child," the Rebel said, wiping her eyes and turning away.

The train roared and puffed leaving the station. María de Jesús put her hand out the window and waved. "See you soon," she called back to the two women standing on the dark platform.

"María, tomorrow we return to our duties, just as if nothing had ever happened to us. You to your school, and I to my kindergarten," the Rebel said as they walked away.

María Villarreal had a private school. Having a sick mother had forced her to give up a teaching position at the Laredo Seminary and open her own school at home. With her three children under Leopold's care, the Rebel too had opened a school, the first kindergarten in Laredo, in a hall that her brother had used during his political campaigns. Her young pupils soon became involved in the Revolution, too. One day, they were to find their school taken over by wounded soldiers. Their picture books and slates under their arms, the Rebel had walked them through the big room. Their work tables had been made into beds, their little chairs, into bed tables. Each child was introduced to the reality of the Revolution at the sight of wounded soldiers who resembled the toy soldiers they used in counting games.

On January 1, 1914, at daybreak, the Carrancistas attacked Nuevo Laredo and were repulsed with heavy losses. The battle was one of the fiercest ever fought in Northern Mexico. Heavy artillery and gatling guns were well handled by the Federals. The Carrancistas, not so well equipped, made repeated attacks and were three times repulsed. All during the day there was the dull sound of guns. During the night there was a lull. At 7:30 the next morning, the main body of Carrancistas under General Pablo González, consisting of cavalry and infantry, advanced on Federal entrenchments on the southern outskirts near the railroad shops. A fierce battle ensued. Both sides fought fiercely for three hours, with the Carrancistas advancing. Learning that the trenches surrounding the heart of town were charged with electricity, they decided to retreat and use strategy to draw the Federals into the open field. After days of fighting, the Carrancistas retreated several miles south to await reinforcements from Matamoros, making Camargo their headquarters.

Meanwhile, on the American side, there was great alarm. An embargo had been declared and the international bridge was closed. When American Consul Garret wired Washington, explaining the situation of Mexican citizens in the war-torn town, they were allowed to cross the river and take refuge on American soil. Aracelito and the Rebel stayed at Pancho's hut while he crossed the bridge to Aunt Adela's house to beg her to cross quickly. Ignacio Beléndez, her husband, was the cashier of the Mexican customs. He refused to abandon the post he had held with honor for so many years. Aunt Adela and her three little girls remained barricaded in their home. Pancho came back with the news, promising to go again to try to convince them to come to American soil.

With a grip on the Rebel's hand, Aracelito refused to leave her until far into the night, hoping to hear from her loved one, Guillermo. He had been well trained, having studied in the military college. Now he was attached to General Pablo González's staff.

"Pancho," the Rebel called the old man. "You must take a message to the first one you find in command of the Carrancistas. Go down the river. General Lucio Blanco and his men are in control of Matamoros and have men along the river. Perhaps you will meet General Murrietta. Tell him that you came from Laredo. That the Constitutional White Cross will care for all the wounded in this vicinity. Tell him Federal reinforcements have arrived from Monterrey."

Pancho sat nodding assent to her words as she spoke. "*Sí mi ama, sí.*"

"And, Pancho," the Rebel begged of him, "stay with them. Serve the general. You will be safer there until the fighting is over."

Going into his hut, Pancho talked more to himself than to the Rebel. "It will not take me long. I had already planned this. My things are packed. Only one thing remains. Lighting a candle, he knelt down by his bed. Everything was dismantled. His bundle of bedding and clothes were rolled like a soldier's pack. Reaching under the bed, he drew out a little carved box.

"My Julia tied this around my neck before she died," he said as he took off a silk cord on which a key was tied.

"Look, *mi ama,*" he said, opening the box tenderly. "Your grandmother gave my Julia this. She said, keep it and someday give it to you. Look, there are two little flags wrapped together. Your mother said they were yours and Leopold's flags. This rose is your mother's model for making her altar flowers. The rosary, the one she had when the Indians attacked us. And this last, the little white flag I made for you one time."

Crying together, they looked at the old, forgotten treasures.

The door was closed and barred. Pancho placed his few belongings in his boat. The two of them stood for a few moments silently, knowing they would soon be engulfed in tragedy and chaos. Then the old man in his boat rounded a bend in the river, going east with the current, and disappeared from sight.

Arriving home, the Rebel found friends awaiting her; the newsboys told her that wounded soldiers were being brought to her place for care.

"Go to the river to help," she told them. "On your way tell the volunteer nurses, Marie, Bessie Moore, and Lily Long, all of them, to come."

Quickly, the kindergarten tables were made into comfortable beds with bed clothes available from her own linens, and those that the Rebel raided from her brother's home. As the wounded were brought in, they were immediately taken to the operating room. The Rebel's little living room was stripped of furniture, equipping an operating room in less than twenty-four hours.

The temporary hospital was soon filled to capacity. Leopold came to his sister's aid, offering her a large building just across the street from her house on his property. By night, the wounded numbered a hundred. The society "Sons of Juárez" offered the Rebel their hall. Soon three emergency hospitals were in use on American soil, all under the supervision of the Rebel and the Constitutionalist White Cross.

During the night, United States reinforcements arrived from Lampazos. American troops were strung along the river banks. Strange to say, the people of Laredo did not run away and vacate the border town. Everybody stayed, watched, and helped. The handful of loyal supporters, who set out valiantly to avenge the death of President Madero, formed the most powerful, mobile armies that Mexican history had ever known. On arriving at Sonora, Carranza and his party were received by waiting generals who were already prepared. They declared, in truth, that Huerta was a usurper, that of necessity all public acts were illegal and that after they had overthrown him, everything that he had done while acting as provisional president of Mexico would be discounted. Being illegal himself, it necessarily followed that all he did was illegal. Victoriano Huerta was repudiated as president as were the legislative and judicial powers of the federation. Governors of states who continued to recognize the federal government's powers, thirty days after the publication of Carranza's famous Plan de Guadalupe, were also repudiated.

In order to organize the army entrusted with the purpose of overthrowing Huerta, Venustiano Carranza, governor of Coahuila, was named First Chief of the Constitutionalist Army. When this army occupied Mexico and order was restored, a general election would be held, delivering power to the man who would be elected as President of Mexico.

Arriving with Carranza in Sonora were Cándido Aguilar, later to become Carranza's son-in-law; Jesús Castro, one of the faithful who stood guard when years later Carranza was assassinated; Alfredo Breceda, later governor of Mexico City, who had been Carranza's secretary; Jacinto B. Treviño, son of General Treviño; and Gustavo Espinosa Mireles, who was Carranza's private secretary. Though of a mature age, Carranza was always surrounded by young men, who were jokingly called Carranza's boys. They were untiring and ceaseless workers. After organizing his temporary government, Carranza left Sonora in the hands of General Alvaro Obregón as military commander, and Roberto Pesqueira, Sr., as governor. Mayor and Hill also had their duties. By some twist of things, he named General Felipe Ángeles minister of war. It took little time for the generals to show their displeasure, arguing privately, however.

Carranza diplomatically sent General Ángeles to place himself under the command of General Francisco Villa, who had mustered a powerful following, and was relentlessly devastating the northern country. His hatred of the *hacendados* in Chihuahua was nonnegotiable. General Felipe Ángeles was second in command and had a brigade of well-trained youths. He treated Villa in a brotherly manner that flattered the puffed up chieftain, who now invited the First Chief Carranza to come to his conquered territory, to establish his government there in safety, while he continued to fight the Federal Army. Clever strategy was Villa's strong asset, together with his rapid troop movements. His fame grew to such a degree that newspapers in the United States in big headlines referred to him as the Napoleon of the South.

Public sentiment in Laredo sided with the Constitutionalists. When news spread that the wounded were being taken to the Rebel's house, neighbors, friends, and sympathizers came bringing mattresses, bed linens, food, dressing, and medicines. A commissary was set up in a small room that had been used as a bath house in the big garden. American doctors were working side by side with Mexican doctors: Doctor Francisco de la Garza, of General Pablo González's staff, Doctor Gilberto de la Fuente, of General Jesús Carranza's staff, Doctor Blum, of General Cesáreo Castro's staff. The four doctors from Mexico made their headquarters at the Rebel's house.

"This is indeed a hall of friendship," thought the Rebel many times as she saw the complete and boundless care given to the Mexican revolutionaries by the Americans.

A phone message, from the northeastern fighting zone to the Rebel, advised her that three more wounded had been brought to the river bank. They would be crossed about sixty miles below Laredo. Leaving the operating room where she was constantly in attendance, she went in search of someone to send. She almost bumped into two young girls waiting to see her. Judging them to be volunteers, she ordered the two startled girls to go to the Orfila ranch and bring in the wounded that were there. When two young men offered their car, she sent them all off. She did not see her young secretary, Aracelito, join the party.

The Rebel went about her afternoon bedside calls. On leaving the hospital, she met an elderly gentleman sitting in the garden. "Señora," he said bowing to her, "I shall wait here for my daughters. You have sent them on a mission. But," he bowed again. "I have not introduced myself. I am Emilio Salinas, brother-in-law of the First Chief Carranza."

Embarrassed at the thought of her abruptness with the girls, the Rebel took a moment before answering. "Yes, Señor Salinas," she looked up at his twinkling brown eyes, "we all serve our country."

Several hours later, after a long talk with him, the Rebel had made a friend of a member of the powerful Junta Revolucionaria, a group of wealthy men on the frontier who supported the anti-Huerta revolt.

Having crossed the river with their wounded and placed them in the car, the volunteers were about to start back to the hospital when a shout was heard from across the river. "Aracelito! Aracelito!" a mounted officer called. "Come back. A word with you."

Taking Pancho's boat, the girl rowed herself across. "Guillermo," she cried, flying into his arms. They walked to the shade of a big mesquite tree. The young officer took the girl's hand. "When you go back," he said, "tell your *jefe* that Pancho was shot an hour ago. He begged me to go tell his *amita*. God sent you, my dear."

Going back some distance from the river bank, they came to Pancho's body. His face was covered with a soldier's cap, his hands crossed on his breast. They knelt beside him.

"He has been with me," said Guillermo. "I gave him the uniform."

"How can I carry this news?" Aracelito wept bitterly. "It is very hard."

Aracelito cried all the way back to the hospital, the volunteers thinking she must have had a lover's quarrel. The Rebel, tired out, had found a solitary bench in the garden. It was mysteriously quiet. She thought of Pancho; he should be coming back soon. She half expected him. Finding her *jefe* in the garden, Aracelito pulled her to her feet. "You must come quickly. Guillermo wants to see you." Seeing the question in the Rebel's eyes, the girl assured her. "The wounded are asleep. Doctor de la Garza is on duty."

They started off, but the Rebel had a premonition that things were not right. On arriving at the place, they found another man in Pancho's boat. "Where is Pancho?" the Rebel asked.

"He is there, across the river, hurt. I'll take you over."

After crossing, the Rebel jumped from the boat and she ran up the bank where Guillermo was waiting for them. "Señora," he said taking her arm, "Pancho died a brave soldier's death."

She stood looking down at Pancho. How small he looked lying there.

"I have sent to Camargo for a coffin," Guillermo spoke, breaking the silence.

"Here we can easily dig," said Aracelito pointing to a place where the nervous horse had pawed the ground.

When the soldier came with the coffin, the two men dug the grave. Soon, the warm earth was caressing the body of the brave soldier and faithful servant. A few branches and a large rock on which Guillermo wrote Pancho's name marked the grave. "Go with God, Pancho," whispered the Rebel.

On the way home, the Rebel took the front seat with the chauffeur, leaving the lovers in back to repeat their vows again and again. The soldier from Camargo had brought Guillermo orders from General Pablo González for a few days' leave to be spent in Laredo on hospital inspection. Again there were skirmishes and more wounded brought to the banks of the Río Grande. Citizens with their cars and buggies were bringing the wounded to the house on 811 Flores Avenue. There were one hundred and fifty men in the three hospitals, with five in private homes. There was a doctor for every fifteen men, and a nurse for every five wounded. The presence of so many wounded soldiers from Mexico in the United States, and the fact that their commanders made frequent trips of inspection, brought many newspaper men. The news transmitted to the fighting zones encouraged the Constitutionalists and angered the Federals.

The time allotted Guillermo was drawing to a close. Together, he and Aracelito had discharged their duties at the hospital enjoying each other's company. Guillermo became helpful to the Rebel, who had now won his confidence. Finding her resting in the garden, he walked over to her and sat down on the grass at her feet. Silent for a while, he kept slipping his knife into the soft ground again and again. Clearing his throat, he spoke to her in a low voice. "I want to marry Aracelito. I had told my general I would approach her mother. We will have a quiet wedding. When the General occupies Nuevo Laredo, Aracelito can go with me."

A pang of fear and joy mingled in the Rebel's heart. Fear that in the coming battle he might be wounded, joy because Aracelito's faith in Guillermo had been proven.

It was a perfect wedding; she so young and beautiful, he gracefully majestic, of military bearing. Aracelito, kissing the Rebel, said proudly, "Now I am Mrs. Guillermo Martínez Celis, the wife of a brave Constitutionalist."

Misunderstandings arose regarding the war work in Laredo and Mr. Randolph Roberson, American consul in Monterrey, Mexico, conceived the idea of asking Washington for help with the Mexican wounded on the American side. He wired Representative John N. Garner, stating that in his opinion the aid of the National Red Cross was needed. This was uncalled for, as the people of Laredo had devoted untiring care to the wounded. When, after an exchange of telegrams, the Rebel was told of the matter, it was a shock to the entire staff. Doctors had worked without compensation; people had opened their homes to the soldiers.

The National Director of the American Red Cross was to arrive in Laredo on the sixth of January, 1914. The Rebel and her corps spent the night before fumigating, disinfecting, and cleaning. Tearing down red cross emblems they had been using, they substituted them with white crosses for fear that their good will would be misinterpreted. Mr. Ernest Bicknell, National Director, with Mr. McGarth and several nurses, arrived and inspected the hospitals. Bicknell issued a statement that the American Red Cross had found no reason to interfere with the work of the White Cross; instead they were to be commended for what they had done. The Rebel and her corps were much relieved when they read the report. The well-meant but untimely interference had brought fresh laurels to the volunteer nursing corps.

In the heat of enthusiasm, no regard of violation of international law was thought of by the people of Laredo, but trouble again arose. The Federals protested at so much care and leniency for the Carrancistas. In Presidio and Marfa, 3,000 Federal soldiers were being held prisoners in American camps, having fled across the border when 6,500 rebels had attacked Ojinaga. The Federals had taken refuge in the United States, carrying arms. The Rebel wondered how long she could keep her Mexican wounded. The hospital was surrounded by American soldiers. But as the days went on and the wounded got better, the problem had to be faced. The men could not leave the hospital and go about on American soil; they would be arrested. General González sent word that every man should return to his post the minute he was able to stand. So it was planned to spirit them out.

To the American soldiers they all looked alike, these natives of Laredo and the Mexican soldiers. So the hospital traded a milkman or two who came to deliver cans of milk for a soldier or two, sending them out past the guards. It was hours before the escape was discovered. But when it was, the Rebel was reprimanded. The wounded were counted ever so many times a day. When five poor fellows actually died, many more were reported dead. The undertaker came. Towards evening the dead were carried out, their bodies wrapped in sheets. No one looked at the dead. One day, however, one of the guards did open a coffin.

"Why put in this man's shoes?" he asked.

"It is a Spanish custom," the Rebel replied feebly. But that was the end of the coffin escapes.

Other ways had to be thought of. It happened that a loyal doctor lived across the street from the hospital. Although there was plenty of equipment at the hospital, the men who could walk were taken across the street to the doctor's home to be treated. The nurses went with them. Soon the returning number began to lessen. The captain of the guards made loud objections.

"Nurses," said the doctor shaking his fist and banging on his desk, "if any of these men are getting away, I'll blame you for it."

In the presence of the captain, the Rebel promised to nail shut the back gate on the hospital grounds. By this time the number had dwindled down to fifty.

"If another man leaves this place, I'll shoot every one of you," the captain shouted down at the crying Rebel. "Can't you see the Federals are howling about their Ojinaga prisoners. If we turn them loose, it will mean that many more to fight against you."

In reviewing the patients, they realized that thirty-three would not be able to leave for another month. The next day, two big army moving vans drove up and, without warning, American soldiers went into the hospital and carefully took out the wounded.

"Please leave them," the Rebel pleaded.

"We would like to leave them here, Señora," smiled the captain, "but they don't seem to want to stay. They disappear."

When available influences failed, the Rebel and her nurses obtained permission to visit the patients at the Army post, to bring them their mail and clean clothes. The Rebel got a lawyer, Mr. Otto Weffing, who called personally on the governor of Texas and wrote letters to Washington, pointing out that the Ojinaga Federal prisoners had crossed over with arms, while the Laredo soldiers had been brought over unconscious and wounded into a private home. Hospitality had been violated by imprisoning these men.

A great number of young boys, fourteen and fifteen, were in the fighting lines. Among the wounded at the hospital was a woman, Petra Mejía, who had followed the troops under hazardous conditions. She was on the battlefield when a spark from a bomb ignited her clothes, burning her painfully.

Captain Rodolfo Villalba, whose leg was almost fractured by a bomb explosion, was a useful man on General Cesáreo Castro's staff. He was a newspaper man, young and fearless. His only brother and inseparable companion had become blind just before the tragedy in Mexico. The brothers knew it was their duty to join the Carrancistas, but the afflicted one would be left behind. In an anguish of preparations, Rodolfo gathered all the material he could to facilitate the writing of messages. In the dead of night, Rodolfo left his brother in a cheerful room with a piano and a guitar. His room soon became the scene of gatherings where news was transmitted from the battlefields to those waiting to hear from their loved ones. It was Rodolfo's intention to join General Pánfilo Natera, who had led the revolt in the central states. News of Natera's righteousness and honesty pleased the young writer, and he sought his camp. It was a hazardous trip, becoming impossible, because of the rapid movements of the Federal troops. He finally reached Monterrey and joined up with the Constitutionalists at Matamoros. He spoke English and sang, constantly encouraging the wounded. He, too, was moved to Fort McIntosh where he soon made warm friends.

It was the latter part of March when the Rebel received the first letter from General Pablo González, of the Constitutionalist northeastern military sector, thanking her for her care of his soldiers and her efforts to secure their release. Though she was not personally acquainted with him, the brave young commander had become an idol to her. She spoke of him so often that the hospital staff always saluted his photograph that hung in the tiny entry. The solicitude for his men, his self-sacrifice, and his loyalty to the First Chief were the subject of many stories told by soldiers and doctors who knew him.

After the Carrancistas' victorious entry into Matamoros, the Rebel received a telegram from Adolpho. He had been in Mexico City, and had decided to stay there. This was the last and only message she was to have from him for many months. Affiliated with the Constitutionalists, their cause had become the Rebel's life. As it was impossible to get news from Mexico City, she did not learn what her husband's political affinity was. Not until she met him a year later were things satisfactorily explained.

During Don Joaquín's time, there had existed a friendship between the Madero family and the Villegas family, business as well as social connections. Don Joaquín held vast interests in Mexico in mines, in the iron foundry in Monterrey, and in the Torreón smelters of which Don Ernesto Madero was president. When the Díaz regime was suppressing any opposition in 1910, the Villegas interest rose high when Francisco Madero became president. His term was of such short duration that scarcely had things become favorable when Huerta threw the country into confusion. Both the Villegas and the Maderos suffered heavy losses. It was on account of this friendship that, in need of medical supplies, the Rebel wrote asking Don Ernesto Madero in New York for help for her hospital. He immediately sent financial aid. The White Cross had so far been running on donations from private citizens in the United States and along the northern border of Mexico.

From Matamoros came the order for the White Cross Corps to join the Constitutionalists, entering the field of service under direct orders of Venustiano Carranza, the First Chief of the Revolution. The Rebel had notified General Pablo González that her unit would be willing to go anywhere they were needed. When their credentials and money came for the corps to leave for Ciudad Juárez, a hasty inventory was made of the hospital equipment, and it was turned over to Elvira Idar and María Villarreal to be used for caring for the soldiers from the battle of Nuevo Laredo. Until then the corps had recognized only one chief, Pablo González, their honorary president.

That same day, April 3, 1914, the thirty-three Mexican Constitutionalist prisoners, including fifteen who had armed themselves on the Texas side and attempted to cross over to Mexico near Zapata, were released from Fort McIntosh where they had been interned.

The afternoon before the nursing corps was to leave in a special car on the International and Great Northern Railway, a mass meeting was held at Luna Park Airdrome. Nearly a thousand sympathizers assembled in a demonstration in celebration of the Constitutionalist victory at Torreón. Speeches praising Carranza, Villa, and Francisco Madero were made. The crowd passed through the streets of Laredo headed by a brass band, with a banner bearer carrying a big, silk Mexican flag. When the Federals protested from Nuevo Laredo, the City Marshal ordered the gathering to disperse.

There were twenty-six on the Rebel's staff that arrived in El Paso on April 5. Of the men there were those who could act as railroad engineers, firemen, brakemen, telegraph operators, newspaper men, printers, and a photographer. At a moment's notice they could run their own train or do propaganda work when not on hospital duty.

Three of the young volunteer nurses were the Martínez sisters, Ofelia, Clotilde, and Emilia, who had been reared as if daughters in the house of the Rebel's wealthy uncle, who had only one daughter. These girls were the daughter's constant companions. One sewed, doing exquisite needlework; another was Herminia's personal maid; and the third took care of her wardrobe. The girls had not been treated as servants; they sat and worked within hearing distance of the family. They had had good training in nursing, having cared for all the old maiden aunts of the queer aristocratic family, where coats of arms and jewels were scattered about the house. Pedigrees and coats of arms were insignificant things to the younger generation, but these girls, reared in awe and respect for the past, were a comfort to the Rebel.

Three married couples came, the Ruizes, the Portachellis and the Esparzas. They did most of the night nursing, supervising the three to six wards. Two mothers came with their daughters, Catarina and Luz Ibarra, Margarita de León and Catarina de León. The girls, inseparable companions, nursed in the same ward. The two mothers were excellent cooks who prepared the food for the doctors and nurses. Mrs. Lily Honeycutt Long, wife of a doctor, was the Rebel's secretary, capable friend, and companion. A good shot, skillful equestrienne, a perfect nurse, she did not speak a word of Spanish. Federico Idar and Felipe Aguirre were secretary and treasurer of the brigade, and Eustacio Montoya was the daring and talented staff photographer.

With no opportunity but to go forward, the Rebel had left her three children with her brother and his wife. With an indefinite idea of her husband's attitude towards the Revolution, she had set out on an unknown expedition. Before the small band of volunteers stood the available future to which every human being is entitled; that future was their own. Behind them would soon be an abyss which would separate them from the past, from those they loved, from their inheritance. They did not speak of home, nor the ones left behind, but kept their eyes on time. The time piece on their wrists regulated their lives; every minute was counted, every minute belonged to duty at a bedside, at an operating table, at a disinfecting process, or writing letters to someone dear to a dead soldier.

Mexican Consul Juan Burns and Vice Consul Salvador Treviño met the group at the station in El Paso. Until now the wounded soldiers and their officers had been the only official contact the corps had with the Revolution. The confidential agency of civilians along the border were all friends of long-standing of the Rebel. These two men, and Don Rafael Múzquiz, who was the First Chief's most devoted friend, were to usher the corps into the war's activity. Once crossing the border, they could not turn back, but became immediately absorbed in the war's activity, working side by side with great men who were giving their lives for a great ideal.

In a few days, the Rebel was to meet Carranza, the First Chief of the Revolution.

CHAPTER X
The Rebel Meets Carranza

The Rebel and Lily Long were taken to the Mexican Consulate, where they were to remain until further orders. The upper part of the building, above the offices, had several furnished rooms, evidently used to accommodate officials who went to and from Mexico and the United States. The rest of the corps were taken to a hotel nearby. A messenger came to the Rebel's room bringing a card from Señor Múzquiz saying that Señor Juan Burns would call for the Rebel and her secretary in an hour. He would be pleased to have them as his supper guests.

As the party was sitting down, Otto Weffing, the lawyer, joined them. He had read in the *San Antonio Express* about their passing through San Antonio on their way to El Paso. He told the Rebel he had come to see them off. He insisted on being host to the party.

"Señor Múzquiz," the Rebel said, "Señor Weffing was an intimate friend of my father." She told how the lawyer had worked for the release of the soldiers held in Laredo. It was then that Mr. Weffing was cordially accepted, and sat down.

Señor Múzquiz told the Rebel that the next day she must send one of the corps with a card to the First Chief saying the constitutional White Cross was at his orders.

"Señor Múzquiz," she said, patting his right hand that was holding his fork. "You don't know me. I am a sensible rebel. No one, as yet, has ordered me to do anything. My father, my husband, and my brother always let me do anything."

Weffing was choking, trying to attract her attention to silence her.

"Now, Mr. Weffing, don't tease." The Rebel was serious then. "You know I love the soldiers. We have come to serve them. All I want is to be assigned to my post."

"I am fully aware of what you say, but this is a serious undertaking," said Múzquiz. "You must be disciplined. You must learn to obey orders." He shook his fork at the smiling, self-assured Rebel.

"Mr. Múzquiz is right, Mrs. Magnón," the lawyer persisted.

"Well, my dear Señor Múzquiz, you tell Señor Burns to notify our First Chief that we are here, and ready to start."

"Yes, my Señora, I will do that. But you, too, must do so." Múzquiz clung to the formality.

At the Consulate again, the Rebel and Lily prepared to retire. Sitting on the side of the bed, the Rebel took her companion's hand. "Lily, what do you think of all this? Are you willing to take the risk by going on?"

In the semi-lighted room, the tall, blond Lily peered closely at her companion. Without her glasses, she missed the fleeting expressions. "Magnón, I shall not leave you one single moment."

It was then that they heard footsteps slowly ascending the stairs. They heard the steps stop at their door; there was a loud knock. Unlocking the door and peeping out was the motion of only a second. In that time, the officer had pushed into the room and into the Rebel's arms. To the astonishment of Lily, the Rebel had a tight grasp around the officer's waist. Breaking loose, she held the soldier at arm's length.

"Why, María de Jesús. It all came true. Sit down. No, show us your uniform first," the Rebel spoke excitedly.

Putting down her cap and gloves, María de Jesús dusted off her shiny boots with her soft muffler; then she turned around to let her audience see her outfit. Sitting down, she began her story. "I must talk quickly; I am leaving early tomorrow for the border to join General Marcelino Murrietta's staff. But to begin at the beginning... After I left Laredo, I came here and stayed a day before crossing to Ciudad Juárez in hopes of an audience with the First Chief. All morning I waited. Towards noon I was admitted. I had prepared myself carefully. I wore my precious white dress; my hair I braided neatly, and wound it round my head. I looked womanly," she laughed.

"The Chief took a fleeting glance at me and continued to dispatch messages, sign papers, and give orders. Finally, he turned and looked squarely at me. He was holding my card. I had written that I was from Laredo. 'What good news do you bring?' he asked.

"Though it was time for his noon meal, I talked. I started with a flood of information about the battle of Matamoros, Nuevo Laredo, and the White Cross. He caressed his silky beard and fixed his heavy glasses. I was taking too much of his valuable time, but I rushed on. 'I want a commission in the army,' I told him. I want to be in the calvary.'

"He continued to stroke his beard. Someone came in; I feared the interview was over. Slowly he said, 'I will keep your card, and the newspapers you brought from Laredo. We will think over how best you can serve. Call again.' The interview was over.

"You were not discouraged?" asked the Rebel.

"No, Señora," she said. "But a month passed and I began to think there was no chance for a foolish girl. I was not going back to you defeated. Meanwhile, Villa had captured all Chihuahua. I wanted action. Then I thought that I could easily pass for my brother, dressed in soldier's clothes.

"I went window shopping and bought these beautiful boots. See, I can stick my dagger in the side." She slipped out the little dagger Pancho had given her. "I took them to my room, and with the empty box under my arm, went to a barber shop. I sat down, loosening my braids. The barber remarked how beautiful my hair was. 'Well, just cut it off,' I told him, and lay them in this box. Give me a man's haircut.'

"The shocked barber went about his business. He deftly laid the shining braids in the box. With a sign, I put on the lid. He handed me a mirror. It was a perfect hair cut. I gave him a big tip."

"What happened next?" Lily asked, forgetting her timidity.

"Then I came across a shop that sold army goods. I told the clerk I wanted a lieutenant's uniform for my brother who was sick. I would try it for a fit. He rushed around. I shook my head until he touched this one.

"All night I tossed in bed waiting for daylight so I could get up and dress myself. I was up early and dressed, no squeaky boots, no wrinkles in my pants. A knock at the door upset me. It was urgent. I opened the door gingerly. It was a telegram from the First Chief's secretary saying the *Jefe* would see me that very morning."

"María, María de Jesús, the miracle," the Rebel smiled.

"I had my breakfast and crossed at the bridge. I showed my telegram, told them I was not returning. At the Provisional headquarters I walked past the guards who saluted me. To the officer at the reception room I presented the telegram, and was ushered in. The *Jefe* drew back a bit. He expected the golden-haired girl. I walked up to him with the shoe box. Handing it to him, I uncovered it. He looked into the box; fixing his glasses, he looked at me. His secretary entered.

"'This young officer is a lieutenant going on a special mission,' he said, fumbling in the inner pocket of his vest and drawing out a paper. He read it and sealed it in an envelope."

"'You shall go immediately to Chihuahua. Find General Manuel Chao. Give him this. Avoid open roads; there is still danger. You will have an escort on your return,' said the *Jefe*.

"I found General Chao. He seemed pleased with the message. Then I came back. Oh! Señora Magnón, how happy I am to see you," the words poured out as she clasped the Rebel's hand. "But, she added soberly, "I must go. So it is until we meet again." Putting on her cap and gloves she slipped out of the door. For a few minutes the sound of her footsteps on the tile floor came back to the two in the dark room. Then there was stillness in the big, quiet building.

The next morning the Rebel and Lily were hopeful of their plans. They were sitting at the breakfast table in a restaurant across from the consulate when a young officer approached them. After the usual courtesies he said he had come for them by orders of the First Chief. Lily went to their room for their credentials and letters from General González. As they sat waiting to be taken to the First Chief, the Rebel examined the papers fondly. They still had a clinging fragrance of Laredo. The postmaster had taken them personally to the Rebel's home because he knew they would be leaving early, too early for the mail carrier delivery. He stood in the doorway saying goodbye, still holding the mail in his hand.

"It may be for awhile, or forever," said the Rebel. "Please open the letters and read them."

"I congratulate you," he said after reading the letters from General González. And like a true Frenchman, a tear glistened in his eye when he said, "Aurevoir."

These same letters she was holding now could pave the way smoothly to begin her work for Carranza. The guard opened the door just then and announced them. The First Chief was standing by a chair near a table. The room was long and heavily draped in rich red plush. Their footsteps made no sound on the thick carpets. As the Rebel advanced, she was possessed by the feeling of walking towards a huge stone statue of a warrior. His uniform was a terracotta hue, like Mexican earthenware. His large gold buttons, each bearing an eagle, shone brightly as the rays of the sun touched them, reflecting playfully on the gilded armchair and making lights on the exquisite marble-top table. She was not frightened as she thought she might be, for as they approached he extended his hand and bowed, cavalier fashion. His face lit up, his eyes twinkled, and a broad smile assured them they were in sympathetic company. On his left was a long elegant lounge; Lily and the Rebel seated themselves, the First Chief taking a gilded chair. Reassured by the pleasant atmosphere, the Rebel turned to Lily for the credentials and records she carried, and was about to hand them to Carranza. "I bring these testimonials," she began.

He was looking far away, not at them. His mind was wandering back thirty years to his home town, Cuatro Ciénegas. "No," he said shaking his head, "I do not need any credentials. I won't even look at them. Keep them; they will do you honor." Then, looking sharply at her, he said, "Were you ever in Cuatro Ciénegas? Are you the daughter of Joaquín Villegas?"

"Yes, I am his daughter," the Rebel said proudly, because to her it had always been like sitting on top of the world to be his daughter. Now his spirit, the fragrance of his soul, the remembrance of his good deeds tied her to his powerful memory.

"Then," he continued, "you must have a burn on your left hand, if you are the little girl who came to Cuatro Ciénegas. You were burnt on your left hand just as I was; the same doctor took care of us both." Looking at Lily, the stranger, he said, "I remember saying that same day we two would be together in a burning experience."

The Rebel showed him her left hand. The scar that for thirty years had been hateful to her now appeared like a proud mark of cast. Pleasure reflected in her face. "It is rather out of place, my Chief, to ask such an insignificant thing, but will you put this all down in writing for me?"

"Yes, I will do that for you. When I am in Chihuahua I will write you that letter."

"I shall remind you," the Rebel answered smiling.

"In your capacity of President of the White Cross I will allow you to observe the silent passages of my life. It will be your privilege later on to report facts about me and my revolt that will be unknown to others."

So it was that the Rebel was present when the great man's path was thick with the smoke of battle, his way bedimmed, and when dark treason surrounded him.

"You are leaving for Chihuahua tomorrow at dawn," he said. "Have everything ready. Dr. José Rodríquez, my staff physician, will be your friend and counselor. He will equip the train and cars necessary for your work. You belong to my staff, having the consideration of the office you hold. You will take orders from me." Rising, he asked whether there was anything she wanted.

"Yes," the Rebel said. "I shall need a small revolver to carry with me in my bag."

"You shall have it tomorrow when you cross into Mexico," he said. "Your train leaves one day before mine. You should arrive in good time to see our entry into Chihuahua. Governor Manuel Chao has orders to receive the Constitutional White Cross.

The next morning, in her bag the Rebel carried a small revolver, an envelope containing a telegraph pass and a railroad pass for any line, and in her bosom a cross sent to her by Pope Leo XIII.

With the whole rich state of Chihuahua under control of the revolutionaries the city of Chihuahua became headquarters for the advancing Carranza government that established itself there with astonishing rapidity. The various divisions of the army were represented, as well as every department of an established government. As before, the people of Chihuahua were active partisans in revolutionary outbreaks. Hidalgo in 1810 in an effort to overthrow Spanish rule was expected there with two of his lieutenants. In 1864 President Benito Juárez made that his provisional capital for a short while, just as Carranza was now doing.

Pancho Villa had easily triumphed in Chihuahua, knowing so well the high mountains of the Sierra Madre range, the isolated peaks, the windows of the Concho River, and the growing fields. In a country ideal for guerrilla warfare, Villa had become the idol of the peons. He confiscated millions of acres of land for the people to the detriment of the great Terrazas estate; the wealthy Terrazas family sought refuge in the United States. Don Enrique Creel was another great landholder. Could anyone wonder why Villa had become an idol, with his land distribution giving Mexican farmers in that section a chance to own and control their share of the land? In Sonora, changes had not been so abrupt; Generals Maytorena and Obregón were more conservative. General Lucio Blanco in Matamoros had also distributed land until told to stop. The First Chief was checking the sweeping movement with moderation.

The Constitutional White Cross, on arriving at Chihuahua, was met by Colonel Joaquín Bauche Alcalde and two assistants. The Rebel and Lily Long with Felipe Aguirre, the treasurer, and Federico Idar, of publication and propaganda, were taken to a hotel centrally located, while the rest of the brigade was to stay at a hotel nearby. The city was congested with people ready to welcome the First Chief on his arrival early the next day.

"My brother, Manuel Bauche Alcalde," said the Colonel, "also in the army, publishes and directs the newspaper *Vida Nueva*. He has asked me to put his daily at your orders."

"Do you hear that, Idar?" said the Rebel. "Call on the Colonel every day and report any news we receive from Laredo."

"Indeed, Madam," said Bauche Alcalde, "we already know of you and your work. Consul Juan Burns of El Paso has notified us of Señor Múzquiz's orders for all your mail to be sent to the First Chief's headquarters. You are to call for it there. That is quite a distinction," he said looking steadily at the Rebel.

After a little rest and preparations of the next day's plans, the Rebel and her party went down for supper in the hotel. While supper was being served, the Rebel noticed a constant going and coming from a room nearby, the headquarters evidently of some important officer. Cautiously, Federico inquired. Lieutenant-Colonel Francisco Manzo, of the 4th Battalion of Sonora, was there with his staff. Captain Abelardo Rodríquez, his intimate friend, was his paymaster. Manzo, the son of a wealthy family, was scarcely twenty-six years old; Rodríguez, "the youth who knew no fear," was twenty-four. As a compliment to the First Chief, General Alvaro Obregón had sent his best battalion to be his bodyguard in Chihuahua.

Visiting the nursing corps in their hotel, the Rebel told them that the governor had ordered them to rest for three days. When the festivities were over, they would be assigned to their hospital. Dr. José Rodríguez would be assigned to their hospital. Dr. José Rodríguez would be on the same train with Carranza. The next morning the corps was to be ready to greet the First Chief's party. In the morning, the voices of troops patrolling the streets, bugle calls, and the sound of spurs and guns downstairs made Lily say, "Magnón, let's go down for breakfast quickly so we can be back to our balcony before the parade starts. They must be on the outskirts of the city now."

They saw Lieutenant Manzo's headquarters abandoned, doors wide open, a sentry standing guard. A glimpse in the room betrayed the hasty departure; uniforms and clothes were strewn about on the floor.

"Magnón," Lily said, "how I would love to go in and give that room a thorough cleaning."

The Rebel and Lily occupied the balcony with Federico and Felipe. They could see the rest of the corps waving flags and holding bags of confetti ready. On the official train, an outline of the formation of the parade had been planned. So when the train rolled into the station at Chihuahua, a procession was quickly formed. All along the way from Juárez to Chihuahua crowds greeted the First Chief, extra passengers boarding the train, mostly politicians. When the Constitutionalists arrived, they were exhausted and overworked from their speech-making. A tremendous reception awaited them. The nurses with their enthusiastic cheering caught the First Chief's eye as he passed. At the head of the parade were Francisco Manzo and Abelardo Rodríquez. Marching through the streets, the parade went to the residence that had been prepared for Carranza and his staff. From the terrace of this house, patriotic speeches and oratory stirred the multitude. General Francisco Villa's band pealed forth Mexican music. Then it was all over. The big banquet, the hand-shaking, and the tired city took on a weary aspect.

In their room that night, the Rebel said to Lily, who sat braiding her blond hair, "Lily, this will be my prayer." Looking out over the great city, she spoke her thoughts out loud. "Dear Lord, as the modest violets give their fragrance from beneath the brushwood that conceals them, please let the kindness and sweetness of my brigade, though unseen, breathe forth their fragrance in restoring the sick and wounded, in kindling the fires of patriotism and courage."

Sitting on her bed, the Rebel emptied her large black bag on the soft covers. "Look what I have here, Lily. After my prayer it doesn't seem consistent, but it's practical."

There was the little revolver the Chief had sent, a copy of President Washington's farewell address, and the farewell message of President Díaz; the first was a masterpiece of wisdom, the other a sad hyperbole. She looked at the tiny photograph of her husband and their three children. Then dumping them back hastily, she turned off the light. But the lights from the plaza made the room half-lit.

"Lily," the Rebel asked, "are you crying?"

"No, Magnón," came back her clear voice. "Are you?"

Creasing the sheet in folds over her breast, the Rebel spoke to her friend. "In these last few months I have outgrown many things. I feel almost ascetic in my tastes. Luxuries that can be bought, the reward that ambition procures, the exquisite sense of love. They are naught to the happiness of drowning oneself in service to one's fellow man."

"Magnón," Lily said, half asleep, "tomorrow is a new day."

"Yes, Lily, every day shall bring a new tomorrow until we triumph."

Two uneventful days passed for the members of the Rebel's brigade. They went sightseeing. Not so for the Rebel and her secretary. The morning after the parade as they went down to breakfast they noticed that the headquarters of Lieutenant Colonel Manzo was dark. On inquiry, they were informed that he was quite sick; he was feverish and had a choking sensation. He would not call a doctor. They knocked gently on the half-open door. Captain Rodríguez greeted them.

"Our *Jefe* is sick; he cannot receive visitors."

"Magnón, what is this man talking about?" said Lily, pushing the captain away. She drew a chair towards Manzo's bed and took his pulse. "Tell the assistant to bring ice and to get the hot water bottle from our room for his feet."

"No," said the captain in good English. "I will go for them. Give me the key to your room."

"Find out that man's name," said Lily when he had gone. "He will be of use to us."

When the Rebel asked the sick Manzo his companion's name, he said, "I am Manzo, and he is Abelardo."

That was the introduction. Thereafter they were so called, and as they too belonged to the Chief's staff, the four were constantly in contact with each other. From that day on to the entry into Mexico City, the 4th Battalion and the Constitutional White Cross were together.

When Rodríguez returned, Manzo said to him, "These people know what they are doing. I want them to nurse me till I get well. And mind you," he said to Lily, "I have to be well tomorrow."

Next day, the patient had fresh linen, new pajamas, and a high pillow. Lily brought the looking glass. "See how well you look. But you must stay in bed all day today."

Governor Manuel Chao and Captain Joaquín Bauche Alcalde, his assistant, called on the third day, and after a few words of greeting, the Rebel and Lily were driven to a beautiful mansion, just across the street from where Carranza stayed. The house was one of the Terrazas'. Having been abandoned, General Villa had put it on the confiscated list. It was to be the headquarters of the Constitutional White Cross while they were off duty. Every night, two nurses would take turns in resting there, accompanying the Rebel.

The young governor to whom María de Jesús, the lieutenant, had delivered her message, assumed a friendly attitude toward the organization; he was an asset in furthering their success. He was much esteemed by the First Chief; and though he belonged to General Francisco Villa's staff, he was loyal to Carranza. It was he who took them to the Municipal Palace to see the First Chief. They were not announced; the Governor preceded them and ushered them into his presence.

Again in the elegant brilliancy of a palace the Chief received them standing, as was his usual way. After a ceremonious bow, he asked them to be seated. The governor remained standing as he had pressing duties. "General Manuel Chao and General Villa, the military commander of the state, have orders to facilitate your work," explained the First Chief. "Tomorrow you will be assigned to your hospital. It is an improvised one; you will have enough to furnish it as soon as your train is unloaded. It is a hacienda on the outskirts of this city. The wounded from the recent battle of Chihuahua and vicinity will be brought in." Carranza adjusted his glasses. "There are other buildings that have been hurriedly occupied and converted into hospitals for the wounded."

As he was speaking, his secretary, Gustavo Espinosa Mireles, came in with a silver tray, presenting him the correspondence. Looking it over hurriedly, Carranza sorted it out, taking letters and a telegram addressed to the Rebel. Holding them in his hand, he returned the rest, ordering his secretary to attend to the mail. Carranza first looked at the telegram, holding it gingerly in his hand, running his finger slowly over the corners. The Rebel lost no motion. She decided he was a lonely man. Alone in his plans, alone in his thoughts. It was not easy to fathom him and his ways. But he was exceedingly interesting.

Slowly, he drew a pen knife out of his left pocket and deliberately opened the envelope. No one had ever opened her mail. Her father had respected it; her husband had, also. Carranza, smiling, extended his hand and delivered to her the telegram. After she read it she handed it back to Carranza. While he was looking at the telegram, she looked at the letters and handed them to her secretary. The telegram was from Colonel Carlos Fierros, on General Pablo González's staff, stating that they had taken Nuevo Laredo and had been greeted on their arrival by the 2nd Brigade of the Constitutional White Cross. His general was much impressed. The Rebel's old home in Nuevo Laredo had been burned, and the town had been burning for three days and nights.

"I am happy," she said. "We now have Nuevo Laredo and all of Tamaulipas."

"Well," said the Chief, "you do not seem too unhappy about your home."

Looking at him the Rebel spoke with feeling, more feeling than she had intended. "It was my birthplace. The place where my mother died, my mother who visualized me with a white flag in my hand." Then smiling, she recalled to him, "It was there that my father declared me a rebel when we were attacked."

The Chief touched the gong on a nearby table and his secretary entered. The Chief showed him the telegram. Mireles bowed to the two men, read it, and handed it to the Rebel. Addressing Carranza he said, "*Mi Jefe,* we are receiving news from Nuevo Laredo from General González. They have control of the wires all over the state. Their next move will be to Monterrey where General Francisco Murgía, Luis Caballero, and Antonio Villarreal are advancing."

Just outside the door, after their interview, Lily gasped, "Magnón, we are one of them; and I swear we will not fail them."

In a short while, the Rebel came to know Carranza's cabinet members: Rafael Zubarán, Minister of Foreign Relations, a polished gentleman of a forceful pen. He was discretion personified. Jesus Acuña, Secretary of the Interior, a persuasive and scholarly writer; Jacinto Treviño, Secretary of War, who had been educated in the Military College at Chapultepec. His assistant, Juan Barragán, was only nineteen, jovial, and a fine soldier; his mail was heavy with fan-letters. Alfredo Breceda, Secretary of State, a staunch friend of the Chief's, was a brilliant lawyer with a well-balanced mind. Isidro Fabela, connected with Foreign Relations, was a lawyer, who became one of the fourteen members of the Hague International Tribunal. They were all between twenty and thirty. Alberto Peraldi, nephew of the Chief, a youth of pale countenance and inexhaustible energy, was Carranza's personal telegraph operator. There was Ignacio Bonillas, who in later years was the indirect cause of the downfall of Carranza. All of these men were to be constantly in the Rebel's path as the cabinet, too, moved with the advancing army.

The hospital that the Constitutional White Cross was to use was a confiscated hacienda belonging to Señor Enrique Creel that had been abandoned. It had enormous rooms, a wonderfully equipped kitchen and every comfort. A large inside patio was made into a beautiful garden. The hospital was soon put in order, each member became a unit, finding ways of accomplishing their assigned duties. Floors scrubbed, windows shining, beds prepared, wards numbered and named. The doctor's quarters were supplied with medicines; his apartment neatly furnished. The large dining room was equipped with clean tables. Big pots of water were kept boiling night and day on special *braceros*. There were plenty of local volunteers who came to work as assistants. They were to remain taking over the hospital work when the moving unit of the White Cross left for another state.

The governor and his wife took special interest in the hospital, bringing provisions, medicines, and money on their numerous visits. Taking off her jewelry, beautiful Luz Corral, General Villa's wife, asked that it be sold for the hospital. "What do I care for them?" she said tearfully. "I want peace so that I can enjoy my husband's company. Now I am always frightened."

Elena de Bauche Alcalde, called the mocking bird of Mexico, gave a concert for the benefit of the hospital. The Rebel asked her to be president of the White Cross organization in the state of Chihuahua. She was the wife of the director of the newspaper, *Vida Nueva*. On leaving, the Rebel knew the hospital would be in good hands. The high ideals of the nurses and the institution of the White Cross were successfully placed before the public through the press. In the columns of their paper, the two generals gave reports of meetings and activities, lessening the propaganda burden on the Rebel.

The original Laredo unit of the Constitutional White Cross was to travel constantly with the moving army, leaving brigades and branches in every city where time allowed. Beside taking over the base hospitals, assigning minor duties to local supporters and co-workers, this unit had other obligations. The Rebel established a bureau of secret service. News of importance was given directly to her regarding movements of troops so that she could supply loyal nurses and doctors as territory was gained. Each one of the members of this original unit was later assigned to the staff of generals commanding different zones, forming their own individual brigades. That is how the Rebel succeeded in keeping control until the White Cross acquired full recognition with the victorious army of Carranza.

One morning, the Rebel and Lily were on duty. Every day they took their turns assisting the doctors in the operating room. On this occasion after inspection, as the Rebel was standing on the porch, she noticed an accumulation of bandages, cotton, and gauze. She knew the trash would cause the spreading of germs. Walking thirty paces towards the center of the patio and looking around, she was satisfied that there would be a good place for her purpose. She called Felipe and Federico and, standing on the spot she had selected, told them to dig a square hole deep enough to burn all the refuse. "Call me when you finish," she told them.

The Rebel returned to her duties. Some time passed. She was busy going from bed to bed, talking with the wounded, when Federico touched her arm and beckoned her to follow. Supposing that they were finished, she walked directly to the spot. Felipe used the pick several times and a strange sound came from the ground. "You see," they both said at the same time.

"There is something buried here; it seems to be a coffin," said Federico.

"Dig a little further up where there is not the same sound," suggested the Rebel.

After more digging, the shovel slid easily and they began digging in a diagonal direction, uncovering to their surprise an iron door, heavily bolted. As they had both worked in railroad shops, they soon pried the floor open. An iron staircase of twelve steps led to another door which was easily opened. There before their eager eyes was wealth not Aladdin and his lamp could rival. Bags filled with coins leaned against the walls; stacked neatly on shelves against the four walls were deposited collateral, mining shares, and industrial shares. It was as if a bank had been buried underground. In the center of the room was a massive mahogany table on which rested a magnificent bronze bust of Señor Enrique Creel, president of the bank. Awestruck, the Rebel stood while one of the boys ran to call Lily.

"Lily," said the Rebel to her wondering secretary, "Take note of all this quickly."

Looking around in amazement, all Lily could say was, "Magnón! Magnón!"

Coming to her senses, the Rebel ordered Felipe and Federico to get some boards big enough to cover the hole. When they returned, they all swore to tell no one. As soon as the boards were placed and dirt spread on them, the Rebel told Federico to go immediately and tell Governor Chao to come and bring his secretary. He was not to be told anything.

"Felipe, you await the governor's arrival and call me. I will invent something to keep everyone busy," said the Rebel as she and Lily returned to the Hospital.

In a short time, the governor and Joaquín Bauche Alcalde came on horseback. The Rebel was notified. "Felipe," she said, "Tell Ezequiel Ruiz to keep the staff busy. There will be an inspection to keep the doctor busy in the office."

By this time, Federico was walking toward the find. Hastily shoving aside the boards, he led the way down the steps, Lily and the Rebel following.

"Does anyone else know of this?"

"No, Governor Chao. We have just now found it, quite by accident," replied the Rebel.

Walking around with his secretary close behind him, he told him to take notes. Lily handed the Governor the paper she had written. They walked out silently. Once outside, the governor said, "Not a word of this. Put back the boards and plenty of dirt. Get a *mozo* to press the ground down hard."

CHAPTER XI
Villa, the People's Idol

In the afternoons, the First Chief rode on horseback with his secretary, Governor Manuel Chao, and five or six high officers to visit the hospital. Carranza chatted with some of the newly arrived wounded, inquiring particularly about the nurses, which pleased them greatly. A photograph was usually taken on these visits, as Carranza was often accompanied by different officials. Francisco Villa sent his band to play in the patio of the hospital, saying it was a tonic for the patients.

Montoya, the official photographer of the Constitutional White Cross, never had an idle moment. The Rebel liked him. He was loyal and eventually became the semi-official photographer for the First Chief.

"Montoya," the Rebel said repeatedly to him, "photographs are history, and you must not let anyone have a negative or sell the pictures. They are my personal property. I pay for the supplies."

On one of the Chief's visits to the hospital, Captain Jesús Valdez, paymaster on Carranza's staff, presented a letter to the Rebel. It was not addressed to her in the Chief's handwriting as was his custom. Thinking it of little importance, she handed it to Lily. When they were at home, the secretary drew out the letter from among the rest and exclaimed, "Magnón, this letter is written in English, addressed to the Chief."

It was from a Doctor Brady of El Paso, Texas. He had done some dental work on the Chief and had been sent fifty dollars as agreed upon for the work. The letter read: "It has been a high honor to serve such a distinguished patient. I therefore return the money you have sent me, acknowledging receipt of same and begging you to use it for some good purpose. Wishing you success."

At the bottom of the letter the chief had written to the Rebel: "Please accept this money returned me; use it for the hospital, for the wounded, or any good purpose."

"Long, what will I do with this money?" asked the Rebel, folding the money thoughtfully.

"Give it to Montoya," was Lily's quick reply. Only yesterday he said he was almost at the end of his film. We may be leaving soon. Perhaps, he will not be able to get more material easily."

"You think this is a good purpose?"

"I certainly do. Ask the Chief tomorrow."

They told Carranza the next day and he approved.

Montoya was sent immediately to El Paso to buy what he needed. Seeing his clothes threadbare, the Rebel added another fifty dollars. Her brother kept her in expense money. "Buy yourself a uniform and brown shoes, Montoya," said the Rebel. "Get one like the soldiers wear."

The First Chief was pleased to see the uniformed Montoya on his return. The photographer had taken a picture of the First Chief on horseback and had sent it to him as a surprise.

Often in the evening the Rebel and Lily visited the First Chief, relating their adventures of the day. It afforded him amusement and relaxation from his own affairs. Next day, he would sometimes write a letter to the Rebel referring to some particular part of their work. It was through Doctor José María Rodríguez, Carranza's medical attendant, that the Chief kept in constant touch with the Rebel. After his daily visits to the hospital, the doctor went to the nurses' home to bring important official documents. Many of them were in English, having been translated. They comprised diplomatic exchanges, war messages, and communiques.

In the operating room where the newly wounded arrived from the battlefields, the staff got news about generals and their troop advances. The Rebel's brigade was conscious of the confidence placed in them. During their rest periods, the nurses went to the Rebel's home in the city. There while recounting their day's experiences they worked on propaganda materials, campaign emblems, flags, and photo buttons, some with pictures of Madero and Carranza, others of generals of different divisions. Later, as they traveled from town to town as the trains stopped for the Chief to greet the crowds, and while official orators spoke, the nurses threw into the crowds their propaganda materials from open windows. Some of the men of the brigade mingled with the people, distributing literature about the Constitutional White Cross, inviting people to join. This went on all during the Revolution until the Chief reached Mexico City.

The First Chief sent his chauffeur twice a week to the Rebel's headquarters with a polite note offering her the use of his car for the afternoon to make sick calls, solicit cooperation, and to visit places of interest. Once, as the chauffeur respectfully opened and closed the door of the car, his coat flew open and Lily noticed in his pocket a rolled up American magazine. Relieving him of it gently, Lily smoothed it out on her lap. To her surprise, it opened to an ear-marked page.

"Lily," the Rebel said in a whisper, "this chap speaks English." They had both noticed how attentive he was to their conversations.

"Magnón, he is an American. I'll bet he's writing for this magazine."

Seeing in the mirror what was going on in the back seat, he wasn't able to keep his secret any longer. "Señoras," he said, "no one knows who I am. I enlisted with General Carranza to be near him to get news and pictures. It is my hobby to pass as a chauffeur. Once I was in Anna Gould's service."

Finding them friendly, he continued. "Does your photographer speak English?"

"Yes, enough."

"He should come with you. I can help him with his work."

During their talk, the Rebel and Lily found out that the young reporter was worried about Carranza's welfare as well as his personal safety. They did not ask him many questions, respecting his secret information. Later, he was to fall in love with one of the brigade nurses, Catarina. But he did not tell her until they arrived triumphantly in Coahuila.

On leaving them that afternoon, he said solemnly, "You are on dangerous ground. The Commanding General had spies in all the divisions of the army. He stops at nothing."

They knew he meant General Villa.

When they arrived at their residence, Panchita, the head nurse, and Ruiz, her husband, were waiting for them. Without stopping to hear what she had to say, Lily told them to prepare their own supper and make themselves comfortable. She and the Rebel would go out again but return soon. The chauffeur took them to the hotel where Lieutenant Colonel Manzo had his headquarters. He joined them at supper. This friendly standing invitation was important to the Rebel, as they talked freely, and Captain Rodríguez spoke English. Here Lily had occasion to become acquainted with many phases of the Revolution.

This night, however, the Rebel was worried, especially so because of the chauffeur's warning. Without much ado, she began talking as soon as they were seated. "My lieutenant, why did you point your guns in the direction of the First Chief's residence? You had them in the open square after midnight."

"What a question," he said. "General Villa is the Commanding Officer. I was ordered by the First Chief to place myself and my battalion at his orders." His answer seemed to satisfy him, for he settled back smiling. "General Villa ordered guns there, so guns were there."

"You would have blown up my residence, too? It was also in the way," the Rebel said. She was shocked at his bland attitude toward the First Chief's safety.

"Orders are orders," he said, looking around. Then he whispered to her. "Tell me, now. Did I shoot?"

"Perhaps, you were not ordered to shoot?"

He did not answer her question, only added, "Your boys knew all about it."

She shook her head. "They did not sleep all night. I heard them up." Raising her eyebrows as if in doubt, she said, "I thought there might have been news from the hospital."

"Now, my lieutenant, be serious," she pleaded. "I have to leave early. Please listen. This morning, Lily and I were practically alone, as Montoya was shut up in the darkroom. I heard someone coming up the stairs. It was strange, as I seldom receive anyone without being notified first by the *portero*. There was a clang of spurs and advancing footsteps. I went to the head of the stairs quietly, leaning over the banister but without speaking, as I did not recognize the officer. At the foot of the stairs were soldiers, seemingly awaiting orders.

"'Good day, my captain,' I said. 'What can I do for you? Anybody hurt? More wounded?' All this volley of questions seemed to confuse him.

"'No, Señora,' he said. 'I have orders from my General Villa to take all the silverware and fine china dishes. We know there is plenty of it here. Please turn it over to us. Our *Jefe* is giving a banquet tonight.'

His companions, who had been nervously waiting, now began to come up the stairs.

"Well, my captain, even if you bring a written order, and I see you have none, I will not allow you or anyone else to remove one thing from this house while I am here."

"Did you get frightened?" Manzo asked smiling.

"No, I did not," she replied looking at him seriously. "I told him the house was assigned to the White Cross, and everything in it must be respected. Just then, Montoya and Idar came out, and leaning over the railing, they began to exchange words with them.

"Idar walked down the stairs towards them; we followed. At that moment, the servants came out and Idar told them to serve coffee and refreshments to the men who were leaving."

Without waiting for Manzo to comment, the Rebel turned to Lily and nodded and they arose to go. "I suppose we are being watched wherever we go. Even at the house the servants must be spying on us," she commented with finality.

The silver that Villa's men had wanted was a collection of valuable silverware, vases, and statues. It had been discovered one day when Lily, attracted by a shiny spot on the wall, had carefully peeled some of the wall paper off with a knife. To her astonishment, she uncovered a glass wall cabinet built the full length of the dining room. It had been hurriedly covered with wall paper that matched the other walls. The servants must have known about the treasure and notified some of Villa's officers.

The owner of the great house, Terrazas Muñoz, had been an acquaintance of the Rebel's father. Everywhere she went, the Rebel met old friends who were to testify to her honesty, thus gaining much good will for the revolutionary cause.

"We will make a hasty inventory and turn it over to Captain Valdez," said the Rebel when the silver was discovered. "We will do this in every place we occupy."

In the beginning, the Rebel expressed a stern wish to her brigade that they would always respect as sacred any property entrusted to them. On receiving any private home assigned as headquarters for the Constitutional White Cross, Felipe Aguirre, the treasurer, made an inventory of everything there. Placing the list on the wall at the entrance of the house, it remained there until the house was turned over to proper authorities. The organization was then free from any further obligation. Most of the time the houses were taken over for officers' headquarters, as the building was considered confiscated property. It was in these homes, away from the nerve-racking hospital duty while apparently resting, that the brigade simply changed from one duty to another. Here, beside propaganda work, they did their secretarial work regarding local hospital work.

The Rebel could vouch for her brigade's honesty and loyalty. They received no salary, expected no reward. Living quarters and living expenses were provided them through paymaster Valdez while on hospital duty. After that, it was up to the Rebel to provide for them. The Rebel dared to make the statement that all of the Chief's co-workers worked and gave service alike. She never heard of anyone of them getting a salary or receiving remuneration. It was a Revolution of the people.

When the Rebel and Lily arrived home from supper, Panchita and Ruiz, who was director of the hospital, were still seated at the table over their second cup of coffee. Ruiz began speaking immediately. He had received an urgent message for the Rebel, and as it required an immediate answer, he had opened the letter. It was from the Department of Hacienda (treasury), signed by Don Serapio Aguirre. He needed as many of the Rebel's staff as available to help him in the post office building that evening.

Leaving it to Ruiz to select a group, the Rebel and Lily retired until time to be called. A telephone message came from Señor Aguirre a few minutes later, asking to be received. A hurried refreshing toilet, a change into uniforms, and Mr. Aguirre arrived. Like all the rest of the young officials, he was courteous. Bowing, hat in hand, he had, however, no time for idle chatter. He quickly told the Rebel that General Francisco Villa had issued sixteen million pesos in paper money. He needed help in his department to sort out, make packages, and file numbers of the bills. The money was to be sent out to paymasters in his division. They needed the technical last touch from the trained brigade. The Rebel did not wait for Aguirre to go into detail because it was confidential and would involve a certain responsibility. It would be an honor to have her staff help. They worked several nights, shut up in a guarded room.

This issue was popularly called "Bilimbigues." It was put into circulation by Villa and was rapidly accepted. Everybody was promptly paid off, all merchants honoring it. Though easily destroyed, its face value was to last until the government became stable. Suddenly canceled, later, hundreds suffered great losses. Perhaps because it was so easily defaced, it did not make its return to the treasury.

The government was to move on quickly at any time to Torreón, where Villa was making the way clear for the First Chief to proceed to Durango and Zacatecas. General Alvaro Obregón and General Alvarado were triumphing in Sinaloa, Jalisco, and Guanajuato. General Zapata was waging the war in Morelos.

Beside hospital workers to be contacted, there were social leaders to be won to the cause. It was the powerful rich, who wielded the scepter of charity with their lavish benefit entertainments, that gave the nursing organization its prestige in new territories. To convince the rich of their civic duties during the Revolution was not easy, especially to the terrified bourgeoisie and aristocrats whose faith had been centered on the despised idol, Porfirio Díaz.

It was from the group of women organized by the loyal aristocrat, Marie de Carturegli, that two great women came to serve the Revolutionary Forces of the North. Doña Panchita Verduzco fed soldiers in her own home, moving from place to place wherever she saw that there was need, always advancing with General Obregón until she arrived in Mexico City. She was known to the troops as "Mamá Panchita".

Another brave woman from Sonora was the beautiful Lupita Juárez. She turned over her home to General Carranza, reserving the servant's quarters for her three little children and her brave husband, who handled the railroads in the north. Far into the night she stood over an open fireplace making pots of hot coffee, and handing out hundreds and thousands of tortillas to the troops that passed by. Finally, boarding a caboose, she continued to feed the soldiers until they all came to Mexico City.

While the Rebel was visiting one of the hospitals, a young girl, almost a child, approached the Rebel asking for permission to become a nurse. She had been hunting for the Rebel since she had heard about the brigade's arrival in El Paso.

"You are too young, child," the Rebel said, putting her hands on the girl's shoulders. She was thinking of the responsibility of the care of this beautiful child, scarcely fourteen. However, as the Rebel went about her visit, the girl clung to her hand, evidently determined to have her way and stay.

"Does your mother know about this?" the Rebel asked.

"No, señora," she answered shaking the black curls that hung about her fair face, her large round eyes pleading.

"Where do you live, child?"

"I ran away from my home in El Paso, following the Revolutionists," was her simple answer.

"You must not go around by yourself," the Rebel exclaimed. "You must write your mother. Meanwhile, you may stay with us." The Rebel smiled at the happy girl.

Adelita soon became the joy and pet of the brigade. In one of the deep barred windows of the hospital she would sit, and while sewing or rolling bandages, she sang. Soon there was an echo to her singing. News of these nightly serenades reached the Rebel, who thought them quite harmless and refrained from reprimanding the girl. There were other things more important going on. Adelita's mother had been contacted. The Rebel pondered what she would do with Adelita if the brigade were ordered to move suddenly.

In Villa's territory, Chihuahua, Carranza had organized the government. Manuel Chao as governor was a fearless man, a good soldier and a scholar. He was well prepared for his post. But Villa, who was the Military Commander, soon became displeased with Chao.

One morning when the First Chief, accompanied by Doctor José María Rodríguez, was on a horseback inspection of the camps, they noticed excited activities around General Villa's headquarters. Riding back hurriedly towards their residence and meeting Colonel Juan Dávila, Carranza's trusted bodyguard, the Chief sent him to find out what went on. Lawyer Alfredo Breceda had also suspected something strange. Going up to Colonel Manzo, he inquired of him why troops were forming. The First Chief had not given orders to march.

"My General Francisco Villa has given these orders, I thought with the First Chief's consent," Manzo answered.

Breceda walked quickly into Villa's headquarters. Everything was lively. Villa was giving orders. Seated near the door was General Chao reading a newspaper. Showing it carelessly to Breceda, pointing to the paper as if actually reading it, Chao said, "In a few minutes I will be shot. Villa is naming a firing squad."

Seeing General Ángeles about to leave the room, Breceda joined him. They both passed the guards at the door undisturbed. Breceda hurried to the First Chief to report what was taking place. Dávila had returned without any news. On hearing Breceda's news, Carranza gave Dávila orders to search for Villa and bring him immediately.

In a little while, Dávila, a great big Sonoran and a handsome athlete, stood by Villa's side. Taking him by the arm, Dávila said. "My General, the First Chief wants to see you at once. You are to go with me."

General Villa pulled back a bit, and while he did not refuse to go, he insisted he had something more important to do.

"It can wait. You are going with me now. Those are my orders," Dávila said, pulling him along.

"Boys, I'll be back presently," Villa shouted over his shoulder.

The First Chief was standing near the door of the great audience hall when Villa entered all smiles. The irate Chief exclaimed, "Where is General Chao?" Holding Villa by the shoulders, he shook him.

"Dead by now! I have ordered him shot."

"Take back that order immediately," shouted the Chief. "Dávila, say that General Francisco Villa recalls the order. Bring Chao here."

Villa did not conceal his amusement when Chao appeared pale as a ghost.

"Now," said the First Chief in a relieved tone, "let's have breakfast."

Seeing the Rebel and Lily with Federico Idar leaving their headquarters, Doctor Rodríguez motioned them to his car. He told them all what had just happened, suggesting that they be punctual at their daily visit to the Chief. He might have important orders for them.

The hospital had, by this time, been almost turned over to local nurses, under the supervision of the First Brigade. Señora Elena Bauche Alcalde had already organized her board of directors; her civic workers were in good order. All were Chihuahua personnel and apparently strong for Villa and Ángeles, who formed part of the Constitutional Army.

"Magnón," Lily said frequently. "There are angry faces about us."

From Laredo had come good news to the Chief concerning the Nuevo Laredo branch of the White Cross. Elvira Idar, as president of the zone, had taken over the Nuevo Laredo hospital. Señora Juana Zapata de Lassaux was president of the organization for the state of Tamaulipas. She was loved by all classes, and was unselfish in her work for the nursing corps. Dynamic María Villarreal and doctor's assistant Magdalena Pérez were important co-workers. Elvira Idar was an excellent nurse. She had the backing of plenty of newspaper publicity. Her five brothers had always been connected with some newspaper work, besides having their own weekly. With these three to direct, the Second Brigade of the White Cross was ready to follow General Pablo González and General Jesús Carranza into the state of Nuevo León.

As soon as the Rebel and Lily presented themselves at the palace, they were announced and received immediately. The First Chief looked tired, the strain of sleepless nights and worry having taken its toll. After a few moments of silence following their report, he said very slowly, "You must be ready to leave Chihuahua in twenty-four hours. Give orders to your brigade to pack things most necessary for emergency purposes. A squad of soldiers will be ready to take everything to the train. The wounded, as I see by your report, are well enough to be transferred to a hospital in town. Doctor Angel Castaneous will continue in charge."

"What about the valuables hidden in the underground room in the hospital?" the Rebel asked.

"I know nothing about it," replied the Chief.

"You have not been told?" asked the astonished Rebel. "Please send for General Manuel Chao. He can tell you."

The First Chief rang his gong and advised his confidential man, Don Pancho Serna, to get Chao. When Chao arrived, the First Chief asked what he knew about the hidden treasure at the hospital.

"I remember," Chao said putting his fist to his forehead, beating his head several times. "Joaquín Bauche Alcalde went with me when you," he said turning to the Rebel, "sent for us. I was going to notify the Secretary of the Hacienda. We were no sooner out of the hospital when

General Villa's escorts met us, saying it was urgent for me to meet the General in Torreón. But now, I must go at once to the hospital."

Chao and Joaquín Bauche Alcalde were the most trustworthy friends that the Rebel had. She could hardly keep on talking; she wanted to rush out and see what General Chao would do. But the Chief continued.

"You and your secretary and three of your best men will travel in my car. The nurses will occupy the car next to ours where there will be minor officers of my staff. It will be more of an office. We will go to Torreón, then to Durango. On the train, I will talk further about this trip."

It was not long before Chao, his secretary, and the three White Cross men, Idar, Montoya and Aguirre, returned to the Chief's office.

"*Mi Jefe,*" Chao began, "there is nothing left in the way of cash in the hidden room, only bonds, mining shares and a railroad collateral in the same order as we found them. Moving one of the safes we found an opening large enough for a man to crawl through. It looks as if the bags of money had been dragged out. The property is very large. Someone must have been spying, although we saw no one at the time. The place is guarded, and no one is admitted to the hospital after hours."

"I would have gone without saying anything further, as I had forgotten the incident," said the Rebel to the Chief. Then quickly recalling the incident at their residence, the Rebel told Carranza how she had defied the soldiers who had come to take away the silver from the White Cross headquarters.

"You were very brave," said the First Chief, looking thoughtfully at the Rebel as he twisted the gold chain that secured his watch to his belt. "Braver than I," he laughed. Then completely serious he continued. "We will leave earlier than I intended. You are to be at the station at 6:30 in the morning. I will tell the doctor."

The Rebel and her group went straight to the hospital. The packing was done quietly so that no one would suspect anything. Every box was labeled with a great Constitutional White Cross. When things were ready, the ambulances came for the wounded. The Chihuahua nurses going with them did not stop to consider anything unusual in the change. Drays hauled away the supplies and equipment, one of the men from the brigade going with each load. The doctor had not shown up; perhaps Doctor Rodríguez was conferring with the Chief.

With the brigade was Adelita, who by now was exceedingly popular and well known because of the ardent admirer who had written a song to her. Until now there had been sung only the ribald "La

Cucaracha" that the soldiers had brought back from Sonora and Sinaloa. It was the troops' most popular tune until their arrival in Torreón where the love song "Adelita," or "The Woman the Sergeant Adored," became the favorite. Adela's young soldier, Sergeant Antonio del Rioarmente, who had composed the song, had gone on to Torreón in a troop train to guard the way for the First Chief.

At the hospital, the Rebel and Lily stayed behind with Portachelli. Idar and Aguirre searched the grounds thoroughly. Finally, Montoya, who had been on a hunt by himself, came in gasping for breath.

"There is a small house made in the wall. You can just see the door; it looks like it might go into the street. But I saw a light through the key hole. I pushed it open and there were two old people, a man and a woman. I asked them to let me take their pictures, but they refused, saying their *amo* would kill them. They were left to guard the place."

Thinking it might be the clue to the lost money, Montoya and Idar went back and examined the walls of the hut. After a long while, they found a door in the wall that had been covered with adobe. Opening the door, they saw such pitch blackness they dared not go in. Afraid they were being watched, they left a guard at the place and returned to the hospital. Going to a nearby street corner, Idar hailed a policeman, who in turn called another on horseback. They supervised the locking of the big gate, then they rode off after signing a paper of the brigade's release of the hospital that Aguirre presented.

At the Constitutional White Cross headquarters, the brigade had orders to have supper and see that the servants cleaned up and got to bed. It was important to have them out of the way. Across the street at the Palacio Gamus, where the Chief resided, the Rebel could see much activity. She sat in the dark, watching intently. The nurses did little talking at the supper table. After supper, they prepared their clothes and bathed. They felt sad at leaving Chihuahua, but did not complain. They dressed, and as the night grew longer, gathered around the Rebel and said the rosary, praying for their loved ones.

In that semi-darkness there was a soft knock, first at the iron gate, then on the glass door. Two of the men went down.

"Where is your *jefe*? I wish to speak with her," came a voice from below.

Going downstairs, the Rebel and Lily were surprised to see the First Chief's chauffeur.

"I was sent by the doctor," he began, "to tell you that all the brigade except you and three assistants are to go with me to the train and take their places. I have just put the *Jefe*'s auto on the platform. I have a city car to use now."

The nurses with their baggage went in groups, taking one or two of the men assistants with them. It was almost dawn when the last left. On the last trip, the chauffeur told the Rebel he would call them at five. He would sleep in the car and keep watch at headquarters. Of course, no one slept, especially as they soon noticed shadows of soldiers leaning against the building. They were found to be Colonel Manzo's men, who were guarding the place. Across the way there was another group.

As the chauffeur entered in the early morning, Manzo's men retired and the others crossed the street and waited. Ruiz, one of those who had stayed behind, already had his papers ready to be signed. Leaving the house after a last look, they got in the car. Just as they were closing the doors an officer stepped up.

"The keys please. This will be the headquarters of my *Jefe*."

"Very well," the chauffeur said. "Ruiz, he had better sign your papers. There will be no one at the train to do it."

The officer signed it, another placing his signature, too, evidently his secretary. Then the chauffeur folded the paper carefully and placed it in his pocket.

At the station after coffee and a good breakfast, the chauffeur told them he would not see them again until their arrival in Torreón, unless something happened on the road. The newsboys were on the street selling the *Vida Nueva* early morning edition. When the Rebel was handed one, she read that the Constitutional White Cross was leaving for Chihuahua on the same train as the First Chief. She did not have to wait long for the First Chief, his staff, and the usual crowd. Don Pancho Serna, the Chief's confidential man, told the Rebel to follow him to the train. Lily and the three men were now considered medical assistants, to be constantly at the doctor's orders.

The Rebel was sorry to leave the place. She had loved her busy time in Chihuahua. She wondered, as the train picked up speed and houses began to fly past the window, what was to become of the First Chief's followers. General Ángeles was among those people. Villa seemed to like him and respect his views. God alone knew how all the intrigue and planning, fighting and dying was to end. The grey of morning turned pink and blue, and then came the clear white light of a new day.

The Rebel noticed that Governor Chao was on the train, as Lily pointed him out. "Magnón," she observed, "there is the governor. I bet the First Chief was afraid to leave him behind."

"Nonsense," the Rebel said. "He is a brave man. We are traveling to Torreón where Villas's army awaits the First Chief."

"Magnón," Lily said, "what do you think will happen there?"

"We will have friends in Torreón, General Felipe Ángeles and his aviator, Colonel Federico Cervantes. I met them both at the Military College at Chapultepec."

Lily and the Rebel had taken their seats near the back of the car. In the adjoining coach the brigade traveled. Sitting across from them were Federico, Felipe, Ruiz, and the doctor. Young Adelita had found her place with the nurses, who spoiled her with attention.

Seeing the seat next to the Governor vacant, the Rebel walked over and sat beside him. She wanted to thank him for having asked Lily and herself to be with his wife when their baby was born. They had also been invited to the christening. It had been the Rebel who wrote the account for the *Vida Nueva*. The First Chief liked the article. A few days later when the city of Chihuahua turned out for a benefit given by Señora Elena Bauche Alcalde, he invited the Rebel to use the box next to his for her party. He then asked her to write up the event.

The Rebel had promised Chao's young wife to keep watch over him for fear of a new appearance of treason. The men of the brigade knew this and became his unofficial bodyguard, although he had a faithful staff. He told the Rebel that he was going only as far as Durango with the First Chief. He would not stay away longer from his wife.

The Chief called the governor, and the Rebel returned to her seat. As they were nearing a town, they prepared to go out on the platform to greet the crowd. Once in the station, the governor and the First Chief stood beside Lawyer Isidro Fabela, one of the secretaries, who made a speech. A young girl presented a huge bouquet, which was later on handed to the nurses.

CHAPTER XII
"The Girl Whom the Sergeant Adored"

Colonel Paulino Fontes was in charge of the First Chief's train, such as it was. At that time, the First Chief was glad enough to get any kind of rail transportation. Carranza and his party weren't riding in pullman cars but in what had been first class coaches. The road from Chihuahua to Torreón had been dangerous until the past few days. General Francisco Villa, preceding Carranza, had fought and won a fierce battle in Torreón. He had driven the Federals out of the rich state of Coahuila and would soon pursue them into Durango and Zacatecas. The road was now clear for the First Chief to travel on his way to establish the provisional state government in Coahuila. He was to remain there until the adjacent country was pacified. Each new triumph made it more difficult to know Villa's exact attitude on account of his varying moods. He was not quite pleased because General Chao was traveling on the same train with the First Chief.

Fontes, who spoke good English, came in and sat by Lily and the Rebel. Travel was slow because of the recently reconstructed road. He spoke encouragingly about the trip, and the Rebel asked him to go in and tell the nurses the good news. She felt that they were somewhat worried about the journey.

Seeing the First Chief sitting alone, the Rebel walked across the aisle and sat beside him.

"You are creating an army of friends for us," he said pleasantly. "That pleases me. I am glad you came.

"We will remain a short time in Torreón, only two or three days. You will not be able to organize your White Cross until you return. But instruct your head nurse to visit hospitals. See that our wounded are attended by loyal nurses and followers to safeguard against any outbreak instigated by Federalist propaganda."

"I have seen to that," the Rebel answered. "I have ordered my assistants to confiscate the first printing shop they find, and publish immediately two sheets of news. They already have the material. We know what is going on. They are only waiting for an order from Captain Valdez."

He nodded his head approvingly, then added, "I will notify you of the time of our departure from Torreón. Your secretary and three assistants will accompany you. I don't know myself what might happen on this trip." He seemed disturbed, although he appeared unconscious of any imminent personal danger.

The Rebel, wishing to reassure him, spoke what she had been thinking for a long time. "I am glad to believe that there is not one among us who does not wish from the bottom of his heart for the day to come speedily when you will have the Mexican nation united, more harmonious in action than it has ever been." Inwardly, she sighed; while talking bravely, she thought of the insurmountable barriers that had yet to be overcome.

The Rebel excused herself as the Chief was approached by his secretary bringing telegrams. She heard the Chief say after reading the first message that the situation did not look good. He sat for a long time holding the dispatch in his hand.

She went into the next car where the corps of nurses was napping. "Ruiz," she said, sitting next to him, "when we arrive in Torreón, no matter what time it is, find out what newspaper has been confiscated. Felipe Aguirre will get an order from Captain Jesús Valdez to occupy the office. Idar can write on the Chief's forces, González' triumphs at Matamoros, and Obregón's victories. Glorify General Villa's loyalty to the Chief. We must disarm him with praises of his patriotism. Place a big white cross emblem across the front sheet. Bring the papers to me at the headquarters at the hotel. You already know the routine, triumphal entry, the banquet, and dance."

It was late when the Rebel returned to her place. Lily was asleep. The seats had been drawn together and though they were hard, at least it was an emergency resting place. Across the aisle, almost opposite them, the First Chief was sleeping, his hat covering his face. She lay down by Lily and was soon asleep.

It was several hours later when the train suddenly stopped. A few minutes later, the conductor, carrying a dim light on his arm, touched the Rebel's shoulder.

"The Chief says for you both to come," he said quietly. "This is Santa Rosalía. We will stop here for the night. He is waiting for you. Your three assistants will go with me. Only those in this car, the Chief's bodyguard, and part of the 4th Battalion will go."

Reaching the platform, they saw General Chao, Espinosa Mireles, and the chauffeur sitting in the front seat of the waiting auto. In the back Lily and the Rebel got in with the First Chief. Nothing was said by any of them. The night was dark and the road rough. After a short ride, they stopped at the door of an inn, the best hotel in the place. Dim lights flickered in the iron lamps hanging in the big hall. At the threshold, the party stopped. A little band composed of a guitar and three violins played the Mexican National anthem softly for the First Chief. The men solemnly took off their hats.

General Chao, taking the Rebel and Lily by the arm, escorted them to a large bedroom with all the doors standing open.

"The Chief will occupy the first room. He will probably have a light long in the night. My room is next to his, so you can sleep tranquilly. If you need anything, rap at my door," he said, leaving them.

Alberto Peraldi, the Chief's nephew, got busy sending telegrams and taking dictation. The patio was full of officers and soldiers standing in groups. Colonel Fontes arrived with the three White Cross men. They would occupy the room across the hall from the Rebel's, and take turns guarding the two women's room. Lily wasted no time in securing the doors and placing the little revolver under her pillow. They blew out the lamp and said their prayers.

As there were lights and noise in the other rooms, the Rebel lay awake. She could see through the cracks in the door that led into General Chao's room. Throwing himself on the bed fully dressed, he had but a short rest before an orderly came to call him. The Chief wanted him. He returned to nap several times. Finally, before sleep overtook the Rebel, she tiptoed to the two doors and the window, making sure they were locked. Soon she was dreaming of her children and her husband, traversing the endless maze between the dusty little Mexican town of Santa Rosalía and Laredo.

It was late when they were awakened the next morning by Montoya knocking at the door. "Quickly," he called. "The Chief says he's only waiting for you. I have a coach at the door."

On arriving at the station, they had their coffee and pan dulce. After the usual morning salutations, they took their places in the coach. During the night, a lawyer, Calixto Maldonado, and a distinguished woman had boarded the train. She was his wife from a wealthy family of Maderista leanings. They were Yucatecos. From nearly every state came people to be near the First Chief, especially those who had political importance or aspired to some. Each person in turn approached the Chief with his own personal business.

Going to the next car, the Rebel had a long talk with her boys. They had mingled with minor officers during the night and had heard much.

"Montoya," she asked. "What makes you think there might be trouble?" She suspected, but it was better to hear it from someone else. Taking photographs, he had the opportunity of hearing much unreserved conversation.

"Since Villa's victory in Torreón there are bands of Federals lurking about. They might try to wreck the train," was his answer.

"What about it, Portachelli?" she asked, turning to him. "You are one of us. You should know."

"Just what they are all saying," he answered, shrugging his shoulders. "Beside the Federals, the Chief has troubles in his own ranks. There is friction between Villa and the Chief."

"You know this road," she drew the writer Idar aside. "What about the dangerous curve at the halfway point between Chihuahua and Torreón?"

"That would be the place for something to happen. Rocks from the cliffs could be rolled down easily enough and wreak the train," he replied. "But we stayed so long in Santa Rosalía, they may have lost track of the train timetable."

When the daily official business of the corps had been attended to, Lily and the Rebel sat close to an open window two seats ahead of the First Chief. When the Rebel wanted to know what was going on behind her, she took out her mirror and, while apparently powdering her face, could see who sat next to the Chief. She also kept her eye on the road.

The small military guard rode next to the caboose, then came the officers and nurses, and next the First Chief's car behind the engine, cars of the Fourth Battalion. The Rebel noticed that since the preceding night there had been a change in the order of the military escort.

At noon, Francisco Serna came in with a basket of lunches and light refreshments. The *Jefe* sent him across to the Rebel and Lily, who were sitting with Mrs. Maldonado. Then helping himself, he continued talking to Governor Chao.

After a while the Rebel went across to the Chief's seat. Most of the occupants of the car were either trying to sleep or read. Thanking the Chief for sending them their lunch was an excuse to sit near him. They did not talk, but kept their eyes on the road. Suddenly the train began to move a little faster. They were nearing the curve which allowed a full view of the engine as it encircled the mountain. The Chief had his eyes on the engine. The train was now going much faster. A white flag appeared waving proudly above the engine, another hanging from a window. Carranza grasped the Rebel's arm and looked again. The flags were gone.

A few minutes later Idar entered, rather pale. Leaning over the Rebel's shoulder, he whispered, "It is all over. We have passed the danger zone. A few shots were exchanged, but so far away that only those who were on the alert could have heard them."

In the three rear coaches some continued to sleep, some to read. Only Carranza and a handful of the Constitutional White Cross Corps knew what had happened.

The Chief fixed his glasses to look at a message he was being handed. Then he looked at the Rebel, saying strangely, "You are very independent in your activities. Until now, there has been nothing to censure, but there could be."

On arriving in Torreón, the First Chief and his staff received a welcome, but not as magnificent as in Chihuahua. However, they were all tired after the long speeches and the banquet. The Chief withdrew to confer with the leaders of the zone he was about to enter. General Triana and the two Arrieta brothers, Domingo and Mariano, were eager to escort him over their conquered territory.

After a short rest at the hotel, the Rebel called a meeting of the corps in one of the private parlors. General Felipe Ángeles, who was in Torreón with General Villa, had arranged headquarters for them. From the balcony of the Rebel's room she could see across the street the residence that the First Chief and his staff would occupy. General Ángeles' headquarters was nearby in a long official building. There his battalion was lodged.

General Ángeles had left a message for the Rebel. He would call in the morning with Colonel Federico Cervantes, head of his staff, bringing horses for the Rebel and her secretary and one for the photographer. They would visit the battlefield and see for themselves the condition of things. There were still skirmishes and fighting guerrillas in the surrounding country.

At the breakfast table next morning, they were greeted by Colonel Cervantes, who escorted them to the front of the hotel, where three saddled horses were waiting for them. General Ángeles and the Rebel rode side by side; behind them, Colonel Cervantes and Lily. Montoya and the General's aide followed. There was little conversation until they were out of town. The General would turn toward the Rebel once in a while, saying "Loosen your bridle," or "Tighten your bridle." He readily understood that Lily was a better horsewoman than the Rebel.

"You can see this is terrible," General Ángeles said as he shook his head sadly as they approached the scene of the recent battle. "Imagine how many wounded we had, all those dead horses lying about."

As they stood facing the battle scene, while Montoya was taking pictures, the Rebel's horse began prancing about impatiently. Finally, he broke off in a frantic run, having gotten his left hoof entangled in a loose piece of barbed wire that cut and terrified him. Lily and Cervantes caught up with the runaway horse, blocking his way. General Ángeles leaned over and took a firm hold on the reins, talking gently to the horse.

After riding on for several miles over the battle ground, they turned back to the city. Now they were all conversing freely.

"I understand your stay here will be short," said Ángeles to the Rebel. "Or perhaps, you do not intend to go to Durango?"

"I am going with a few of the corps. The rest will wait here until we return," she answered. Then she spoke impulsively:

"My General, I wish to ask you a favor."

"I am at your orders," he answered politely.

"It is necessary that we call on General Villa. We are in his zone. As it is hard to get an interview without great delay, I beg of you to get me an audience this afternoon with him."

"My general receives in the afternoon," he replied after a short, studied silence. "Meet me in his reception rooms. I will announce you and take you in."

They separated at the hotel, the general to review his troops, the Rebel to hold a meeting. The brigade all had dinner together in the great dining hall. It was full of officers from every division. Some were leaving; others had just arrived. There were many *abrazos* and greetings. The brigade, notified of the Rebel's departure in the early morning, had gone to their rooms. She had told them that each one should decide and write what she most wanted, so that the Rebel could get it from the Chief. On returning to Coahuila, she would present their petitions to him. Having been printed in Laredo, their certificates should have arrived. She had left Ezequiel Ruiz and Panchita in charge.

After dinner with the brigade, which was editing the paper, Adelita came into the Rebel's room singing gaily.

"I wish to be married, Señora Magnón," she said. "Antonio has told me he loves me."

"What about your mother, Adelita?"

"I have already written her," came the girl's prompt answer.

"Magnón," Lily coaxed, "let her marry the young man. She will be well protected."

"We will talk it over when he can come to see me," said the Rebel.

"Tonight. He will come tonight. He went off early this morning with his general," the excited girl skipped from the room laughing.

The nurses had all afternoon to do whatever they wished. Adelita strayed away. She could ride well and had followed her sergeant from Del Río. The troops were engaged in combat near Torreón on the road to Chihuahua. Carrying a canteen of water to his general, Carlos E. Martínez, Antonio was about to cross the firing line. Adelita screamed to him to stop. It was too late. A bullet ended his life. Brought back to town by the General's aide, Adelita fainted in the Rebel's arms. Later when she felt better, she decided to join the active fighting, to go to León, Guanajuato, where the fighting was thickest. Nothing else would console her.

Fortunately, Dr. Francisco de la Garza, an elderly doctor who had been in Laredo in charge of the Carrancista wounded in the Rebel's home, had just arrived. He was with General Jesús Carranza's forces near Nuevo León on a mission to the First Chief. The Rebel begged the doctor to take Adelita and two other nurses with him. She would be better off away from Torreón.

Adelita was in León, Guanajuato, when Fierros attacked Lagos de Moreno. The Rebel did not see her again until they found each other in Mexico City. The song continued to follow Adelita, weaving its music into the fabric of the Revolution.

At the appointed time, the Rebel and Lily were at General Villa's headquarters. What a contrast to those of other generals' headquarters. General Ángeles came in. Bowing to them, he went into Villa's office. A glimpse of the inside of the room made Lily shiver.

"Magnon, I'm afraid. Are you?"

"No, not as long as General Ángeles is here," was the Rebel's reply.

After waiting a full half hour sitting on one of the hard benches in the waiting room, General Ángeles opened the door for them to enter. The Rebel approached Villa without an introduction. His harsh manner made her defiant. He was surrounded by his famous bodyguards who adored him. Armed to the teeth, they watched with a steady gaze as the women entered the room, and showed no intention of leaving their chief during the interview.

"We are part of the Constitutional White Cross, working with the army," the Rebel began, determined to dominate the situation.

"You belong to the Chief's staff," Villa replied quickly.

"We belong to the Constitutional Army, serving every division," she answered, taking up the gauntlet. "We come to place ourselves at your orders, to get your permission to work in this zone, which you command."

"*Compadre,*" Villa said, turning to his friend, General Tomás Urbina. "How is this? They want to care for my wounded. What a request."

"Señoras," he turned to them, "I care for my own soldiers."

"So you do. We know it well, my general," she replied immediately. "We congratulate you for all you did for your brave men who were under our care in Chihuahua."

"Oh!" he laughed. "You are head of the White Cross. I have heard much about your bravery. I had no time to call on you there with always a fight ahead. I have no time for calling. I only give orders," Again he laughed, and drawing up two wooden chairs to a small round table cluttered with empty beer bottles, he sat down in one of them.

"I love my soldiers," he said as the Rebel took the other chair. "They are the best in the world. Just as General Felipe Ángeles is the best artillery commander."

Looking straight at the Rebel, tapping the table with his whip, he added, "You are a friend of my General Ángeles?"

"I have known him for many years," she answered tersely. "But we are here to serve all the army, no general in particular."

Hitching his chair up closer to the table, he leaned over to the Rebel, speaking almost in a whisper, his gruff mood changing with the familiar Villa magic, "I shall tell you my story, myself."

He told how he had become a bandit in his youth. In Porfirio Díaz's time, enraged at a grave offense caused by a rich landowner, he had sought justice, but none was meted out to him. No court did justice to the poor in those days. Rich *hacendados* too often outraged the comeliest daughters of the peons. The peons were subject to the law of "el Fugo" (of the peon's running away and being shot in the back by the henchmen of the *hacendados*).

Protesting his lot, Villa fled to the mountains to mete out justice for himself, becoming a bandit who plagued the wealthy landowners. When the Madero Revolution broke out, he joined the cause, becoming a fearless officer. At the treacherous death of President Madero, Villa joined Carranza. Finishing his story, Villa drew the back of his hand across his eyes. His assistant, blowing his nose loudly, looked admiringly at his general.

"I serve my country and the First Chief. I will always be loyal to him. Remember, I will always be loyal." Villa's voice rose loudly in ringing sentences the Rebel was never to forget.

Getting close to the Rebel, Lily begged her to leave.

"What does this *güera* say?" he asked pushing back his chair and giving himself room to stand.

"My general," the Rebel replied, "she says we are taking too much of your time."

"That is true," he said, looking thoughtfully at the blonde, slender Lily until she dropped her eyes in confusion.

"They tell me she is a good shot and rides well," he said waving for the door to be opened.

Escorting them to the door, Villa turned to the chief of staff and said, "These people, they are our friends."

"Magnón," Lily said as the door closed behind them, "I kept praying he would not remember the day he sent for the silverware. What do you think he meant when he said we were brave?"

"Lord only knows," replied the Rebel, glad to be outside again. "I'll ask the general about our interview when we meet again. We will probably not see Villa again for a long time."

American newspapers had charged Villa with innumerable vices and sins: that he was a continual pursuer of young girls, corrupt, immoral, faithless, bloodthirsty, destitute of culture and intelligence. He was said to have no following except the ignorant, whom he inspired with awe. He was rumored to have had an aged couple beheaded because they protested his running away with their daughter. If all the assertions were only partly true, what would happen to Mexico if it were delivered to Villa and his followers? On the same stage with the world's great generals, Villa would be only a rough buffoon with a knack for leading men in a furious charge in battle.

When Villa asked the Rebel what she thought of him, she had pointed to the white cross on her arm. He recognized her official capacity with the army, admitting that his men needed the help of the Constitutional White Cross. There had been over three thousand wounded in the battle of Torreón.

When the Rebel and Lily arrived at their headquarters in late afternoon, the nurses were talking over their war experiences with Doctor de la Garza, and he was entertaining them with news from Laredo. A solemn, brokenhearted Adelita was packing to leave. As they entered, Lily went to salute the doctor.

Esparza, Idar, Ruiz, and Montoya had finished their printing job. Their small paper looked beautiful to the Rebel. "I am sure the Chief will like this," she said. "It is well-timed."

"Montoya, tonight at this last banquet I want you to bring your camera. Take some pictures, then keep your lens where Governor Chao will be sitting. Keep it there. That will also take in the First Chief. If the lights go out, keep your camera in position and ready to take a picture of the Governor's place the minute the lights are turned on.

"Idar, stand behind Chao's chair. When the lights go out, Esparza and Ruiz are to come into the room and go straight to the Chief, then to Villa, and down the table placing a paper at each place. Idar will keep against the wall until Aguirre enters and hands the Governor a telegram.

"Now get yourselves ready. Discuss this with no one. I'll meet you here after the banquet," the Rebel concluded her outline of plans to the men.

It worked out almost exactly as planned. The Rebel wrote a message on a telegraph blank to Governor Chao, demanding his presence because of important news from Chihuahua. Aguirre delivered the message during the time Lawyer Alessio Robles was speaking. Chao read the telegram and waited for Robles to finish. During the applause he pushed back his chair. At that moment the lights went out. Idar in the darkness stood behind Chao's chair, after having been pushed roughly by a waiter. The lights turned on; Montoya took a picture. General Chao's chair was empty. The waiter and Idar were already in the street having a tussle. When Governor Chao had left the banquet, he went directly to the White Cross headquarters.

"Please forgive me for frightening you," the Rebel greeted him. "Nothing has happened to your wife. I was afraid something was going to happen to you. This afternoon as we sat so long in General Villa's waiting room, I overheard remarks and snatches of conversation of what would happen at tonight's banquet.

"Thank God, the danger is over. Go back to the banquet. We leave tomorrow for Durango. Please go back to Chihuahua." The Rebel felt that Chao's luck could not hold forever with Villa around.

Chao returned immediately, and there was no scandal. Everyone was reading and commenting on the Constitutional White Cross' paper. It had praises for everyone's loyalty to the First Chief, and to the united Constitutional Army. Colonel Manzo was proud of it, as was Lawyer Juan de Dios Bojórguez, who was a forceful writer. After the banquet, the Chief went home escorted by Villa and Governor Chao after riding over the city in harmony, making plans for future victories.

Waiting at the station to leave for Durango, the part of the Constitutional White Cross which was leaving gathered in groups. General Manuel Chao approached the Rebel, handing her a large envelope, which Lily placed in her portfolio to be opened later. He spoke only a few words to them before returning to salute the Chief, who was standing on the platform greeting the crowd.

Colonel Fontes escorted the Rebel and Lily to their places in the Chief's car. Lawyer Calixto Maldonado and his wife were in the seat next to them, lawyers Iglesias Calderón and Isidro Fabela in front. Across the way from them was the First Chief. Francisco Serna had brought a table for the Chief to work on; persons wishing to discuss anything with him could sit across from the Chief.

General Felipe Ángeles had gone to Saltillo, where there was fighting, to make the way clear for the First Chief on his return to Torreón, and thence into the State of Coahuila.

Opening the envelope from General Chao, the Rebel took out his picture. On it was written the memorable date of his second escape, May 8, 1914.

"How about General Chao? Will he remain in Torreón until you return?" the Rebel inquired of the Chief.

"No," he answered. "Chao is to return to Chihuahua, where he is much needed."

Understandingly, the Rebel said no more. But Lily was told by the Chief's secretary that Villa and Chao had patched up their differences. Evidently General Ángeles had been the wise mediator.

While talking over things with the Rebel, the First Chief mentioned again that he wanted her to write the interpretation and story of the Revolution for posterity.

"I will try to do it when the Revolution is over," she said. "It is good to see the end of things."

"We will not stay long in Durango. You will occupy a suite in the hotel. I will expect you to dinner the day after our arrival," he told her.

The First Chief's arrival in Durango was equal to none. Thousands awaited him at the station. Cathedral bells rung as prominent citizens proclaimed Carranza's popularity. The mining state with all of its wealth was at the Chief's command. A fine patriot was its Governor Ingeniero Pastor Roaix. The military chiefs of Durango, Mariano and Domingo Arrieta did honors royally, vying with each other to please the Chief, although they were at dagger's point with the governor.

From the balcony of the official palace Miguel Alessio Robles delivered a speech on the promising future for the Constitutionalists. That night Lily and the Rebel stood on the same balcony with the Chief, who introduced them to the Governor.

The next day at lunch, Lily and the Rebel arrived in good time to meet new members of the personnel from Durango. The Rebel sat at a table on the Chief's right, Lily on his left. Next to Lily was Iglesias Calderón. There were many new faces which the Rebel later on learned to know and love. Pastor Roaix spoke warmly of his state, its future in national development. He was a noted geologist who not only loved his state, but knew the value of its abundant resources. After the dinner, Roaix took the Rebel and Lily to visit the famous "Cerro de Mercado" mine. Its unexploited resources could supply the world with metal for an indefinite time.

The Rebel became friendly with the Roaix family. Señora Roaix consented to be president of the Constitutional White Cross in the state of Durango.

On the 13th of May, while they were in Durango, a messenger came to the hotel with a package for the Rebel. It contained a large size photograph of the Chief with an inscription to the President of the Constitutional White Cross. Carranza wrote, praising the Rebel's works with the organization, her cooperation in bringing friends to their aid, and her writing in advocacy of unity for an early triumph of the Revolution. It pleased the Rebel because it was historic approval of her efforts, embarrassing her, however, because there were many more powerful writers around the Chief. These men were her lifelong friends: Felix F. Palavicini, Alessio Robles, Isidro Fabela, and Juan de Dios Bojórquez.

"The march of providence is not bound," she said to Lily concerning the Chief's salutation. "It does not trouble itself to follow out today's consequences on the principle which it lay out yesterday."

To the Rebel, Carranza was a monumental figure, an able statesman. When he addressed crowds from trains, at stations, from portals and palaces, he held the hearers spellbound.

Leonor Villegas de Magnón upon her return from New York to Laredo, Texas, in 1895.

Leonor Villegas and Adolfo Magnón on their wedding day, January 10, 1906.

Portrait of V. Carranza given to Leonor Villegas de Magnón—"A mi estimada amiga Sra. Leonor Villegas de Magnón, 1914."

The Villegas residence at the corner of Farragut and Flores in Laredo, Texas, circa 1890.

Leonor Villegas de Magnón, Alfredo Breceda, secretary to governor of Coahuila, and Lily Long.

International bridge over the Río Bravo/Río Grande between Laredo, Texas, and Nuevo Laredo, Tamaulipas, México, circa 1913.

Mexican residents of Laredo, Texas, march in a demonstration in support of the democratic cause in Mexico. Mounted on the horse, Melquíades García carries a flag promoting return to the Liberal Constitution of 1857.

Leonor Villegas de Magnón and Aracelito García posing with their White Cross flag, 1914.

A group of pupils in Leonor Villegas de Magnón's first kindergarten, 1912.

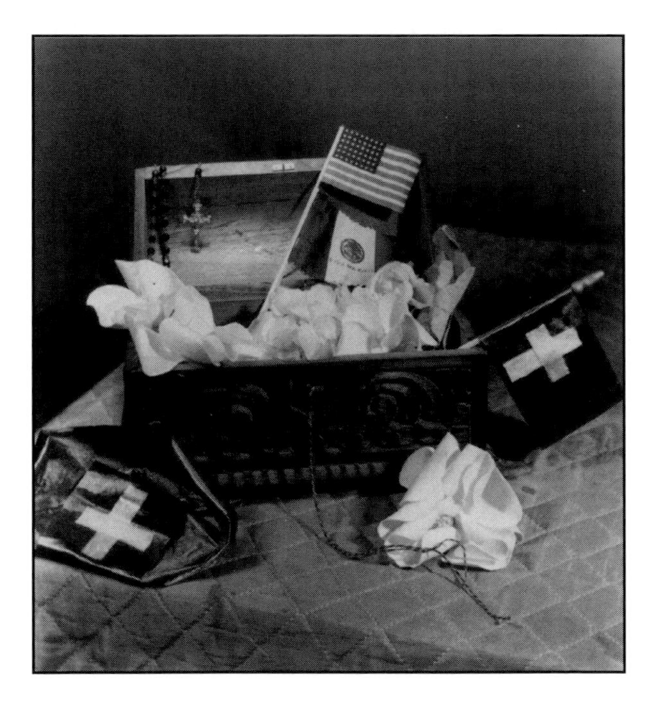

Contents of the carved box Pancho kept for Leonor Villegas de Magnón.

From left to right: Leonor Villegas de Magnón, Guillermo Martínez Celis and Aracelito García.

Leonor Villegas de Magnón offering condolences to the family of a deceased soldier.

At the home of Leonor Villegas de Magnón, 811 Flores Avenue, a group of the first nurses to serve as volunteers along with two editors of *El Progreso*. From left to right: nurses Margarita Alonzo, Elvira Idar, Panchita Ruíz, Angelita Esparza, Leonor Villegas de Magnón, Catalina Guevara, Nena Magnón (Leonor Grubbs).

Another group of volunteer nurses in front of the offices of *El Progreso*. From left to right: Adela Bruni, Leonor Villegas de Magnón, Chente Farías, Paz Martínez, Margarita de la Garza, Tina Merriweather, María Juárez and Blasita Flores.

Medical relief corps and assistants which form the Laredo, Texas Brigade in their Cruz Blanca uniforms. From left to right: standing, Emilia Martínez, Araceli García, Captain Guillermo Martínez, Leonor Villegas de Magnón, María de la Luz Velásquez; sitting, Adelfa Martínez, Librada Leyva, Jovita Garza, Eudelia Esparaza, María G. Martínez, Angelita Gaona, Angelita Ruiz, Catalina Mireles.

Part of the Cruz Blanca Brigade preparing to leave to El Paso, Texas, to cross the border at Ciudad Juárez. From left to right: José Ugarte, Jesusa Guerra, Margarita de la Garza, Gilberto Guerra, Olivia Guerra, Aurora de la Garza, Rafael Rentería, Luis Vela, Aracelito García, Rosa de la Garza, Eduardo Guerra and Jerónimo Marín.

Out of the first groups of medical volunteers. From left to right: unidentified man, Reverend Neftalí Avila (Presbyterian Minister), Leonor Villegas de Magnón, María Alegría. Jovita Idar, Rosa Chávez and Elvira Idar, 1914, 1914. (Courtesy of Jovita López.)

Group of nurses, assistants and doctors with Leonor Villegas de Magnón and Lily Long in front of the Chihuahua hospital.

Hospital in Chihuahua, patio in which the buried treasure was found. Leonor Villegas de Magnón, Lily Long, Dr. José María Rodríguez, Dr. Angel Castellanos, Don Venustiano Carranza.

Lily Long, Venustiano Carranza and Leonor Villegas de Magnón.

General Pánfilo Natera greets Venustiano Carranza in Durango.

From left to right: Lily Long, unidentified man, Leonor Villegas de Magnón, Venustiano Carranza and Luis Caballero.

Leonor Villegas de Magnón, Venustiano Carranza and Constitutionalist officers and nurses.

Alfredo Breceda giving official recognition to the Cruz Blanca. Leonor Villegas de Magnón receives documentation, June 1914.

Members of the Cruz Blanca at Monterrey, June 28, 1914. From left to right: standing (1) Jesús Pérez Fierro, (4) Captain Rodolfo Villalba, (5) María Morales, (7) Coronel Eugenio Canales, (8) Don Faustino García, (9) Eduardo Idar; sitting, (1) María Villarreal, (2) Leonor Villegas de Magnón, (4) Lily Long and her son Robert at her feet.

The 33 Constitutionalists who returned to The Rebel's house at 811 Flores Avenue in Laredo, Texas, after having been detained at Fort McIntosh.

CHAPTER XIII
The Rebel Is Concerned

Among Carranza's friends, his *absolom,* and one who still remains faithful to his memory was lawyer Luis Cabrera. He was of singular strength of character, a master of parliamentary procedure, an eloquent speaker, and a leading thinker in governmental reform. His influence was notable in the Madero Revolution and had impregnated the Carranza Revolution. Félix F. Palavicini was another great man whose wisdom and faith encouraged the Constitutional movement. General Francisco Murguía stands out as a notable military figure. He, too, was to remain faithful to Carranza.

In Durango, a young newspaperman, Gaxiola, had become absorbed in the work of the White Cross Corps. During the trip there, the work was organizing and spreading information about the Constitutionalist nursing corps. Señora Roaix had taken over the nursing and hospital division, and it was running smoothly.

A good-looking young officer, General Pánfilo Natera, had come to Durango to escort the First Chief to Zacatecas, where he was eager for the people to know Carranza. Although the stay in Durango was planned to be of short duration, the military commanders of that zone saw that there might be danger to the Chief's life if he went on to Zacatecas immediately. The extra time during the enforced stay was spent in making future plans.

Gustavo Espinosa Mireles, the Chief's private secretary, was engulfed in unceasing work. The Rebel never remembered his having a single moment of leisure, unless it was during the brief hours of sleep. Nothing passed him by. Newspapers had to be read, reporters interviewed. There was an immense amount of press material to be gotten out. All information sent to headquarters by subordinates had to be acknowledge or answered. He often did his work while accompanying the Chief on long auto trips of inspection through country dominated by Constitutionalists. From early daybreak far into the night, the Chief and his secretaries were busy. All his staff worked long and hard. Their only aim was to reach Mexico City in triumph.

The Rebel and Lily were invited several times to small dinners with the Chief. Alberto Salinas, the Chief's nephew, was often present. Though quite young, he was head of aviation for the Constitutionalists. He was brave and loved adventure. He loved music, too, and the Chief enjoyed hearing him play and Lily sing. These were brief, free moments allowed by the time spent in Durango.

The Chief would ask the Rebel her opinion of some of the dinner guests. "What about Iglesias Calderón?" the Chief questioned with a smile. "Is he a great writer?"

"I think his fingernails are too long," she answered unwittingly. "As he placed his hands on the table I noticed what a long reach! If he clawed anyone's reputation with words as sharp as his nails, it would be a serious matter. Besides, he has it in for Ceballos, whom we consider a strong adherent of yours."

"What about Santos Chocana?" the Chief asked.

"Well, as a poet I like him, although I have not talked much with him yet. He is a Latin, not a genuine Mexican. I hope to disarm him with kindness," she replied.

The nerves of the Chief's party were being taxed by inactivity. Each idle day prolonged the nervous waiting. At one of the banquets, Captain Abelardo Rodríguez was a little late. When everyone was seated, his place remained unoccupied. Finally he walked in, handsome, immaculately uniformed. As he pulled out his chair quietly, he heard someone make a remark about his late arrival. Not in the humor for such remarks, he pulled out his revolver and fired in the direction from which he thought the insult had come. Fortunately, no one was hit, but the Chief ordered Rodríguez's immediate arrest.

The Rebel was sitting at the Chief's right, Lily at his left. These places they always occupied as an honor to the organization they represented. The Rebel immediately pushed back her chair and, excusing herself, stood up. Lily seeing this, followed her. As the confusion brought in stragglers, their vacant places were soon filled. The few who noticed their leaving thought they were only returning to duty.

Abelardo was Manzo's best friend, and a friend of the White Cross. The Rebel felt it was up to the corps to mutely protest his arrest. In a few minutes, she had organized her group for action. The Rebel, Lily, and each of the assistants who had come with them to Durango took turns sitting at the door of Abelardo's prison. When it came time for her conference with Carranza in the afternoon, the Rebel was not present at the Palacio. Word reached the First Chief that the Rebel was protesting Rodríguez's arrest.

Montoya took photographs of the protesting pickets. When he had given them to the Chief, he returned to the Rebel with the news that the official party was to leave early the next morning. They were all to meet at the station.

The next day, Montoya came hurriedly to the Rebel's hotel. "Everyone is at the station. Please come. The Chief is waiting. We are in danger," he begged her.

"Tell the Chief I cannot leave while one of his men is in prison. If the Federals attack here, Abelardo will be considered a political prisoner," was her firm reply.

A few minutes later, Idar came. He called through the closed door of the Rebel's room. "The Chief says, all right, for you to come on."

An order must have been sent to the prison at the same time because, as the Rebel boarded the Chief's car, Abelardo was getting on the one occupied by the Fourth Battalion.

Lily, who could wait no longer, walked back through several cars. Seeing Rodríguez she pleaded, "Abelardo, please behave yourself. You might be president of Mexico one day."

"Please do not let the Chief hear you say that. It will make things worse for me," he replied, looking up at her worried face.

With fighting going on in some parts of Zacatecas, the capital was not in control of the Constitutionalists. However, the Chief resolved to go as far as he could. Some of the staff remained in Durango and new members were added. There was Lawyer Iglesias Calderón, historian of Mexico, Chief of the Liberal Party. At the invitation of the First Chief, José Santos Chocana, a well-known poet and writer, had also come on the trip.

The train moved slowly with guards sitting on the tops of the cars. The military escorts on board were on the alert. Finally, they arrived at a beautiful spot surrounded by mountains. The train could go no further, because the roadbed had not been repaired since it had been torn up by the retreating Federals. General Natera and State Secretary Acuña Navarro had arranged for autos to drive the party to Sombrerete, Natera's headquarters. The Rebel and Lily traveled in a car with Ignacio Bonillas, Secretary of Communication, and two other officers. Since Bonillas spoke English, the conversation was in that language all the way.

The Rebel was thrilled by the marvelous scenery. On both sides of the road were great stones resembling ruins of ancient castles; each mound was isolated from the other so that the site seemed to be the remains of some great, ancient city. But they were soon to see another marvel of human origin a mile or so before entering the town. There extended before them a panorama of great green cactus and maguey plants. At close range, people could be seen walking about among them. It became evident that houses had been built from the cactus and maguey with the insides of the walls plastered with thick mud. No one would have approached the place looking for the colony, it was such a well camouflaged, fortified city.

In Sombrerete, the Rebel and Lily were escorted to the fine residence of the Covalrubio's, whose family included five beautiful young daughters. For their guests, the girls had laid a finely drawn work cloth and served a meal of fried *cabrito,* tortillas, and chili sauce. While they were at supper, an officer called, bringing invitations for the dance which was to start at midnight. The officer said on leaving that the Chief had said to consider the invitation an order for the young ladies and the Rebel. The Rebel replied at once that she and her secretary were too tired to attend.

As the girls went off to dress, Señora Covalrubio came over to the Rebel, taking her hand. "You see what happens," she said sadly, "we are glad, my husband and I, to help the Revolution, but the officers are very demanding with our daughters. They are asked everywhere. The entertainments get rough toward morning, and it makes the officers angry when their father takes the girls home. I am always afraid that he will get impatient, and that would start trouble."

The Rebel suggested having her White Cross boys escort the young women. The white crosses on their arms would insure respect and safety for the party. At midnight, a coach was standing at the door and the girls left with members of the Rebel's corps. Lily went to bed and was soon oblivious to her surroundings, but the Rebel could not go to sleep. She heard the muted voice of the girls' mother saying her rosary, repeating the lulling prayers, adding to each bead, "God help our daughters."

Toward morning, the mother came into the Rebel's room. Kissing the astonished guest's hand, she cried, "Thank God they are here."

No sooner had the house gotten quiet than a band of troubadours started a serenade. The Rebel put out her light. Five songs were sung, one for each girl. Sending the mother for refreshments, the Rebel decided to talk to the young soldiers. Through the barred window, she handed them the fine wine and tacos, speaking gently to them. "Boys, your general is a fine man. Follow him. This campaign may be a perilous one, and these girls will be the ones to nurse the wounded. You may be among them. I beg respect for them."

They listened quietly, then one spoke up, "Si, Señora," he said. "You are right. We leave in the morning for the capital of Zacatecas. There will be fierce fighting."

They sang one more song, "Adiós, Adiós." When the last notes of their soft voices had died, and as the guitar chord had ceased echoing, the sounds of their footsteps on the stone pavement came back through the darkness to the women listening in the house.

In the morning after breakfast, the mother came to the Rebel's room. Feeling that her family was in constant danger, she wanted to speak to the First Chief to ask him a favor. The Rebel promised to send a note to the Chief asking him to call before he went to his afternoon conference. The girls prepared refreshments for their prominent guest and practiced several songs for him.

At three o'clock, the Chief and Espinosa Mireles presented themselves. The family was introduced. In a flutter, the girls brought their guitars and sang. While they were having the *merienda,* the girls told some of their adventures during the reign of terror caused by the retreating Federals. Finally, the mother and father were left alone with the Chief. They begged him for a "Salvo Conducto" for themselves and their daughters to Mexico City as soon as Zacatecas was in the hands of the Constitutionalists. The Chief ordered his secretary to write them two official letters for their safety: one addressed to the Political Chiefs and governors and one for local authorities, for their safe conduct.

For two hours the Chief and his secretary relaxed in the convivial atmosphere. Before leaving, Carranza told the Rebel to be ready to leave early the following morning for Santiago Papasquiaro, where General Pánfilo Natera wished the Chief to see the fortifications. It would be a dangerous trip, because at any time the train might come to a destroyed roadbed, or a bridge might be blown up as they approached. Generals Domingo and Mariano Arrieta's troops would be guarding the rear.

The trip was a short one, the train arriving in time for the group to have their two o'clock dinner in the town. The Chief's office was next to the Rebel's apartment. When they called for their mail there, an incident occurred that showed the mounting tension of the times. The Rebel's mail was brought in and laid on the Chief's table. Taking it up to hand to Lily, Carranza noticed that some of the letters were opened. At that moment his military aide, Colonel Treviño, whom he greatly esteemed, walked in.

"Why were these letters opened?" the Chief asked gruffly.

"This can happen easily," the Rebel said, hastily shocked by the Chief's tone. "They must have been opened by mistake."

The Rebel developed a sick headache and, as soon as she got to her room, threw herself on one of the comfortable beds. When Montoya called, she asked him to photograph the banquet, and to try to reach Colonel Treviño and ask him to come to her room.

When the young Colonel entered, the Rebel had gotten up and was sitting near an open window. "Colonel," she began earnestly. "You are one of my best friends. Please do not be angry about the letter incident. The Chief meant no offense, he is overworked and tired."

Smiling, Treviño bowed gallantly. "I must hurry to the banquet," he said. "I will be missed."

As he walked out, he passed another of the Chief's aides, Pancho Serna. They did not speak to each other. Serna had come with an invitation for the Rebel and Lily to attend the banquet. Feeling ill again, the Rebel asked Lily to send the Chief their regrets and to request him to send Doctor Rodríguez over in the afternoon. Lily wrote, assuring the Chief that they could easily hear the speeches during the banquet, as their room overlooked the patio where the meal was being held. When the Rebel closed her eyes to rest, Lily left the room. Two hours later, there was quiet downstairs.

The Chief and Doctor Rodríguez came up to inquire about the Rebel. Lily was writing a letter to her husband in Laredo. It would soon be vacation for her two daughters, and she wanted them taken to San Antonio to her sister's home. She begged her husband to bring her ten-year-old son to Saltillo to meet her.

The Rebel did not open her eyes as they entered the room. At that moment, she did not care whether she lived or died. She had never had any friction with any member of her beloved Constitutionalist Army. Seated by the foot of the bed in a chair strategically placed by the doctor, the Chief could be seen by all of them. After a brief examination, Dr. Rodríguez handed some pills to Lily, who then poured water from a Mexican jug. She gave them to the Rebel, who, as she sipped the water, secretly slipped the pills from her mouth. She was determined to fight the problem out her own way.

Looking at the Chief, she said fearfully, "You are not angry?"

"No," he said. "But I am going to ask you a favor. I beg you not to make excuses for me when I rebuke my officers. I saw Treviño leaving your room just before dinner."

The Rebel lay still. She was rapidly reviewing her life. She wondered what her father would have done. Finally she received her inspiration in her Grandmother's dying words. "Do your duty, never hesitate. Leave the rest to God."

How easy it would be for her to flare up and throw everything to the wind and quit. Shaking up her pillow, she looked at the Chief, a great, indomitable, fearless man, lonely without realizing it. "Chief," she said, "my coming here had a purpose. I shall accomplish my purpose."

Closing her eyes, she continued. "You can argue, but you cannot fill my mind with doubt. You need many friends. Without you, the army can accomplish nothing. You are their standard of hope. But you can do nothing without your followers. There can be no retracing of steps now until you bring peace and do justice to the oppressed millions."

Sitting thoughtfully, the Chief had even forgotten to adjust his glasses. The Rebel was looking tired, so Lily brought coffee. Quietly, they sipped it. There was a knock at the door, and General Natera came in and had coffee, too. He had brought an invitation for the Rebel and Lily to the dance that night in the hotel. The dance was to start early, contrary to custom, for the Chief had ordered an early departure for the next morning. It was four o'clock in the afternoon when the Rebel and Lily were left alone.

"You must sleep, Lily," the Rebel said. "Call the *mozo* and ask him to have our bath ready at six. I shall be well by then. We'll have our supper here at seven, in our room. "I am better," she said joyfully. "I feel almost lighthearted. All that was weighing on my soul has vanished."

At eight, the Rebel and Lily dressed and went downstairs to the dance. The Chief was in his room, threshing things out with his generals and his secretary. Again, there was dissension. As they descended the stairs, they were met by the boys of the corps; each of them had found a friend who wanted to join the brigade.

The music began and the young elite of the town began arriving with their parents. The large crowd testified to General Natera's popularity. The Rebel danced with Espinosa Mireles several times. She noticed that Santos Chocana, the poet, had arrived. Greeting him, she begged him to give some of his recitations. He consented to give two of his favorites. The girls kept applauding, and he became the lion of the party immediately.

The dance broke up slowly, the guests leaving reluctantly. For those who had not left, General Natera came in with an armful of flowers. As the ladies passed by him, he handed them gardenias with a gallant, low bow. At last, the Rebel, Lily, and Santos Chocana were alone.

As the two women were going upstairs to their rooms, General Natera called to them, saying he had been to see the patient, and left flowers in her room for her.

It is a Spanish custom to linger almost as long over the goodbyes as at the actual event. Leaning on the banister of the balcony outside their room, Santos Chocana insisted on talking. Finally, he decided that he would leave the next morning, going straight to Torreón to join Villa's division. He was satisfied with what he had seen and heard of the Carranza government and its armies.

At the station next morning, Iglesias Calderón was looking scornfully at Ceballos, who was nervously playing with his cane. Ceballos was to go to Villa's division, though he would have preferred staying in rich, aristocratic Chihuahua.

The Chief approached the Rebel as she and Lily were standing with their group. The corps was well organized and alert. Cordially, he looked over the little group. "You are better disciplined and organized than my own staff," he said to them.

"What is in for us today?" the Rebel meekly asked the Chief. "These writers around you do not agree. They are like blank checks of intellectual bankruptcy."

Colonel Fontes came up just then and ushered the party to their places on the train. The Generals Arrietta took over the train guard. General Natera was there. He was quite handsome, having the crimson olive skin so prevalent in the central states of Mexico, where the cool breezes are tempered by a slightly heating sun.

The next day in Durango at the usual conference with the Chief, the Rebel showed him a letter saying, "I will have to leave as soon as possible. My corps needs me. We have been here much longer than I anticipated."

"I will be delayed here at least another week," the Chief replied. "The stay in Torreón will be short. Since it is urgent for you to be with us later, you had better go now, so you can be ready to leave for Saltillo.

"When we enter the capital, it will be a historic return to the cradle of the Revolution. Much has happened since our declaration there. Three-fourths of Mexico is now under our control."

"Since the trains are running unhindered to all border towns," the Rebel said, "I have promised to relieve my corps and let the Laredo nurses who have been in Tamaulipas join us."

The Chief was listening and nodding his head approvingly. Quickly, she took advantage of his good humor. "What about our popular Governor Pastor Roaix and his wife? Perhaps, they will go with us to Saltillo."

Immediately, he handed out the olive branch of reconciliation to her, by confiding his plans. "Yes, they will be with us." Then hesitating, he continued. "He will be on my staff. When we arrive in Mexico City, he may be in my cabinet."

CHAPTER XIV
Supper with Ángeles

A day later, an exploring train with a few cars left Durango for Torreón. The trip was a pleasant one; the Rebel and her brigade occupied an entire car working on propaganda material, distributing it at every station. Popular Montoya threw photographs and small emblems to the crowds. He was returning to Torreón, although he longed to stay with the First Chief.

Members of the brigade who had remained in Torreón were lined up at the station to welcome them back. General Felipe Ángeles and Colonel Federico Cervantes, mounted on beautiful horses, waved their welcome, but did not dismount. The Rebel and her corps had quarters at the hotel they had occupied before. The Rebel planned an important meeting for that evening, and after a late supper, they all gathered in her room to hear about the Durango trip and to make future plans. They were going soon to Saltillo. Half of the brigade was to precede the Rebel there to begin organizing and be at the station when the First Chief's train arrived.

It was late when they retired for an uneventful night of quiet sleep. At daybreak the sound of shots fired in rapid succession coming from the patio of the hotel awakened the Rebel and Lily. Throwing open the window in her room facing the street, the Rebel saw General Felipe Ángeles and Colonel Cervantes waiting for their horses. It was the usual early morning hour for inspection. She beckoned frantically to them. Quickly, the men crossed the street and ran up the steep stone stairs. The Rebel's room faced an open porch overlooking the patio. Approaching the stone railing and looking below, the general indicated what the trouble was.

General Villa, having made a surprise entry into town, was furious because the First Chief had not yet arrived from Durango. He and his men had caroused all night until they were exhausted, yet still craved excitement. Coming to the hotel, he had become enraged at the manager and the servants for some petty annoyance. Villa had the Chinese hotel help herded into a large fountain where in good times clear water sparkled down into a small pool. Now it was not so clear. The Chinese were made to get into the pool and march around in the water that was up to their knees. At first glance it was a ludicrous sight, then suddenly Villa ordered his men to drag each Chinese out by the pigtail to an open rice field to be shot. Screaming, jumping, and hopping as Villa's men fired at the ground about their feet, the poor devils were dragged away. One was badly wounded and could not walk.

Swiftly, the Rebel and Lily ran downstairs, General Ángeles with them. They knelt beside the wounded Chinese.

"My poor baby," he muttered in pain. "Please, my poor baby. My wife."

"Tell us quickly," the Rebel said, "where is your wife?"

"The long dark street from the market," he whispered, "at the Chinese shop." Villa's men returned for the last Chinese. The Rebel and Lily stood back silently.

"Too bad these things happen. Drinking is a vice," General Ángeles said, walking away to see what would happen next.

They found Carlota Foo, the young mother, ill in bed. She lay with a wet cloth covering her face, a baby by her side. For two days, she had awaited her husband's return; now she found out he had been killed. Quietly, she passed away; the shock had killed her.

"Lily," the Rebel said, "can we save the baby?"

"I'll try," was Lily's answer as she cradled the baby in her arms.

While they talked to the Chinese who had gathered about them, day dawned. The sun was bright, but the body of Carlota was still. The Rebel and Lily secured the papers of birth and certificate of death. Getting together what money they had, Panchita was sent with the baby on a military train to Ciudad Juárez to give the child to Carlota's mother.

After a long day spent with the Chinese, the Rebel and Lily returned to the hotel and looked forward to an early supper. The long corridor that led to their room was dimly lighted. All the doors on either side were closed, except one about midway down the hall, which was half open. The Rebel, glancing in, saw an officer sitting at a desk, his back toward the door. Apparently he had been writing, although his head was resting in his hands. When they went down to supper, the man was still sitting in the same position. The Rebel couldn't get him out of her mind. After a brief meeting with the corps, she begged to be excused.

"Let's walk slowly," she said to Lily, "and stop in front of that open door."

Looking cautiously, they saw that the officer did not move. They stepped inside the room and closed the door quickly. Lily went up to the man, felt his head and pulse. "Magnón," she said, "let's get him to bed. He has high fever."

Between the two of them, they carried him. They unbuckled his belt and laid his pistol on a small night table; off came his coat and boots.

"Magnón, I'll get him ready for bed," Lily said. "Better go and get our kit, some alcohol and towels."

After a lot of doctoring, he opened his eyes. Looking toward his desk, he asked anxiously about his papers. He had been making out his report. The Rebel assured him that no one had entered the room. Everything had been taken care of. Again, he sank into unconsciousness. It was fully midnight before he roused again. Feverishly, he looked about him, then at his nurses.

"How good you are," he said. "I am General Frausto, Attorney General of the Army. My papers? . . ."

"Your reports have been carefully put away," the Rebel told him.

They sat up all night watching the sleeping patient. At dawn they summoned Ruiz to relieve them. He was instructed to lock the door and permit no one to disturb the sick man. After gathering up the available newspapers, the general's mail and their own, they went down for an early breakfast. They would be in their room all day. Ordering a light breakfast, they took it up to the general's room. No one was told about their high-ranking patient. The three of them took turns caring for him.

Later, they found out that he was supposed to have gone to Durango. Because of something that had come up, he had decided to stay. They understood perfectly the ever-changing moods and orders of Villa, the military commander, who could throw a whole army into an unexpected change. However, for Lily and the Rebel it was good luck that brought into their path Ramón Frausto, one of the finest brains of the Constitutionalist Army. He was an able lawyer, a writer, and a Veracruzano. His convalescence was of short duration. He was young and full of energy. He became a fast friend of the White Cross. Later on, he sent the Rebel his photograph as a token of gratitude. He lauded their work.

A few days after their return to Torreón, General Ángeles sent a message asking the Rebel and Lily to have supper with him and his staff. Montoya, who had been taking pictures of the general that day, came in at that moment to show them to the Rebel.

"Montoya," she said, "we are going to be guests of General Ángeles tonight. If we delay, please come and say we are needed. It will be an excuse for us to leave."

On arriving at Ángeles' headquarters, Lily and the Rebel were met by Colonel Cervantes. After saluting the general, they were ushered into the dining room. An atmosphere of camaraderie prevailed. It was like a brilliant party from a play. Some recited, some sang. Near the Rebel sat Joaquín Bauche Alcalde. It was the last time she was ever to see him. He was killed in combat soon after, loyal to the Division of the North.

General Ángeles was sitting next to the Rebel. Very informally, slowly folding and unfolding his big, colored napkin, he began asking her questions.

"Tell us about your trip. How is it you preceded the First Chief? We hear he will return later than intended."

"We had important business," Lily answered immediately. "We came on when we learned the Chief's stay here would not be long enough for the work we had planned,"

"Fortunately," continued the Rebel, "our brigade acted wisely, and most of the work had already been done."

"You are right," a young officer answered from the other end of the table. "They helped us in the tremendous undertaking of clearing the surrounding country, where dead soldiers and horses were filling the air with stench."

As he spoke, the Rebel recalled scenes from something she had read years before from *The Scottish Chiefs*. She remembered how she would lock herself in her clothes closet and read by candlelight, lest she be reproved for her late hours. She had loved those Scots, her heart beating as fast as she read, longing to be able to save them from prison and death.

An officer of General Ángeles' approached him, bowing in troubadour fashion. He wore his hat like the rest, tilted up on one side, with the colors of his regiment over his shoulder. He looked quite picturesque, handing the general a telegram. The Rebel watched the general's face closely, noticing the quick, worried look that flickered in his eyes. "More trouble," she thought.

Carefully folding the message, he slipped it into the side pocket of his coat. He looked straight ahead. All his staff was quiet, at attention. They dearly loved him.

Montoya appeared as they were taking their coffee. He was offered a seat after speaking softly to the Rebel. Abruptly, the general pushed his chair back. He assisted the Rebel to her feet. His staff rose, exchanging troubled glances.

A constant drizzle had made the night chilly. The Rebel had not brought a wrap. Ángeles noticing it, took off his coat and threw it about her shoulders. They didn't have far to walk to the hotel. As they were on their way, a group of officers met them, saluting the general. He joined them, and they stood back at some distance talking.

Taking her hand out of the coat pocket, the Rebel saw the telegram slip out and lay partly open on the sidewalk. In an instant, she noticed that it was from General Villa. Quickly, she put it back in the pocket. In a few minutes, the General joined Lily and the Rebel, apologizing for the delay. When they reached the door of the hotel, he told them good night.

"My general, you are forgetting your coat," the Rebel reminded him. "You see, I could have kept the coat, and the mysterious message that upset you so."

"I am going to answer it immediately," he replied.

"I almost know what it says," she said as she helped him on with his coat.

Ángeles felt in the pocket to see if the telegram was still there.

"Now, you know how honest we of the White Cross are," she said looking up at him unflinchingly.

"We also are honest, we of the Division of the North," was his ready answer, with a quick smile at her seriousness.

Later on they found out from General Frausto that Villa had wanted to wreck the train that Carranza was traveling on to Torreón. General Ángeles had not approved. It was foolhardy, especially so, as General Villa had already gone on to Saltillo to await the Chief's triumphal entry.

As Lily and the Rebel passed General Frausto's room, he came out, as if he had been awaiting them, and asked them in.

"You had supper at General Ángeles' quarters with his staff," he said solemnly. "Do you think the Chief would like that? You have a responsible place in our army as head of the Constitutionalist White Cross. Do you not realize how important it is to be careful?"

"General," she replied, "you are the supreme judge of this army. We will never fail you. I have known General Ángeles a very long time and how fine he is."

The General stood up, but before he had a chance to say anything else, the Rebel added quickly, "Until now we have had only praise for the many fine men of this Revolution. We feel that you will be our best friend."

The Chief's arrival in Torreón was hardly noticed, because it was unexpected. Only those occupying high government posts greeted him. He would stay only a few days to rest.

Wherever he was, there were always letters to be dictated, telegrams to answer, orders to be given regarding the wounded. Time meant only service. All were ready to move and act at a moment's notice. Thirty minutes after arriving in a city, town, or hamlet, the Provisional Government was in working routine. Cases were unloaded and sent to their respective buildings. Signs were put up indicating temporary quarters. By now the signs were showing the effect of much travel. Nurses and doctors were immediately assigned, each to their work; very little had to be said concerning their duties. There were moments of relaxation, a little entertainment, a supper, a few hours at the theatre. Everything had a political significance or a revolutionary purpose. Things were done with extraordinary rapidity.

On the eve of the brigade's departure for Saltillo, there was great excitement. The private dining room of the hotel was completely occupied by the Constitutional White Cross and their guests. It was the first time they had been allowed the privilege of entertaining formally. Durac, the writer who was Carranza's chauffeur, was present, talking to the nurses, Clotilde and her mother. Lily and the Rebel sat apart from the group, enchanted with the happiness of their faithful corps.

General Felipe Ángeles and Manuel Bauche Alcalde came in to say goodbye. Manuel Bauche Alcalde was writing for his newspaper about the work of the brigade and its future plans. Both he and General Ángeles had helped make the corps' hospital work a success in Chihuahua and Durango. General Ángeles drew up a chair, sitting at the table across from the Rebel. Bauche Alcalde, speaking English, began talking to Lily and taking down notes.

General Ángeles spoke to the Rebel in a low voice. "You will be leaving at dawn. It is possible that Huerta, on seeing his forces routed and the fall of his government imminent, will do something rash."

At that hour, the Constitutional forces were approaching Mexico City from every direction. The reactionary General Orozco had some support. General Zapata had a powerful army in the south, and though not of the Northern Army's way of thinking, the uprisings and succeeding triumphs over the Federals had helped the rebellion against Huerta. General Obregón was advancing from the northwest. General Pablo González was entering Nuevo León. Generals Cándido Aguilar and Guadalupe Sánchez were in Tabasco and Veracruz fighting Felix Díaz's Federal forces. General Eulalio Gutiérrez was winning in San Luis Potosí. All the successful Constitutional forces were to be represented in Saltillo on the triumphal entry of the First Chief.

"It is right," Ángeles continued, "that the First Chief have a clear road to enter Mexico. He is, after all, our leader. This I keep repeating to my General Villa. But he is full of fight.

"It is understood, of course, that every living Mexican will stand united in case of foreign invasion." This last sentence he said looking directly at the Rebel for the first time.

Lily was too busy to hear. The words cut the Rebel's soul. She thought of her brigade. Everyone of them had an American mother or father. They had come from the United States to Mexico.

"Why have you taken up Villa's cause?" she said, leaning forward and looking into his kindly eyes, yet not wishing to hurt him. "Am I to understand that only in the case of foreign invasion will we all be united?"

"Yes," he answered. "That is the way it is. Remember, at first I was with the First Chief. He appointed me Minister of War because of my military experience."

"You were happy to serve the First Chief," she quickly replied to relieve him of unhappy thoughts. "Just as you faithfully served President Francisco Madero as his Minister of War."

Dismissing the waiter who had served them, he continued. "I hardly dare to hope that you and your brigade will remain with our Division of the North."

"No, General," she said shaking her head. Then challenging him she said, "Go with us!"

"I cannot," he said. "The Chief sent me to Villa. When jealousy and treachery threatened the Chief, he called me, and talking things over, he thought it best that I go with General Villa and remain under his command. General Villa has a greater following and plenty of money. He does not hesitate at anything. Someone should be near him who is better balanced, better educated."

"My general," she said, not wanting to believe his words, "we were all one army with lofty ideals and high hopes."

"The Chief himself sent me to this man," he insisted. "Now I know his ways. I know his army. They love and trust me."

The brigade was rising now from their tables. Approaching General Ángeles, they said goodbye and thanked him for the courtesies they had received from him during their stay. Following the party, the Rebel and the general walked through the open patio under the shining stars. The bright, clear moon traveled freely above on its ordained orbit.

"So you remain with the First Chief," he said thoughtfully. "I, with the Constitutional Chief of the Division of the North."

"It is late," was her reply. "It will soon be dawn."

They stood silently for a few moments at the railing overlooking the garden. *La aurora de la mañana* (the dawn of a new day). May it be a bright one for both of us." She spoke half aloud as he walked away from her into the graying morning light.

In her heart pounded the words, "Do your duty. That is best. Leave to God the rest."

The Rebel was restless after she had gone to bed. Finally, Lily said, "Magnón, you are troubled."

"Lily, no one knows what Villa might do next. Let's get up and be ready to go," the Rebel replied, getting out of bed and putting on her clothes.

General Frausto was waiting for them at the station. He handed the Rebel a copy of the telegram he had sent to Saltillo, asking for suitable quarters for the White Cross. He told her that he would see her in Monterrey regarding her work.

"General," she said clasping his hand. She was touched by his kindness. "I will consult you on everything of importance regarding our organization."

Again they were in their places, this time on the road to Saltillo. The traveling family had added another woman to the group. The popular and gracious wife of Governor Pastor Roiax, with her ten-year-old son, who was very spoiled, had joined the party.

At noon, the train stopped at San Pedro de las Colonias. A big banquet was held after the ceremonious greetings and cheering. The Rebel sat at the Chief's right, Lily at his left. Lawyer Isidro Fabela made a speech lauding the generals' triumphs that assured their future unity and success. He reminded them that scarcely a year had passed and their people had now almost won the war. Miguel Alessio Robles, the official speaker, aroused the audience with words for greater deeds of bravery.

It was a short stay, as the Chief preferred leaving at an early hour. The next day would be the first anniversary of the Revolution. It was on that day that he had left his office as Governor, rebelling against the assassination of President Madero.

The train was crowded. People from every sphere of life wanted to be in Saltillo to greet the Chief. All day, there was a continual flow of passengers getting on. Room had to be made in the coaches for them. The Chief's car, however, was restricted to those high officers who had been with him step by step on his campaign.

Just as the train touched the state boundary line, it stopped. The whistle began blowing and continued to blow until all on board the train had marched through General Venustiano Carranza's car to salute him as the First Chief of the Revolution. Officers embraced him, addressing words of congratulations. Everybody was excited. So it was that the Rebel, Lily, and a select group of the brigade were among the fortunate ones to greet Carranza at that happy hour, when he was returning to Coahuila, the state of his birth.

Great wooden arches erected by a Monterrey beer company and a Torreón cotton firm stood on the boundary line between Coahuila and Chihuahua. Decorated with bright colored paper, they bore the historic date of General Carranza's triumphal entry to Coahuila: June 7, 1914. It was an event of great joy. The army was returning victorious to establish the provisional capital of the constitutional government. The cradle of the Revolution was once more in the possession of the Constitutionalists.

Isidro Fabela, Carranza's Minister of Foreign Relations, sent telegrams to Constitutionalists General Roberto Pesqueira and Rafael Múzquiz, diplomatic agents in Washington; to Samuel Belden, Consul to San Antonio; and to Consul Carrillo in El Paso advising them of the occupation of Saltillo, Huerta's last stronghold in the North.

Generals with their staffs coming from all sectors filled the old city of Saltillo to overflowing with uniformed men. An immense crowd was gathered at the station with a delegation from Laredo and Monterrey.

The First Chief told the Rebel that she should go to his residence. His wife and daughters, as well as the family of Doctor Emeterio Flores from Laredo, would be there. Lily's husband, Doctor George Long, with their small son, awaited her. They were to take charge of the brigade temporarily. Lily was eager to see her husband and find out whether he was on General Pablo González's staff.

"Magnón, orders are orders," Lily said in a matter of fact voice, trying to mask her excitement at seeing her family again. "We will see you in the morning."

The Rebel finally consented to allow Lily to go when she found out that Lieutenant-Colonel Martínez Celis, who was Araceli's husband, was coming for her. He had been sent by General Pablo González to escort her to the First Chief's residence. The brigade was to occupy the family residence of Doctor José María Rodríguez, which was a great honor.

Venustiano Carranza, after a year's hard fighting, passed down streets scattered with roses. Young women with arms full of flowers bestrewed them in his path. There were also tears for the ones who would never return. Speaking to his people, Carranza promised to return to Coahuila to solve the agrarian question. Everything would be his who employed energy and intelligence in cultivating the soil given him, he told the huge crowd.

At the Chief's residence, the Rebel was met informally by Carranza himself. He beckoned to his nephew, Alberto Salinas, to call Señora Carranza. When the Rebel was introduced to the First Lady of Mexico, it was recalled that they had met once before in Laredo on the eve of the Rebel's departure for Cuidad Juárez. When the Chief added that Señora Magnón was head of the Constitutional White Cross, his wife only nodded. She had known that for some time.

Carranza asked his wife to assign a room to the Rebel, as he wanted her to spend that eventful night in their midst. The Rebel was escorted to her room, which the maid told her was next to that of the Chief's nephew. While she was getting ready for supper, the maid prepared the bed for the night.

When the Rebel entered the dining room that night, everyone was seated except the First Chief. He was standing at the head of the table; his wife was seated at the other end. Beside her was the Rebel's place, so that they both sat directly opposite the *Jefe*. On Carranza's right was General Pablo González, Division of the North East. He would now become division general. He had the greatest number of soldiers at that time, some of the finest generals, and high officers in the army. All of them were loyal to Carranza.

Although the Rebel and General González had never met, it was through him that she had formally entered the Revolution. Both of them were curious to know what the other was like. They caught themselves in sly glances at each other. The general wore big, dark glasses, though it was night. He looked like the photograph he had sent the Rebel the night before she had left for El Paso.

On the Chief's left was Iglesias Calderón. No other high officers were seated at the table. All were civilians. Espinosa Mireles sat between the Chief's daughters, Virginia and Julia. Opposite them, Alberto Salinas between the daughters of Don Emeterio Flores, a fine old man who had been one of Don Joaquín's friends. There was Don Felícitos Villarreal, an aristocrat from Nuevo León, Treasurer of the Revolutionary Party. Don Nicéforo Zembrano and Don Manuel Amaya, wealthy men both of the Junta Revolucionario, had come from Laredo.

Don Melquíades García, Consul in Laredo for the Constitutionalists and one of the First Chief's most loyal friends, had been entrusted with the commission of escorting the Chief's family from San Antonio to Saltillo. He had returned to his post immediately. He was expected to be named Mexican Consul General in Laredo. He was a man well qualified for any high post, but with the possibility of Huerta's being overthrown at anytime, he was needed on the frontier where he was well liked. He knew the politics of the rebellious Mexican exiles who had recently settled there.

The guests were served a true Mexican frontier supper: *cabrito al horno* with chili sauce, rice a la Veracruzana, vegetable salad, plenty of Mexican pies, candied fruit, and coffee. A congenial atmosphere surrounded the Chief. During supper, members of the First Chief's staff and military chiefs had been gathering in the drawing room to offer congratulations to Carranza and his family.

After supper, Espinosa Mireles approached the Rebel, inquiring if she was not happy with all the great assembly of Constitutionalists.

"Not entirely," she answered. "It is the first time I have been away from my brigade. It seems disloyal. Please take me to headquarters. I won't be missed."

"Indeed not," he answered firmly. "The Chief wants you here."

She looked up gratefully at him, thinking there was one in the large gathering who appreciated her work.

She slept peacefully that night and awakened early the next morning, knowing the Chief to be an early riser. However, the drawing room was occupied by General Pablo González and visitors from Laredo. Laredo seemed to surround the General, she thought to herself. After breakfast, she begged General González to send Colonel Guillermo Martínez-Celis for a car to take her to White Cross headquarters, asking him to make excuses for her to the Chief. Although Señora Carranza had been affable, it was easy to see that she longed to be alone with her husband.

CHAPTER XV
The White Cross Is Nationalized

In the General's car, the Rebel and Guillermo Martínez-Celis had time to exchange news. Aracelito had remained in Monterrey and would precede him to Mexico City, where they would remain for an indefinite time.

"Will our General Pablo González be military commander in Mexico City?" the Rebel inquired.

"That will take time," Martínez-Celis answered. "Things look bad."

"Huerta or Villa?"

"Both, I am afraid," was his candid answer. "General Villa and his men are leaving for Torreón tomorrow."

When they drove up to the quarters that had been assigned the White Cross according to the address that Francisco Serna had given her, they were shocked to see the beautiful home occupied by a cavalry regiment of Lieutenant Colonel Manzo's. Horses were in the drawing room eating hay from an open Steinway grand piano; horses stabled in the downstairs rooms looked out on the street through the barred windows. Soldiers were giving away the household belongings to passersby: furs, dresses, cooking utensils, a sewing machine. Everyone who passed was given a present.

Time had wrought a psychological change. Triumph had gotten in the blood. For some few it was the satisfaction of the Constitutionalists' winning; for others it worked havoc in all directions. There was envy. General Alvaro Obregón's division thought that General Pablo González's division of the North East were better clad. Perhaps, being in contact with border facilities afforded certain commercial ventures. The Division of the North, an army of sixty thousand commanded by Villa, was thought by many to be made up of unruly ruffians, wild money-spenders and despoilers.

Villa's army had entered Saltillo first, then turned the capital city over to the First Chief's men. Villa had waited, seemingly peaceably, the First Chief's coming. It was the first time that representatives of all the forces had been together. But after feasting and congratulating each other, a spirit of discontent began to spread, ambitions and jealousies coming to the surface. When Villa made his departure from Saltillo with his army, a group of loyal Constitutionalists gathered at the station to say goodbye. All of them noticed the amiable disposition of Villa at his departure.

The creation of new divisions complicated things to a great degree. General Pánfilo Natera was made commander-in-chief of the Central Division in the states of Zacatecas, Guanajuato, and a portion of the state of Jalisco. General Villa would be subordinate to General Natera when Villa's army was in that zone, where a large part of the army had mobilized to combat unexpected Federalist resistance.

The same day Villa left Saltillo, General Carranza had elevated to the rank of division general, among others, Pablo González, Francisco Villa, and Obregón. With the arrival of the First Chief in Saltillo, the announcement of the official cabinet of the Constitutional government was expected. Personnel for all government office heads was to be named. Don Manuel Amaya was regarded as the future Secretary of Foreign Relations. Luis Cabrera was Secretary of the Treasury, and his assistant was to be Rafael Nieto, a shrewd and successful business man. The expected announcement was set aside. All this was now in the ink stand.

The Arrieta brothers, encountering a strong Federal army in Durango, sent an urgent message to the First Chief for aid. Five thousand men were needed from Villa's division. The First Chief called General Villa long distance and ordered him to send the required men. Villa protested, saying five thousand men were too many. He did not want to lose them; rather, he preferred to muster out all his division and defeat the enemy himself. This the First Chief did not want; such a large force would be a menace so close to the capital and with a quickly crumbling Huerta government. Villa and his men would be placed in an easy position for the conquest of the City of Mexico. Villa had to be held in abeyance, as was later the case with Obregón's army.

The First Chief consulted with General Pablo González, the least ambitious of his generals, who was there with him. They both agreed that all factions would meet at a given point and await the command of the First Chief to enter the capital in an orderly manner, according to rank. General Villa, still holding the line, spoke in open rebellion to the Chief's orders. He said in plain terms that he no longer held Carranza to be supreme head of the army. Villa would take things in his own hands.

The happenings that followed occurred in such rapid succession that when it was all over, the Rebel took weeks to recall clearly the many facets of those eventful days.

The Rebel was standing by, awaiting orders. Her official appointment as head of the National White Cross had been planned for the twelfth of June as her birthday present. Seeing things in such a turmoil, she spoke to Colonel Breceda and asked that it be conferred at an early date. On the eighth of June, the day after their arrival in Saltillo, the Constitutional White Cross was officially recognized by the First Chief and became known as the National White Cross. The Rebel, as President of the organization, was recognized for her previous activities from 1910. Carranza signed the memorable document of recognition.

The gathering Constitutional army was becoming more menacing to the Huerta government. In spite of his reiterated friendship for the American Ambassador, Huerta now displayed an insulting and threatening attitude toward the United States. The American government sent ships to Veracruz to remove any United States citizens who wished to leave Mexico. These ships were escorted by a United States Naval vessel which was bringing Red Cross supplies and food. The United States was still withholding recognition of Carranza, despite his army's controlling over three-fourths of Mexico.

Huerta had refused to honor the American flag and had arrested American State Department messengers. Matters grew worse, provoked by Huerta. The American occupation of Veracruz took place. While the First Chief was facing this state of international affairs, internal rebellion was brewing in his own army.

Argentina, Brazil and Chile, becoming alarmed with the situation in Mexico, offered their services as arbitrators. Carranza promised nothing, playing for time. He remained unmoved when the United States occupied Veracruz. The quarrel was between Huerta and the United States, not between the majority of the people of Mexico, who were represented by the Constitutionalists. The possibility of Huerta's continuing to govern Mexico was rapidly becoming less and less. The A. B. C. nations at Niagara Falls were even considering a list of names for the position of President of Mexico. During these trying days in Saltillo, the Rebel saw the Chief often enough to understand what General Felipe Ángeles had meant about worse times awaiting the Revolutionists.

It was at this time while looking over their correspondence that Lily found an unopened letter from North Carolina. On reading it, she was amazed to find in it a letter of introduction to Mr. Josephus Daniels, Minister of Navy in President Wilson's cabinet. A friend of the Rebel, having learned that she was involved in the Revolution, had hastened to offer help. She wrote that her uncle, Senator Overman, was also in the cabinet. If the Rebel wished to present any communication to the President of the United States, it could be gotten to him.

The Rebel showed the correspondence to the Chief.

"Are you going to answer this?" he asked, frowning.

"Yes," she replied, "I am going to ask for time, time enough for us to reach Mexico City. I shall send her your photograph."

"No! No!" Carranza said roughly. "President Wilson and I will never clasp hands."

To her offer of mediation, the First Chief remained noncommittal. His answer was that of Napoleon: "God is on the side of the largest army." On this point, a strong united army, Carranza and Villa were to suspend their differences of opinion for the time being. Soon, news came of the triumphs of Generals Luis and Eulalio Gutiérrez in the state of San Luis Potosí. The First Chief could now plan on leaving Coahuila, proceeding to Nuevo León.

In Saltillo, the Rebel met Ignacio Magaloni, a lawyer from Yucatán, a good friend of the Chief. He was an elderly man, a scholar, rather than a soldier, who valued human life. In the days of adversity for the Constitutionalist cause, he brooded over the plight of his rich state, lamenting the decline of the export of henequen and the state's greatest resource. He liked to write poetry, which had a strain of melancholy. On the Rebel's birthday, he sent a bouquet of gardenias and a sorrowful poem about the ingratitude she could expect for her work. It ran on and on till, pausing in its reading, she called a nurse and asked her to put the flowers in water.

That same night, there was a grand concert in honor of the Chief's wife and daughters. The National White Cross had a box near the Chief's. Magaloni would accompany the Rebel and Doctor and Mrs. Long. The Fourth Battalion in new uniforms was guarding the entrance of the theatre. Colonel Juan Barragán, an Adonis and, until now, a playboy, had recently grown grave. On his youthful face one could see the trace of new burdens of responsibility. Colonel Jacinto Treviño, though of military bearing, was now even more preoccupied. They all seemed to take the intervention as a personal affront. There was a forced gaiety about the gathering that hurt. It hit Magaloni just right. The next day, he could write a sad poem.

Later that night, after some hours of sleep, the Rebel was awakened by a sound at her window. Without putting on the light, she approached it quietly. Two slim trembling hands grasped the bars at the window. A pair of large shining eyes focused on the Rebel.

"Please let me in. I must see the Rebel," came the breathless voice of a woman.

"Who are you," was the Rebel's startled reply.

"Can't you see my cross?" came her answer. She seemed in pain.

"Come to the front door. I will meet you," the Rebel told her.

"Coronela," the Rebel gasped. "How did you get here?"

She took the girl to her own room and had scarcely gotten the half-fainting girl to bed when Lily opened the door.

"What is it, Magnón? Can the doctor come in?"

"No, Lily. Please, just you and I. She is Carmen de la Llave, a Colonel from Tabasco and Veracruz." The Rebel spoke in answer to the question in Lily's eyes.

Light coming from the next room was bright enough to show the girl's bloodstained clothes. Holding a short skirt of rough red flannel up to the light, the Rebel saw the two bullet holes in it.

"Magnón! She is wounded." Lily showed the Rebel two places where bullets had grazed the girl's legs. They dressed the wounds themselves. Although Doctor Long kept tapping impatiently at the door, they refused to let him in.

After having some hot coffee, the girl revived somewhat. "Please, señora," she said clutching the Rebel's arm, "no one must know I dared to do this for my general's sake."

She slept, watched over by the Rebel. The girl was suffering from shock and loss of blood. Towards morning, La Coronela sat up and had an early breakfast. She was kept in bed despite her insistence that she be allowed to get up.

"I must see the First Chief and deliver a message from my General Miguel Alemán," she told the Rebel earnestly. "I rode hard through the state of Veracruz, sometimes getting off and walking to rest my horse. As I was nearing a train, my horse was shot; I was hit in the leg. That did not matter. I could still walk. I found a Constitutionalist train headed north, boarded the caboose and lay on the floor all day. But," she added, smiling broadly, "I did not die. I got here."

The Rebel sent a message to Magaloni, saying that she needed him. He did not fail her, arriving with an enormous bouquet of red roses.

"Please do not dismiss your coach," the Rebel said as she met him in the parlor. "I'll meet you in the dining room in a few minutes."

The Rebel took a tray up to the Coronela, who was dressed in one of the Rebel's best dresses. "As soon as you finish supper," she told the girls, "go out and get in the coach that is standing outside. Wait for me."

After a hasty supper, the Rebel and Magaloni excused themselves from the members of the corps gathered in the dining room and got in the coach with the Coronela. The Rebel then asked Magaloni to secure an interview immediately with the First Chief before Carranza began his evening session of conferences. It did not take the Coronela long to deliver her message. Then together the three of them drove to the station where the Coronela, whom the soldiers called Marietta, was to leave.

Marietta had a love song written about her. The tune had spread quickly among the music-loving soldiers of the southern camps. In a running strain it started:

"Marietta falls in love with a young officer."

("Marietta se enamora de un joven militar.")

The love story continues through many stanzas, interspersed with the chorus:

"Marietta, do not be a flirt."

("Marietta, no seas coqueta.")

"Because the men are very bad."

("Porque los hombres son muy malos.")

"They offer many gifts."

("Ofrecen muchos regalos.")

"Instead they beat you down a lot."

("Y lo que dan son muchos palos.")

As the Coronela hastened to board the train later that night, an officer, his head out of the window, was whistling the tune. It was to be many years after that night that the Rebel met the Coronela in Mexico City in a tragic manner. As the train passed from sight, Magaloni was silent. Later the next day, he, too, left Saltillo.

General Ramón Frausto returned to Saltillo and sent the Rebel a note that he would call the same day. She was glad to hear from him, for now she could complete her plans for going to Monterrey.

At a meeting with the brigade, the Rebel told her plans for a reception for the high officers of the army in honor of the First Chief. It would be a mark of gratitude from the White Cross. She wished all the corps to be present, as well as those who had helped in Laredo. Federico Idar and Felipe Aguirre would go to Laredo and buy uniforms for the men to wear at the reception. They would act as hosts. The nurses, wearing white dresses, were to stand in the receiving line. It was to be an elaborate affair.

After the reception in Monterrey, there would come changes in the brigade personnel. To Ezequiel Ruiz and his wife Panchita, Señor Felícetos Villarreal, Secretary of Finance, was to give an assignment in the Customs. The three Martínez sisters wished to continue in action and were to be transferred to General Jesús Carranza's staff with Clotilde as head of that brigade. Doctor and Mrs. Long would go with the Rebel as far as San Luis Potosí and there join General Luis Caballero's staff. Lily and the Rebel asked General Frausto to make the White Cross headquarters his during his stay, so they could finish their program for the proposed reception. He assisted them, though he was very busy.

Diplomatic negotiations continued between Mexico and the United States. Some foreign countries had no scruples about recognizing Huerta, but the United States was not so inclined.

At home, Villa had to be appeased. Lázaro de la Garza, Villa's financial advisor at Juárez, Eusebio Calzada, Director General of Villa's railroads, and Roberto Pesqueira, the Chief's diplomatic agent to the United States, conferred with Villa. It was finally agreed that Villa would assist General Pánfilo Natera in driving the Federals out of Zacatecas. Meanwhile, Carranza conferred over leased wires with Rafael Zubarán, his Minister of Foreign Relations in Washington. These talks, in regard to mediation proceedings, were not entirely secret. Luis Cabrera, one of Carranza's advisors, was in Washington, supposedly to attend the conferences. He left for New York, his mission unknown.

Telegrams poured in from all over the Republic of Mexico, proclaiming loyalty to Carranza, resenting outside interferences in Mexican internal affairs. Despite foreign displeasure at the civil strife in Mexico, hostilities could not be suspended until Huerta had been driven from power.

As he had promised, General Ramón Frausto spoke to the Chief about the Rebel's wish to give the reception in Monterrey the night of the Chief's arrival. Carranza accepted the invitation, promising to arrive on the hour at her residence on the seventh of July. Frausto sent a telegram to the Governor, Antonio I. Villarreal, to prepare quarters for the National White Cross in Monterrey.

News came from Laredo that Manuel García Vigil, editor of his own newspaper, *El Radical,* had been cowardly attacked by three Huertista sympathizers. Bullets fired from different directions struck him in the cheek and ear and pierced his arm. The gunfire had damaged expensive plate-glass show windows of a store. A mob soon gathered. When the sheriff handcuffed García Vigil and took him off to jail, the crowd was beyond control, gathering in threatening confusion around the jail and courthouse. A hurried session was held and, after a midnight trial, Vigil was released.

The joy of the people proclaimed itself all night. Vigil was carried through the streets, jubilant, making speeches at every corner. At dawn he was forced to seek medical attention. He wired the Rebel later that day that he wanted to enter the army. He was a graduate engineer of Chapultepec Military College. Wanting to confer with the First Chief, he could not leave Laredo until he had the money to pay off his employees. The Rebel wired him a hundred dollars. He arrived in Saltillo the day of the Rebel's departure for Monterrey, remaining in the National White Cross quarters to meet General Ramón Frausto. The Rebel had explained to Frausto about Vigil's sudden appearance. Vigil joined General Pablo González's army, later becoming a general under General Alvaro Obregón.

On the train to Monterrey, the Rebel and Lily had an encounter with a man of uncertain political affiliations whom they had heard much about. The women were both much concerned about the American intervention that was holding on so stubbornly. George C. Carothers, a confidential agent from the United States, sat beside the Rebel. For a few minutes, Lily and the Rebel were silent. The Rebel looked from the willowy, unselfish American Lily to the fleshy, sphinx-like American Carothers. She could not fathom his diplomacy. Constantly with Villa's army, he seemed to favor that internal division to the Carranza forces. He was now on his way to Washington.

"Mr. Carothers," said the Rebel, mustering up her courage, "I understand that the aim of the American people is not to crush Mexico, but to help them eliminate Huerta. By so doing they will favor the Mexican Revolution, of which Carranza is First Chief. He is the only man who can bring order."

Carothers leaned forward slightly to better catch the Rebel's words. Although appearing to have heard her, he was noncommittal in his short answer.

"Magnón," Lily whispered, "he is not a friend of the First Chief. I showed him the newspaper that said in a few days the Constitutionalists will be on their way to the Mexico City. He read it several times, but made no comment."

After a few moments of heavy silence, the Rebel invited the agent to the reception to be given by the National White Cross in honor of the First Chief and the military forces. Dr. Long talked to him about the aid Texas had given the wounded in Laredo. The doctor wanted Carothers to carry a good impression of the character of the First Chief's cause.

In all social upheavals, grafters, demagogues, and wolves of the social body prey upon innocent individuals with insatiable greed that becomes steadily rapacious in its voracity. These people without morals have caused more destruction and grief in the world than all the pestilence mankind has ever endured. It was fervently planned that no sympathizer of Huerta would ever be President of Mexico.

At the station in Monterrey, the Laredo group with its White Cross flag awaited the Rebel's brigade with Governor Antonio I. Villarreal. After greetings and *abrazos,* the corps went to the beautiful mansion of the Sada Garza family. A housekeeper who had been left in charge of the house received the Rebel. The owners of the place, wealthy Díaz *científicos,* had long since fled to the United States.

Making a hurried inventory of the place, the Rebel noticed a small theatre in the basement where the young people celebrated and entertained the family at festivals. Also in the basement was a thoroughly equipped kitchen for the household servants. There were long tables and cupboards filled with china, silverware, and aluminum cups. Adjoining were their sleeping quarters. The house suited well the needs of the White Cross brigade. After supper, the corps adjourned to the office, studio, and library. Though separated by carved mahogany doors, these rooms could be thrown into one large hall.

At almost noon the next day, Governor Villarreal and his staff doctor, Luis Cervantes, called at White Cross headquarters. Looking down into the round reception hall, Lily saw the two officials. She stood thoughtfully at the polished oak rail of the staircase. The rail bound a circular hall, which led to seven bedrooms on the second floor.

"Magnón, quick," Lily said, as she rushed into the Rebel's room. "We have company. The handsomest men in the whole army. I'll greet them while you get ready."

The Rebel had just started to work on a speech of greeting for her reception. Pushing away her papers, she scattered them about the room in her haste. She had risen early that morning to inspect hospitals, so she was well dressed in a sweepingly graceful pink dress and stylish white shoes. Her sister-in-law had sent her an appropriate wardrobe, knowing that the Rebel would meet many old-time friends in Monterrey. It was a typical July day when Monterrey, in spite of its high surrounding mountains, had its hours of dense heat.

Villarreal and Doctor Cervantes began talking when the Rebel came downstairs. Time ran into noon, and the visiting continued after a well-served luncheon. Looking for the Governor, some Laredo friends were sent to White Cross headquarters, so long was his visit on that important day of the reception.

While very young, Villarreal had belonged to "The Precursors," the early pre-Revolutionary liberal party. When the Flores Magón brothers were exiled, Villarreal, too, had left Mexico for St. Louis,

Missouri, with his father and sisters. There, he and his two sisters had published a revolutionary newspaper. Villarreal was persecuted by Díaz followers and was finally arrested in St. Louis. While he was in jail, the paper continued to be circulated by his two sisters, Andrea and Teresita, to liberal sympathizers.

During President Madero's short term, Villarreal was Ambassador to Spain. There, he fell in love with a girl whose family was from Mexico. Their property in Chihuahua had been confiscated. He had known Blanca in Mexico during the Madero Revolution. She was a very young girl then, with her hair in long braids, which he delighted in pulling. He did not dream that in a few short years they would be married. When the Carranza Revolution broke out, Villarreal left his wife and son with her family in Spain, and returned to Mexico. Villarreal was usually accompanied by Isidro Fabela, sometimes by General Nafarate or General Luis Caballero. They called often and had dinner or supper at the National White Cross Headquarters.

The long awaited reception took place on the seventh of July, 1914. The brigade, standing in a semicircle in the great reception hall of the headquarters, awaited the Chief. Exactly at eight o'clock, Governor Villarreal, Lawyer Isidro Fabela, and General Caballero arrived. They stood at the entrance, where they greeted the Chief and escorted him into the parlor.

Two hundred invitations had been given to the governor to address, so there would be no mistake regarding alliances and rank of the guests. The two elegant parlors were ablaze with lights that were reflected in the gold furniture and mirrors. Flowers were placed on all available tables and on the floor. An orchestra played softly. Many of the guests were seated. Others were standing, as the invited guests had asked others.

Radiant in pale yellow satin, the tiny, brunette Rebel made a speech of greeting. Doctor Francisco de la Garza gave the history of the National White Cross. The doors of the spacious dining room were then thrown open. A large banquet table was decorated with floral designs, as only the nimble fingers of Indian artists can create. Seeking to emphasize the friendship of the two nations before American news correspondents, the Rebel asked Lily to accompany the First Chief. Queenly in pale blue tulle and satin, Lily walked with the Chief to the place of honor at the table, sitting at his right. The Rebel entered with General Pablo González. At her left sat General Antonio I. Villarreal, next to him nurse María Villarreal from Laredo.

The supper was a magnificent success. As the last glasses of wine were being sipped, Clemente Idar arose and made a brilliant speech.

He could sway the multitudes in English or Spanish. He spoke of the friendship between Mexico and the United States, lamenting the conduct of Huerta. He referred to the current policy of the United States of not wanting to acquire Mexican territory, and of President Wilson, who scorned the very suggestion of the violation of Mexico's sovereignty. Idar quoted Professor Hale, who had wisely remarked that it would be a fool's act, indeed, to barter the confidence of a hemisphere for what could be gained by open interference in Mexico's internal problems.

Later, a military escort arrived to take the First Chief to a meeting at the theatre, which by this time was filled with military men from all over the Republic. The function was more political than artistic. Orators had gathered to offer allegiance to the First Chief. The White Cross was represented by male members of the corps.

Carothers and Durac, the American newsmen, had attended the reception and had gone with the group to the theatre. It was in the early morning hours that the Rebel and Catarina sat together awaiting a return visit from Durac. Attentive to Catarina for the past few weeks, Durac had offered to pay for the girl's education before their marriage. Catarina eagerly awaited the American to find out his final plans.

To the practiced eye of the Rebel, the manner of Durac's entrance into the softly lit parlor told her what the man had decided. His hesitancy at the door, the hard set of his jaw, his exceeding politeness all passed over the girl's unsuspecting mind. The Rebel left them alone, going into the adjoining parlor in her role of chaperone. The visit between the two was a long one; Durac continually emphasized Catarina's youth, which until now had been her greatest charm. The importance of the girl's career was brought up; he did not wish to stand in her way.

"Señora Magnón," Durac spoke to the Rebel from the doorway, "I must go now. My train leaves in a few minutes."

The Rebel rose, her satin party dress lustrous in the half light. "Yes, señor?" she asked, already knowing his decision.

"Catarina is staying, señora. She . . ." He stopped, seeing the firm expression of the Rebel's mouth.

The girl was silent, having just been convinced of something; she was not sure what. The three of them stood wordlessly for a few minutes, the room looming large about them. The lights burned cruelly bright; the sweetish scent from the flowers was heavy and old now.

"Do you wish to go to the door with Mr. Durac, Catarina?" The Rebel spoke in rapid Spanish.

There must have been no farewells, for the heavy door shut immediately. The sound of the departing car, coughing as the hard-pressed accelerator filled the night with a harsh sound.

The next morning at a meeting attended by General Frausto, who was staying in one wing of White Cross headquarters, Doctors Rodolfo Villalba and Francisco de la Garza extended thanks to the faithful members of the corps. New officers of the brigade were named. Jovita Idar was to become the Rebel's secretary when Lily left the unit at San Luis Potosí. María Villarreal was named Inspector General of Hospitals. These women had been with the corps in Laredo. Aguirre continued as treasurer, the rest of the men staying with the corps for further assignment.

The White Cross was planning to go to San Luis where General Eulalio Gutiérrez had been appointed governor and General Pablo González, Military Commander. Meanwhile, there was local work to be done in Monterrey, and luck played into the Rebel's hands. Señora Angelina S. Meyers, who belonged to the powerful Zambrano family, accepted the presidency of the White Cross in Nuevo León. Merging several societies over which she presided, into one, she formed her White Cross unit. This woman of culture and prominence was a fortunate acquisition in furthering the effectiveness of the White Cross work in the rich industrial state of Nuevo León.

Meanwhile, news came from Zacatecas that General Villa was again on the rampage. General Obregón had just triumphed in Jalisco; many wounded were still lying on the battlefield when Villa sent him a telegram requesting him to come to Torreón. There was to be a conference with a committee of the North East Division representatives: Generals Cesáreo Castro, Antonio Villarreal, and Luis Caballero. The Division of the North, Villa's forces, sent José Isabel Robles, Ignacio Bonillas, and Doctor Miguel Silva, who was a man of culture.

Before the committee of the North East left Nuevo León, the Rebel received a message that General Luis Caballero had become ill, but was insisting on going on to Torreón. He needed a nurse. Explaining that the mission was secret, the Rebel asked Lily and Doctor Long to go. They did not hesitate, though Lily was tired. They would meet the subject of the controversy, General Ángeles, whom Villa felt had been slighted by General Carranza.

In Torreón, when Lily spoke to the officers of the Division of the North, she boldly defended the First Chief. She also told them that the First Chief had their meeting place under surveillance.

Noticing two chests in the headquarters of Villa's meeting place in Torreón, Lily quickly recognized them as having been part of the Chihuahua booty the Rebel had discovered buried at the hospital. As she was having her luggage taken to the train for their return trip, she pointed out the two chests as belonging to General Caballero and had them put on the train. Lily and the doctor took possession of them for benches. As soon as they arrived in Monterrey, she told General Caballero to take the chests with him. Although Lily turned over the chests unopened, she noticed that soon afterward some of the ragged uniforms of Carranza's soldiers were replaced by new ones.

The White Cross had put in a petition to go with General Pablo González' Division to San Luis Potosí, and had made plans accordingly. Carranza's never-tiring secretary, Mireles, was approached to obtain official permission from the busy Chief. Mireles sent the Rebel a telegram, calling later over the phone, saying that everything was arranged.

The First Chief was leaving immediately for Tampico with General Nafarate for a few days' visit. The people there wanted to know Carranza. He would inspect Tampico's large oil district, encouraging the people and probing into the question of intervention, as there were many Americans there. The troops of General Nafarate and Colonel Manzo's Fourth Battalion were escorting the Chief on this trip. General López de Lara, Governor of Tamaulipas, also went.

The Rebel rushed to the station to see the Chief off. The train was ready to pull out when the Chief hurriedly called out to the Rebel. "I shall see you in San Luis." Some of the Rebel's nurses were with the Chief's group. After the train had left, she stood silently watching until it disappeared behind the high mountains.

"How happy Juanita Mancha would be to greet the First Chief," the Rebel thought. She was head nurse in General Jesús Carranza's forces. Young and brave, she had accomplished much for the Revolution. An ex-school teacher, Juanita did whatever needed to be done, getting information of the Federals, doing propaganda work, or nursing. She spoke a little English, and could interpret for the Chief.

General Jesús Carranza, learning that the Rebel was sending nurses to Tampico, chose Juanita to go to the new fighting zone in Central Mexico to deliver confidential and important information to General Federico Montes. Montes had just waged a successful campaign against the Federals to gain the stronghold of Querétaro, which was now key to final victory.

Perfect for the job, Juanita, dressed as a peon, was seen briefly by the Rebel in San Luis. Mingling with the brigade, Juanita then proceeded ahead of Montes, gathering information about Federal troop movements for Generals Jesús Carranza and Montes.

On the First Chief's return from Tampico, he was to go immediately to San Luis, with the Fourth Battalion of Sonora continuing as his escort. Jesús Carranza's forces were to follow in another train as rear guard. General Pablo González's troops planned on leaving some days ahead of the advance guard. It was with this division that the Rebel and her corps were going. The brigade now consisted mostly of young men and women from Laredo who had worked for General González's division on the frontier.

The Rebel had little fear of being misunderstood by her subordinates. She was confident that she could handle things her own way with little interference. Traveling with her were Lily and Doctor Long, with their little son, Doctor Luis Cervantes, and Doctor Blum. The Rebel could pull away from them at a moment's notice and follow developments with María and Jovita, Aguirre, Idar, Portachelli, and Montoya to help. She made no plans too far ahead of time. Things were done on the spur of the moment's need, as they were presented.

Among General Pablo González's officers was General Francisco Murguía, second in command, who was considered the bravest of Carranza's military planners. The Rebel, an ardent admirer of bravery, sought Murguía's division. It went first, always—his tired, fearless soldiers, ahead of all the others. Perhaps, General Murguía saw in her the fiery instinct of the Apache, the persuasiveness of the Comanche. In an atmosphere of bravery and daring, she could more easily work out her plans.

During the day's traveling on a shabby train, sitting on hard benches, there was much talking and getting acquainted between the White Cross corps and the general's staff. The Rebel noticed two young officers, Colonel Guillermo Castillo y Tapia and Lieutenant Ricardo González. These two, the Rebel decided, would make a fine team for action in case of danger. One commanded a squad of artillery, the other a group of explorers. Both were very congenial and resourceful. They promised to help the nursing corps secure food, and to provide them with a few comforts during the trip.

Danger threatened the advancing Constitutionalists on all sides. Some scattered detachments of depressed Federals, defeated and driven toward the center of Mexico, sought refuge in the country surrounding San Luis. They formed guerrillas and attacked without warning, pillaging villages and destroying communications.

Late in the afternoon of the first day, some of Lieutenant González's men came into his car excitedly. It was probably bad news, as the Lieutenant shook his head and made frantic gestures to Colonel Tapia, who rushed to General Murguía's car. In a few moments, the train slowed down to a labored, creaking stop. The bridge ahead had been blown up.

The general threw a line of soldiers on guard around the cars. More troops scrambled up on top of the coaches, which were already occupied by soldiers and their wives. The Rebel, signaling to her people, got off the train. Noticing a handcar, she beckoned to María, two staff doctors, and her four aides. They all jumped on the car at the same time as Colonel Castello y Tapia and Lieutenant González. The officers looked surprised at the Rebel's actions, but signaled an artillery squad to follow on a hand-pushed car. Calling to Jovita to care for any casualties in case of fighting, the Rebel turned to face the stiff breeze on the hand car. As they moved swiftly along, Montoya handed his precious camera to her while he helped propel the car. The two young officers began singing gaily at the top of their voices as the car sped along the unguarded tracks.

Behind them, General Pablo González ordered the troops to set up camp and await a report of the damage. The army would have to wait there until the road was cleared and the bridge reconstructed. Meanwhile, General Francisco Murguía had detached the engine from the troop train, and with a car full of soldiers was slowly advancing toward the wrecked bridge. A bright, full moon guided them. Making occasional stops, the Rebel's party lighted their little hand lanterns and inspected the handcar and the track ahead. Towards daylight they arrived at the bridge.

Everyone went to work to clear the debris. Women who had come from surrounding ranches were sent home to bring food. The wounded were taken in carts to nearby villages. News reached the improvised camp at the bridge that skirmishes between Federal guerrillas and González's men had taken place around the halted troop train, but the Federals had withdrawn.

The train had set out from Saltillo on the sixteenth of July. It was late the next day when the train, after crossing the repaired bridge, reached a place between Venado and Bocas, about a hundred miles from San Luis. General Murguía ordered his troops to camp there for the night. Soon, the soldiers and nurses were rounding up wagons and tents. The lights from camp fires and *braceros* were bright against the dark night. Peopled with a shadowy army, the troop camp was laced with the soft sounds of soldiers' wives at their endless tasks of making tortillas and putting their babies to sleep.

Carrying a lantern in his hand, General Murguía made the rounds with the Rebel, María, and Jovita. He talked to all his chiefs. Away from the stress of battle, he was close to his men. In battle, he gave orders once, his fierceness belying his kind nature. He asked the Rebel and her nurses to his boxcar, where there was an improvised table made of boards laid across some beer cases. They had a soldiers' feast of *cabrito,* tortillas, and chili sauce; there were no knives or forks except the sharp mesquite sticks for spearing the meat. It was a good, earthy meal.

After supper, General Murguía's band formed along the side of the car and played until midnight. Then, the General had the car swept out with branches, and army blankets were stretched on the floor. Some of the officers rolled their coats for pillows for the nurses. Placing a guard at the door, Murguía left the Rebel and her companions for the night.

"I shall come early," he told her. "If we are to stay here, we will look for a place to have our hospital. My men have been out scouting. There is a big abandoned hacienda near here on a lake. Perhaps, you had better stay there."

"No," she replied,"we are too tired. We will stay here."

Fortunately, they did, for news came through that night that the Federals were converging on San Luis, pursued by General Carrera Torres.

Quickly in the early morning, Colonel Castillo y Tapia had his squads ready with their rapid-firing guns. The Rebel and María began filling their cauldrons with fresh water in preparation for any necessary hospital work. Montoya was photographing the two of them when General Murguía came driving along in his car. Lily Long was in the back seat.

"Magnón, come here!" she shouted to the Rebel. "The general says I must be the first to shoot."

"To shoot? What is the idea, general?" the astonished Rebel asked.

"She must shoot first," he replied. "My men have heard what a good shot she is."

Taking one of the general's guns, Lily leaned out of the window of the moving car. Quickly she shot at two birds flying past. Both fell to the ground. The general stopped the car, picked up the quail and held them high for his men, who were forming their ranks nearby, to see.

Throwing them to an aide, he said, "I shall have them for breakfast. We will return in an hour."

Murguía inspected all his troops; receiving his reports, he handed them to the Rebel to hold. Afterwards, he conferred with his general in command. At breakfast, Murguía did not share his birds, but gave the corps a fine meal of *ranchero* eggs that people from neighboring ranches had brought.

News came during the morning that the train could go forward to San Luis, although the trip would take until evening, as the road was still being repaired. When the army boarded the train, there were people from the surrounding countryside who got on with the troops. At every stop the train made, excited men and women greeted the soldiers, wishing them a speedy victory.

Before abandoning San Luis, the Federals had destroyed everything that might be of use to the Constitutionalists. When the Federalist governor had been captured by the incoming troops, he was tied to a wagon and dragged through the streets of the town. Churches had been pillaged; the monastery and hospital damaged. Some of the havoc had been done by the pressing Carrancistas.

The traditionally aristocratic city of San Luis, seat of learning and a religious stronghold, boasted one of the largest universities in the Republic. Built in the heart of the city, shrouded by enormous eucalyptus and fruit trees, the university buildings were looted and wantonly defaced. Here was the observatory where students from all over Mexico came to study astronomy. Corridors of old paintings in the university had been chipped and scratched by the knives and guns of irresponsible soldiers. The terrified populace was leaving the city afraid of a worse fate if they stayed. General Eulalio Guitérrez and his brother, Luis, and General Carrera Torres had not been able to control the situation. The fighting had been fierce.

On the evening of July twentieth, after four days of interrupted traveling, General Pablo González, Military Commander of the Central Zone, entered San Luis with 60,000 men. With González, besides a large number of officers, were a great many writers. There was General Manuel W. González, a keen critic, writer of biting anecdotes, Colonel Alfredo Rodríguez, who was Chief of Staff, Federico Elizondo, and Fortunato Zauzau.

When the troop train arrived, the city was in utter darkness, under martial law. Constitutionalist guards on horseback patrolled the deserted streets with lanterns hanging at the sides of their saddles. There was no welcome. The air was filled with breathless tension.

"¿Quién vive?" shouted sentinels to passersby. "Who lives?"

Those who answered "Villa" were stopped. Again the sentinel repeated his question, aiming his gun at his terrified victim. If Carranza was the answer, the guard would put away his gun and be on his way.

The Rebel was being escorted by General Francisco Murguía and Doctor Blum. The brigade followed them quietly down the dark, empty street. No lights came from the grilled windows to show the way. A man on horseback approached. Introducing himself as Doctor

McKaller, General Eulalio Gutiérrez's staff doctor, he dismounted and shook hands with the Rebel and Lily. He was to escort the Rebel's party to the nearest safe place available. In the morning, he would call and take them to their quarters.

The doctor left them at an impressive doorway that loomed massive and forbidding above them. A sentinel came out of the darkness to escort them through the deserted building. Following him up a wide stair with carved stone banisters, the Rebel could not imagine where they were being led. At the head of the stairs they were handed a box of candles and told to select their own bedrooms.

Too tired to inspect their surroundings, the Rebel, María, and Jovita went into the first room they came to. Magnificent doors with stained glass panels opened into a spacious, elegantly furnished bedroom. Deep red plush portieres and handsome lace drapery hung over the windows overlooking the dark street. María and Jovita quickly undressed and crawled into the wide bed. The Rebel threw herself on a large, comfortable lounge. Looking through the glass panels in the door, the Rebel could see small, dim lights. She was about to turn away when Lily opened the door. Silently, the Rebel went out to meet her, closing the door behind her.

"Magnón," Lily spoke softly, "Doctor Long is asleep, but I couldn't sleep, thinking about you."

"Yes, we will soon part, Lily," the Rebel answered thoughtfully. "Stay close to General Caballero. He is loyal to the Chief. Our Chief will need many friends in his triumph, even more than before."

They walked over towards the stone railing overlooking a large, dim hall filled with gold-painted furniture. The Rebel remembered seeing the same kind of delicate furnishings in Versailles.

"Let's get a lantern from the sentinel at the door," suggested the Rebel. "We can explore this castle, even if we can't sleep."

Arousing a sleeping guard to take his place, the sentinel took a lantern and led them through the dark corridors. They came first to the chapel. Rich vestments were thrown on the floor from the half open drawers of a massive carved chest. Fine linens and lace vestments were hanging half-caught by the hasty ransacking of drawers. The altar was desecrated and the statues of the saints riddled with bullets.

The Rebel found out from the guard that they were in the palace of the Reverend Archbishop Montes de Ocas. This high prelate had sponsored the rich pilgrimages to Rome that the Rebel's husband had organized in 1902 and 1903. When the Rebel knelt down and prayed amid the shambles, even the guard knelt, taking off his cap.

The guard wanted to take them on further, but the two women had seen enough. He whispered to them that the next day the priests were to be sent off to the frontier. Only the Mexican priests would be permitted to return.

Gallantly, the sentinel gave the Rebel his flickering lantern and left them. They felt small and lonely in the great, shadowy, marble hall. Leaving Lily at her door, the Rebel went alone. Setting the lantern down in a little empty niche, she left it burning. Somehow the light, though small and uncertain, gave warmth and hope in the immense darkness of the bishop's palace.

When dawn came to the silent city, no church bells summoned the townspeople. Remembering the many dangers that had befallen them, the people remained in their houses, waiting for servants and tradespeople to bring them news of what kind of creatures the Carrancistas were. As a further precaution, they decided to lock their doors as well as their hearts against the conqueror.

Doctor McKaller, an American who had come to Mexico with a mining company, was an early riser. Arriving at the bishop's palace, he sent the sleepy guard up to arouse the sleeping brigade. He was impatiently awaiting them when they appeared downstairs; starting off at a brisk walk, his broad brimmed hat at a jaunty angle. The corps followed him breathlessly to a nearby restaurant.

"Doctor," the Rebel said as soon as she had caught her breath after sitting down at the table with him, "surely the bishop's palace will not be our headquarters?"

"No," he replied, "but it was the safest place for you last night. You will occupy Doctor Soberón's home that has been confiscated by the governor."

"But, Doctor," the Rebel said, disturbed by the change in routine, "we are to stay here only until we organize the hospital and care for the wounded. I could stay at the hotel, and the rest of the corps at the hospital."

"No," the Doctor answered her thoughtfully, "better stay in the Soberón house. The hotel has been taken over for General Pablo González and his men. Besides, the hospital has to be thoroughly cleaned. I have orders from the governor to give you any help you need to put the place in order.

"Ezequiel Ruiz, our propagandist, can handle a crew of soldiers, or prisoners, for the clean-up job," the Rebel replied. "We want everything in good order by the time the First Chief arrives."

"Wait until you see the hospital," the doctor said smiling. "It is the most wonderfully designed building I have ever seen."

Work in San Luis was not as it had been in other places. Finding echo in the hearts of the citizens of the newly conquered state did not come easily. Viewing the disorders and crimes of the fleeing Federals, the people were not soon convinced that in order to construct the new it is often necessary to witness destruction of the old.

Walking up the wide stairway of the San Luis hospital, her brigade trailing some distance behind her, the Rebel was overcome with wonder at the beauty of the place. Reflecting the sun back into her face were dozens and dozens of windows.

"I am patterned with brilliance," she thought to herself. "It must be a good omen, after the dark night."

Built in the shape of a wheel, the immense hospital building was walled with windows. The central unit was a circular building. On one floor was the round operating room, out from which fanned the wards, like spikes. Each ward was separated from the other by gardens planted in between each building. Outbuildings were laid out to continue the pattern of the wheel.

When the corps took over the hospital, the work was divided among them, each one having command of a crew of workmen. Although the nurses hastily prepared beds, no sheets could be found. The storerooms were empty, and there were no medicines or chloroform. Sitting at her empty desk, holding her hands to her forehead, the Rebel thought and prayed. Only a miracle could make the place ready for use in time.

Just then Doctor McKaller entered the room. "Señora," he said as he saw her, "you are exhausted. This is a tremendous job."

"No, doctor," she replied, smiling at his concern, "I am only trying to collect my scattered thoughts."

"You shall go with me to the governor," he said. "But first, let me take you to a wonderful woman who will help you. She is a Britisher, married to a Spanish dentist. She loves Mexico."

"First, you must give a report to the governor," the Rebel spoke, rapidly making plans. "Then we will tell this woman that we need sheets, lots of sheets and pillow cases, bedding of any kind. I'll ask the governor for an order to cover expenses. With luck, in a few hours we will be ready to receive our wounded."

"What?" exclaimed the doctor. "That's impossible."

"Doctor," she said fervently, thinking of the situation in San Luis, "the religion of our people cannot be destroyed. It has been stamped on their souls through generations. I have prayed. Help will come."

After inspecting the hospital, the doctor looked into the operating room. Thoughtfully shaking his head, he said, "I shall take the responsibility of bringing an operating table or two from some of the doctors' offices. There are three at Doctor Soberón's. I shall bring one and leave a receipt to be paid later. I might also find some chloroform there."

Several operations had already been performed without anesthesia, the nurses holding the men, trying to comfort them. There was plenty of alcohol available, which helped soothe the sore bodies of the wounded men.

Accompanied by María, Jovita, and Lily, the Rebel and Doctor McKaller arrived at the home of Mimi Eschausier to explain their needs for the hospital. A smiling, well-trained maid escorted them to the drawing room. The doctor walked about the room, nervously working his hands in his pockets.

The Rebel took in every detail of this room. The exquisite taste of the lady of the house was a meter of her bountiful grandeur. Bright with its burnished golden light, a harp stood in a corner, half draped with a rich cloth. An open piano, on which stood a tall venetian vase of red roses, filled one part of the room. The music file was replete. A guitar and mandolin lay carelessly on a gilded French divan. Dresden figures on the marble mantle completed the impression of art and culture.

As the Rebel sat wondering about her hostess, Mimi Eschausier appeared. She was tall and well proportioned, a rosy blonde with blue eyes. A ripple of laughter had preceded her, filling their hearts with assurance of her good will. The Doctor advanced and, with a low, gentlemanly bow, saluted the queenly woman who was to be the answer to the Rebel's prayer.

Seating herself by the open piano, she graciously inquired about their work, mingling questions with gay repartee. Signaling to the maid, she told her to prepare tea and to ask her daughters to come to be presented to the guests. The two young girls who were introduced by their mother with a deep maternal pride were both adopted. One girl had an olive complexion and warm coloring. She was Indian. The other child was Spanish, with fair skin and dark eyes; her hair was raven black. Both children were groomed to perfection.

When tea was served, the Rebel, her heart filled with joy, had to control herself, lest an outburst of tears fill her eyes, betraying her. Squeezing the lemon vigorously into her tea, she had an excuse to wipe away the emotional tears.

Before the visit had spent itself, everything was arranged. The beautiful Mimi would organize the White Cross in the state of San Luis Potosi, as president. She had vast holdings, including a large hacienda, which she loved and where she took good care of her peons. Familiar with all walks of life, she belonged to the aristocratic circle of

San Luis. Her work would have to fight against a current of opposition for a time.

Returning from their visit, they separated at the door of the hospital, Jovita and María to supervise the supper hour, Lily and the Rebel to call on the governor.

At the Governor's Palace, Eulalio Gutiérrez stood in greeting as Doctor McKaller introduced Lily and the Rebel. A strong man of wonderful physique, his great brown eyes viewed everything with a boundless serenity. In civilian clothes, he looked even better than in his smart uniform. The governor called his secretary, who filled out an order and handed it to him for his official signature. The paper was handed to the doctor, who bowed himself out.

The governor had just received a committee of Catholic women, who had come to plead for protection of the priests and against further anti-Catholic action.

"I have promised them that nothing further will take place, but they must abide by my orders," he said calmly. "The churches will be closed until the final triumph over Huerta. They can help if they obey orders."

When the Rebel and Lily returned to the hospital, the nurses greeted them with the news that Señora Eschausier had already canvassed the town, and local merchants had sent out load after load of bedding, underwear, and pajamas. The hospital was now equipped with the necessities to properly take care of the wounded.

General Pablo González, the Military Commander, had numerous army details to thrash out before the arrival of the First Chief. With a large army, González and his men were to move on, preceding Carranza, to insure the Chief's safety. The last Federal defense to be taken was the rich state of Querétero, another Catholic stronghold, which had suffered from combat and destruction by troops of both sides.

The First Chief now had the religious question to face, added to Villa's increasingly arbitrary acts. There was also the possibility of outside intervention by the A B C powers meeting at Niagara Falls. Looming uncertainly from the south were the strong figures of Zapata and Orozco, who would have to be considered in the peace settlement. All this would have set back any leader, if the young people around Carranza had not been so well balanced and resourceful.

Word came that Huerta had finally left Mexico on July fifteenth, escorted to the port of escape by a battalion of loyal soldiers. Lawyer León de la Barra had been named Provisional President to keep order in the capital.

At the hospital in San Luis, among the wounded brought in from the surrounding villages was the body of a soldier who had been killed, and his critically wounded wife, who was dying. After the death of his mother, their little eight-year-old son came pitifully, silently to the Rebel and, laying his small head in her lap, cried bitterly. The child stayed at the hospital until some arrangements could be made for him. According to orders, the parents were buried together in a cemetery called El Saucito near the child's home, so that he could always remember the place. The little boy was formally adopted by one of General Pablo González's staff, and the Rebel soon became fond of the child, for he continued to spend much of his time at the hospital. He became the mascot of the corps, and Mimi Eschausier taught him to read and write.

Advancing rapidly, the First Chief arrived in San Luis. After a wild greeting by the troops, he went to the hospital with General Luis Caballero, whose division was now the First Chief's guard, along with the Fourth Battalion. After a small social gathering of welcome in the office of the hospital, the Chief visited each wounded soldier, handing him five pesos for cigarettes. Standing at the door of the ward, he made an inspiring speech, telling the men they still had work to finish, and praising them for their sacrifices. He reminded them of the planned triumphal entry soon to take place into Mexico City.

The Chief approached the Rebel, asking her to be ready with those who were to accompany her to Querétaro. They were to leave the next morning very early. Lily would not go with General Luis Caballero to Mexico City. It was already August. They had been in San Luis a month. General Federico Montes had been notified to receive the Rebel and her corps at the train, as they were to stay in Querétaro until further orders from the First Chief. The corps was not to go to Teotihuacán to await the arrival and grouping of high officers and their escorts before the official entry into Mexico City. The Rebel asked no questions, accepting what she was told. In Querétaro, she would find out the information she needed.

As usual, people crowded the depot to see the Chief's departure. On the back platform of the train stood Doña Virginia Salinas de Carranza, the Chief's wife, and their two daughters, with General Caballero and his staff. There were military trains ahead of them and behind them.

The Rebel saw Colonel Carlos Fierros, a Laredo youth, who had risen rapidly in rank. On arrival in Mexico City he was to be made a general. It was but a few days after his promotion that he became deathly ill. When he died, the Rebel went to his funeral. The young warrior had fallen to disease, the insidious enemy that uses neither gun nor knife.

The Chief was now traveling in the best of Pullmans with one drawing room occupied by his family. In the rest of the car were diplomats, division generals, and the Chief's own staff. In the National White Cross car, General Fontes made the corps comfortable, providing tables and typewriters which attracted reporters and writers whose company the Rebel dearly loved. After the train pulled out from San Luis, the corps' work fell into routine again. The brigade made dozens of propaganda insignias, most based on the First Chief. On this trip, they were no longer in General Pablo González's forces, but with General Teodoro Elizondo, who was to remain in Querétaro. Also staying would be General Ramón Frausto and Calixto Maldonado and his wife.

During the day Colonel Carlos Fierros came with a message for the Rebel from the Chief. She was expected to spend the night with two companions in the Chief's car. This she promptly and decidedly refused, thanking the officer.

"Is that all?" he asked politely. "No supper with us?"

"No," the Rebel answered, "I have my brigade to instruct. The time is short."

"But the Chief wants to talk to you," he insisted.

"Then he may come in to see us," she nodded, smiling. "We probably won't see him again until he is installed in the president's chair. On that day, we will see how the land lies," she concluded so softly that Fierros could not make out her last words.

Fierros, who had been one of her co-workers at the Madero outbreak, and again at Carranza's call to arms, knew the independent Rebel. With a little questioning smile, he bowed and withdrew.

Towards evening when the train made a short stop, the Chief got out and walked thoughtfully up and down the station platform. Colonel Fontes made a sign to the Rebel. Thinking he was calling her to supper, she got off with her nurses. In front of the station restaurant, a Chinese man was ringing a bell furiously and insistently. As Fontes escorted them to the small, dark restaurant, the First Chief stepped up and detained the Rebel.

"I am going to beg of you to remain in Querétaro," he began immediately. "I will send you a wire when it is time to join us. It is right and just that you and your brigade enter Mexico with our victorious armies.

"Teotihuacán would be hard for all of you. There are no accommodations. My family," he said nodding toward the train, "is safe in the Pullman. There are many women who will meet us in Teotihuacán, wives of officers, who have long been awaiting their loved ones. General Montes will take you to a suitable residence in Querétaro. I will let you know when to come," Carranza stood looking at her, stroking his white beard.

"My general, we do whatever you wish. You know that," she replied.

In the clear moonlight she saw a rare, broad smile light his face. Winking back at the twinkling stars, she thought, "What pranks the stars play with our plans."

Going into the cafe, she was handed a sandwich and a bottle of hot coffee. When the train began moving a few minutes later, the Rebel and her nurses ran out laughing and talking to board a car. A wide door opened to them, and hands appeared to lift them inside. It was the car that carried the Chief's automobile. For a long time, the women sat in the open doorway, swinging their feet and talking, looking out into the night, planning the coming day of triumph. The train was making no stops, so the guards lit their lanterns and their cigarettes, and eased watch.

When the Rebel decided that she and her companions would spend the night there, the guards provided blankets for the nurses and spread them on the floor. The Rebel climbed in the back seat of the Chief's car, and María got in front.

"You have captured this fort," one of the guards said good humoredly. "You may sing, snore, or make plans. We will keep guard. It is good to hear women's voices in the night."

Early the next morning, the guards called the Rebel and her nurses in time for them to fix up and be ready when the train arrived at the depot. They found a sheet for the women to step on in getting out of the box car. Coming up to the crowd around the First Chief, the Rebel heard him tell General Federico Montes to take the White Cross corps to the home of Señor Isaz, one of the richest men in Querétaro.

CHAPTER XVI
Resignation

The First Chief was standing near the train as an official was addressing the crowd. People had even come from Mexico City to escort the Chief to the capital. There was a hurried breakfast and a rush of cars forming to accompany the First Chief to El Cerro de las Campanas on the outskirts of the city. It was on this site that Maximilian, Miramón, and Mejía had been executed. The visitors who wrote their signatures in the register there were mostly high ranking officers. Jovita, María, and the Rebel also signed their names.

Returning to the station, the First Chief presented General Federico Montes to them as governor of the state of Querétaro. Amid waving and cheering, the Chief's train left for Teotihuacán, followed by other trains loaded to full capacity.

During the time in Torreón, the Rebel had met a fearless writer, Alfonso Peneche. Hardly had she time to know him when he was off to the front. She remembered often his scorching words and scornful attitude towards the mercenary and avaricious ones in the Constitutional Army. Evidently, he did not forget the White Cross. Some time later, he wrote the Rebel asking her to take into her corps the bearer of his message: a woman whom he assured the Rebel was a brave and loyal worker for the cause. After consulting with her corps it was decided to take the woman and give her easy work. Evidently, she had met with many hardships.

As the Chief's train pulled out of Querétaro, the Rebel caught sight of Peneche flying past. Hanging to the railing of the last car, halfway over the platform, he was waving wildly to Idar.

"See you at the Cosmos," he shouted.

How strange that he should say that, thought the Rebel. She had already made reservations at the same hotel for her corps. The owners of the place were old friends of the Rebel. General López de Lara, the future governor of Tamaulipas, was to make his headquarters at the Cosmos, too.

The house where the National White Cross lodged was superb. It accommodated Generals Marcelino Murrieta and Teodoro Elizondo and their staffs, and General Ramón Frausto. There were two dining rooms. The Rebel organized the household so that the servants could wait independently on the staffs of officers and soldiers and the National White Cross in separate quarters. In the house was a family chapel that had been closed by the governor.

General Federico Montes called to escort the Rebel and her corps to the hospitals. "You'd better carry your rosaries," he said laughing. "Let them be seen, for the population here is very religious.

Prominent women of the city boarded the train, while the First Chief was on an inspection tour, to complain bitterly to Señora Carranza.

"The poor soul," the Rebel replied. "Señora Carranza and her daughters must be very tired. However, they are Catholics."

Although the stay in Querétaro was to be a short one, the White Cross set about immediately putting the hospitals in working order. News came that at the Red Cross Center there were some wounded still uncared for. Trying to locate the place was difficult. At one house, the men of the corps were drenched with water poured on them from an upstairs window while they were inquiring about the wounded men.

Continuing their search, they noticed a man suspiciously guarding a great gateway. Idar and Ruiz approached him, asking for information about the wounded soldiers. The man shook his head woodenly, standing closer to the gate. The guard's feeling inside his coat made the men more sure that here was the place. Idar, in a quick move, jerked back the man's coat, revealing a ring of keys hanging on his belt.

Unlocking the heavy wooden door and entering the courtyard, they heard groans coming from the building. Through the high, dusty windows they peered into a long hall. Lying on beds were wounded men, unattended.

"Why are these men here alone?" the Rebel asked the guard.

"The Red Cross has no money," he grumbled. "Everyone left them, saying they were Carrancistas. People here are afraid to help for fear of the Federals."

When the boys threw open the great doors of the hall, the Rebel stepped inside the threshold. Horrified, she saw one of the soldiers kneeling in the middle of the room praying wildly. The men were all thirsting for water.

"Captain," the Rebel gasped. "What is this?"

"Señora," he said trembling feebly. "We are starving. We have been here for four days. No water, no food, no medicines!"

In the confusion of the going and coming of Federals and Constitutionalists, the men had been neglected and forgotten. In the mad rush to be in Teotihuacán in time to enter Mexico City with the Chief, the sixty wounded had been shunted off to the Red Cross Center and abandoned. They were so badly wounded, they could do nothing for themselves. Even the water had been cut off.

Doors from the hall were opened and rooms were found to be stacked with supplies and medicines. A perfect kitchen was clean and ready for use. Immediately, the men of the brigade installed themselves in the guard's quarters, taking charge of the keys and relieving him of his watch. However, he was left free to come and go as he wished.

The new-found hospital and the wounded soldiers were now the responsibility of the White Cross. Captain Del Toro and his men, separated from the rest of their division of wounded, had found their way to Querétaro after the Federals had abandoned the city. They belonged to General Lucio Blanco's division, which was already in Teotihuacán. General Montes was their commander, but he would be leaving the next day. General Elizondo was to remain in command.

Several hours later, the Rebel, María, Jovita, and Montoya returned to headquarters to rest and talk with General Elizondo. As they entered the house, the Rebel rushed to the stairs. From somewhere a young officer appeared and, running after the Rebel, caught and hugged her.

"Who is this young man?" María asked, laughing. "Someone from Laredo?"

"Remember the night the wind blew me in on Pancho's skiff?" the young officer said, hugging them again and again,

"María de Jesús," the Rebel exclaimed. "Come on up to our little sitting room. It's good to see you."

As soon as they had entered the Rebel's sitting room, María de Jesús took a message from her tunic. It was from General Marcelino Murrietta to the Rebel.

"I am tired," the girl said after they had visited a few minutes. "I would like to take a bath and sleep."

"I shall order your supper, and you can sleep as peacefully as you did in Pancho's hut," the Rebel replied. She couldn't help pampering the strange, beautiful girl who gave so little thought to her own safety.

Meanwhile, Jovita, the Rebel's secretary, was busy with her nightly report. Gathering news, she would wire it along the line to the frontier and Laredo. From the beginning of the Revolution, the Rebel had a pass and time allotted her for transmitting news over the Constitutionalist wires. Now Jovita had taken the job.

The Rebel also got news by wire of her children, who read eagerly all the accounts of the progress of the White Cross from the home of her brother Leopold in Laredo. But there was no news regarding Adolpho, her husband. For almost a year, she had not heard a single word from him. This worried her, although she appeared indifferent to her personal affairs. It was her constant prayer that her work would be for the honor of her loved ones and the glory of her beloved Mexico.

The large drawing room at headquarters in Querétaro had been converted into a club room where the household gathered in small visiting groups. There was talk of past glories, of plans for future ones, and of the burning anxiety to be among the first to enter the city with the Chief. Yet, the White Cross corps went on silently gathering up the wounded and caring for them regardless of the nebulous plans of the uninjured fighting men.

Several days passed uneventfully for the brigade, save for the constant attention given the wounded. General Elizondo had showered attentions on the nurses, always lamenting that there were so many wounded that could not be left alone when the call came for him to leave.

One day about two weeks after the White Cross had come to Querétaro, General Elizondo came to the hospital with a telegram for the Rebel. It was from headquarters, signed by Gustavo Mireles: "The *Jefe* says you are to come immediately with the White Cross." General Elizondo had orders to leave, also.

When she had read the message, Elizondo solemnly handed her a little revolver he kept in an inside pocket. Looking at her carefully, he said, "I am leaving this to you."

"It is, indeed, something I might need," the Rebel said slowly, turning the pistol in her hand. She had given Lily the pistol the First Chief had given her in El Paso.

The General turned and walked toward the door, not hurrying. The Rebel, watching his bright, polished boots on the red tile floor, did not raise her head to say goodbye. It was when the boots spun around toward her that she threw back her head and met the General's questioning eyes.

"What have you decided?" he said softly. "Is it to be honor, or duty?"

"General," she said, looking straight at him, still fingering the pistol. "I shall stay here with my wounded."

All that day, she went about in a feverish state of mind. How unjust it would be to leave the helpless wounded in less-trained hands. Yet, how unfair to her brigade to deprive them of the moment of gratification and honor in Mexico City. Somehow, she prayed, the problem would be solved.

Doctor Blum, Doctor Osuna—she must find someone for a last look at her patients. She went to General Elizondo's headquarters. He had just come in after a few hour's rest.

"General," she said, "come with me and see the forgotten squadron."

As they started out together, the Rebel's plans crystallized in her mind. General Elizondo helped her into his car and, getting in himself, closed the door.

"To the little hospital," he called to the driver.

"Wait, my general," she said impulsively as the car started. "I have decided to do both. I shall take the wounded. We will be in time for my White Cross to enter Mexico. "You are the commander. Take me to the railway station. I want two cars—cattle cars, boxcars, it doesn't matter. If you will give orders to turn them over to me and have the cars hitched on your train, we will be leaving with you tomorrow," she concluded.

At the railway station a few minutes later, the Rebel was handed a written permit, which she had watched the general sign. It was almost supper time when the general left the Rebel. She could use his car to complete her plans. The boxcars had to be readied by early morning. Cleaned, disinfected, and whitewashed, the cars were stocked with medicines and provisions. Two coal stoves were put in for heat, and last, the mattresses for the wounded.

At the clinic, the soldiers were told of the plans, and their wounds were carefully dressed. The nurses were handed a list of names of the men for whom they would be responsible. María, the Rebel and Doctor Osuna would go in the first car with the more serious cases. María de Jesús and the men of the brigade would guard the cars. By midnight, everything was ready, and the wounded were carefully transferred to their traveling quarters. The conductor had provided red lanterns to hang at the door of each car. Satisfied with their move, the Rebel went to report to General Elizondo. Everything in the clinic had been cleaned up and the doors locked. The keys were turned over to the proper authorities. They were now ready to leave the city of Querétaro.

Early in the morning, about two o'clock, the train pulled out. The two White Cross cars were hooked on last. On top of the cars rode the men of the brigade. Fastening cords from the roof down to the Rebel's car, they made it easy for her to keep in touch with them. As they rode through the darkness, the Rebel held watch over her group. Perhaps it would be the last time she would have the privilege of overseeing them.

On and on the train traveled. Day came and passed swiftly into evening. The wounded slept, rocked by the moving train and comforted by the attentions of the nurses. As the train went through a deep ravine between high mountains, a lawless group jumped off low hanging cliffs, clinging to the half open doors of the boxcar in which the Rebel kept vigil.

"We want this car," a grizzled, dirty man in an officer's uniform shouted to the startled people in the boxcar.

"Who are you to give orders?" the Rebel demanded, jumping up and taking her gun from her bag.

"See for yourself," the man replied tossing a greasy card at her feet. "Dinamitero del Centro." The card gave his profession as a train dynamiter.

Pulling the cords for help from the men of the brigade, she barred momentarily the entrance of the dynamiting team. Soon help came, and the renegades were taken by surprise from above, tossed and fought on the floor of the moving car. María de Jesús got word to the engineer to get on faster. When the leader regained consciousness, he told the brigade that he was from Aguas Calientes. He had not heard of the First Chief's triumph on his dynamiting mission across the continent toward Mexico City.

On the outskirts of Mexico City, María de Jesús came to the Rebel. One of the badly wounded soldiers was resting his head in her lap while she was feeding him through a glass tube. She dared not move her aching limbs, lest she disturb him. She beckoned María de Jesús to come close.

"I have just overheard a conversation," María de Jesús whispered. "A plot to kill the First Chief tonight. I have the address of the place they think he will go."

With difficulty, the Rebel pulled out a small notebook from her apron pocket. She glanced over it quickly at first, then hesitated, comparing the address María de Jesús had to hers.

"I know the place," she said. "María, mingle with these men. Follow them when we arrive. You know where we will lodge. Wait for me there. Then we will go together."

How long the remaining few hours of traveling seemed. The Rebel remembered the night in a little town where the train had stopped on the way to Torreón. Knowing of the constant danger to his life, the Chief handed the Rebel an address to a house in Mexico City.

"Keep this," he had said. "If anything should happen to me, find your way to Mexico City and notify my loyal people there. They are always in danger."

General Jesús Carranza had also given the same address to the spy, Juanita Mancha.

At midnight, after twenty-four hours of travel, they arrived in Mexico City. Trains were still arriving at the then Colonia Station. The intricate railroad switching and unhitching of car after car, and sidetracking them after they had been unloaded, delayed the White Cross for some time.

It was August 14, 1915. General Carranza had arrived in Mexico City that morning. The doors of the National Palace had been thrown open wide to receive him.

On the front page of the great daily newspaper, *El Imparcial,* was the picture of the Rebel and her brigade. Her corps had been highly honored. At the station, she was handed a letter from the editor of the paper, Reyes Spíndola, who had published the paper for many years and had been dean of the newspapermen during Díaz's time. However, Spíndola was soon to be replaced by the editor of *El Liberal,* when the government began immediately confiscating newspapers.

Ambulances were provided, and the White Cross wounded were taken to a recently improvised Red Cross hospital in the center of the city, just two blocks from Hotel Cosmos. The Rebel left the train to report to General Luis Blanco, accompanied by his cousins, Evita and Trini Flores Blanco, who were stationed in the city. They had come to the train to go with the Rebel to his headquarters.

When the two señoritas, Trini and Evita Flores Blanco, had come to Laredo at the beginning of the Carranza revolt, their beauty and charm had captivated many hearts. They were the idols of the newspaper men, especially the editors of the liberal Spanish daily.

Young Trini had been in charge of the telegraph office in their home in Monclova. Their mother, famous for her beauty, died young, and their father had devoted his life to the two little girls, though he was never very strong. Spending playful hours around the telegraph office, Trini soon learned to decipher messages. After her mother died, Trini became telegraph operator and had sent the younger Evita to San Antonio to school.

In 1912 when the two girls reached Laredo, they were already identified with the Madero Revolution of 1910. They had passed many messages for Madero while he was struggling to overthrow Díaz. They had kept secret communications hidden deep in the center of their mattresses. Any information the Revolutionists sent, they relayed without charge. The sisters had many friends among telegraph operators throughout Mexico.

In Laredo, the Revolutionary Junta thought it would be helpful for the two sisters to return to Mexico, where they could intercept important messages. Since they were accepted among the Federals without serving them, it would be feasible for them to cross the line into Federalist territory, accompanied by their father. They reached Mexico City after many difficulties, and towards the last of Huerta's control, they got possession of the telegraph office in Tacubaya, the key to the Zapatista camp on the outskirts of Mexico City. They were then in a position to intercept all messages to and from the surrounding areas. Morelia was entirely cut off from communication by the girls' cohorts. The Federalists did not even know when General Pablo González arrived and established his headquarters in Tacubaya.

The Rebel returned to the hotel immediately after leaving General Blanco. With María de Jesús, María Villarreal, and Jovita she started walking toward the Alameda. No one spoke. It was almost two in the morning. They had not had a moment's rest since their departure from Querétaro. Although it was August, the night was chilly and a persistent drizzle had made puddles on the sidewalks and filled the air with a clinging mist. Walking beside the Rebel, María de Jesús told her that the First Chief was still in the National Palace, receiving group after group of soldiers congratulating him and their chiefs swearing allegiance.

"The First Chief looks tired, but he has to bear it," María de Jesús said. "He is surrounded by dissent and rebellion."

"Yes, I can imagine," the Rebel replied dryly. "We shall go back to the hotel as soon as we find the place we are looking for."

They walked rapidly through the dark streets. The Zapatistas had control of the power and light plant, and the aqueduct and water supplies, which was part of their plan for entering Mexico.

They stopped uncertainly in front of a great open archway. Then going into a big patio, the women went up a stone stairway into an open hall whose banister overlooked the dark patio they had just left. A dim light coming from one of the many windows gave the Rebel courage to knock at the door. A thin, pale woman holding a lighted candle in a heavy silver candle holder opened the door slowly, the small, flickering light casting giant shadows in the immense darkness.

Pushing her way inside gently, the Rebel entered a large parlor, where she stopped suddenly. Before her was a life-size painting of the First Chief, covering an entire wall. At the foot of the painting, on the floor, banked up like fallen snow, was a fine linen sheet.

"Have you had this hanging on the wall all this time?" not believing, the Rebel asked the wraith-like woman. "It is a miracle you have not been betrayed."

"It has been completely covered with this cloth," the woman replied. "It had the appearance of a solid wall. Tonight we ceremoniously pulled off the draperies so the First Chief could see it."

"No!" the Rebel exclaimed. "He must not come here tonight. His life is in danger. Can you get a message to him?"

Noticing the woman's questioning look at the warning, the Rebel smiled at her own brusqueness. "Tell him, if he asks," she said gently, "that the President of the White Cross sent you."

"He will know at once," the woman replied calmly.

The Rebel handed her the paper the Chief had once given her. It was only an address. The Rebel had fulfilled her mission. The address was lost to memory. It had been the symbol of refuge to the Chief's loyal followers in the face of death and disloyalty.

When the nurses got into bed for a few hours sleep just before dawn, the Rebel had already formed her plans. Next morning, calling Idar and his sister, Jovita, she said, "Federico, get your typewriter. We shall lock ourselves up today, and no one will disturb us."

That day they drew up an account of all the war work of the National White Cross and a list of their expenses. Then a resignation was written. The First Chief was free now to appoint new members for a peacetime White Cross. Having accomplished their purpose, the corps were eager to return to their homes, but they would always respond to a call. Copies were made of the resignation to send to members of the Rebel's scattered corps. They would be free to choose their own future. The whole staff in Mexico City signed the resignation.

Alfonso Peneche had looked for the corps all day. Finally, at supper time he came into the Rebel's room. Pulling a document out of his pocket, he thrust it into her hands.

"Read. Read," he said dramatically. "I am going to the newspaper right now. It shall appear tomorrow."

The Rebel read the paper as Peneche stood by awaiting her opinion. It was a strongly worded patriotic document of loyalty to the Chief. He had written his resignation, so Carranza could set freely in choosing his officials. The Rebel handed him her resignation, asking him to take it to the government newspaper, also. She had already sent the original to the First Chief. He would probably not see it for some days, as government business was piling up on secretaries' desks.

General Luis Blanco had ordered Doctor Luis Cervantes to take charge of the wounded the Rebel had brought from Querétaro, and it was not many days before a number of them could walk from the Red Cross Center to the Hotel Cosmos to have their wounds dressed.

General I. Villarreal, who was making his headquarters at the Jardín Hotel, a block from the Cosmos, sent a message to the Rebel that Adolpho, her husband, was staying at the Jardín and wanted to see her. Adolpho had decided to stay with his group until he had talked with the First Chief, making clear his political affinity. The Rebel answered immediately. She wanted very much to see him. But it would not be best. She was leaving Mexico soon to join her children, but she would return to him as soon as possible. Yet, it was a month before she could leave for Laredo.

At first, it seemed impossible to get out of Mexico City. There were no trains. Then word came that trains and cars were being moved. Evidently, some important person was leaving on a special train. The Rebel told her staff to get ready to leave. The railroad men of the corps could stay if they liked. Montoya was to take a message to the Chief after the corps had left. The Rebel, María, and Jovita and a few others packed their scanty belongings and went to the depot.

As the corps stood making plans for getting a way back to the frontier, a conductor came along.

"It looks as if you were going somewhere," he said hailing the Rebel.

"It certainly does," she answered. "We have passes on all trains, so make room for us."

"All right," he said easily. "Follow me. I have orders not to take any passengers, but I am head of this line all the way to Nuevo Laredo. Go to my private car; I have a good cook. Only men in charge of divisions along the road are going."

They had no sooner gotten settled, when Montoya arrived with a news reporter. He told the Rebel that a messenger had arrived from the First Chief with a bunch of keys and orders for the Rebel to take over the Capucín College for the National White Cross headquarters. The reporter was instructed to say nothing except that the corps of the White Cross was leaving for Laredo for a much needed rest. They were, however, ready to return for any emergency.

If the Rebel ever did anything right in her life, it was this withdrawal. She had better plans and rewards for her co-workers. They had served as selflessly as any group. A year later when the Rebel again met the Chief, he told her that he had held the keys that she had so rebelliously returned in his hand a long time, wondering what force had moved her to refuse them. Her giving up control at that moment made him consider, too, moving out of the pit before it was too late.

The trip to the frontier was without event, and the corps scattered as soon as they reached Laredo. The Rebel's home was not where her children were, but with her brother. Leopold had recently been elected mayor of Laredo.

The First Chief, after a few short months in Mexico City, had felt it too insecure to remain there. He was in constant danger, what with the growing dissatisfaction, exhausted nerves, and unlimited ambitions. The pharisaical Porfiristas continued to act as when they had surrounded Franciso I. Madero, circumventing him and his government. Carranza was not disposed to fight over again battles now ended. The great problem before him was to inspire his own people to help him restore the union and integrity that a battle weary Mexico had lost.

In April, 1914, to prevent a German munitions vessel from entering Veracruz, the United States had taken possession of the Mexican port. On November 23, at the request of Carranza, the Americans withdrew. A few days later, the First Chief came there with his cabinet to establish his government temporarily while awaiting his formal election to the presidency. Intermittent waves of Villa's and Zapata's forces had driven the Carrancistas out of the Mexican capital. Generals Cándido Aguilar and Guadulupe Sánchez, whom Carranza treated as a son, surrounded Veracruz, protecting the First Chief from attack.

Carranza now named his staff: Lawyer Luis Cabrera, Secretary of the Treasury; Jesús Urrieta, Secretary of Foreign Relations; Lawyer Felix F. Palavicini, Secretary of Education; Lawyer Rafael Zubarán Capmany, Secretary of the Interior; Lawyer Francisco Escudero, Supreme Court Justice; Lawyer Ignacio L. Pesqueira, Secretary of War. General Alvaro Obregón was in Sonora battling insurrection in the West. General Pablo González had returned to quiet the frontier.

General Eulalio Gutiérrez, as provisional president, established his government in Mexico City. Loyal Carrancistas on his staff were: General José Isabel Robles, Secretary of War; Engineer Valentín Gama, of Development and Agriculture; General Lucio Blanco, Secretary of the Interior; Engineer José Rodríguez, Secretary of Communication. It was Gutiérrez's mission in taking charge of affairs in the capital to keep order and bring ambitious politicians and military men to some understanding with Carranza's policies. Villa remained the greatest power obstacle. When he moved into Mexico City with his forces, Gutiérrez fled to San Luis Potosí.

The convention called in Aguas Calientes was handicapped by the powerful forces at Villa's command, which threatened the attending members. There were many prominent generals at the convention which was being held to name a successor to the First Chief, nominating him as President. Carranza's representative objected to the proceedings because the *Plan de Guadalupe* stated that elections would not take place until the country was at peace. When Villa's forces were routed from the capital by Obregón's army, he headed for Chihuahua, fearing that General Pablo González might secure a hold. On arriving there, he had two of General Maclovio Herrera's brothers beheaded. Fortifying himself in Tamaulipas, Maclovio Herrera vowed to kill Villa, to avenge his brothers. Obregón was in Tampico with his own well equipped division and many generals, García Virgil, Federico Montes, and Jacinto Treviño, who were all artillery officers. Scarcely had Obregón time to put his camp in order, when Villa and Ángeles reached Saltillo from the West. There, fierce fighting raged for several weeks.

While this struggle was going on, the First Chief made his headquarters on the island of San Juan de Ulloa, the famous, old political prison. The walls of the damp dungeons could tell horror tales of savagery and merciless treatment of political prisoners for over a hundred years of Mexico's stormy history.

Immediately, the First Chief transformed the little island into a place of production, where the cells were thrown open and visitors with special permits allowed to visit. There was the sound of machinery running, of smiths forging hot irons, transforming rude metal into fire arms and ammunition. The island became a military and political camp. During certain hours, the Chief received diplomats and high officials who were ferried to the island.

Meanwhile in Laredo at the first outbreak of fighting, the Rebel received a telegram on October 7. General Reynaldo de la Garza, in Nuevo Laredo, Military Commander of that zone, sent the Rebel an official notice to take possession of the military hospital in Nuevo Laredo. The Rebel and her select corps of workers renovated the interior of the war-damaged building. Soon, aid began pouring in from the American side. The Rebel donated more than two thousand pesos worth of supplies for the hospital.

The fighting now became fierce in the surrounding country. Nuevo Laredo was garrisoned by General Maclovio Herrera. He had good doctors and a brave staff of officers. News came of an impending attack. Villa wanted General Herrera as much as the General wanted Villa. Fighting had already broken out at El Ebano, near Tampico.

María de Jesús, the General's most trusted officer, was dispatched to Monterrey to report on fortifications and the number of troops marching toward Nuevo Laredo. The Rebel was again faced with the task of caring for an army of wounded soldiers.

CHAPTER XVII
War Flares Again

The Rebel left the hospital in Nuevo Laredo one night to go to her brother's home to rest. Rebecca, the head nurse, had promised to call her if the fighting started. American doctors were also put on the alert.

After a warm supper, she asked to be excused, and retired to her room, more to pray than to sleep. She feared for General Herrera's safety. Pressing her hands together, she looked at the burn scar on her hand. It was her destiny to be bound to the country across the river and its people. Had the months of swift-paced duty now suddenly ended, leaving her only uncertainty and loneliness? Where was the fulfillment she had expected on her return home? The revolution had ended in a hollow triumph, with dissatisfaction, greed, and reaction holding rein on the victory.

A disagreeable, teasing rain, beating insistently against the window, racked the Rebel's shattered nerves. Holding her mind to her prayers by sheer force of will, she watched night envelop the city, a city whose inhabitants had for many nights kept vigil for the coming battle across the river. Gloomy clouds gathering above showed that a storm was brooding where, "in the vast greatness of Texas a tempest can achieve the height of its magnificent awfulness."

Fear was a thing unknown to her, a word she had never recognized. On the battlefield, attending to duty amid the fire of deadly machine guns, she had stood watching the ravages of guns and bombs. Yet, on the faces of the dead strewn about, fear had yielded to a triumphant expression of another world.

In the parlor the old clock struck ten slowly and heavily. The density of the atmosphere and the increasing darkness added to the solemnity of the Rebel's thoughts. Sitting, watching the gathering storm, she saw the tall, wet weeds move in the garden, pushed aside by the impact of a weighty body. There was someone next to the window, enveloped in the darkness.

"Come," she heard a familiar voice say. "There's no time to waste."

Sliding out of her rocking chair, looking back at her inviting warm bed, she tapped on the window in reply. Dressing quickly by the light of the always burning holy candle in its cupped brass holder, she slipped out of her room and down the long, dark hall. Once outside, she was met by her tall, slender messenger. As the darkness closed about them, they bolted for the other side of the street. The night police, patrolling the streets, were silent specters, unwilling servants of the law. How they cursed the clinging, stinging rain. Approaching the two, a policeman grumbled, "Fine night to be prowling around."

When the lightening flashed, he recognized them. The bridge was only a few paces ahead. As they walked toward it, Federico Idar explained their mission to her.

"Tomorrow the big fight is on. The Federals will attack. Monterrey has already fallen into their hands, and they are advancing rapidly. General Maclovio Herrera is preparing to meet them."

Guiding the Rebel along the street, he continued, "Traitors have spread insidious tales about town that Herrera will let stray bullets go over to the American side. At Fort McIntosh, soldiers have received their call to duty. At this moment they are prepared to shoot back."

"Did you see them?" the Rebel whispered, afraid of his answer.

"Yes," he answered. "They are scattered for miles, undercover, in the brush. Even their cannons are camouflaged. I heard a sergeant say roughly, 'If any of those blooming, bastard Mexicans fire one shot this way, they'll find hell.'"

The international bridge was opened only to those with special permission; being in the hospital service, the Rebel and Federico Idar were allowed to pass quickly.

"Go straight to General Herrera," Idar said rapidly. He had the fire and fearlessness of a Comanche. To him a patriotic duty was a moral command. "Tell the general that he is being betrayed. He must give explicit orders to his men."

"Yes, yes," she replied. "But tell me how to start."

"No," he said shaking his head. "One cannot plan these things. Go and look at him. He is brave and just. You'll know what to say."

"But will he believe me?" she insisted. "I am only a woman in the hospital service. It's true I have talked to many generals; they have faith in me. But tonight, will I convince him tonight?"

Federico was silent. The Rebel watched him as he looked from one side of the bridge to the other.

"There," he said pointing to a stone tablet in the middle of the bridge. "Read that. What does it say?"

"Peace, peace, and only peace," her soul cried out, but she could not read it aloud. She remembered the woman who had placed the emblem there between the two nations. For an instant, they leaned over the railing, above the sleeping waters.

"Texas here, Tamaulipas there," Idar said thoughtfully. "This must not happen." Now he spoke calmly, for his mind and heart were at peace.

The Rebel, too, laid her patriotic fears before the words proclaiming peace. As they redoubled their speed confidently, a calmness was about them. There was a prevailing silence. The sky had cleared; the storm was raging elsewhere. Here in the night was peace, peace so perfect that their souls were jubilant.

Once past the guard on the Mexican side, the two were soon inside the general's camp. A few minutes later, with a squeeze of the hand and an unexpected shove, Federico left the Rebel just inside the door of a dimly lit building. She found herself in a small room; soldiers at arms were keeping vigil quietly. A clock's ticking loudly was the only sound.

"What do you want? Have you the password?" the guard demanded.

"I don't know the password. I have only this." The Rebel showed him her nurse's badge.

A slight rustle came from across the room, and a woman in white, wearing the same emblem on her arm, approached. The soldier left them.

"I must see the general," the Rebel told Rebecca.

The nurse clasped her hands. What could she do? She was under the general's orders. She was also under the Rebel's.

"The general is very ill," she said. "The doctor has just left. I am to give him his last medicine, a hypo." There was no acquiescence to the Rebel's demand. The nurse was just stating a fact.

"Get your medicine," the Rebel said gently. "While you do, I'll speak to him. Perhaps he will understand."

Looking behind her into the general's' quarters, the nurse went on without speaking.

Groping in the dark chamber, the Rebel saw an agonizing figure. A dim light in the far corner of the room showed her the general's bed. Quickly she approached. There was so little time left. A decision had to be made. Only a moment and the nurse would be back with the sleeping potion, and her efforts to rouse him would be in vain.

She leaned over him until the heat of his burning fever engulfed her like tongues of fire. She placed her hand on his brow. How hot and dry he felt. Touching his hand, she spoke softly to him.

"My general, do you understand? I am a nurse at the base hospital."

"I am sick," he answered feebly. "Did they send you?"

"Everything is ready for tomorrow," the Rebel said. "I have come for one last order. Quickly, general, can you give it? It is important."

As if out of a daze or a terrible dream, he pulled himself together. The wet cloth on his forehead fell on the Rebel's hand. He pushed back the bed clothes.

"Time to fight," he said in a husky, faraway voice.

"No! No, my general, not now. Just time to give one order before you go to sleep. You shall be well. You shall command."

"Quickly," he said, staring vacantly about the room. The hollow adobe walls echoed his words, "Quickly, quickly, quickly."

"General, call your officer. Tell him your soldiers must be miles away from the border. No shot must cross the Río Grande. Let your men meet the enemy far out in the hills of Tamaulipas."

"Nurse! Nurse," he called, and Rebecca came. "My officer in command, quick."

The Rebel held the sleeping potion, while Rebecca dragged in the guard, followed by the officer in command. In military terms, and in a strong voice, the general gave the order that not one shot must cross the Río Grande. A few minutes later, the troops began mobilizing; moving silently and quickly out into the night. The Rebel knelt beside the general while Rebecca gave him his hypo.

"¿María de Jesús, *dónde está*? Has my Lieutenant María de Jesús arrived? It will soon be morning. Let her come in at once." The general kept talking until he fell asleep. María de Jesús did not come.

Outside the general's headquarters, the Rebel met Federico. On their way to the bridge they noticed the general's aide rubbing down Firebrand, his master's horse. The horse was a beautiful, almost flawless thoroughbred whose long wavy mane and silken tail were the pride of the general. Herrera had often remarked that there were few horses like Firebrand. A small neat H branded on the horse's cheek had been put there by the Indian who had given the horse to the general. As they drew near, they heard the aide talking to the horse.

"Tomorrow you will no longer be the general's horse," the boy said.

"What?" said the Rebel, surprising the boy. "Why should he not belong to the general? Why such foreboding?"

"No, it is not that," he answered. "But my general has promised Firebrand to his Lieutenant María de Jesús if she fulfills her mission."

Federico stayed behind and watched on the Mexican side. The Rebel went on alone. Crossing the bridge, her eye caught a flash of light along the river's edge. Having reached the American side, she strayed along the river.

"Halt!" a voice ordered. "Come closer and tell who you are. What is your business?"

Approaching the bright spotlight, the Rebel stood tall and spoke clearly, her voice reaching across the empty darkness.

"Captain Austin?" she asked, recognizing his voice.

"What do you know about this fight?" he asked, walking up.

"Captain, you promised me after the other fight, when General González's wounded men were here, that you would always remember me," the Rebel reminded him.

"Yes, I remember you. What's up now?" he asked.

"Well, you see," she said, almost choking, "I want you to fight back. If there is just one shot, you let go."

"Those are our orders," he replied.

In the early dawn, the rasp of the telephone awakened the Rebel. It was from the hospital. She was to come quickly. The general had been killed.

She arrived across the river in time to receive the body of General Maclovio Herrera to lay him in state. From Rebecca the Rebel learned that, after sleeping several hours, the general awoke, and ordered his horse and ridden forth to join his troops in action. Only he would command them when they met the enemy. No argument was strong enough to stay him.

Hardly had he ridden beyond the outskirts of the city, when a breathless soldier rushed to meet him, handing him a small packet. At that same moment, a bullet pierced the general's body. He fell clutching the message in his dying grip. María's mission was completed. The officer in command reading María de Jesús' message gave sharp orders. The battle that followed was won by the Constitutionalists. Outside Nuevo Laredo there now stands a monument in commemoration of the brave general.

After the General's funeral, the Rebel's thoughts returned to María de Jesús. What would María do on her return, finding her general dead? Herrera's forces, now under command of General Luis Caballero, marched into Monterrey, routing the enemy and forcing them west towards the hills of Coahuila.

Days followed with the usual bustle and excitement and clamor of a disorganized population. The officer in charge reviewed his army, rewarding the brave and making provision for the dead and wounded. Although María de Jesús was not there to be commended, she had fulfilled her orders.

The hospitals resumed their quietude, their routine, their monotony broken only by families coming to visit the wounded or to mourn their dead. Satisfied that the hospitals were supplied with competent nurses and loyal doctors, the Rebel joined the advancing army with another corps of nurses to be of service in the next encounter, and to look for María de Jesús.

From camp to camp the Rebel searched, working until night overtook her and until the last battalion had put up its tents and built its fires. María de Jesús was not to be found. Day after day the Rebel searched. Some said the young officer had been shot, others, that she had joined the enemy.

Orders to advance were delayed. Fortifications and trenches were being built or reconstructed. The governor proclaimed martial law, and the streets were deserted after dark. News reached the Rebel that an exploring squad was about to leave by train. She boarded the train with them to continue her search. As the train picked up speed, the fearless soldiers relaxed their vigil. Happy in the thought that no enemy confronted them, they indulged in games and singing.

A bullet struck inside the car. The train came to a sudden stop, and a fierce skirmish took place, bullets flying. It was the last effort of the retreating army to delay the pursuit of the Constitutionalists. When the train rolled back to the station, the Rebel was weary and unnerved from the battle; she returned to her quarters.

As soon as she opened the door of her room, she saw María de Jesús. María was sitting on an old wooden box beside the Rebel's bed, her elbows resting on her knees, holding her head between her hands. Raising her eyes at the Rebel's entrance, she did not move.

"María de Jesús?" the Rebel exclaimed rushing over and embracing the girl.

"Did my general get the message?" the girl asked plaintively.

"You have won Firebrand," was the Rebel's reply.

"Then, I shall ride with him in the next encounter," the girl said, raising her shining blue eyes, and tossing her thick hair. "I shall be brave like my general. We will always win."

"María de Jesús," the Rebel said as she sat on the bed by the girl and took her hand. "The general was buried in a shroud of glory. They left it to me. I lined the inside of the coffin with white, white lilies all around his bier, great white ribbons hanging from a bell made of flags. Brave generals stood beside him, and twelve young girls all in white, daughters of generals, held calla lilies and sang softly. The Americans were there too."

Speechless, María listened. The Rebel had overpowered her with a volley of words, speaking of the general. Suddenly the girl dropped her head, sobbing loudly.

"Thank God, my general won," she cried.

"María," the Rebel asked, changing the subject. "How did you get here? Why did you not take the message to the general yourself? What was the delay?"

"I will tell you everything," replied the girl. "But give me a little water first."

The Rebel went to the windowsill, where she had a clay water jug. Close beside it was a little bottle of *mescal*. Filling the glass with water, she looked at María. Silently the girl nodded her consent. As if eager to begin her story, she tilted back her head and quickly swallowed the drink.

"María, you have not eaten. You are hungry," the Rebel said.

"No, more water, please."

Drawing the pillow to the edge of the bed, María de Jesús rested her head without changing her sitting position. Her short, bobbed hair made a light of flame on the dusty, grey pillow. Pale and defeated, she began to tell of her experiences.

"The enemy's preparations for battle were going on," she began slowly. "I had reached the nearest encampment towards our lines. My mission was finished. I had the needed information for our side."

"María, were you alone? Where was your aide?"

"Francisco had orders to abandon my quarters, taking with him only the duplicate of the message. If I should fail to reach the general, he would take my place."

"Where did you leave him, María?" the Rebel asked, wondering how swiftly Francisco had traveled.

"We passed through the ranches as peons, with *aqua miel* and corn. No one discovered who we were. As we reached the last encampment, we had nothing more to give. Fearing for our safety, I told Francisco we should part. If I was not at my *compadre* Pedro's inn by daybreak, he must go on with the message."

"And then, María, what happened?" the Rebel asked. She noticed the girl shiver and close her eyes. Bringing water, the Rebel bathed María's forehead. After a few minutes of silence, María resumed her story.

"In my *huaraches* I had concealed the message, the drawings of fortifications, marking with red ink the important points, telling the number of the forces. I made a copy for Francisco. I trusted him; he, too, loved the general."

"He left you at what time, María? He must have ridden hard and fast, some ten hours," the Rebel observed.

"It was near Cerro de la Silla. It gets dark early in the mountains; perhaps, it was about seven. We were on this side. One could make the ride in ten hours.

"The general was killed at five, at daybreak," the Rebel added. "And you, what did you do?"

"We parted, he galloping one way, and I the other. A little later I got off my horse close to a shack. A jug of water was hanging on the wall outside. I took it down carefully to fasten it to my saddle. But my trembling fingers let it slip, and the jug fell to the ground. The frightened horse shied, and a soldier sprang out from somewhere and held me at bay.

"You know I am brave. I could have disarmed him, but I thought better of it and told him I was on my way to a tavern close by. He said he would go with me; we could dance.

"He whistled to another guard and, forgetting all about the horse, he took my arm and off we marched a good two miles. All the way, the soldier talked of home and his sweetheart, but mostly of his many battles. He wanted to drink and dance. It would soon be time for him to return to battle again.

"At the tavern there were dim lights and music, and much drinking. Outside the door I saw a demijohn on a bench. I drank deeply. A soldier coming by, pushed my companion aside, saying to me, "'*Hermanita*, you are just in time. We shall dance before I leave this place!'"

"Did he recognize you, María?" asked the Rebel.

"No. I did not look much at anyone. I was afraid someone would know me. Soon, we began dancing. Soldiers were crowding the place. Some raised their goblets to the ballerina, that was me; others frowned at my companion. A drunken fellow came up to my partner.

"'My captain wants to dance with this girl.'

"'Keep away, you common soldier,' my partner replied.

"I was hoping they would fight and I could get away. But no," she said shaking her head. "The captain approached me. Horror stricken I looked at him. I was so tired, and now a new partner. I kept thinking of Francisco with the message. Surely, he would arrive at dawn. I kept on dancing. I danced and danced, until suddenly the strap of my *huarache* broke."

"Was it the one with the message in it, María?" asked the Rebel.

"Yes, yes. That one. I slid down, squatting on the floor, determined to stay there all night. Finally, I pulled off the *huaraches*. The dancing crowd kicked one away. To my horror, the captain picked it up, holding it on his dagger.

"'What a tiny foot my Cinderella has,' he laughed.

"I felt like shouting to the drunken captain. I had no arms. My dagger was in my boots, and my gun, I had given it to Francisco.

"Then the music started its jingling rhythm, and the captain whirled me around barefoot.

"'Bravo,' he shouted. 'She dances well.'

"The other *huarache,* which I had hidden in my *rebozo,* fell to the floor. It was kicked from one to another. I slapped the captain and ran to the door. A soldier had gotten the *huarache,* and he and the captain were struggling for it. Then the message fell out!

"Staring at the captain, I could not move. My mind was on Francisco and the message he had. I demanded my *huarache* from the captain.

"'Not so quick, my Cinderella,' he said tauntingly. 'General Ángeles shall know of this.'

"'Men, take this traitor. March her to the graveyard. We will shoot her like a dog when I get orders from my general.'

"Up against a tomb they stood me. The moon was shining. The firing squad formed not twenty feet away. Something about me must have appealed to the officer in charge. He asked my dying wish.'

"'First,' I said in a fearless voice, 'A good bottle of *mescal,* and then I shall talk to the soldiers."

"Meanwhile, General Ángeles had been given the news. He sent back word to make me talk, to get news about Herrera."

"Did they bring you the *mescal,* María? You talk so well, you did not need it."

"That's true. But I did not want to feel death. I drank the *mescal,* then I told them my second wish: for one of the men to go to my quarters at Chonita's place and get my uniform. I must die like a soldier, not a spy."

"María," spoke the Rebel, "at that moment General Herrera was asking for you."

"The soldiers laughed and said 'more lies,'" the girl continued. "But the captain sent a soldier on horseback to bring the uniform."

"What about the message from General Ángeles' headquarters?" the Rebel asked.

"The captain of the firing squad had sent a second messenger to the general, saying that I was a lieutenant in the command of General Herrera.

"General Ángeles replied that I should die like a soldier. When my uniform was brought, I stood behind a tall cold tomb and changed my clothes. I was happy, so happy because my general would know that I died like a brave soldier.

"The first messenger from the general's headquarters returned, running breathlessly. He said they were not to shoot until I had talked. Then up rushed a second messenger, saying that the general was much surprised that I was an officer, and that I must die.

"A third messenger arrived on his heels with the order to put me in a boxcar where prisoners were kept. A few minutes later, I was pushed into a dark boxcar nearby. Sounds of cursing, dull commands, and firing lasted all night. Exhausted, I fell asleep.

"All the next day and the next, I rode in the closed boxcar. The battle had been won by our people, I heard from prisoners that were thrown into the car with me. They also told me that my General Herrera had been killed. Ángeles and Villa retreated to Torreón, and we were taken to prison.

"General Ángeles came into my cell.

"''Tis well done, María de Jesús of General Herrera's forces,' he said looking thoughtfully at me. 'I wish our ranks had such brave women; then we would not retreat.'"

"Were you afraid of General Ángeles?" the Rebel asked.

"No," María replied. "He seemed a true warrior. So I murmured that we needed men like General Ángeles on our side."

"Soon, I hatched a scheme to escape. Families of the prisoners and their friends began visiting the jail. Seizing one of the women who was near my open cell, I dragged her in and took her clothes, leaving my uniform behind. I closed the cell, and passed by the guards carrying the cooking vessels and the food she had brought.

"I found the road to the border. Sometimes walking, sometimes getting a ride, I reached Juárez and crossed to El Paso. Then I begged food and stole a ride on the train, arriving in Laredo only yesterday.

"When I found you were not there, but had advanced with the troops to Monterrey, I came on. General Luis Caballero told me you would be here."

"María, you are indeed brave," the Rebel spoke admiringly, trying to reassure the exhausted girl.

"But how am I to get others to believe my story?" said the girl, wringing her hands, and pacing the floor now. "You believe it, do you not?"

"Yes," the Rebel replied. "Place yourself under orders of General Marieta. I shall get the proofs for you."

CHAPTER XVIII
Fitful Winds of Dissension

General Alvaro Obregón was head of the First Chief's fighting forces. Wealthy reactionaries and *científicos* were having their cause defended by General Pascual Orozco, a faithless, one-time Maderista.

Loyal Jesús Carranza, in command of Constitutionalist forces in the Central Zone, was of different temperament than his brother. He was a good fighter at his advanced age. When the Rebel first met him in Saltillo, she was surprised to find the successful warrior an affable and easygoing man.

After hours on the battlefield, he loved nothing better than finding a piano and, still in his dusty uniform, sitting and playing his favorite songs of many stanzas. Suddenly wheeling about on the piano stool, he would look at his small audience, smiling, even if everyone was serious. Turning again to the piano, he would continue to sing more improvised verses.

He never won a laugh from the Rebel, for as much as she admired his courage, there was something pathetic about most of the funny things he said and did. At one such concert, General Pablo González, sitting next to María Villarreal, remarked, eyeing the Rebel, "Is she always so solemn? We thought her very lively."

"Girls," the Rebel said presently, "we must go. We still have duties tonight."

She wanted to get away from that room and General Carranza's performance. Everyone had enjoyed his songs; the Rebel thought the entertainment otherwise. Perhaps, she sensed tragedmy for him in the future.

After the famous expedition to subdue General Pascual Orozco, the General's train was returning to Mexico City. It was a fine convoy, with many soldiers and plenty of money. All this excited the vengeful envy of his chief-of-staff. Along the train were four members of the White Cross: Juanita Mancha and the three Martínez sisters. They had been with this division since the Rebel had taken on a new staff.

Somewhere on the road near San Gerónimo, General Alfonso Santibáñez, the Chief-of-Staff, ordered the train stopped. Leaving the major part of the troops on board, he proceeded with a select squad into the woods. Those left on the train were ordered to remain there. Marching quite a distance, Santibañez took General Jesús Carranza and his faithful companions as prisoners. He ordered the general to write a letter to the First Chief asking for ransom to be sent immediately, or Jesús Carranza and his party would be killed.

As the messenger was delayed in returning, Santibáñez proceeded to have a deep hole dug to meet the measurements of the tall form of General Carranza, who was subsequently shot and thrown head first into the pit. His two feet sticking out of the soil were mute grave markers. On the sole of each shoe were printed the initials J.C.

Among those on his staff were three young men: his son, Abelardo; his nephew, Ernesto Peraldi; and Leonardo Vidaurri, of Laredo. They were made to dig their own graves, only to be shot in the back as they stood on the edge of the freshly dug trench.

Still no messenger arrived. Upon returning to the train, Santibáñez took the money and fled for Cuba. Meanwhile, hiding in a tree, the messenger and bearer of the First Chief's answer had witnessed the atrocities. He had a hard time locating the place, having been blindfolded by the murderers on being brought there from the train in the beginning.

The stern rebuke which the First Chief sent was the reply of a stoic and patriot. He refused to send ransom.

> My duty as First Chief of the Revolution makes it impossible for me to negotiate with bandits, no matter at what price, or personal sacrifice, or what my sufferings might be. If my son were in my brother's or my nephew's place, I would observe the same conduct regardless of heartfelt anguish.

Carranza could not establish such a cowardly precedent. He dispatched troops to capture the assassins, but it was too late. They had fled. The bodies were located by the messenger, a newspaper man and teacher. He had been spared, by chance, to carry the ransom note.

The First Chief received the body of his beloved brother while he was still in Veracruz. On looking at the sleeping form, the Chief was shaken with grief. He called his secretary, making a noble gesture.

"Find the wife and children of this treacherous murderer. They shall have a pension that they may use for their moral education, that they might be better citizens."

Arriving in Mexico City, the horrified Martínez sisters returned immediately to Laredo. They went to San Antonio, finding quiet, gentle work in a dress factory, far from the sound of guns and the cruelties of men.

The Rebel had been at home scarcely a month when news came of General Jesús Carranza's murder. The country was at peace again for a time. The First Chief was organizing his government to return to the capital.

The Rebel received a telegram from her husband to join him in Veracruz, and the prospect of being with him again after so many months was an immediate cure for her loneliness. Leaving the Nuevo Laredo hospital in the hands of the municipal authorities, she traveled with her three children to Monterrey and thence to Tampico, where she was met by Adolpho. He was now in the Department of the Treasury. His superior was Rafael Nieto, Under-Secretary.

Travel was slow. Trains were now subject to military maneuvers, commanded and escorted by military guards. It was the same with boat travel. It took weeks to get a boat to Veracruz. However, things were made easy for the travelers from the border through the aid of General Manuel García Vigil, an early friend of the Rebel and Adolpho.

A few days after the family had arrived at Veracruz, the Rebel was notified that the First Chief would receive her at his island headquarters. Eager to see him, she came to the pier with one of her sons, and showed a sailor-guard the Chief's telegram. He signaled a boat to ferry her across to the famous Isle of San Juan de Ulloa where the Chief had isolated himself to work on future plans.

It was a hazy afternoon as they rowed away from the mainland toward the island. The Rebel recalled that Napoleon, when imprisoned on Elba, had been visited only once by Josephine.

Guards allowed the Rebel and her young son to land on the fortified island. It was the hour of rest, blacksmiths leaving their anvils, mechanics turning over their day's work to foremen. Men were lining up to leave on a huge barge, while another set of men were disembarking for the next day's output of guns and ammunition.

Up a narrow stone stairway toward the grim fortress covered with dull grey moss, the Rebel was led by a guard who called out a visitor's presence. The Chief's private secretary, Gerzain Ugarte, greeted her and took her to the First Chief's chambers that served as his sleeping quarters and office.

Entering the Chief's room, the Rebel's eyes fell immediately on a statuette of Napoleon that stood on his desk. Grabbing it, she went toward an open window facing the grey waters of the Gulf, with its gigantic waves dashing monotonously against huge rocks. At that moment, the First Chief entered the room and greeted them. His eyes looked quizzically from the Rebel's face to the statuette in her hand.

"How horrible this is," she replied to his look. "I was going to throw it into the water. This already reminds me too much of Elba, and Napoleon's last days," she waved her hand to include the whole island.

For her graduating thesis, years before, the Rebel had written about Napoleon. Being a woman, she could not forgive him for his disloyalty to Josephine. Although the board of regents of the school had all been men, she was awarded the medal for her writing.

The Chief took the statuette and looked at it with a startled expression. "I'll throw it myself," he said, solemnly taking it from the Rebel and flinging it out to the dark waters below. The statuette hit a projecting rock, then disappeared forever.

Fixing her mind on the reason for her visit, she handed the First Chief her report of recent events on the frontier. She offered him a project for the termination of the National White Cross which would benefit her corps. It now seemed advisable to continue the Red Cross that had been organized by Señora Cassío in the last years of Díaz. Continuation of the Neutral White Cross also seemed possible, for a wealthy Spaniard had recently died, leaving that organization over a million and a half dollars.

The Rebel told the First Chief that in a few days she was going to Mexico City to place her sons in military school. Later, she wanted to take them to New York, while she attended the Nursing Center of the National Red Cross and received her credentials.

Casually, she suggested to the First Chief that she contact high Catholic prelates in New York, finding out their feeling toward Mexico. The Chief had mentioned the idea to her some time before. The Rebel thought that perhaps quieting the Catholic question would unite Mexico in every phase, its being a Catholic country. At that time, there was bitter Catholic resentment against the government. Churches had been confiscated and libraries, public health units, and schools had been established in their stead during General Eulalio Gutiérrez's short term, causing discontent in high Catholic circles.

Angel Lagarde, who was Adolpho's direct chief, was moving to Mexico City to establish his office of government supply, transforming it to the military. Adolpho, with his family, accompanied Lagarde on this move. On reaching Mexico City, the Rebel took an apartment at the San Carlos Hotel until they could find a furnished house.

"This is just the place I'd like to have," she told her children, pointing to a nice house one day as they drove about the city looking for a place to live.

Stopping the car at a nearby store, she asked the name of the person to whom the house belonged. Hardly had the proprietor finished speaking, when the Rebel went confidently up to the house and rang the bell. Soon, she was in the embrace of Mrs. Edward Butler, who had been her first neighbor on Calle Bucarelli. Mr. Butler had died and his wife wanted to return to the United States. Within a week, papers were drawn up and the Rebel and her family had moved to the Butler house.

At the military college the Rebel chose for her sons, she was informed that the First Chief was the school's patron and the young students would form a guard of honor for him on state occasions.

The Rebel's family enjoyed the year 1916 spent in Mexico City. She saw again her former secretary, Aracelito. The girl's husband, Colonel Martínez Celis, was chief-of-staff for General Pablo González, who was the First Chief's commanding officer. With troops stationed in Tacubaya, González had opened the way for the First Chief to reoccupy Mexico City.

Many who came to see the First Chief were welcomed at the Rebel's home. Señor Andrés Patino's family were visitors. Patino had been the treasurer of *El Progreso,* the frontier's liberal newspaper. Through the Blanco sisters in Tacubaya, where Trini was chief telegraph operator, the Rebel kept in touch with the Chief's activities and with military movements. The group of friends met once a week for music, singing, and dramatic readings. Although a pleasant atmosphere of friendship existed among them, the First Chief was still striving hard to hold his place as head of the Revolution.

The congress that had gathered in Aguas Calientes to decide whom the presidential nominee was to be had found no agreement between Villa and Carranza. When Villa, with a great show of arms, had surrounded the convention's location, those who could escaped to Mexico City where another convention was being held. There was also opposition to the First Chief.

Carranza's best friend, Luis Cabrera, after making a warm defense of the Chief, quietly left the hall. Going to Carranza's headquarters, he asked the First Chief to go with him to the assembly without letting him know how great was the opposition. Arriving unannounced, Cabrera opened the doors and walked in proudly with Carranza. Taken by surprise, the astonished gathering in an emotional state rose as one person and, applauding wildly, declared Carranza President of Mexico. The United States wired recognition.

President Carranza offered Adolpho the post of Consul General in San Francisco, California. Much to the Rebel's chagrin, her husband refused the post, saying that was for a financier, not a diplomat. He would have to work hard to make expenses for educating their children. Some days later, Adolpho was made president of a group of confiscated banks in Veracruz. He was also on a monetary commission with Rafael Nieto, the Under-Secretary, and Luis Cabrera, Secretary of the Treasury.

Adolpho was to be sent to New York City on a monetary mission. The Rebel, although she loved her home in Mexico, decided it was best to educate her children in New York; and the family left together.

Sitting on the deck of the Morro Castle, sailing toward Cuba on their way north, the Rebel had time to let events of the past years flow through her mind, recalling her corps of volunteers who had so bravely faced a civil war, which now seemed endless. Aracelito and her husband had spent many happy months at the Rebel's home, while General Pablo González was in Mexico City. Adolpho had come to love the two young people. When Guillermo was sent to the frontier where there was fighting, Aracelito had followed, but she could not save him from a treacherous attack. Young and lovely, robed in widow's weeds, she returned to Texas to live with her mother.

Doctor Long, the faithful Lily, and their little son were with General Luis Caballero's staff, stationed in Saltillo when she contracted a severe case of smallpox. Her son, Robert, contracted the same dreaded disease. Doctor Long would not accept other professional aid when General Caballero offered. Day and night he watched by his wife's bedside. In her feverish unconsciousness, she asked constantly for Magnón. After the illness, no marks remained to mar her fair complexion. Doctor Long had placed olive oil on each spot with a tiny, soft pigeon feather. The General and his staff poured attentions on her.

The Longs were well rewarded by the events of the past three years. When at the outbreak of the Revolution, on the eve of their departure for Mexico, they had consulted with Leopold regarding the sale of their Laredo property, he had advised them not to sell. By the time they returned, their holdings had more than tripled in value, owing to the exodus of rich Mexican exiles to Laredo. Selling what they had, they moved to San Antonio.

Mimi Eschausier had left San Luis Potosí after the second attack on the city. Her hacienda confiscated, she hurriedly gathered what she could salvage from her city home and went with her family to San Antonio.

The Rebel thought of the uncertainty of the First Chief's future. He was now President, struggling to stabilize his government against a powerful military machine of his own making. How many times he had said to her, "I make many generals. Who will make me a general?" How sad and wistful it had sounded.

Carranza reminded her of a sturdy oak whipped by the fitful winds of dissension. So deeply rooted was he that only the greatest of passions, ingratitude, could destroy him. On the Chief's second entry into Mexico City, the Rebel had occupied a balcony next to the presidential staff. She had watched his firm, resolute walk. He had leaned over the balcony rail before a sea of people and waved the flag of Mexico and rung the famous Hidalgo bell of liberty.

Slipping away unnoticed, the Rebel mingled with the crowd to hear what the multitude felt. She was not convinced of their sincerity. Reactionaries for the moment were holding back. Numerous women, vowing he loved them, appropriated the Chief's smile to themselves. A wave of shame came over her as she turned away from the mockery of the great man's works.

The Rebel had been closely associated with the First Chief for many months. She had seen women flock eagerly about him, rendering homage, merely for their own gratification at the time of his high triumphs. On Carranza's part, there was never any lack of chivalry. Of the two loves in his life, one was his adoring wife, Virginia Salinas de Carranza, by whom he had two daughters: Virginia, who later married General Cándido Aguilar; and Julia, who has remained unmarried. His other attachment was to his second wife, whom he married a year after his first wife's death. They had several children. Not beautiful, but accomplished, his second wife had been a teacher in Saltillo University while Carranza was governor there during Madero's time.

"What do you do with so many adoring women?" the Rebel had once said on seeing so many women sitting in the audience hall of the Palace.

"What do you want me to do?" he had answered smiling, stroking his silken beard. "I make friends of them by trying to grant them their petitions and listening to their troubles, do you remember?" he added seriously. "I reproved you for consoling my officers when I had reproved them. You said you did not want them to be my enemies."

She remembered only too well. She promised him to continue work in her field of nursing. In that way she would be in point of contact with the revolutionary movement, yet removed from the politics and ambitions of the men who were carrying it forward.

On board ship she was surrounded by her thoughtful, confiding husband, and her longed-for children. They occupied two state rooms: one for the two boys and their father, and the other for herself and her daughter. They sat at the captain's table. He was her husband's good friend.

At the pier in New York, they were met by Mama Eloise, who was living there. Almost immediately, the Rebel contacted Clason Point Military Academy on the Sound. On visiting the school, the boys were refused admittance, the rector saying it was too late for further registrations. The Rebel could not accept his refusal.

"I have come a long way," she said after a few moments silence. "Here they will be close to their sister's school. I am determined that they be accepted."

"What can they do?" he asked her.

"They play handball, the violin, and a wind instrument," she replied, reciting each accomplishment slowly and positively.

"That is enough," he stopped her. "I will make room for them."

The next day, the Rebel and her family went in search of the girls' school, Mount St. Ursula. With distances so great in New York, an entire afternoon was needed to locate it. With trembling hands, the Rebel finally rang the familiar door bell. The door opened by some mechanism, and a voice which sounded familiar to the Rebel asked them to enter. So happy was she that she was actually pushing Adolpho in the direction from which the voice had come. They were directed to open the door and wait in the empty drawing room. After what seemed an eternity, a nun appeared.

The Rebel hurried over to greet her, but alas the nun did not remember the small, dark woman. The Rebel had forgotten that twenty years had passed since she had been a student there.

"Sister, there must be someone who remembers me," she said, repeating her name, Leonor Villegas, for the nun.

The children became excited at their mother's persistent words.

"Adolpho," she said, turning tearfully to her husband, "this is no place for my child, if no one remembers me."

She was caught in her husband's warm embrace. To the Rebel, life had become a ridiculous blank.

Just then the door opened softly, and the Reverend Mother walked over to the Rebel.

"Is this our little Leonor?" she asked, touching the Rebel on the arm. "And this, the father of Leonor's children?"

"You do not remember me," the Rebel replied accusingly. "I shall not leave my child here."

"Come," the nun said, leading them to a small room across the hall. "This is my office. We never allow visitors to enter this room. But I want you to see for yourself," she said, looking at the Rebel. "We have never forgotten you."

Hanging above the Nun's desk was the picture of the Rebel's graduating class of 1905.

"You see, Leonor," the nun said, "we remembered you and prayed for you. You always seemed so far away."

Busy days of shopping followed. Each boy had to have his trunk filled with all the required clothes. Shopping had to be done for the little girl. Leaving the children with Mama Eloise, the Rebel begged her not to spoil them, for the old woman was enjoying having Don Joaquín's grandchildren with her for the first time.

When everything was in readiness for school, Adolpho suggested some sightseeing. He did not want the children to appear ignorant. Mexico was, after all, a foreign country full of wild people always at civil strife. One afternoon, tired out from sightseeing, the children sat in quiet corners in the hotel sitting room, writing letters. The Rebel, nearby, looking at a magazine, had to fight back the tears. She would soon be separated from her children again.

Then it was as if an apparition had stolen into the softly lighted room. It took all the courage the Rebel had to sit there and watch the tall, straight man coming toward her. Half smiling, General Felipe Ángeles came up beside her. He told her that it was through the Reyes Retana brothers, exporters in New York, that he had learned of their arrival.

Adolpho had been in contact with the Reyes Retana and Figueroa Company for some time. He had sent them a shipload of henequen from Yucatán. Handled through the Mexican Treasury Department, the sale was a financial success. The henequen had been sold and paid for before it arrived in New York, for it was most urgent to secure money for General Cesáreo Castro's troops in Oaxaca. Adolpho had been scouring the country to find ways of obtaining funds for the payment of Mexican soldiers. He had also sent a shipload of mahogany to be sold in the United States.

Her joy at seeing General Ángeles was great. Now she would be able to get all the truth regarding María de Jesús González. She recalled that their last meeting had been at the time Villa had rebelled. Afterward, the blame had been laid at General Ángeles' door for being the intellectual background for Villa's actions against the First Chief.

The Rebel ordered coffee for the General, as he drank nothing stronger. Sitting low in a soft armchair, he told the Rebel the same story as María de Jesús had.

"May I," asked the Rebel, leaning toward the General, "if God ever inspires me to write about the Revolution, write all this that you have told me as a fact?"

"Yes, yes, of course," he repeated, nodding his head solemnly.

The general was in New York on private business, he told the Rebel. His wife and children were with him. As he talked, the Rebel was filled with a deep sense of tragedy for the lives and high plans of the men of the Revolution. She looked at him sadly. How he had been set, as if by a mocking fate, on the road that had led him so far away from his original beginnings.

Adolpho came in and saluted Ángeles. He too was hardly able to restrain his surprise at seeing him. Ángeles stayed to have supper with them and, seated at the table, he began immediately asking questions about Mexico.

"My general," Adolpho said laying his hand on Ángeles' arm, "make up your mind to come back to Mexico with me. Now is the right time to patch up your differences with the Chief."

Ángeles turned livid. But the Rebel saw that it was not what Adolpho had said, but the presence of someone in the back of the room. Ángeles was being followed; the man was sitting nearby, his face hidden behind a magazine. Hastily excusing himself, Ángeles walked quickly out a side door used by the waiters.

The family continued their supper, but Adolpho got up and went to the small drawing room and, sitting opposite the man, began reading a newspaper. From her place at the table, the Rebel could see her husband. The man evidently thought that Ángeles would come back, for he continued to sit there waiting.

When supper was over, the Rebel beckoned to her husband and they went up to their rooms. For the next few days, they heard nothing of General Ángeles.

The Rebel's two boys were most eager to go to school. They had learned that several of their friends from Colegio Militar in Mexico were attending the school on the Sound.

At the invitation of the Reverend Mother at Mount St. Ursula, the Rebel took her daughter to visit the school the day she went to stay. As they entered the drawing room, the Rebel was surprised to see the room filled with people and decorated with flowers. Finally, a great bell rang and they all got in line, walking into the familiar dining room.

It was the annual alumni meeting of all ex-graduates. The Rebel was to be the honored guest.

The United States had declared war on Germany. Adolpho rushed back to Mexico. Meanwhile, General Felipe Ángeles had disappeared. He had left for Mexico to rejoin Villa.

CHAPTER XIX
The Pattern Is Completed

With her children in school, the Rebel began her Red Cross studies. Thomas Beesley, speaker for the Red Cross, held conferences on the work of the organization. At the same time, the Rebel contacted several writers, hoping to change their opinion regarding President Carranza's administration. During the summer vacation, instead of returning to Mexico, she took her children to a summer school on Lake Champlain, where she met Catholic prelates who showed an interest in the Catholic situation in Mexico.

In the grave international situation, Mexico declared herself neutral, having nothing to offer after years of civil war. President Carranza, still not able to please all the various supporters and factions of the revolutionary movement, was continually confronted with outbursts of opposition. He set about to purge the opposition by force.

General Pablo González, after several unsuccessful assaults with his large army against the strong man of the south, Emiliano Zapata, decided on the age-old Mexican method of planting a traitor in Zapata's ranks. Zapata was murdered in April, 1918, as he came unsuspectingly for an entertainment at Colonel Jesús M. Guajardo's camp. Guajardo was the man General González had chosen to kill Zapata. For his success at murder, Guajardo was made brigadier general with a bonus of $50,000 pesos. Emiliano Zapata, the idealist with the dreamy eyes and graceful bearing, handsome in his tight-fitting charro suit and always looking to the welfare of his *campesinos*, no longer roamed the south.

At Zapata's death, a cry of indignation arose from all over Mexico. The Zapatistas, their leader murdered, dispersed into the mountains, sadly disarming and becoming poor farmers again. General Muggersa, an ardent advocate of Zapata's doctrines, when he became governor of Morelos, carried on Zapata's program of dividing huge estates among the peons.

Meanwhile, General Felipe Ángeles had arrived in El Paso on his way to reenter Mexico. Closely followed by spies of the Mexican government, he was arrested for plotting rebellion on United States territory. After many hardships and much expense, which he could ill afford, he secured his liberty. A few days later, he crossed the Rio Grande with a small group of followers. Colonel Federico Cervantes remained in El Paso to organize troops and follow later. He had in his forces many Chapultepec-trained officers whom he knew to be loyal to Ángeles. These men, like Ángeles, had high ideals for creating a new Mexico. They planned a strong, clean army, such as General Bernardo Reyes had dreamed of. Then they, too, were arrested, and some of them imprisoned in Leavenworth, Kansas, for a time.

When General Ángeles finally reached Cuchillo Prado in Chihuahua, he was informed that the meeting with Villa would be a few weeks later in Tasesihua. There was great rejoicing and celebrating among Villa and his men when Ángeles arrived to join the forces.

Ángeles soon took it up on himself to instruct Villa's untrained troops in military tactics to replace Villa's guerrilla warfare practices. Instructions in the art of war took too much time, and though Villa was an adept pupil, he could not be convinced out of his old way of sudden wild charges of calvary. Ángeles' tactics were too slow and methodical.

Secretly rushing off with a select band, Villa attacked small towns along the border of the United States on wild murdering and looting sorties. Little by little, Villa and Ángeles grew apart. Ángeles' ambition was to build a new army and retake large cities; he couldn't condone Villa's banditry and ruthlessness.

One of the men of Ángeles' company invited Ángeles, whose funds and reputation were now very low, to share a cave with him and his wife. Ángeles accepted willingly, for he was ill and in need of solitude and rest. Betraying him, the men went to a nearby village with news of Ángeles' whereabouts. Gabino Sandoval personally captured him.

Born in the State of Hidalgo, June 13, 1869, Felipe Ángeles at fourteen attended Chapultepec Military College, when General Juan Villegas was director; later, Ángeles was to become director himself. In his youth he loved cockfights, fascinated by the fierce attacks of roosters fighting to the kill. In college, he excelled in mathematics. He made improvements in firearms and artillery when he entered the army. All through life he was distinguished for his modesty, his fine appearance, and great intellectual capacity. He was always scrupulously groomed, whether in civilian or military dress.

A faithful friend of Madero's, Ángeles was the last man to see the ill-fated President as he was taken from the National Palace, a prisoner.

Ángeles himself became a hunted man. Fleeing from the murderous Huerta, he joined Carranza's forces in the Northwest in the great revolt that formed after Madero's government crumbled.

At his court-martial trial, Ángeles prepared and made his own defense. Though the trial was lengthy and cruelly drawn out, it afforded Ángeles an opportunity to express his brilliant mind on political questions. He was court-martialed as a soldier. Clara Kraus de Ángeles, his wife, was sick when General Ángeles was being tried, and she died without knowing her husband's fate. Isabel Ángeles addressed a heart-rending telegram to President Carranza's daughter, begging clemency for her father, reminding her that she too had a warrior father. She received no answer to her pleas.

General Ángeles died a soldier, giving the order for his execution on November 26, 1919. His last words were for his wife and children. Ángeles, whose military genius might have placed his nation on a sure footing, was a gallant soldier who might have led his people into an intelligent peace. Ironically, six months later, the First Chief was to meet death by the cold bullet of a passionless executioner.

Villa, the bandit, continued to range free in the state of Durango. Not until July, 1923, after Carranza's death, was the volatile rustic killed. Villa's habits were known, and on a trip to town from his hacienda to purchase supplies, he was ambushed, his car riddled with bullets. His life was no more violent than this death.

Away from her homeland, the Rebel in New York continued working for Carranza's cause, not knowing his own generals were against him. When Carranza found out that those nearest him were plotting his overthrow, he decided to choose as his successor a civilian, not a military man. Determined to select a man not directly involved in the post-revolutionary struggles, he unfortunately missed the mark. As much as the Rebel admired the First Chief, she could not countenance his choice of Ignacio Bonillas for presidential candidate.

On April seventeenth, 1920, the Rebel received a letter from Carranza telling her of a new outbreak headed by Adolfo de la Huerta, a close friend of General Obregón. "Perhaps," he wrote, "you know of it already."

It was hard to believe the news. She had visited the Mexican Consulate often while Don Adolfo de la Huerta was in New York. There she had talked to Amado Nervo, the famous Mexican writer, before his departure to South America as ambassador. Both men had expressed their admiration for President Carranza.

The Rebel did not wait any longer. From the letter, she foresaw the coming disaster. She packed. Taking Mama Eloise, who was staying with her, back to her hotel, she said her last goodbye. She was never to see her alive again. Together with her children, she left for Laredo to await events. Don Melquíades García, still Mexican Consul on the frontier, was hopeful of a peaceful settlement, but day by day the situation grew worse.

President Carranza, on seeing himself abandoned by his former trusted supporters, Obregón and González, now became more determined to force the issue of Bonillas for president. Relying on the fact that he had loyal followers in Veracruz, commanded by General Guadalupe Sánchez, Carranza secretly arranged his departure for that state to establish his government there. Frantically, without order or system, train cars were loaded beyond capacity with documents, money, and too many people. Early at dawn, the heavy trains began moving on the outskirts of the city; because of the congested line, the last of the long convoy was attacked.

Although it was too late to capture the president when General Obregón gave orders to intercept Carranza, orders were telegraphed all along the line to seize the First Chief and bring him back, preferably alive. Slowly and cautiously, the trains in compact formation moved toward the destination where they were to be met and escorted by Guadalupe Sánchez's troops from Veracruz. Orders to leave had been so hurried that no provisions had been made for food or comfort. All those who had heard of the change of location of the government had rushed to accompany the president. Adolpho had been ordered to transfer a certain amount of collateral and money to the Veracruz banks, where he was president. The Treasury Department also was carrying all the money available in a special car.

During the headlong rush to arrive at the agreed meeting place, many times the engines stopped for lack of water; then the passengers would take all the buckets and vessels available and from some faraway water hole bring water, passing the buckets from man to man. Again and again, the buckets went swinging back and forth. Finally, the engine puffed and pulled a short distance to stop for the last time.

When a cloud of dust appeared on the horizon, unarmed people on the trains clamored out to welcome the arrivals. Shots from the oncoming troops of Guadalupe Sánchez broke out suddenly against the famished and dazed passengers. General Murguía, brave and undaunted, rushed the length of the long convoy, shouting, swearing, urging the hysterical passengers to fight. Giving his horse to the First Chief, he begged him to flee, and by another, longer route find his way to safety in Veracruz.

A few who heard Murguía, hurriedly mounted to accompany the Chief. A score of military cadets joined the company. Feverishly, they rode deep into the wild coast country, with no food and little money.

Adolpho, hearing of the Chief's flight and seeing the attacking enemy, threw himself off the train and into the woods. Walking all night and all day in the direction of Mexico City, he passed through wild-animal-infested country with no provisions or water. Finally, waiting near a road hoping to get a ride, he heard the rattling sound of an old car. A car full of women with a chauffeur drove up and stopped on hearing his call. They allowed him to get in, but as they were starting off, a man who had also been hiding nearby came running up to the car, begging to be taken along. When he found out there was no room for him, he brought a valise he had hidden and asked Adolpho to take it to Mexico City with him. Adolpho told the man he would be at the San Carlos Hotel.

On arriving at the hotel, Adolpho ordered his supper brought to his room. A porter put the valise in a corner, near Adolpho's bed. After a hot bath and a good supper, he went to sleep exhausted. Later, as if in a dream, he began hearing the sound of footsteps walking up and down the hall outside his room. Too fatigued to investigate, or even to order food, he lay in his room all day. Toward evening, he became conscious again of the walking in the hall. Dressing, he opened the door swiftly and peered out. There stood the owner of the valise.

Pushing Adolpho aside, the man sprang into the room, closing the door. "*Hombre,*" he said smiling, "I thought you were dead. Where is my valise?"

Adolpho pointed to the corner. The man rushed over and, grabbing the bag hastened toward the door. Just as he was about to leave, he looked suspiciously at Adolpho, then dropping his suitcase on the floor, he opened it. Adolpho watched amazed as the man quickly counted through bundles of paper money.

"Everything is all right," he said. "I put eighty thousand pesos in here." Patting down the bills neatly, he closed the valise and left the room and Adolpho without another word.

Meanwhile, the First Chief was hurrying to escape his pursuers. An officer with a few men had joined him, suggesting a place where they might find shelter for the night. Carranza agreed to follow. Turning to the cadets, he begged them to return; it would be easier to travel unnoticed with fewer bodyguards. Reluctantly, some of them left.

When the forlorn group reached the small town of Tlaxcalantongo, located at the base of a range of mountains in Puebla, it was the twentieth of May, 1920. They had ridden frantically without respite. It had been a terrific journey. Hounded by the strain to escape, traveling in constant rain and dense fog, they were exhausted and needed sleep. General Rodolfo Herrero showed the Chief the hut he was to occupy. Trusted by Carranza, Herrero had been presented to the Chief by General Maríal as the man to lead him to safety.

Seeing a small candle used to light the little room melting all too hastily, the Chief asked that it be used prudently. They would continue their flight early the next morning, and the candle would be invaluable then. At Carranza's faithful side, Secundino Reyes, who had been with the First Chief since the early days of the Revolution, prepared the Chief's resting place. Unsaddling Carranza's horse, he took the saddle blanket for a pallet, putting the saddle for his head.

In the same damp hut were lawyer Manuel Aguirre Berlanga, Secretary of the Interior; the Director of Telegraph, Mario Méndez; Carranza's private secretary, Pedro Gil Farías; and his two loved assistants, Captains Octavio Amador and Ignacio Suárez. General Herlidero Pérez, under the direction of General Herrero, made the arrangements for the group.

Stretching his tired body upon the thin pallet, the President asked his secretary if there was not some place a little better for them to stay; perhaps a hut with a board floor. Farías told him they had the best house in the village.

"Then, we will remain here," Carranza answered with resignation. "There is nothing better to do."

Turning to Captain Suárez, he asked him to tell the others not to unsaddle their horses, they might have to make a quick flight during the night. Suárez answered that all the horses had already been unsaddled, for they were very tired. There seemed nothing to do but await a message from General Maríal. Carranza spoke a few words to his faithful officers.

Later in the night, General Murguía, who was commanding the scant escort, brought in a messenger with a letter from General Maríal at Xico. Carranza was awakened. He lit the candle and, raising up on his elbow, read the message out loud.

"Early tomorrow, General Lindero Hernández, who is trustworthy, will send troops to meet your expedition and direct you to Villa Juárez."

"Now we can sleep safely," the Chief said. "I could not feel at peace until this message came."

A few hours later in the storming thunder and rain, a shot rang out in the darkness. Carranza was wounded. The message had been a ruse to locate him.

"What's the matter?" called out Berlanga. "What has happened?"

"My leg is broken," Carranza called out. "I cannot rise."

A second shot echoed bluntly. Captain Suárez rushed to the president, lifting Carranza's head in his arms. He tried to drag Carranza outside, but the Chief pulled himself to a seated position on his improvised bed.

"Señor, my Chief," Suárez began, speaking to the Chief in a tender and respectful manner. He heard the dying man's death rattle, the shortened breath, and felt the last pulsation of the great heart. Carranza was dead.

No one moved. Suárez holding the heavy body said, "The President has just died. Take note of the hour: exactly twenty minutes past four in the morning."

Soldiers belonging to Herrero and commanded by his nephew, Ernesto Herrero, disarmed Carranza's followers. Captain Reyes, the Chief's aide, kneeling reverently beside the body lying on the floor, covered Carranza with the coat from the foot of the Chief's pallet.

Carranza's body was placed on a litter hastily built of rude lumber, and brought to Mexico City. He was buried in a fourth-class grave in Dolores Cemetery. It was the humblest: those were his wishes. Several years later, the body was moved, and friends of Carranza secured a monument for the place of his burial.

The Rebel, with the door closed to further work in Mexico, remained in Laredo. Adolpho, as soon as he was able, joined her. There was no place now in the government for Carrancistas. For the first time in ten years, the Rebel took up a strangely quiet life removed from politics, upheaval, and war. For the time being the action of the Revolution was pushed aside, forgotten, to make way for a new era in Mexico's tempestuous history. If the hour of need ever came again, the Rebel vowed to herself, she would be ready to serve. Too many memories were gathered in the recesses of her mind to allow her to be content with the peace of forgetfulness.

Commanded by the dead, and wishing to do justice to the worthy nurses and brave women who so patriotically defended their country, the Rebel watches the outcome of the years that flamed at white heat in the fiery crucible of the Mexican Revolution.

Appendix I

Chronology of Events
Surrounding the Mexican Revolution

1857		New Constitution proclaimed by Liberals.
1859	Sep 28	Juan Nepomuceno Cortina, a Texas-Mexican rancher, captures Brownsville, Texas, with the help of his vaqueros from rancho El Carmen.
1861		Benito Juárez, President.
1861–65		Civil War in the United States. Texas-Mexicans in Southern Texas served as Confederate and Union soldiers. The Río Bravo is an international boundary and waterway which cannot be blockaded by the Union Navy. The waterway becomes the major point of exit for Confederate cotton to the world market.
1862–67		French military intervention, Emperor Maximilian.
1867–72		Benito Juárez, President.
1872–76		Sebastián Lerdo de Tejada, President.
1873	Sep 16	Ricardo Flores Magón born in San Antonio Eloxochitlán, Oaxaca.
	Oct 30	Francisco Madero born at Hacienda El Rosario, municipio de Parras, Coahuila.

The Beginning of The Rebel

Year	Date	Event
1876		General Porfirio Díaz's *Plan de Tuxtepec,* designates himself Restauration Military Commander in Chief.
1877–80		Porfirio Díaz's first term as president begins. His ascendency to the presidency begins a 34-year period known as the *Porfiriato.*
	Jun 12	Leonor Villegas (de Magnón) born in Nuevo Laredo, Tamaulipas.
1879		The Texas-Mexican Railroad connecting the Port at Corpus Christi, Texas, eastward to Laredo, Texas, is completed. Trade goods will be shipped from the port to Laredo and then on to Mexico on the Mexican National Railway.
1880–84		Manuel González, a close friend of Díaz, becomes President. Díaz remains the power behind the scenes, waiting to return to the presidency.
1881		Sara Estela Ramírez born in Villa de Progreso, Coahuila.
	Feb 3	Andrea Villarreal born in Lampazos, Nuevo León, Mexico.m
1882–85		Leonor Villegas attends Ursuline Convent, San Antonio, Texas.
1884–1911		Díaz, President, from his second to his seventh term as President of the Republic of Mexico.
1885–89		Leonor Villegas attends Academy of the Holy Cross, Austin, Texas.
1885	Sep 7	Jovita Idar born in Laredo, Texas.

1889–90		Don Catarino Garza, journalist and editor from San Diego, Texas, proclaimed a Texas-based rebellion against President Porfirio Díaz. An attack on Guerrero, Tamaulipas, failed, and the invaders returned to the United States.
1892–95		Economic crisis in Mexico.
1889–95		Leonor Villegas attends Academy of Mount Saint Ursula, Bedford Park, New York City and receives teaching credentials.
1895		Leonor Villegas returns to Laredo, Texas.
1900	Aug 7	Jesús Flores Magón founds legal review *Regeneración*.
1901	Jan 10	Leonor Villegas marries Adolfo Magnón and moves to Mexico City.
	Feb 5	First Liberal Congress, San Luis Potosí.
1902	Jul 16	Ricardo Flores Magón edits *El Hijo del Ahuizote*.
1903		Juana Belén Gutiérrez de Mendoza founds *Vésper,* Guanajuato, Mexico.
	Mar	Founding of Anti-reelectionist Club Redención, with its newspaper *Excélsior*.
	Jun 20	Jovita Idar receives teaching credentials, Holding Institute, Laredo, Texas.
1904		*La Mujer Moderna,* directed by Dolores Correa Z. through 1908, Mexico City.
	Jan 3	Ricardo and Enrique Flores Magón, and other Liberal political exiles arrive in Laredo, Texas.
	Nov 5	*Regeneración* reissued from San Antonio, Texas.

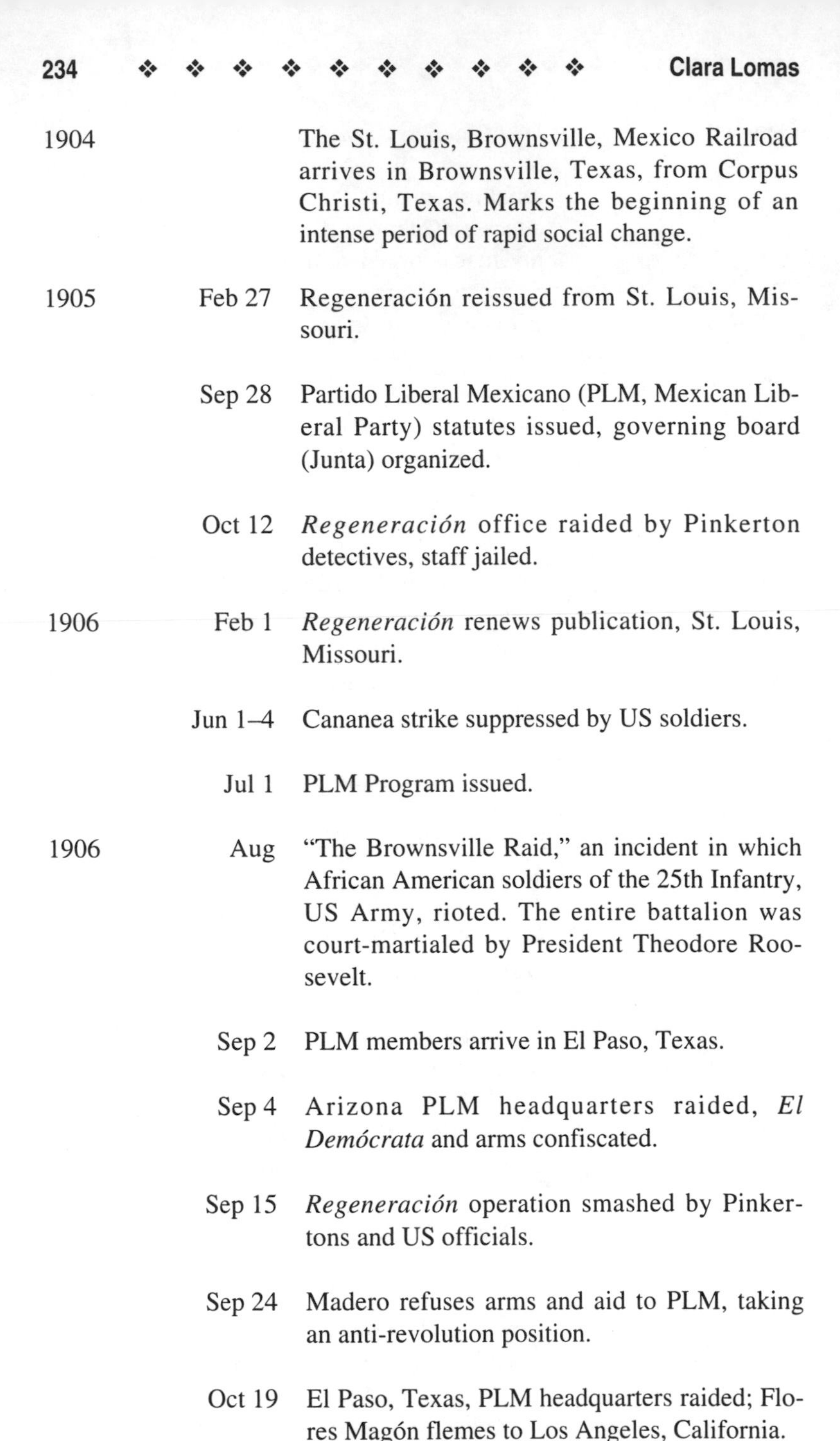

1904		The St. Louis, Brownsville, Mexico Railroad arrives in Brownsville, Texas, from Corpus Christi, Texas. Marks the beginning of an intense period of rapid social change.
1905	Feb 27	Regeneración reissued from St. Louis, Missouri.
	Sep 28	Partido Liberal Mexicano (PLM, Mexican Liberal Party) statutes issued, governing board (Junta) organized.
	Oct 12	*Regeneración* office raided by Pinkerton detectives, staff jailed.
1906	Feb 1	*Regeneración* renews publication, St. Louis, Missouri.
	Jun 1–4	Cananea strike suppressed by US soldiers.
	Jul 1	PLM Program issued.
1906	Aug	"The Brownsville Raid," an incident in which African American soldiers of the 25th Infantry, US Army, rioted. The entire battalion was court-martialed by President Theodore Roosevelt.
	Sep 2	PLM members arrive in El Paso, Texas.
	Sep 4	Arizona PLM headquarters raided, *El Demócrata* and arms confiscated.
	Sep 15	*Regeneración* operation smashed by Pinkertons and US officials.
	Sep 24	Madero refuses arms and aid to PLM, taking an anti-revolution position.
	Oct 19	El Paso, Texas, PLM headquarters raided; Flores Magón flemes to Los Angeles, California.

1906	Dec 4	Nationwide textile strike begins in Mexico.
1907–11		Economic crisis throughout Mexico.
1907	Jan 8	Río Blanco massacre, textile strike ends.
	Jun	*La Voz de la Mujer* founded in El Paso, Texas.
	Jun 1	First issue of PLM's *Revolución,* Los Angeles, California.
1908	Feb 17	In "Creelman interview," Díaz welcomes "opposition" party.
	May 30	Díaz announces he will run for another term.
	Jun	PLM announces it will fight for Anarchism.
1909		Nellie Campobello born.
1909	Jan 31	Madero's *La sucesión presidencial en 1910* appears, El Partido Nacional Democrático (National Democratic Party).
	Nov	General Bernardo Reyes exiled; Ateneo de la Juventud founded, Mexico City.
1910		Madero's anti-reelectionist campaign repressed; Nicasio Idar, Jovita Idar's father, becomes owner and publisher of weekly *La Crónica,* Laredo, Texas; Teresa Villarreal founds *El Obrero,* San Antonio, Texas.
	May 10	Mexico's Secretaría de Relaciones Exteriores receives report of two Maderista periodicals in San Antonio, Texas: *Monitor Democrático,* directed by Paulino Martínez; *La Mujer Moderna,* directed by Andrea Villarreal.
	Jun 5	Madero arrested in Monterrey, jailed in San Luis Potosí.
	Aug 21	Sara Estela Ramírez dies, Laredo, Texas.

1910	Sep 24	Díaz "re-elected."
	Oct 5	Madero escapes from prison, his *Plan de San Luis* declares elections null, calls for upraising, flees into US exile.
	Nov 20	Revolution breaks out in Puebla, Aquiles and Carmen Serdán respond with bullets to arrest notice; Elena Arizmendi organizes *Cruz Blanca Neutral* (Neutral White Cross) to serve during short-lived Madero revolt.
1911	Mar 6	President Taft orders 20,000 soldiers to Mexican border, naval units to Gulf of Mexico and Pacific.
	May 9	Madero establishes his government in Ciudad Juárez, Chihuahua.
	May 25	Díaz resigns.
	May 31	Díaz leaves Mexico for exile in Europe.
	Jun 7	Madero enters Mexico City triumphant.
	Jul 12	Colonel Blanquet's troops kill 80 Maderista soldiers, Puebla.
	Aug 12	General Emiliano Zapata, Southern agrarian movement leader, declares their demands be met.
	Aug 27	Madero-Zapata truce; General Victoriano Huerta routs disarmed Zapata forces; Zapata then plans revolt against Madero.
	Sep 14–22	El Primer Congreso Mexicanista (First Mexican Congress) takes place in Laredo, Texas.
	Oct	Jovita Idar founds La Liga Feminil Mexicanista (League of Mexican Women) to provide free education for Mexican children.

1911	Nov 28	Zapata demands redistribution of land.
1912		*El Progreso* founded by Leopoldo Villegas, edited by Santiago Paz and Oswaldo Sánchez, Laredo, Texas.
	Feb	General Bernardo Reyes returns from US exile in San Antonio, Texas, and declares revolt. He was captured in February of 1912 and spent a year in jail.
	Feb	Insurgents against Madero occupy Ciudad Juárez.
	Mar 3	Pascual Orozco, a former Maderista, proclaims himself against Madero.
	Apr 14	Alvaro Obregón rises against Orozco.
	Jul 3	Orozco defeated by government military General Victoriano Huerta's forces.
	Jul 15	Casa del Obrero Mundial founded by Díaz Soto y Gama and others.
1913	Feb 9	*Decena Trágica* (Tragic Ten Days) begins.
	Feb 11	Madero names General Huerta commander in chief of government military forces.
	Feb 18	Huerta betrays Madero, assumes power.
	Feb 22	Madero and Vice-President Pino Suárez assassinated.
	Mar 4	Woodrow Wilson assumes US presidency.
	Mar 17	Nuevo Laredo attacked by Jesús Carranza's military forces; Leonor Villegas de Magnón forms medical relief group, assisted by Jovita and Elvira Idar, María Alegría, Rosa Chávez and Dr. M. M. Dávila, to care for all wounded

1913		soldiers; Huertista General Blanquet solicits group's services; group opts to declare itself Constitutionalist.
	Mar 26	Venustiano Carranza proposes the *Plan de Guadalupe*, calls for revolt, names himself *Primer Jefe del Ejército Constitucionalista* (Constitutionalist Army First Chief).
	May 10	Lucio Blanco, Constitutionalist General, captures Reynosa, Tamaulipas.
	May 18	Leonor Villegas de Magnón founds *La Cruz Blanca* (The White Cross), Laredo, Texas.
	June 4	Blanco captures Matamoros, Tamaulipas, and holds it for two months. The Carrancistas hold Matamoros until March of 1915.
	Oct 10	Huerta dissolves Mexican Congress.
	Nov 5	*Pluma Roja,* an anarchist feminist biweekly, founded by Blanca de Moncaleano, Los Angeles, apparently ran through 1915.
1914	Jan 1	Nuevo Laredo, Tamaulipas, attacked by Constitutionalist forces; La Cruz Blanca reassembles over 50 nurses and over ten doctors; 150 soldiers treated at Leonor Villegas de Magnón's Laredo home.
	Feb 3	President Wilson lifts arms embargo supporting Revolution.
	Apr 2	Francisco Villa occupies Torreón.
	Apr 3	Constitutionalists held at Fort McIntosh are released.
	Apr 5	At General Pablo González's request, La Cruz Blanca brigade of 26 leaves to Torreón, Coahuila, via San Antonio and El Paso, Texas.

1914	Apr 7	Nicasio Idar dies.
	Apr 19	La Cruz Blanca arrives in Torreón, establishes temporary hospitals, works on revolutionary propaganda, founds new brigades in Durango, Santiago Papasquiaro, Torreón and San Pedro de las Colonias, Chihuahua.
	Apr 21	U.S. Marines occupy Veracruz port to prevent a German munitions vessel from entering, thereby blocking arms to Huerta.
	Apr 23	Revolutionary forces occupy Monterrey.
	Apr 24	US-Mexico diplomatic relations are severed.
	May	Casa del Obrero Mundial closed down by Huerta police.
	May 12	Revolutionary forces occupy Tampico and Tuxpan.
	May 13	La Cruz Blanca in Durango.
	May 15	Revolutionary forces occupy Tepic.
	May 20	Revolutionary forces occupy Saltillo; Niagara Falls Conference begins; Carranza authorizes and renames *La Cruz Blanca Nacional* stationed in Saltillo.
	Jun	Jovita and Clemente Idar join La Cruz Blanca in Saltillo as its secretary and journalist, respectively.
	Jun 23	Revolutionary forces led by Villa occupy Zacatecas.
	Jul 11	Revolutionary forces occupy Acapulco.
	Jul 15	Huerta driven from power, exiled.

1914	Jul 16	Revolutionary forces occupy Guadalajara, Guaymas.
	Jul 17	Revolutionary forces occupy San Luis Potosí, Colima, Aguascalientes.
	Jul 27	Revolutionary forces occupy Guanajuato.
	Jul 29	Revolutionary forces occupy Quéretaro.
	Jul 30	Revolutionary forces occupy Morelia.
	Aug 4	Revolutionary forces occupy Pachuca.
	Aug 5	Revolutionary forces occupy Mazatlán.
	Aug 8	Revolutionary forces occupy Toluca.
	Aug 11	Revolutionary forces occupy Tlaxcala.
	Aug 13	Revolutionary forces occupy Cuernavaca; Carranza orders La Cruz Blanca to meet him in Tanepantla.
	Aug 15	Constitutionalist forces led by Obregón enter Mexico City.
	Aug 20	Carranza enters Mexico City and assumes power.
	Sep 14	La Cruz Blanca returns to Laredo, Texas; unsuccessful negotiations to have Zapata recognize Carranza.
	Sep 22	Villa breaks from Carranza/Constitutionalists.
	Oct 1–4	Governers/Generals' Convention convened by Carranza, Mexico City; Villa and Zapata refuse to attend; Carranzam resigns as military and executive chief; convention members refuse his resignation.

1914	Oct 7	Villegas de Magnón receives office telegram to take possession of military hospital in Nuevo Laredo, Tamaulipas.
	Oct 11– Nov 13	Aguascalientes Convention with Villistas and Zapatistas; Carranza refuses to attend; convention disavows Carranza as First Chief.
	Nov 6	Eulalio Gutiérrez, Provisional President, through May 28, 1915.
	Nov 23	US Marines withdraw from Veracruz port at Carranza's request.
	Nov 29	Carranza government moves to Veracruz; Zapatistas occupy Mexico City.
1915–17		Texas-Mexican and Mexican attacks on Anglo ranches, irrigation works, military camps and railroad crossings. The attackers were known as *Los Sediciosos* and were supposed to be part of the *Plan de San Diego.* During this period hundreds of Mexicans were disarmed and executed by the Texas Rangers and sheriffs of South Texas. Anglos fled to Corpus Christi, Texas, and Texas-Mexicans crossed the border into Mexico. More than 70,000 US regular and National Guard troops were mobilized into South Texas.
1915	Jan	Carranza's agrarian-reform decree.
	Jan	Plan de San Diego promulgated at San Diego, Texas. It called for an armed uprising to begin on February 22, 1915. All Anglo males over 16 years of age were to be killed, but women and children were not to be molested. The plan sought to return the territory between the Nueces River and the Rio Bravo to Mexico. The two principal signers of the Plan were two

1915		well-known Texas-Mexicans, Anizeto Pizaña and Luis de la Rosa.
	Feb	Carranza-Casa del Obrero Mundial alliance; Carrancistas defeat Villistas and Zapatistas.
	Mar 27	General José Rodríquez leads a Villista attack on Matamoros, Tamaulipas. Over 200 wounded Villistas are allowed to cross to the United States at Las Ruscias, five miles west of Brownsville, to receive medical assistance. They later travel to Laredo and cross into Nuevo Laredo and rejoin the Villistas.
	Apr 16	Fort McIntosh soldiers scatter for miles on border waiting for stray bullets from Mexico to shoot back, Laredo, Texas.
	Apr 17	General Maclovio Herrera killed in Nuevo Laredo, Tamaulipas.
	May	Venustiano Carranza visits Matamoros, Tamaulipas.
	Jun 27	US federal agents arrest Huerta and Pascual Orozco, El Paso, Texas, imprisoned in Fort Bliss.
	Jul 2	Díaz dies in Paris.
	Jul 25	Sediciosos burn a railroad bridge of the St. Louis, Brownsville, Mexico Railroad South of Sebastian, Texas.
	Aug 2	Small detachment of US Calvary along with civilians and Deputy Sheriffs attack Rancho El Tule looking for Mexican bandits.
	Aug 8	Sixty Sediciosos attack Las Norias, a section of the King Ranch, 70 miles north of Brownsville.

1915	Aug 30	Sediciosos burn the railroad trestle 12 miles north of Brownsville.
	Sep 1	Fresnos Canal Company irrigation pumping station burned to the ground 14 miles north of Brownsville.
	Sep	Villistas attack train at San Ysabel, Chihuahua, killing 17 US citizens. Carranza declares Villa an outlaw.
	Oct 11	Carranza returns to Mexico City.
	Oct 17	The St. Louis, Brownsville, Mexico train is derailed six miles north of Brownsville. Four passengers are killed. Seven Mexicans in the vicinity of the wreck are arrested and four are executed by the Texas Rangers.
	Oct 19	President Wilson recognizes Carranza's government.
1916	Jan 13	Huerta dies in El Paso, Texas.
	Mar 9	Villa attacks Columbus, New Mexico; 27 die.
	Mar 15	General Pershing's Punitive Expedition invades Mexico in search of Villa.
	Oct–Dec	Mexico/US talks on Punitive Expedition, Altantic City.
	Nov	Jovita Idar establishes *Evolución,* Laredo, Texas.
	Dec 1	Querétaro Constitutional Convention.
1917	Feb 5	Constitution promulgated, based on PLM Program.
	May 20	Jovita Idar marries Bartolo Juárez.

1918	Aug	Librado Rivera and Ricardo Flores Magón sentenced to fifteen and twenty years, respectively, in US prison.
1919	Apr 10	Zapata assassinated.
	Nov 15	Felipe González arrested, executed, Chihuahua.
1920	Apr 24	Obregón and Pablo González against Carranza.
	May 7	Carranza leaves to Veracruz.
	May 21	Carranza assassinated, Tlaxcalantongo.

The End of The Rebel

1920	May 24	Adolfo de la Huerta, Provisional President through Nov 30.
1920–24		Alvaro Obregón, President.
1921		Jovita Idar Juárez moves to San Antonio, Texas.
1922		Ricardo Flores Magón dies in Fort Leavenworth Federal Penitentiary, Kansas.
1923	Jul 20	Villa assassinated.
	Aug 30	US-Mexico diplomatic relations reinstated.
1924–28		General Plutarco Elías Calles, President.
1928		Jovita Idar founds free kindergarten for Mexican American children, San Antonio, Texas.
1940	Feb–Dec	Jovita Idar co-editor of *El Heraldo Cristiano,* San Antonio, Texas.

1941	Feb 14	Secretary of National Defense, Mexico City, acknowledges Leonor Villegas de Magnón's services to the Revolution, recognizes her as a veteran of the Mexican Revolution.
	May 16	Leonor Villegas de Magnón receives *A la lealtad Mayo de 1920* (Loyalty to May 1920) medal from the Venustiano Carranza Association.
1942		Leonor Villegas de Magnón, member Institución Auxiliar Femenina de Voluntarias para la Defensa Nacional (National Defense Auxiliary Women Volunteers).
1943		Leonor Villegas de Magnón employed Dirección General de Estadísticas (Department of Statistics), Mexico City; recognition by women's club, Club Femenino, Protector, Cultural, Recreativo, Defensa y Amparo de la Mujer, for her humanitarian work.
1945–47		Leonor Villegas de Magnón works at Rancherías Camargo, Tamaulipas, on her *parcela.*
1946	Jan 2	Leonor Villegas de Magnón receives *Presidente Madero* medal from Agrupación Patriótica Nacional, Mexico City.
	Jun 15	Jovita Idar dies, San Antonio, Texas.
1949		Mexican House of Representatives approves veteran pension bill, 10 pesos a day.
1951	Apr 9	The Naylor Company of San Antonio, Texas, refuses to publish *The Rebel on the Río Grande Border.*
	Oct 29	Simon & Schuster Publishers, New York, refuses to publish *The Lady Was a Rebel.*
	Dec 14	The MacMillan Company, New York, refuses to publish *The Lady Was a Rebel.*

1952	Jan 26	University of Texas Press, Austin, refuses to publish *The Lady Was a Rebel.*
	Jan 31	The Bruce Publishing Company, Milwaukee, Wisconsin, refuses to publish *The Lady Was a Rebel.*
	Apr 25	Andrea Villarreal applies for *Mérito Revolucionario* (Revolutionary Merit) medal for work with *Vésper,* other publications, Juntas Revolucionarias Precursoras, propaganda for 1910 and 1913 Revolutions.
1954	Jan	Leonor Villegas de Magnón requests to see Mexican President Adolfo Ruiz Cortines.
1955	Apr 17	Leonor Villegas de Magnón dies in Mexico City.
1963	Jan 19	Andrea Villarreal dies in Monterrey, Nuevo León, Mexico.

Appendix II

Bio-Bibliography of Historical Characters

Acuña, Jesús (1886–1916)

A lifelong Madernista and a principal supporter of Carranza. In 1913, he formed a regiment of 600 men to defend Carranza's Plan de Guadalupe. Personal secretary to Carranza during the campaign against Victoriano Huerta, President of Coahuila 1914–15, and Secretary of State and Chief of Staff in Carranza's pre-constitutional government.

Aguilar, Cándido (1889–1960)

A hero of many revolutionary battles fought in Veracruz and a principal force there behind the Revolution. He served as governor of Veracruz from 1914 to 1916. He also occupied the posts of Secretary of State in Carranza's cabinet during 1916 and 1918. After Carranza's death, he was exiled to the US twice and finally granted amnesty by Cárdenas in 1939.

Aguirre, Felipe (? - ?)

Aguirre was staff treasurer of the original Cruz Blanca brigade which traveled from Laredo to El Paso, Texas, then from Ciudad Juárez, Chihuahua, to Mexico City.

Alvarado, Salvador (1880–1925)

A supporter of the anti-reelectionist movement during the seventh reelection of Díaz, and one of the first to take up arms on behalf of Madero. As a Constitutionalist and Carrancista, he became governor and military commander in Yucatán from 1915 to 1918. During this time, he was known as a great social reformer. He established a chapter of the Casa del Obrero Mundial; he organized a conference for both teachers and feminists; he founded schools of Agriculture, Arts and Trades, Fine Arts and Law; he passed important legislation concerning land redistribution and protection for workers; and he returned many Yaqui Indians, who had been sold as slaves in Yucatán, to their homeland in Sonora. In 1917, he was designated as the military commander for the Isthmus and the entire southeast region of México. In 1919, he founded the newspaper, *El heraldo de México*. He was a powerful military-political figure and was even considered as a presidential candidate in 1920 and served as Secretary of Housing that same year. He was later forced to flee the country several times and was finally assassinated in 1925.

Amaya, Manuel (?–?)

One of the first to join the Constitutionalist movement and a loyal Carrancista. He served as Head of Protocol for the Secretary of State in 1913.

Ángeles Ramírez, Felipe (1869–1919)

One of the top students, and later professor, at the Colegio Militar during the Porfiriato. He opposed the military's injustices against the Yaqui Indians in northern Mexico. In 1912, Madero named him director of the Colegio Militar. He supported Carranza and became his Secretary of War. In 1914 he joined Villa, represented him in the Convention of Aguascalientes, then parted from him after conflicts over military strategies. After Carranza's triumph, he took refuge in New York where he was politically active in the Alianza Liberal Mexicana until 1918. He returned to Mexico to oppose Carranza but was arrested and executed on November 26.

Arizmendi Mejía, Elena (?–1949)

Founder of the Cruz Blanca Neutral (Neutral White Cross), the medical relief group of the Madernistas. José Vasconcelos refers to her under the pseudonym "Adriana" in his works *Ulises Criollo* and *La Tormenta.*

Arrieta León, Domingo (1874–1962)

He began his military career in the anti-reelectionist movement of 1910 in his home state of Durango. Together with his brothers, he backed the Plan de San Luis and began fighting on November 20, 1910, and took the city of Durango in May 1911. In 1913 he and his brother Mariano directed the Durango forces in favor of the Plan de Guadalupe, fighting against the Huertistas. In August of the same year, the Arrieta brothers met with Carranza as he traveled to Sonora; Domingo was promoted to General and named as military commander of the state. He remained loyal to Carranza and in 1917 was elected governor of Durango.

Arrieta León, Mariano (1866–?)

The brother of Domingo and a co-agitator with him in the fight against Díaz and later against Huerta. He also was a loyal follower of Carranza and served as the Constitutionalist governor of Durango for several months in 1915.

Barragán, Juane (1890–1974)

Joined the Revolution in the fight against Huerta by equipping the servants of his father's hacienda with guns, horses and the call to arms, "Viva Carranza." He served under Jacinto B. Treviño, accompanying Carranza through northern México and into the capital. He remained faithful to Carranza during the campaign against Villa and was an essential member of the Estado Mayor. In 1917, he was the governor of San Luis Potosí. He was also the founding member of the Partido Auténtico de la Revolución Mexicana (PARM) and wrote the classic work *Historia del Ejército y de la Revolución Constitutionalista.*

Bauche Alcalde, Elena (?–?)

President of the Cruz Blanca, Chihuahua brigade.

Bauche Alcalde, Manuel (?–?)

An outspoken supporter of the Madernista movement and later of the Constitutionalist movement. He served in the Eastern Division in Veracruz under General Cándido Aguilar. He was later sent by Carranza to Tamaulipas with the reporter Alfonso Barrera Peniche to report on the campaign against General Caballero.

Berlanga Aguirre, Manuel (1887–1953)

Governor of Jalisco beginning in 1915 and later the first Chief of Staff in the Carranza administration from 1917 to 1920. He also wrote several important legal works on the Mexican Revolution.

Blackaller Sisters: Carolina, Rebeca, Margarita, Francisca and Adela (?–?)

In 1913 they all joined the Constitutionalist movement, working in a hospital in Monclova, Coahuila. They also worked as volunteer nurses in hospitals in Piedras Negras, Coahuila, and Matamoros, Tamaulipas.

Blanco, Lucio (1879–1922)

He entered the Revolution during the Orozquista revolution and was one of the first to follow Carranza against Huerta. In the military, he served in many different posts and under many different commanders. It was during this time that he became acquainted with and a rival of Alvaro Obregón. In 1914 he left the Constitutionalist Army and joined the Convención. Under the government of the Convención, he was the military commander of Mexico City and the Chief of Staff in Gutiérrez's cabinet. After the success of the Plan de Agua Prieta, he was exiled, but from Texas he conspired with Francisco Murguía against his old enemy Obregón. He was assassinated in 1922 after crossing the Rio Grande into Tamaulipas.

Blanquet, Aureliano (1849–1918)

A military man from the age of 28, Blanquet was loyal to the government of Porfirio Díaz until its end. He hated the Revolution and in 1913 played an important role in the Decena Trájica. In that same year, he led the fight against the Constitutionalists, serving in Huerta's second cabinet as Secretary of War and of the Navy. With the fall of Huerta's government, he fled to Cuba to escape reprisals for his opposition to the Constitutionalist movement and for his participation in the death of Madero. He returned to Veracruz in 1918 and allied himself with Félix Díaz in order to fight against Carranza. He fell into an arroyo several days later and died. The Carrancistas found and decapitated the body and then sent the head to Veracruz, where it was on display for several days.

Bojórguez, Juan de Dios (1892–1967)

He served as Mexican minister in Honduras, Guatemala and Cuba, as the chief of the Labor Department, as governor of Baja California Sur and as Chief of Staff. A prominent intellectual and director of the newspaper *El Nacional.*

Bonillas, Ignacio (1858–1924)

Born in México but raised and educated in the United States, he returned to his native Sonora and became a man of means. A Madernista from 1910 on, and later a Constitutionalist. He served in Carranza's government, filling several lower level positions. His diplomatic career began in 1917 when he attended the Atlantic City conferences with the Mexican delegation. Soon afterwards, he was the Mexican ambassador in Washington for two years. In 1919, he became a presidential candidate with the backing of Carranza, but this was one of the reasons for the Agua Prieta rebellion. He was charged falsely by Obregón and fled with Carranza to Tlaxcalantongo. He then returned to the United States, where he lived until his death.

Breceda Mercado, Alfredo (1886–1966)

A signer of the Plan de Guadalupe and a friend of Don Venustiano. He served Carranza in several confidential commissions, both in the Constitutionalist movement and in his government. In 1917, he became the military commander and governor of San Luis Potosí and then, in 1918, governor of the Distrito Federal. He was also sent as a diplomat to Sweden and Panama and was the author of *México Revolucionario*.

Burns, Juan (1884–?)

A local politician in the state of Chihuahua and a consular agent for the Constitutionalist regime in El Paso and Galveston, Texas. Later, he served as the consulate general in New York and Tokyo.

Caballero, Luis (1880–1934)

A Constitutionalist who fought against Huerta and the Convención in the state of Tamaulipas. He was proclaimed a general by his own troops. After the Revolution, he became the inspector of the army and president of the Superior Military Court.

Cabrera, Luis (1876–1954)

A competent attorney and writer who helped organize the Reyista political movement, Cabrera did not support the Madero campaign, but he became one of the most noted legislators during the Madero presidency for several speeches of historical significance—one of which was an ideological antecedent to all land reform in México. He was the founder of the Escuela Libre de Derecho. He lived in exile in the United States during 1913, but was asked by Carranza in December of that year to be the Constitutionalist's confidential agent to the United States, and later Secretary of Housing. As Carranza's top aide, Cabrera was responsible for a social reform program and a new constitution that could cope with surging political, social and economic demands. In 1917, he was sent to South America as a representative of the Mexican government. With the fall of Carranza, he was given his liberty on the condition that he would stay out of politics henceforth. He never again became personally involved, but his criticisms and ideas continued through his writings.

Calles, Aureo L. (1887–1957)

A Constitutionalist who carried out several military commissions, including Chief of Operations in Tabasco, Chiapas, Yucatán and Colima, Infantry Commander under the Secretary of War and Navy and Subsecretary of National Defense during the Alemán administration.

Calzada, Eusebio (1870–?)

A Constitutionalist first, he later became a general in Villa's army when he was given command of the military trains.

Cantú, Severo (?–?)

Cantú was one of the original Cruz Blanca staff members who traveled from Laredo to El Paso, Texas, then from Ciudad Juárez, Chihuahua, to Mexico City.

Carranza Garza, Venustiano (1859–1920)

Carranza was educated at the National Preparatory School in Mexico City but he abandoned his studies for agricultural pursuits on his family's ranch in Coahuila. His political career began in 1887 when he was elected municipal president of Cuatro Ciénegas. Due to conflicts with the governor Garza Galán, Carranza resigned his position. When Galán attempted to reelect himself, Carranza rebelled yet convinced Díaz that his rebellion was not anti-Porfirista. Bmmernardo Reyes mediated the conflict and helped Carranza reestablish himself politically. Carranza once again became municipal president and was a representative in the Coahuila legislature and a senator to the Union Congress. Carranza temporarily served as the governor of Coahuila in 1908 and he believed himself to be the next governor of the state but Díaz and the Científicos opposed the election due to Carranza's involvement with the Reyistas. Despite the opposition, Carranza ran for governor but was defeated by Jesús del Valle, thus beginning his career as a political oppositionist. Carranza eventually distanced himself from Reyes and joined the Madernist movement just before fleeing to the United States for a short period. Madero named him Secretary of the Armed Forces, even though he was a civilian, and Carranza became governor of Coahuila once again. Carranza organized auxiliary forces to restrict the Orozquistas from entering Coahuila in 1912. In 1913 Carranza rebelled against Huerta and initiated the Constitutionalist movement. He sent Eliseo Arredondo to collect information and to negotiate an agreement with the supposed national government in Mexico. He launched the Guadalupe Plan on March 26, 1913. In the Plan, Carranza openly opposed Huerta and the Legislative Powers of the Federation as well as any state governments that still recognized Huerta after thirty days; he named himself Head of the Constitutionalist Military in defense of the 1857 Constitution. The Plan also named Carranza temporary president in Mexico City until official elections could be held and peace restored. While crossing through country he had designated as refuge for the revolutionary leaders, Carranza formalized his first national government and put together his cabinet. The year 1914 marked the beginning of his confrontations with Villa, which escalated into Villa's disregard for Carranza's orders and subsequent occupation of Zacatecas. Despite the internal conflicts among the Constitutionalists, Carranza defeated Huerta in 1914 and claimed Mexico City. At the Torreón Convention, Eulalio Gutiérrez assumed the presidency and Carranza declared his own rebellion. He re-organized his troops and made several additions to his Guadalupe Plan. Carranza ultimately reclaimed Mexico City and his government thus gained recognition from the United States. Carranza organized a constituent congress and promulgated the Constitution on February 5, 1917. He won the election for President of the Republic on May 1, 1917, and began reorganizing the powers and administration of the country, redistributing lands and reestablishing labor and civil rights. Carranza continued his political career as a diplomat before he was assassinated by Rodolfo Herrera's troops in Tlaxcalantongo on May 21, 1920.

Carturegli, Marie de (?–?)

An aristocrat from Sonora who organized a group of women to serve the revolutionary forces of northern Mexico as propagandists and nurses.

Castro, Cesáreo (1856–1944)

A delegate to the convention of the Partido Nacional Anti-Releccionista in April 1910 and a seconder of the Plan de San Luis, he took up arms on November 20, 1910. He defended Madero in 1912 against Orozco and his forces. Then following the rebellion of Huerta, he joined Carranza and signed the Guadalupe Plan. He was a loyal friend to Carranza and in 1914 was promoted to General in the Constitutionalist Army. From 1916 to 1917, he was the governor of Puebla. With the fall of Carranza, Castro emigrated to the United States but later returned to the Mexican political scene.

Castro, Jesús Agustín (1887–1953)

A Madernista who served in the revolutionary forces in Durango until 1912. In 1913 he fought in the Ciudadela during the Decena Trájica against the insurrectionists. With the fall of Madero, he fled north with those who remained loyal to Madero and joined the Constitutionalist forces under the command of Lucio Blanco. After the Constitutionalist occupation of Mexico City, Castro was named governor and military commander of Chiapas, where his first act was to free peons and servants from their debts. In 1917 and 1918, he served as Secretary of War and Navy and in 1918 was also promoted to division general. He later served as governor of his home state of Durango.

Ceballos, Ciro B. (1873–1938)

A writer for and editor of *La Revista Moderna* and director of *El Intransigente*. Primarily an admirer of Bernardo Reyes, Ceballos later pledged loyalty to Carranza. He served as director of the Biblioteca Nacional during the Constitutionalist government.

Cervantes Muños Cano, Federico (1883–1966)

A military man who had received his degree in México, but had gone to Europe to train in the French army. He returned to México in 1913 and joined Francisco Villa's army. After the triumph of constitutionalism, he was exiled to the United States, where he organized an anti-Carranza movement to no avail.

Chao, Manuel (1883–1924)

A Constitutionalist who served in the Northern Division under the command of Francisco Villa. He was promoted to General by Carranza, and served as governor of Chihuahua in 1914 until Villa tried to depose him and execute him. Later, Chao was the governor of the Federal District during the presidency of Gutiérrez and later returned to the north to fight with Villa against Carranza. When Villa's forces were defeated, he fled to Costa Rica, but returned and joined the Delahuertista rebellion in 1923. He was shot and killed in Chihuahua in 1924.

Creel, Enrique (1854–1931)

A businessman from Chihuahua, he also served in Porfirio Díaz's cabinet as Secretary of State, where he pressured the United States government to fight against the revolutionary movements of both Madero and Magón. He was exiled when Madero came to power. He was also the owner of the abandoned hacienda that the Constitutional White Cross confiscated and used as a hospital.

Dávila, Juan (?–?)

He joined the Constitutionalist Army in the fight against Huerta. He signed the Plan de Guadalupe and accompanied Carranza in the failed attack on Torreón.

Díaz, Felix (1868–1945)

Porfirio Díaz's nephew, he was sent as the Mexican consul to Chile. Díaz later served as the Chief of Police in Mexico City during the Díaz regime. In the army, he earned the rank of brigade general, but he asked for retirement when Madero came to power and set himself as a sworn enemy of Madero. He started a rebellion in Veracruz on October 16, 1912. In that same month, he was court-martialed and sentenced to death, but Madero halted the execution due to public sentiment, and Díaz was sentenced to life in prison. In February 1913 he was one of the leaders in the Ten Tragic Days, in which Madero was overthrown. He fled the country when Huerta gained power, but returned to fight against Carranza in 1916. None of the movements he led were successful, and once again, he left the country.

Díaz Mori, Porfirio (1830–1915)

Díaz began his political career in 1854 in Oaxaca. In 1877 he became the Constitutional President, the post which he occupied until 1911. In 1908 the decay of the Porfiriato became evident with the rise of the Anti-Reelectionists. The Liberal Party began organizing strikes and armed movements against the Porfiriato in 1906. As a result of electoral fraud on the part of Díaz, the armed Madernist movement gained power. The fall of Juárez provoked Díaz's resignation and he fled the country for Europe, where he died on July 2, 1915.

Eschausier, Mimi (?–?)

President of the original Cruz Blanca brigade in the state of San Luis Potosí.

Escudero, Francisco (?–?)

A lawyer and journalist, Escudero was affiliated with Constitutionalism and was given a position in the Departments of State and Housing in Carranza's first cabinet. It wasn't long before he broke ties with Carranza and joined Villa as a member of Villa's staff in the government that he formed in Chihuahua.

Esparza, Santos and Angelita P. de (?–?)

This couple formed part of the original Cruz Blanca brigade which traveled from Laredo to El Paso, Texas, then from Ciudad Juárez, Chihuahua, to Mexico City.

Espinosa Mireles, Gustavo (?–1943)

An attorney and a Constitutionalist, Espinoza Mireles served as Carranza's personal secretary from 1913 to 1915. Then, in 1915, he returned to his native Coahuila and served as provisional governor, filling the post that Jesús Acuña held up to that point. He resigned to run for the office of constitutional governor and won, beating out Luis Gutiérrez, thanks to the backing of Carranza. During his term, he supported the land and agricultural reforms and convened a worker's conference in 1918, out of which was created the Confederación Regional Obrera Mexicana (CROM).

Fabela, Isidro (1882–1964)

A lawyer who began his political career by supporting the candidacy of Madero in 1910. He served in many different public offices after this, including state representative in the national congress. From this position, he fought against Huerta's government and defended the freedom of the press from attacks by the Secretary of Justice, Rodolfo Reyes. Due to many pressures, he fled to Cuba, but returned to México when Carranza came to power and served as chief clerk to the Secretary of State. He participated in the Niagara Falls Conferences, the withdrawal of the Marines from Veracruz and the declaration of neutrality by Mexico at the outbreak of WWI. He was in Europe when Carranza was killed.

Flores Blanco, Trini and Evita (?–?)

Maderists and Constitutionalists from Monclova, Coahuila, who from their family's telegraph office, would intercept all Federalist messages to and from the Monclova surrounding areas.

Flores Magón, Enrique (1877–1954)

Flores Magón has been considered a forerunner of the Mexican Revolution parallel to the rest of the members of the Magonista group.

Flores Magón, Ricardo (1873–1922)

Born in San Antonio Eloxochitlán, Oaxaca, on September 16, 1873, Flores Magón has been considered the leader of the precursory movement which led to the Revolution of 1910. Along with other opposition journalists, he was jailed for several months in 1903. After his release in early 1904, he went into exile in Texas and from there tried to re-establish the opposition newspaper *Regeneración*, to create liberal clubs (PLM groups) and to launch a revolutionary movement in Mexico. Persistent harassment by President Díaz's foreign agents forced the PLM radicals to flee to St. Louis, Missouri. PLM activity nonetheless persisted and spread throughout the U.S. Southwest to Texas, Arizona, New Mexico, and California. Headquarters for the PLM leadership were established in San Antonio in 1904 and in El Paso in 1906, where more oppositional newspapers were published. The years between 1907 and 1910 were ones of intense activity for Flores Magón and the PLM. While the leadership was being arrested in California and Arizona, the forty to sixty-four PLM groups organized on both sides of the border were attempting to foment rebellion in Mexico and escape arrest by U.S. and Mexican authorities. By the time most of the PLM leaders were released from prison in 1910, the political situation in Mexico had dramatically changed. After two unsuccessful armed efforts to establish "local political revolutionary hegemony" in Baja California and Texas in 1911 and 1913, respectively, and a very successful campaign launched by Mexican consular agents to discredit them as traitors, the PLM lost their influence in the border communities. Flores Magón died in prison in Leavenworth, Kansas, on November 21, 1922. PLM member Librado Rivera contended that Flores Magón had been assassinated.

Fontes, Paulino (?–?)

A Constitutionalist who participated in the campaign against Villa under the orders of General Obregón. Carranza named Fontes general director of national railroads. In 1920, he accompanied Carranza to Tlaxcalantongo, Puebla, and he later earned the rank of colonel in the Constitutionalist Army.

Frausto, Ramón (?–1919)

A constitutionalist general, and a representative of Guanajuato in the Constituent Congress of 1916–17.

Gama y Cruz, Valentín (1868–1942)

An engineer and member of the International Trade Commission between México and the United States. Carranza named him Dean of the Universidad Nacional, 1914–15. He was the Secretary of Agriculture and Public Works during the presidency of Eulalio Gutiérrez.

García de Martínex, Araceli (?–?)

Leonor Villegas de Magnón's first secretary, she was a volunteer of both the medical relief groups which assembled for the March 17, 1913, and the January 1, 1914, Constitutionalist attacks on Nuevo Laredo, Tamaulipas. She was also advisor to the second brigade of the Cruz Blanca in Nuevo Laredo.

García Vigil, Manuel (1888–1924)

A journalist who sympathized with the Reyista movement during his youth, García Vigil later supported Madero, then became a loyal Carrancista until 1920. During his stay in the Laredo, Texas, area in 1913, he was editor of his own newspaper, *El Radical* (The Radical). He served in General Pablo González's forces and was a Carrancista delegate to the Convention of Aguascalientes in 1914. He was governor of his native state of Oaxaca until 1923. He was executed in 1924, following his support of the Adolfo de la Huerta uprising.

Garza, Pablo de la (1876–1932)

De la Garza joined the Constitutionalist movement in 1913 and earned the rank of Colonel. He fought under Pablo González in Coahuila, Nuevo León and Tamaulipas. He was promoted to General in 1914 after taking Monterrey and was represented by Ramón Gámez in the Convention of Auguascalientes. With the fall of Huerta, he became the military commander and governor of Guanajuato. With the split in the revolutionary forces, De la Garza took charge of the government and military command of Nuevo León. He served as Attorney General under the Carranza administration from 1918 to 1919. He was exiled immediately following the triumph of the Plan de Agua Prieta.

Garza, Reynaldo (?–?)

Garza began his participation in the Revolution in 1911. He was a delegate to the Constituent Congress of 1916–17, and later earned the rank of brigade general and served as chief of arms in various parts of the Republic.

Gaxiola, Macario (1890–1953)

Gaxiola fought against Huerta and became a general and battalion commander in the Army of the Northwest, commanded by Obregón. As a delegate to the Convention of Aguascalientes, he voted for the retirement of Carranza. Gaxiola supported the Agua Prieta Plan and later served as governor and senator for his native state of Sinaloa.

González, Manuel W. (1889–?)

González joined the Madernist revolution alongside Sánchez Herrera. In 1913, he joined the Constitutionalist forces and was the personal secretary for General Pablo González. He achieved the rank of brigade general, fought in several battles against Carranza and ultimately became Secretary of the Economy. González also published several works on the Revolution.

González, María de Jesús (1881–?)

González emigrated to the United States, where she worked as a hotel administrator in San Antonio, Texas, that accommodated many revolutionaries, such as Francisco Madero. She was an economic supporter of the Revolution and, when Madero gained power, she moved to Monterrey. In 1913, she returned to the United States and converted her house into the headquarters for the conspiracy against Huerta.

González Alemán, Miguel (1884–1929)

In 1910 he joined the Madernista movement and took up arms against Díaz. A Constitutionalist and Carrancista, González Alemán was commissioned by Carranza in 1915 to strengthen general Obregón's troops in Celaya, Guanajuato. After a decisive victory over Villa, he was promoted to the rank of Division General. In 1920 he joined the Agua Prieta movement. He committed suicide in 1929 before being taken prisoner by government troops in Mata de Aguacatilla, Veracruz.

González Garza, Pablo (1879–1950)

González Garza was brigade General of the Murguía forces. He was later chief of military operations of the Veracruzan Huasteca.

Gutiérrez, Eulalio (1881–1939)

With the rise of Madernism, Gutiérrez returned to the military, recognized the San Luis Plan and took up arms against Díaz. In 1911 Gutiérrez and his brother were defeated and held prisoner until May when the Juárez Treaty granted their release. In February 1913 he became municipal president of Concepción de Oro and soon after joined the Constitutionalists. In March Gutiérrez and his brother attempted to take Saltillo and participated in the defeat at Torreón. Gutiérrez became brigade general in September with orders to operate in Coahuila, San Luis Potosí and Zacatecas. He was a representative to the Aguascalientes Convention and was part of the War Commission. In 1914 Gutiérrez was designated Provisional President of the Republic. His cabinet was made up of distinct representatives from all political corners. Despite the liberal scope of his presidency, Gutiérrez was practically held prisoner by Villa and Zapata during their occupation of Mexico City. Villa threatened Gutiérrez's life upon his request for certain restraints of power among the Villistas and Zapatistas, and Gutiérrez subsequently moved his government to San Luis Potosí. His brother Luis remained loyal to Carranza and refused to recognize Gutiérrez's presidency. He went into exile in the United States but was granted amnesty shortly thereafter. In 1917 he began propagandizing against Carranza and later emigrated again to the United States, where he supported the Agua Prieta Plan. Gutiérrez died in Saltillo on August 12, 1939.

Hernández, Lindoro (1875–?)

Hernández joined the forces of the Western Division to fight against Huerta. In 1922 he was pursued for the rebellion at Murguía and was later named Chief of the Civil Guard. Hernández ultimately achieved the rank of brigade general.

Hernández, Teresa G. Vda de (?–?)

Hernández was one of the original Cruz Blanca staff members who traveled from Laredo to El Paso, Texas, then from Ciudad Juárez, Chihuahua, to Mexico City.

Herrera Cano, Maclovio (1879–1915)

Since 1909 Herrera Cano sympathized with the Anti-reelectionists and in accordance with the San Luis Plan he took up arms in November 1910. Before the defection of Orozco, Herrera Cano fought in defense of Madero and later with Villa's forces against Emilio Campa. When Villa was apprehended by Huerta, Herrera Cano took over his position for the Battle of Benito Juárez. In 1913 Herrera Cano was one of the first people to rebel against Huerta. Herrera Cano united with General Chao's forces and attacked Camargo. Once he achieved the rank of brigade general he fought alongside Villa in Torreón and the indefinite occupation of Juárez. In 1913 Herrera Cano became a Villista hero in the Tierra Blanca victory and by 1914 he was one of the most important military leaders. Before the revolutionary split, Herrera Cano continued to recognize Carranza as the Military Commander. This infuriated Villa and he sent Chao and Rosalío Hernández to kill Herrera Cano and his family. Herrera Cano resisted and ultimately defeated the Villista troops. Carranza named him Military Commander of Coahuila. On April 17, 1915, Herrera Cano and his troops moved toward Nuevo Laredo, Tamaulipas, on a train convoy, but he was killed by his own troops when he neared the train on horseback.

Hill, Benjamín G. (1847–1920)

Hill was liberated from prison by Madernist forces in 1911. He was named prefect of the district of Arizpe and fought against the Orozquistas. He later became prefect of Hermosillo and denounced Huerta and formed one of the Sonorense Constitutionalist circles. Hill defeated the Huertistas at La Concentración and in April 1913 he entered Alamos. From there he reconstructed the South Pacific Railroad. Shortly before the Battle of Santa María, Hill joined Obregón's forces. Hill controlled the entire Obregonista military campaign up to the occupation of Mexico City in 1914. Carranza named him governor and military commander. In the Battle of El Bajío Carranza was wounded and named Hill his successor and top confidant. Hill assumed responsibility for the troops up until their victory at Trinidad where he was given the rank of division general. He ultimately became Secretary of the Armed Forces but died just days before taking his position.

Huerta, Victoriano (1854–1916)

During his youth Huerta excelled in the Colegio Militar as one of the finest strategists. In 1911, after Emiliano Zapata put forth his Plan de Ayala, accepting Orozco as chief of the Revolution, Madero named Huerta commander of military forces in Northern Mexico against Orozco. In 1913 Félix Díaz, Porfirio Díaz's nephew, along with Bernardo Reyes, escaped from prison and placed Mexico City under a state of siege from the Ciudadela. During La decena trágica (Tragic Ten Days) of battles in the city, Huerta betrayed Madero in an uprising. Huerta conspired with Henry Lane Wilson, US ambassador to Mexico, and Aureliano Blanquet, he arrested President Madero and Vice-President Pino Suárez and forced their resignations. Pedro Lascuráin, Secretary of Foreign Relations, became president for a few minutes, but resigned and allowed Huerta to "legally" become president. Two days later Madero and Pino Suárez were assassinated. Francisco Villa, Venustiano Carranza and Alvaro Obregón rebelled against Huerta under the Plan de Guadalupe, which initiated the second violent phase of the Mexican Revolution. Although the German government supported him, President Woodrow Wilson actively opposed Huerta. On July 15, Huerta resigned and left for Europe. In 1915 he went to New York where he was under strict surveillance by the US government. He was arrested along with Pascual Orozco on June 26 and died in Fort Bliss, El Paso, Texas, on January 13 of the following year.

Ibarra, Catarina and Luz (?–?)

This mother-daughter team was part of the original Cruz Blanca brigade staff which traveled from Laredo to El Paso, Texas, then from Ciudad Juárez, Chihuahua, to Mexico City.

Idar, Clemente M. (1883–1934)

Born in Laredo on November 11, 1883, Idar was a journalist and public speaker well known for his labor-organizing efforts in the United States and Latin America. He was a propagandist for Maderism and later for Constitutionalism. As a labor leader, he represented both Samuel Gompers, President of the American Federation of Labor, and William Green, leader of the United States Labor Union. He was a major contributor to his family's weekly newspapers, *La Crónica* and *Evolución*. He was responsible for advising Leonor Villegas de Magnón on organizing the Cruz Blanca into a national and international medical corps. In a May 8, 1914, letter to Villegas de Magnón, Idar counsels, ". . . Sra. Magnón: Ud. tiene gran porvenir. Ud. ha encontrado un sendero cubierto de buena ventura. [...] Use Ud. el tacto y el talento de las grandes mujeres. [...] Debe contestar [a Carranza] haciendo que se advierta y se note que [Ud.] ya es una de las futuras damas de la república. [...] Pida autorización al primer jefe para ramificar la Cruz Blanca en todo el territorio que domina la revolución [...] parar establecer una asociación nacional [...] y así [...] deja Ud. establecida en México esa institución benéfica como vivo testimonio de su trabajo revolucionario." (Mrs. Magnónm: You have a great future. You have found a path filled with good fortune [...] Use the tact and talent of great women. [...] You should reply [to Carranza] making it clear that you are one of the future ladies of the Republic. [...] Request authorization from the First Chief to create brigades of the Cruz Blanca throughout the entire country. [...] Thereby [...] you will have established in Mexico a charitable institution as a vivid testimony of your revolutionary work.) He died on January 27, 1934 in San Antoino, Texas.

Idar, Federico (1892–1938)

Federico was the only son of Nicasio and Jovita Vivero de Idar who was born in Mexico. He was born in Monterrey, Nuevo

León, on May 2, 1892. Like his sisters Jovita and Elvira, he volunteered to work in both the medical relief groups which assembled to care for the wounded soldiers of the March 17, 1913, and the January 1, 1914, Constitutionalist attacks on Nuevo Laredo, Tamaulipas. He served as staff secretary of the original Cruz Blanca which traveled from Laredo to El Paso, Texas, then from Ciudad Juárez, Chihuahua, to Mexico City. After the Revolution, Idar remained in Monterrey and was elected state senator to the Mexican congress. Like his brother Clemente, he traveled extensively throughout Latin America, unionizing workers, and was a major contributor to and correspondent for his family's *La Crónica* and *Evolución*. He dedicated his life to defending the interests of railroad laborers, an act for which he was assassinated in Mexico City on March 12, 1938, while he was serving as senator of the Republic.

Idar, Jovita (1885–1946)

Born in Laredo, Texas, on September 7, 1885, she was educated at Holding Institute, a Methodist institution, from which she received her teaching certificate in 1903. In addition to teaching, she was a committed journalist, editor and publisher. She worked for her family's *La Crónica,* and intermittently collaborated as contributor and copy editor for other newspapers, such as *El Progreso* (Progress) in Laredo, *El Eco del Golfo* (The Gulf's Echo) in Corpus Christi and *La Luz* (The Light) in San Benito. She was an active organizer of El Primer Congreso Mexicanista (The First Mexican Congress) and was elected president of the Liga Femenil Mexicanista (League of Mexican Women). Idar also worked as a volunteer nurse for the Cruz Blanca and traveled with the original brigade from Monterrey, Nuevo León, to Mexico City. In 1916, she founded the weekly *Evolución,* which was published until 1920. That same year she moved to San Antonio, Texas where she opened a free bilingual kindergarten and worked with the Democratic Party, organizing El Club Demócrata, one of the first political bases for Spanish-speaking people in San Antonio. In 1940, she coedited the Methodist journal, *El Heraldo Cristiano*. She also worked for the census through the 1950s, and served as district judge, as Conference Officer for the Women's Society of Christian Service from La Trinidad Methodist Church and as interpreter for doctors with Spanish-speaking patients at the Robert B. Green

Hospital Clinic. Idar died on June 15, 1946, in San Antonio, Texas.

Idar, Nicasio (1853–1914)

Born in Point Isabel, Texas, Idar moved to Laredo, Texas, "after living in Corpus Christi and attending schools there. He was primarily a journalist and commercial printer, although he also served as an Assistant City Marshall and a Justice of the Peace in Laredo." He published *La Revista,* a Masonic review, and *La Crónica,* a weekly independent newspaper. Idar belonged to the Sociedad Mutualista Benito Juárez in Laredo and was vice-president of fraternal lodge system La Orden Caballeros de Honor. Idar was also the labor organizer of *ferrocarrileros.*

Idar de Fuentes, Elvira (1892–1925)

Bookkeeper of her family's weekly independent newspaper, *La Crónica.* She volunteered to work in both the medical relief groups which assembled to care for the wounded soldiers of the March 17, 1913, and the January 1, 1914, Constitutionalist attacks on Nuevo Laredo, Tamaulipas. She was vice president of the first Cruz Blanca brigade and director of hospitals of the second brigade. Idar died on August 3, 1925, leaving her two-year-old daughter, Jovita Idar Fuentes, to be raised by her aunt, Jovita Idar. Jovita Idar Fuentes de López and Guadalupe Idar, Aquilino's wife, have been responsible for supplying most of the information we now have on the Idar family.

León, Margarita and Catarina de (?–?)

This mother-daughter team was part of the original Cruz Blanca brigade staff which traveled from Laredo to El Paso, Texas, then from Ciudad Juárez, Chihuahua, to Mexico City.

León de la Barra, Francisco (1863–1939)

A lawyer who served in many capacities, León de la Barra was ambassador to the United States and Secretary of State during the Díaz administration. He was the provisional president of México from May 25 to November 6, 1911, under the Juárez Treaties. He later served as Secretary of State in Huerta's first cabinet and was governor of the state of México. With the fall of Huerta, he left México to live in Europe, where he served as the president of the Mixed Arbitration Courts created by the Treaty of Versailles at the end of World War I.

Llave, Carmen de al (?–?)
(aka La Coronela and Marietta)

A Constitutionalist colonel and messenger from the states of Tabasco and Veracruz. According to Villegas de Magnón, she inspired the revolutionary folk song "Marietta."

Long, Lily Honeycutt (?–?)

Leonor Villegas de Magnón's second secretary, Long, traveled with the Cruz Blanca from Laredo to El Paso, Texas, then from Ciudad Juárez, Chihuahua, to Monterrey, Nuevo León. In Monterrey, she was joined by her husband, Dr. George Long, and together they became part of General Luis Caballero's division.

Madero, Ernesto (?–?)

The uncle of Francisco I. Madero, Don Ernesto was the Secretary of Housing during Madero's presidency and president of the Torreón smelters. Upon Huerta's capture, Don Ernesto fled to Cuba.

Madero González, Francisco I. (1873–1913)

Madero began his political career after completing an extensive education in Mexico, the United States and Europe. He organized the Independent Democratic Party in 1904 and edited *El Demócrata*. He later felt the need to expand to the national level of politics and joined the Magonist faction. His publication of *La sucesión presidencial* (The Presidential Succession) openly proclaimed his opposition to Díaz and he subsequently organized the Anti-Reelection Party. Madero was nominated for president at the National Independent Convention of the Anti-Reelectionist and National Democratic Parties in 1910. He campaigned across the country, despite Díaz's open resentment toward him, was jailed in San Luis Potosí, but released upon Díaz's re-election. He took up arms upon his release and joined the revolution but quickly fled to the United States, where he stayed until he completed the San Luis Plan and proclaimed the July 10th elections illegal. Upon his return Madero launched an armed attack, which began in Puebla. After Madero successfully gained the occupation of Juárez, Díaz resigned and Madero ultimately moved in to claim Mexico City. Despite the gains made by the Madernists, there were many growing problems within the party. Huerta invaded the National Palace on

February 18, 1913, and reclaimed control of the government. Madero was assassinated during the invasion.

Maldonado, Calixto (1885–1942)

A lawyer from Mérida, Maldonado was the vice-president of the National Anti-Reelection Party until he was imprisoned in 1909. He was apprehended again in 1910 under the suspicion that he participated in the happenings in Puebla. An orator and writer, Maldonado published *Los asesinatos de Madero y Pino Suárez: Como murieron* (The Assassinations of Madero and Pino Suárez: How They Died). Maldonado died in Mexico City in 1942.

Mancha, Juanita (?–?)

An ex-school teacher, Mancha became head nurse in General Jesús Carranza's forces. A brave woman, she also served as a spy, propagandist and messenger.

Manzo, Francisco (1884–1940)

In 1913 Manzo joined the Constitutionalist cause and fought alongside Obregón. In early 1914 he was the personal bodyguard for Carranza and later became general after the Battles of Celaya and Trinidad. Manzo was subsecretary of the Armed Forces from 1926 to 1929, after which he took up arms against the "renovated revolutionaries." Following the battle, Manzo fled to the United States but died in Guaymas, Sonora, in 1940.

Mariel, Francisco de P. (1885–1943)

A Maderista and a Constitutionalist, he fought under many of the generals of the revolution, including Cándido Aguilar, Pablo González, and Jacinto B. Treviño. He remained faithful to Carranza after the split with Villa, and was with him when he fled Mexico City towards Veracruz.

Martínez Celis, Guillermo (1894–?)

Celis rebelled against Porfirio Díaz's government towards Benjamín Hill. After the fall of Madero, Celis was an important Obregonista. He was head of the Departamento de Caballería, army and navy.

Montes Alanís, Federico (1884–1950)

A federal soldier who sympathized with Madero's movement, Montes Alanís joined the revolutionary army in 1911. He accompanied Madero when he was taken hostage by General Blanquet and tried to stop his assassination by killing Major Izquierdo. As punishment, he was sent to fight in the campaign against the Constitutionalist Army, but instead he joined the Constitutionalists. In 1914 he was named governor and military commander of the state of Querétaro. José Siurob represented him at the Convention of Aguascalientes. In 1919–20, he served as governor of the state of Guanajuato but was forced to leave this position because of his loyalty to Carranza, whom he accompanied to the sierra of Puebla and there witnessed his death.

Murguía, Francisco (1873–1922)

Murguía joined the Madernists in 1910 and took up arms in accordance with the San Luis Plan. He was a rifleman in the Coahuila troops and supported Carranza against the Obregonistas. Murguía was one of the first to follow the Guadalupe Plan and joined the troops of Pablo González. In 1914 Carranza named Murguía governor and military commander of the state of México. He attended the Aguascalientes Convention where he openly opposed the renunciation of the First Chief. Murguía organized 10,000 soldiers to combat the Villistas in the western region in 1915 and later participated in the Battles of Celaya and Trinidad, where he was given the nickname the Hero of León. In 1916 he became Chief of Operations in Durango and in 1917 in Chihuahua as well as general of the division. In 1920 Murguía remained loyal to Carranza, but after the success at Tlaxcalantongo he was apprehended and sent to prison under the accusation that he lacked military enthusiasm. Murguía managed to escape from prison and sought refuge in the United States. He later returned to México in opposition to Obregón, but no one supported his revolt. He was once again taken prisoner in Tepehuanes, Durango, and condemned to death. He was shot in 1922.

Murrietta, Marcelino (1880–1939)

A teacher and school inspector, Murrietta supported Madero and started several Anti-Reelectionist clubs. He took up arms against Díaz and in the region of Misantla he joined a group of campesinos who fought for Pico de Orizaba. He soon became captain and upon Madero's victory was named Political Chief of Huatusco. In 1913 he joined the Constitutionalist forces in Magdalena, Sonora, and later fought with the Villistas in the Battle of Tierra Blanca. He was the head of customs, prefect of Villa de Guadalupe, president of the Junta Reguladora de Comercio, and he was a representative to the Aguascalientes Convention. In Veracruz the Constitutionalists named Murrietta head of state of the First Division and chief of operations for the central region.

Múzquiz, Rafael E. (1882–?)

Múzquiz joined the Madernist movement in 1911 and upon its demise he signed the Plan de Guadalupe. He was called by Carranza to Hermosillo in 1913 to organize the revolutionary consular service. From this point on, he served as a diplomat and a consular consultant in the United States and Europe.

Nafarate, Emiliano (?–1918)

After the fall of Díaz, General Nafarate became the second chief of the 21st Rural Corps, commanded by Jesús Agustín Castro. He was extremely active in the attacks of La Ciudadela during the Ten Tragic Days, but also perpetrated the fall of Madero. Nafarate was fundamental in the 21st Rural Corps' rebellion and war plan to move from the capital to Tamaulipas to attack the plaza of La Victoria. A short time afterwards, Nafarate abandoned Castro and joined forces with Luis Blanco. With Blanco he participated in the seizure of Matamoros, where he was accused of killing various young members of the "social defenses." Loyal to Carranza, he became the military chief of Matamoros in 1915, when great conflicts with the United States arose over the San Diego Plan. Nafarate was later elected constitutional deputy and was assassinated for political and social reasons.

Natera García, Pánfilo (1882–1951)

In 1910 Natera García joined the Madernist movement, his main objective to gain land. Following Madero's assassination, Natera García became brigade general and commanded the Constitutionalist Central Division. With the support of Villa, Natera García seized Zacatecas and became military commander and provincial governor of the state. He attended the Convention of Aguascalientes, and before the revolutionary split,

Natera García momentarily joined the Conventionalist forces, only to return to Aguascalientes as the city's governor. On August 2, 1915, Natera García resigned his position as governor and disowned Villa. In 1925 Natera García was named chief of commissions inspector for the military and later he became deputy president of the 2nd War Counsel and military commandant of Guerrero and Zacatecas. In 1937 Natera García became the divisionary general and was once again governor of Zacatecas in 1940. Natera García died in San Miguel de Allende in 1951.

Nervo, Amado (1870–1919)

An important and distinguished Mexican poet, Nervo dedicated his life to writing and journalism. Before the Revolution Nervo was a correspondent for *El Imparcial* in Europe, where he became close friends with Rubén Darío. He was later designated secretary of legations from Argentina and Uruguay. He collaborated in the publication of *Revista Moderna* and *Revista Azul*. With the rise of the Revolution, Nervo was the diplomatic representative for Carranza.

Nieto, Rafael (1883–1926)

Upon the capture of Huerta, Nieto joined the Constitutionalist forces as the party's undersecretary and he often headed the dispatch. In 1919 Nieto lost the election for governor and was under suspicion for fraud. On the national level, however, his case was supported by the Obregonistas and by the Congress of the Union who permitted him to assume his position as governor upon the fall of the Carrancistas. Despite Nieto's loyalty to the party, Obregón doubted his military capabilities and ultimately decided to send him to Sweden as a top diplomat. He later served in Italy and Switzerland, where he died in 1926.

Obregón Salido, Alvaro (1880–1928)

Obregón joined Madero in his fight against Orozco in 1912, and he participated in the overthrow of Huerta by Carranza in 1913–14. He commanded the Constitutional Army against Zapata and Villa. Obregón revolted against Carranza when he attempted to impose his own presidential successor and was later elected in 1920. As president Obregón introduced many labor and land reforms, despite his administration's constant conflict with the United States. Obregón was re-elected president in 1928 after retiring to business for a few years, but he was assassinated by a religious fanatic before taking office on July 17, 1928.

Orozco Vázquez, Pascual (1882–1915)

In 1911 the Independent Center of Chihuahua made Orozco their candidate for state governor, but he lost because of claims that he belonged to the "old regime." Orozco maintained his position as commander of the rural areas of Chihuahua, but he was later moved to the state of Sinaloa to avoid the influence of Bernardo Reyes. Orozco showed signs of starting his own movement upon his installation in Sinaloa and in 1912 he openly professed his rebellion against the Madernist government. On March 25 the Orozquista movement launched its Packer Plan, characterized by its personal attacks against Madero.

Palavicini Soria, Félix F. (1881–1952)

Primarily dedicated to journalism, Palavicini Soria founded *El Precursor*. He also published writings on sociological questions and taught at a technical school. In 1908, Palavicini Soria edited *El Partido Republicano* and was a delegate for the Mexican Society of Geography and Statistics at the International Congress of Geography in Geneva. From the beginning Palavicini Soria sympathized with the Madernist cause, and he served as the Secretary of the Anti-Reelection Center. He accompanied Madero in his campaign tour and directed *El Antireeleccionista,* focusing much attention on education. In 1911 he became the director of the Orphans Industrial School, and from there he was a representative for the First District of Tabasco for the 26th Legislature. In the Legislature Palavacini Soria integrated the commission of public instruction and thus achieved a 25 percent raise for educators. Likewise he defended the importance of the National University. Carranza named him Secretary of Public Education in 1914. Palavacini Soria started the Section of Social Legislation, and he participated in the formation of the Guadalupe Plan. In 1916 he became the Constitutional Deputy for Mexico City, and he participated in the Querétaro debates, where he once again defended public education and campaigned for equal rights for men and women and the recognition of nationalized citizens as Mexicans. In October 1916 Palavacini Soria inaugurated the newspaper *El Universal* and later founded *El Globo, El Día* and the magazine *Todo*. He was ambassador to England, France, Belgium, Italy and Spain and later to Argentina. A distinguished author, Palavicini Soria published several works that focused specifically on history and politics. He died in Mexico City in 1952.

Pesqueira, Ignacio L. (1867–1940)

Upon the victory of the Madernist movement, Pesqueira was elected deputy of the district of Arizpe. In 1913 he replaced governor of Sonora José María Maytorena. He assumed the position on the critical date of Madero's assassination, and immediately asked Congress to repudiate the seizure of the government. In August 1913 Pesqueira was named President of the Supreme Court of Military Justice for Carranza's staff, and later he became the War and Naval Secretary. In 1917 Pesqueira was elected deputy for the Constitutional Congress of the Distrito Federal, and later governor of Sinaloa. In 1920 Carranza named him governor of Sonora, but due to the rebellion of Agua Prieta, Pesqueira could not take the responsibility. Pesqueira died in 1940 in Saint-Provence, France, while serving in a political commission from Mexico.

Pesqueira, Roberto V. (1882–1966)

Roberto Pesqueira—a direct relation of Ignacio Pesqueira—was a Madernist collaborator. In 1912 he served in the 26th Legislature, but upon the February military uprising, he immediately left Congress and affiliated himself with the Constitutionalists. In April 1913 Pesqueira joined Adolfo de la Huerta and became a delegate for the state of Sonora to the Monclova Convention, where the Guadalupe Plan was recognized. Pesqueira thus began carrying important political commissions for Carranza. He was a Constitutionalist agent to Washington with the objective of gaining US support, while he also served as a Carrancista financial representative in New York. Toward the end of 1914 he accompanied Carranza to Veracruz, where together with Ramón Denegri he formulated the agrarian reform plan called the Law of Benito Juárez, which later became the 27th Constitutional Article. Carranza's fall from power prompted Pesqueira's retirement from politics. He died in Mexico City in 1966.

Pino Suárez, José María (1869–1913)

Pino Suárez was vice-president during Francisco I. Madero's short-lived presidency. Along with Madero, he was arrested, pressured to resign and assassinated on February 22, 1913.

Reyes, Bernardo (1850–1913)

Reyes began his military career under General Régules and later became an aide for General Ramón Corona. Reyes later became lieutenant colonel under Donato Guerra and ultimately military commander of San Luis Potosí. Reyes fought against the rebellion of Tuxtepec, and subsequently Villa promoted him to general. Reyes made many changes for public works during his term as provisional governor of León. In 1900 he replaced Felipe B. Berriozabál and established himself in political circles, ultimately to be recognized as Díaz's successor. Reyes established the obligatory military commitment with the idea of enrolling educated men as second lieutenants to educate the lower troops. He participated in the publication of *La Protesta,* a newspaper that protested the works of the group Los Científicos, which supported Limantour as successor to Díaz. Reyes was subsequently excluded from the cabinet in 1902, but he reentered the political spectrum as governor of Nuevo León. Due to Díaz's doubt of Reyes' loyalty, Reyes was sent to Europe. He returned following Díaz's fall from power in 1911 and opposed Madero, but he quickly left Mexico again for Texas, where he forged his own rebellion. On December 13 Reyes crossed the border under the false assumption that his troops would follow him. Reyes was held in the Santiago Tlaltelolco jail. Together with Félix Díaz, who was held prisoner at the same time, Reyes planned an uprising. On February 9, 1913, Reyes and Díaz were liberated by General Ruiz. Together with Ruiz, Reyes entered the National Palace with the intention of apprehending Madero. Reyes died in the attack on the Palace.

Robles, José Isabel (?–1917)

Part of the Constitutionalist movement, Robles participated in and led many attacks, beginning with the attack on Torreón. The occupation of Saltillo finally established Robles' position as one of the most important Villista leaders. Robles' expression of personal judgment over one of Carranza's orders marked his military intelligence and changed the political atmosphere for Carranza. Robles was the representative for the

North at the Aguascalientes Convention, which finalized the growing disregard for Carranza as Military Chief. Robles became Minister of War during the provincial presidency of Eulalio Gutiérrez, and in January 1915 he protected Gutiérrez's escape to Mexico City and made his break from the Villistas. Shortly afterwards, however, he re-established his support for Carranza and was commissioned to Oaxaca to fight against the Soberanistas, where he once again renounced Carranza and was captured. Robles was executed on the Campo Marte in Oaxaca on April 2, 1917.

Rodríguez, Abelardo (1889–1967)

In 1913 Rodríguez joined the Constitutionalist forces under Obregón and, upon the defeat of Huerta, he earned the rank of first captain. With the commencement of the fight against Villa, Rodríguez joined the 4th Battalion of Sonora and was wounded in the Battle of Celaya. Shortly thereafter, Obregón promoted him to Lieutenant Colonel. In 1920 Rodríguez joined the Aguaprietista movement against Carranza, which granted him enormous political benefits and positions, including Secretary of Industry, Commerce and Labor as well as Secretary of War. Rodríguez ultimately became the substitute president for the Union Congress. Rodríguez retired from politics and dedicated himself to business before his death in 1967 in La Jolla, California.

Rodríguez, Alfredo (?–?)

Rodríguez was a Constituitionalist in the Western Army, commanded by General Pablo González. He fought against Huerta and participated in the battles of El Ébano acting as the chief of the Army of the Northeast. Rodríguez achieved the stature of brigade general during Carranza's capture and occupation of Mexico City.

Rodríguez, José M. (?–?)

Dr. Rodríguez, a surgeon, supported the Constitutionalist cause with various important responsibilities. He represented Constitutionalism in San Antonio, Texas, and was municipal president of Torreón. In 1916 he was elected deputy to the Constitutional Congress and later became the head of the Department of Health in Mexico City.

Salinas, Emilio (?–1927)

A relative of the Carranza family, Salinas sympathized with the anti-reelection movement and fought against Díaz in 1911. In 1913 he joined with Carranza to fight against the Huerta government, and in 1914 he earned the rank of brigade general. During Carranza's stay in Querétaro, Salinas was named state governor and military commander. He later became a senator for the state of Coahuila in 1918, was nominated for the Counsel of Mexico in San Antonio, Texas, and ultimately became the provincial governor of Chihuahua in 1920. Salinas retired upon the triumph of the Plan of Agua Prieta. He died in Laredo, Texas, in 1927.

Sánchez, Guadalupe (1890–?)

Sánchez earned the rank of captain in his participation with the Madernist movement. Following Madera's assassination, Sánchez joined the Constitutionalists and served in the Western Division under Cándido Aguilar, where he achieved distinction as one of the principal leaders. In 1914 Sánchez was a delegate to the Aguascalientes Convention and later was commissioned to fight against Villa under the orders of Obregón. Sánchez became chief of military operations in Veracruz in 1918. In 1920 he supported the Agua Prieta movement, and in 1923 Sánchez became one of the principal leaders in the rebellion led by Adolfo de la Huerta, in which Sánchez seized the city of Jalapa. Following the defeat of the movement, Sánchez lived in exile before he died in Veracruz.

Sánchez Azcona, Juan (1876–1938)

During his studies in Europe, Sánchez Azcona became friends with Madero and Altamirano. Sánchez Azcona returned to Mexico and eventually began working as a journalist. He was the editor of *El Partido Liberal, El Nacional, El Mundo* and *El Imparcial.* He entered the political spectrum in 1904 as a federal representative but was accused of exposing government secrets to the press. The final decision from the grand jury was a victory for freedom of the press in Sánchez Azcona's favor. He was critical of Los Científicos and an advocate of Reyismo. In 1908 Sánchez Azcona founded *México Nuevo,* and shortly thereafter he affiliated with the Anti-Reelectionists. He served as one of the directors at the party's electoral convention and supported Madero's campaign platform. In the midst of the campaign, Sánchez Azcona fled the country due to official accusations against him. He sought exile in San Antonio, Texas, where he reestablished the publication of *México Nuevo,* participated in the San Luis Plan and was a member of the national board for the insurrection. In the eyes of the United States, Sánchez Azcona was recognized as a Madernist agent and granted asylum in the United States. When Mexican officials presented an accusation against him, the US government maintained his political amnesty. Shortly thereafter Sánchez Azcona crossed the border, joined the Madernist revolt in Chihuahua and later accompanied Madero into Mexico City. Sánchez Azcona became Madero's personal secretary upon his seizure of Mexico City and he participated in the 26th Legislature while he continued his journalism career with the newspaper *Nuevo Era*. During the Ten Tragic Days, Sánchez Azcona was captured along with Madero. He accepted Huerta's offer to his own ministry under the condition that he send him to Europe to cure a supposed hearing problem. Huerta, primarily fooled by the plan, later captured Sánchez Azcona on board a ship bound for Germany. Sánchez Azcona escaped to Cuba, where he formed a junta against Huerta and reentered Mexico to join the Constitutionalist forces in Coahuila. He represented Carranza in Europe, participated in the formation of the Constitution and later was elected senator for Mexico City, only to return to Europe as Minister of Mexico in Spain. Sánchez Azcona continued his political and journalist careers up until his death in Mexico City in 1938.

Sandoval, Gabino (?–1920)

Sandoval was Chief of Social Defense in Olivos, Chihuahua. In November 1919 he captured General Felipe Ángeles and thus earned the rank of Lieutenant Colonel. Sandoval was executed under the regulations of the Agua Prieta Plan in 1920 because of his loyalty to Carranza.

Santibáñez, Alfonso (?–1916)

Santibáñez joined the Constitutionalist movement out of criminal rather than political motivations. He was incorporated in Jesús Carranza's forces in 1914, but in December of that year Santibáñez rebelled and took Carranza hostage. When Venustiano Carranza would not meet the demands made by Santibáñez, he executed Jesús and his troops. Santibáñez was similarly killed by another rebel leader, Eguía Lis, in Oaxaca.

Santos Chocana, José (?–1935)

A distinguished poet and orator, Santos Chocana was first a Constitutionalist and later embraced the Villista cause. He suffered a tragic death in Chile in 1935.

Serdán, Aquiles (1876–1910)

Serdán was the president of the Anti-Reelectionist Party in Puebla and worked closely with the Anti-Reelectionist leaders. Following police hostility during the electoral campaign, Serdán exposed his radical position—including his call for revolutionary acts—in opposition to Madero's expressed caution. When Madero passed through Puebla, Serdán met him with a large contingency of workers, campesinos and students. Upon Madero's defeat, Serdán and his sister Carmen left Mexico for the United States, where they rejoined Madero and planned their return to Puebla. Once in Puebla, Serdán began his clandestine arms operation in preparation for a revolt. Authorities entered his home under suspicion of his activities in September 1910, but to no avail. On November 18, 1910, he and his sister Carmen Serdán responded to a notice of arrest for possession of a revolutionary arsenal by shooting at the chief of police; they were thereby credited for initiating the revolution two days before the date Francisco I. Madero had designated. Aquilles and Carmen Serdán and others held up their resistance battle against the soldiers sent in by the governor, Mucio P. Martínez. The rebels were ultimately forced to surrender, and Serdán was executed after hiding in his basement for fourteen hours. The surviving collaborators were incarcerated.

Serdán, Carmen (1875–?)

Also known by her pseudonym Marcos Serrato, Serdán was active in the Anti-Reelectionist campaign. In 1910 Serdán was attacked by rural forces and the police in her home, but she continued to defend the revolutionary arsenal. She was captured, jailed and later hospitalized at San Pedro. Later she collaborated with the Revolutionary Junta in Puebla, where she distributed arms and was a courier. Serdán also worked as a nurse during the Constitutionalist movement, after which she retired to her private life.

Serna, Pancho (?–?)

Serna participated in the Constitutionalist movement, and during the Carranza government he managed the presidential residencies.

Silva González, Miguel (1859–1916)

A well-known and highly respected surgeon, Dr. Silva entered the political spectrum in the late 1880s and fought against the Porfiristas. In 1909 he joined the anti-reelection movement and began organizing political meetings in his home. Madero named Dr. Silva chief of the movement during his electoral tour in 1910, and later in 1911 he was named interim governor of the state. During his term Dr. Silva reinstated the town councils and political prefectures and thus gained popularity, which brought him to his position as constitutional governor in 1912. Shortly after he assumed power, Huerta separated Silva from the state government with the help of the legislature. Silva reentered the Constitutionalist ranks in the Northern Division under Villa's command. In 1914 Silva represented Villa for the Torreón Pact and before the end of the revolution he participated alongside Villa in battles. Silva organized blood hospitals for the military and later became the personal doctor for Villa. Before the fall of Villa, Silva moved to Cuba, where he continued practicing medicine. He died in Havana in 1916.

Toro, Francisco del (?–1919)

In 1912 Del Toro joined Pascual Orozco in his fight against the Madero government. Before the military uprising, Del Toro joined Huerta. Later he joined another rebel, Chávez García, but was finally captured and executed by government forces in 1919.

Treviño, Jerónimo (1836–1914)

Treviño joined the Liberal cause in 1858 during the French intervention. He later became the governor of Nuevo León and lived the latter part of his life in Laredo, Texas.

Treviño González, Jacinto B. (1883–1971)

Treviño González was a graduate of the Military Academy. He did not take up arms to follow Madero but did help to put down the Orozco rebellion. In 1914 he was promoted to brigade general and placed in command of a regiment that occupied

Pachuca during the Huertista regime. Later he was placed at the head of the office of the Secretary of War. He remained faithful to Carranza when Villa broke away and was sent to San Luis Potosí to fight against him. At San Luis Potosí Treviño González was considered a hero and was promoted to division general. In 1920 he switched his support to the Agua Prieta Plan and became the commander of González's forces. His troops were the first to occupy Mexico City. Toward the end of his life he founded and became president of the Partido Auténtico de la Revolución Mexicana (PARM).

Treviño González, Salvador (?–1914)

Treviño González—brother of General Jacinto Treviño González—first joined the Constitutionalists and later the Madernists. He was killed in the battle of Nuevo Laredo in 1914.

Triana, Martin (?–1934)

In 1913 and 1914 Triana fought against Huerta in the region of San Juan de Guadalupe. One of the most important leaders of the Northern Division, he soon joined the Constitutionalists, where he collaborated with General Obregón in the Battle of Celaya. In 1916 he earned the rank of brigade general. Triana died in Mexico City in 1934.

Ugarte, Gerzain (?–1956)

Ugarte originally identified with the Reyistas, but he later joined the Anti-Reelectionist Party with his friend Luis Cabrera. He was a representative to the 26th Legislature and to the Constituent Congress of 1916–17. Ugarte was the personal secretary of Carranza in 1916. Along with Luis Cabrera and Ernesto Hidalgo, he represented Mexico in 1918 in the unsuccessful convention for world peace in Buenos Aires. From 1918 he was minister of Mexico in Colombia, Ecuador, and Venezuela. He was at Carranza's side at his death. Ugarte died in Mexico City in 1956. His booklet *¿Por qué volví a Tlaxcalcantongo?* (Why Did I Return to Tlaxcalantongo?) is considered a testimonial of great importance in Mexico.

Urbina, Tomás (1877–1915)

Urbina was pursued by authorities, along with Villa, his friend and travel companion. Urbina was one of the first to take up arms in defense of the Madernist cause, and upon its triumph in

1911 he was recognized as colonel. In 1912 he fought against the revolt of Pascual Orozco and later joined the Northern Division under Huerta. In 1913, before Huerta's takeover, Urbina joined a group of campesinos in defense of the Constitutionalists and later assumed "supreme" command of the Durango troops. With them Urbina took control of the state capital on June 18, 1913, and named Pastor Rouaix state governor. Following a series of battles Urbina joined troops with Villa in Chihuahua, and he soon became one of the top leaders of the Constitutionalist Northern Division. Urbina was named Chief of Operations in Tampico, but his failure against the troops of Jacinto B. Treviño in El Ebano cost him his military stature with Villa. Urbina was executed by Rodolfo Fierro in 1915 in compliance with orders from Villa.

Villa, Francisco "Pancho" (1878–1923) (aka Doroteo Arango)

The most controversial figure of the Mexican Revolution, Villa's career as a bandit began in 1894 and was characterized by his constant evasion of the police. In 1910 he joined the Madernist movement and on November 17 he attacked the Hacienda de Chavarría and began his continual search for supporters. He was known for his audacity and organization, and he moved up through the military ranks quickly. With the Battle of Juárez Villa gained national fame and recognition, and he was soon named colonel. After the signing of the Treaty of Juárez, Villa gave over command of his troops to Raúl Madero and dedicated himself to business. In 1912 he showed his loyalty to Madero and rejected an invitation from Orozco to rebel along with his movement. Instead he took up arms again to defend the Madernists. He joined the troops commanded by Huerta and fought alongside Huerta in several battles before earning the rank of brigade general. Huerta ordered Villa to be executed out of jealousy of Villa's intelligence and astute military control. Madero saved Villa's life, and he was instead sent to jail in Mexico City, where he joined the Constitutionalists and crossed into Chihuahua to fight against Huerta in March 1913. By May Villa had an army of more than 600 men and ultimately claimed the northern zone of Mexico as his own. Villa's careful strategic planning earned him the title of general in chief. As provisional governor of Chihuahua, Villa assumed control over Manuel Chao, who had been named governor by

Carranza, and completely changed the atmosphere of the state. Villa began 1914 by taking over Ojinaga and later assumed control over the entire lagoonal region. Villa continued to express his own judgment over military actions in disregard of the orders of Carranza, thus increasing the tension between the two men that had started with Villa's gubernatorial discrepancies. The Torreón Pact alleviated the tense atmosphere, although in their reconciliation Villa proposed strong limits over Carranza's power. Many of Villa's orders from the Torreón Pact went unrecognized, which provoked the conflict of August 1914 in Sonora. During the conflict Obregón nearly shot Villa in the middle of a conference session. The Convention of Mexico City and then Villa's installation at Aguascalientes preceded his designation as chief of operations for the Conventionist Army. In the battle against the Constitutionalists Villa sought to ally himself with Zapata and in December of the same year the Xochimilco Pact was instituted, in which Villa accepted the Ayala Plan. The Ayala Plan included, among other agreements, the idea of choosing a civilian associated with the Revolution for the presidency. In 1915 Villa was repeatedly defeated by Obregón and the Constitutionalists. With very few troops, Villa dedicated himself to antagonizing the Carranza government. On March 9, 1916, Villa attacked the city of Columbus, New Mexico, and provoked the military expedition led by John Pershing. Villa once again began his clandestine activities through 1920. De la Huerta requested Villa's surrender and, on June 26, Villa signed the Sabinas agreements, which obligated his surrender of arms and his retirement to the Hacienda de Canutillo, Durango. The exact details of Villa's assassination are unknown, but it is thought to have been a repercussion of De la Huerta's rebellion. He died on June 20, 1923, in an ambush in Chihuahua.

Villarreal González, Antonio I. (1879M–1944)

Villarreal's political career began in 1896 in the midst of the Magonista era. In 1909 he sympathized with the Anti-Reelectionists and, months later, during the rise of Madero, he formed part of a group of professors who joined the armed fighting. His first operations in Chihuahua led him to earn the rank of colonel. After the fighting ended, Villarreal participated in the Convention for the Constitutional Progress Party. With the initiation of Madero's presidency, Villarreal became the consul-general of Mexico in Spain. Upon the successes of the Ten Tragic Days, Villarreal returned to Mexico to join Carranza's movement. He became general and assumed responsibility over the Northeastern Army. Following a series of battles Villarreal became brigade general, and in 1914 Carranza named him governor and military commander of Nuevo León. Villarreal met with Zapata in Cuernavaca in hopes of establishing a conciliation among the revolutionaries. He presided at the Convention of Aguascalientes, where he was commissioned to meet with Carranza, but he abandoned the Conventionalists and joined the Constitutionalists once again. After breaking with Carranza, Villarreal returned to Nuevo León and later went into exile until 1920. Upon his return to Mexico, Villarreal became secretary of agriculture and was later a candidate for senator of Nuevo León. In 1927 he fought against the Re-electionists, but two years later he was the presidential pre-candidate for the National Anti-Reelection Party. In 1934 he ran for president again, this time supported by the Revolutionary Confederation of Independent Parties, but he lost to Lázaro Cárdenas. Following his defeat, Villarreal turned from politics to journalism and became the editor of *Excélsior*. He died in Mexico City in 1944.

Zapata Salazar, Emiliano (1879–1917)

Zapata's military career began in Morelos, following his instruction under a Latifundista-Porfirista professor. Zapata's astute horsemanship led him to work closely with Díaz's top aides. Zapata entered the political spectrum in the gubernatorial elections of 1909 in Morelos in support of the opposing candidate, Patricio Leyva. In 1910 Zapata participated in the conference at Villa de Ayala where the San Luis Plan was discussed. Toward the end of the year Zapata sent Pablo Torres Burgos to meet with Madero in the United States, which resulted in the taking up of arms on March 10, 1911, in proclamation of the San Luis Plan. Following several battles and the recuperation of land, Zapata assumed the position as chief of operations for the Maderist movement in Morelos. Despite the agreements made in the Juárez Treaty, Zapata refused to disarm his troops and thus provoked Francisco de la Barra to proclaim him and his troops bandits. Over a thousand troops were sent by Huerta to combat Zapata. Madero met with Zapata in August to recognize his troops but made no concessions concerning agrarian reform, Zapata's primary concern. Shortly thereafter the federal government repeated its call for violent action, and Zapata retreated to Guerrero and Puebla to rebuild his troops. Madero met once again with Zapata when he became president, but still reached no agreement. In 1911 Zapata launched the Ayala Plan, which clearly reflected the ideology of the Morelense campesinos and called for equal rights as well as land rights for the indigenous peoples of Morelos. With the plan Zapata openly recognized Pascual Orozco as leader of the Revolution and proclaimed violent action the only means to establish justice. During 1912 Zapata and his troops fought intensely and violently. Huerta sent Zapata a commission to establish a peace agreement, but Zapata assassinated the courier and sent a letter back repudiating the Huerta government. In May he reformed the Ayala Plan and proclaimed himself leader of the Liberator Army. Zapata did not recognize the Guadalupe Plan and continued his conquests up to Mexico City, but the Constitutionalist forces blocked his entrance to the city. At the Aguascalientes Convention Zapata finally convinced the others in attendance to renounce Carranza. Then allied with Villa, Zapata recognized Eulalio Gutiérrez as provisional president. The Zapata movement gained national fame upon the siege of Mexico City at the end of November. On December 4 Villa and Zapata held a conference at Xochimilco, where they allied both militaries, and Villa accepted the Ayala Plan and agreed to hand over arms to Zapata. In 1916 Zapata's movement was attacked by the Constitutionalists, and little by little the previous gains of the Zapatistas were taken over by Carranza. By 1918 Zapata had become a guerrilla with little future. He was assassinated on April 10, 1919, and is still considered the symbol of the dispossessed campesinos.

Zuazua, Fortunato (1890–1938)

Zuazua joined the Madernist movement in 1910, and later in 1913 he joined the Constitutionalists under General Pablo González. Zuazua collaborated with Lucio Blanco in the seizure of Matamoros, where he was promoted in the military ranks. Loyal to Carranza, Zuazua fought Villismo in 1915, ultimately under the command of Jacinto B. Treviño. In 1916 he earned the rank of general. Zuazua served during the interim of De la Huerta and continued in the political spectrum until his retirement. Zuazua died in Temple, Texas, in 1938.

Zubarán Capmany, Rafael (1875–1948)

A member of Carranza's cabinet in 1913, Zubarán Capmany served as the Secretary of the Interior until the middle of 1915. He was the adviser to Carranza and played a key role in the signing of the pact with the Constitutionalist Army. Zubarán Capmany soon distanced himself from the Carrancistas and joined the Liberal Constitutionalist Party. He was the municipal mayor of Mexico City, senator, diplomat, and secretary of industry and commerce during Obregón's government. Zubarán Capmany died in Mexico City in 1936.

Appendix III

Autobiographies of the Mexican Revolution Published between 1920 and 1955

Anti-Carrancista

Capistrán Garza, René. *Andanzas de un periodista y otros ensayos.* México?: s.n., 1950s?

Anti-Maderistas

Esquivel Obregón, Toribio. *Mi labor en servicio de México.* México: Edictiones Botas, 1934.

Huerta, Victoriano. *Memorias del general Victoriano Huerta.* San Antonio, Texas: Librería de Quiroga, 1915?

Moheno, Querido. *Mi actuación política después de la decena trágica.* México: Ediciones Botas, 1939.

Reyes, Rodolfo. *De mi vida: Memorias políticas, 1899–1914.* Madrid: Biblioteca Nueva, 1929.

Carrancistas

Aguirre, Amado. *Mis memorias de campaña: Apuntes para la historia.* México: s.n., 1953.

González, Manuel. *Con Carranza: Episodios de la revolución constitucionalista, 1913–1914.* Monterrey, N.L., México: J. Cantú Leal, 1933–34.

———. *Contra Villa: Relatos de la campaña, 1914–1915.* México, D.F.: Ediciones Botas, 1935.

Luquín, Eduardo. *Tumulto: Memorias de un oficial del Ejército Constitucionalista.* México: s. n., 1937.

Urquizo, Francisco L. *De la vida militar mexicana.* México: Herrero Hermanos Sucesores, 1930.

———. *"Recuerdo que...": Visiones de la Revolución.* México: Ediciones Botas, 1934, 2 vols.

———. *México, Tlaxcalantongo, mayo de 1920.* México: Editorial Cultural, 1943.

———. *3 de Diana.* México: Publicaciones Mundiales, 1947.

Maderistas

León Ossorio, Adolfo . *Mis confesiones.* México: s.n., 1946.

Luna Morales, Ricardo. *Mi vida revolucionaria: Con aportaciones históricas del movimiento social y político del ciclo contemporáneo de México.* Tlaxcala, México: R. Luna Morales, 1943.

Palavincini, Félix Fulgencio. *Mi vida revolucionaria.* México: Ediciones Botas, 1937.

Pani, Alberto J. *Apuntes autobiográficos.* México: Librería de Manuel Porrúa, 1950.

Romero, José Rubén. *Apuntes de un lugareño.* Barcelona: Imprenta Núnez y C., 1932.

Vázquez Gómez, Francisco. *Memorias políticas 1909–1913.* México: Imprenta mundial, 1933.

Non-Partisan

Molina Font, Julio. *Halachó, 1915.* México: Editora Internacional de México, 1955.

Novo, Salvador. *Return Ticket.* México: Editorial "Cultura," 1928.

Ramírez Garrido, José Domingo. *Así fue . . . [artículos de combate, por] J.D. Ramírez Garrido.* México: Imprenta Nigromante, 1943.

Obregonistas

Almada, Pedro J. *Con mi cobija al hombro autobiografía: Por el general de división Pedro J. Almada.* México: Editorial Alrededor de América, 1930s?

Porfiristas

Gamboa, Federico. *Mi diario.* Guadalajara: Imprenta de "La Gaceta de Guadalajara," 1907–20.

Pani, Arturo. *Una vida.* México: s.n., 1955.

Soldadera

Poniatowski, Elena. *Hasta no verte, Jesús mío.* México: Era, 1969.

Villistas

Brondo Whitt, E. *La división del norte 1914 por un testigo presencial.* México, D.F.: Editorial Lumen, 1940.

Gavira, Gabriel. *General de brigada Gabriel Gavira: Su actuación político-militar revolucionario.* México: Talleres Tipográficos de A. del Bosque, 1933.

Guzmán, Martín Luis. *El águila y la serpiente.* México: Editorial Anahuac, 1949.

Zapatistas

Galindo, Miguel. *A través de la sierra diario de un soldado.* México?: s.n., 1940s?

Appendix IV

Glossary

a la Veracruzana: Veracruz style
abrazo: a hug, usually given in a cordial greetings
agua miel: honey water
alcalde: mayor
amo-a: the boss, master or mistress

bodega: storeroom
bracero: brazier, ametal pan or pot to hold hot coals

cabrito al horno: baked goat
casuelo: a stewing pot
científicos: scientists
compadre: the godfather of one's child, a close friend
compañero: companion, friend
copita: literally, a little glass; figuratively, a drink

encargado: the person in charge of doing something
esquifero: skiff, small boat

güera: blond woman

hacendado: hacienda owner
huaraches: sandles

jacal: a humble living quarter or shack
jefes: the bosses

merienda: a late evening meal
mescal: the chepest grade of liquor made from the agave cactus
metate: a stone for grinding food in the kitchen
mozos: literally, young men; means workers or servants

nacimiento: a nativity scene

padrinos: godparents
"Pase usted": Come right in.
patrón, patrona: the owner or boss
pitahaya: a type of cactus
portero: doorman
portón: a large door
posadas: literally, inns; refers to the Christmas pageant of Mary and Joseph seeking shelter

qué bonita: how pretty

ranchero eggs: eggs fried sunny-side up on a tortilla with hot sauce
rebozo: an shawl
romería: popular fiesta or ritual involving a trip or short pilgrimage

salvo conducto: a note of safe passage
siesta: an afternoon nap or rest

torero: bullfighter

¿Y María de Jesús, dónde está?: And where is María de Jesús?

Appendix V

Onomastic Index